The Employment Interview Handbook

Robert W. Eder
Michael M. Harris
Editors

SAGE Publications
International Educational and Professional Publisher
Thousand Oaks   London   New Delhi

For information:

 SAGE Publications, Inc.
2455 Teller Road
Thousand Oaks, California 91320
E-mail: order@sagepub.com

SAGE Publications Ltd.
6 Bonhill Street
London EC2A 4PU
United Kingdom

SAGE Publications India Pvt. Ltd.
M-32 Market
Greater Kailash I
New Delhi 110 048 India

Printed in the United States of America

Library of Congress Cataloging-in-Publication Data

Main entry under title:

The employment interview handbook / edited by Robert W. Eder and
    Michael M. Harris.
        p.   cm.
    Rev. ed. of: The employment interview, 1989.
    Includes bibliographical references and index.
    ISBN 0-7619-0648-7 (cloth: acid-free paper)
    ISBN 0-7619-0649-5 (pbk: acid-free paper)
    1. Employment interviewing.   I. Eder, Robert W.
    II. Harris, Michael M.
    HF5549.5.I6 E48 1999
    658.3'1124—dc21   99-6163

This book is printed on acid-free paper.

01 02 03 10 9 8 7 6 5 4 3 2

Acquiring Editor:	Marquita Flemming/Harry Briggs
Editorial Assistant:	Mary Ann Vail
Production Editor:	Astrid Virding
Editorial Assistant:	Nevair Kabakian
Designer/Typesetter:	Janelle LeMaster
Cover Designer:	Candice Harman

Contents

To my wife, *Janice*, and my two sons, *Collin* and *Derek*.
—Robert W. Eder

To my wife, *Pat*.
—Michael M. Harris

Preface

Overview

When the *The Employment Interview: Theory, Research, and Practice,* edited by Robert W. Eder and Gerald R. Ferris, was published by Sage Publications in 1989, scholars and advanced practitioners were just beginning to rethink the employment interview's value. Up to that time, the general consensus in the literature was that the interview was a poor selection device, tolerated primarily because it was the only personal opportunity for applicants and interviewers to exchange information with one another. Researchers lamented the widespread practitioner reliance on the relatively unstructured, face-to-face interview to arrive at employee selection decisions, despite the interview's questionable validity in predicting job success when compared with other selection techniques (such as biographical information, work samples, and ability testing).

In perhaps the single most important development in the 1980s, validation studies on a new type of interview, the "structured interview," offered the promise of superior selection accuracy, resurrecting the value of the interview as an employee selection method. A series of meta-analytic studies (i.e., quantitative reviews of the literature) published in the late 1980s and early 1990s, as well as continued primary research, consistently reported a larger mean validity for structured interviews than for unstructured interviews.

With a less cynical attitude toward the employment interview, researchers began to explore new theoretical frameworks for studying the interview event and to address methodological challenges in testing these more dynamic theories. It became clear that myriad factors (e.g., applicant strategies, preinterview impressions, interviewer-applicant interaction dynamics, interview content, and interview context) influence interview decisions. Scholars and advanced practitioners began to ask how the interview might be used to assess expanded notions of applicant "fit" with the organization's values and culture and how applicants were reacting to these new structured interviewing procedures. Practitioners quickly adopted these structured interviewing techniques through books and workshops, raising practitioner confidence in the improved efficacy of their interviewing. Using a medical metaphor, the health of the employment interview has greatly improved over this past decade.

Development of This Handbook

This handbook builds on the successful format of Eder and Ferris's 1989 edited volume. The basic integrative structure is retained, respective streams of research are updated, and new lines of promising research are examined. Thirteen authors from the Eder and Ferris volume return, and they are joined by 28 new authors, all of whom make significant contributions to the advancement of employment interview knowledge. In the 1989 volume, an integrated framework was constructed and then contributing authors were sought to write chapters on different facets of the framework. In this handbook, we decided not to be constrained initially by the framework, but instead began by asking leading interview scholars of the past decade to share their latest thinking on promising lines of research that have the potential of advancing interview practice. The result is a handbook that reflects original, cutting-edge scholarship and advanced practice.

Coherence across the chapters was accomplished, in part, through the editing process on initial drafts to minimize redundancies across chapters, improve readability, and, where needed, enlarge a chapter's scope. Authors were asked to summarize the existing research and were encouraged to stretch their thinking to propose new needed research, and to comment on the importance of their research for testing theory and enhancing interview practice.

As in the 1989 volume, we provide an organizing framework at the end of Chapter 1 to group research efforts that address similar key variables; we also offer introductory comments at the opening of each part of the handbook to describe how the chapters relate to one another within the organizing framework. Finally, the handbook concludes with a commentary/discussion section that highlights key contributions across the contributing chapters to advancing employment interview research and practice.

The handbook is particularly appropriate for use by (a) researchers and graduate students, as a resource for stimulating new research streams on employee selection in general and the employment interview in particular; (b) instructors, as a textbook supplement for industrial/organizational psychology and human resource management seminars on employment practices; and (c) advanced practitioners, as a reference source for auditing and updating employment interview procedures and policies. Edited research volumes, with their emphasis on advanced empirical work, frequently create initial difficulty for readers unfamiliar with the topic. Therefore, in Chapter 1 we provide the reader with the history of employment interview research, placing many of today's diverse research efforts and ongoing debates in historical perspective.

Becoming an Informed Consumer of Research

Also, we would like the reader of this book to become an informed consumer of employment interview research—past, present, and future. No single empirical study is ever perfect, methodologically. Trade-offs are often made between concerns over controlling for a variety of internal validity threats to hypothesis testing in a study and concerns over the external validity, or generalizability, of the study's findings to actual interview practice. The employment interview is a complex phenomenon that still mystifies interviewers and applicants alike. When we attempt to study actual interviews and the outcomes of interest to us, there are so many subtle dynamics operating that it is difficult to rule out something we did not observe or measure as a plausible alternative explanation for what we think we have found.

Not surprisingly, researchers have often conducted interview research in relatively controlled settings, where specific subtleties of interest can be examined and the potential efficacy of an intervention can be tested. However, the more removed these studies are from actual interviews, the greater is the concern over what the study's findings mean for real employment interviews. In place of "live" employment interviews, the stimulus studied may be a narrative description, audiotape, or videotape of an interviewer-applicant exchange. Often, these stimuli are responded to by college students who are asked to take on the role of interviewer or applicant in the situation. Unlike supervisors or coworkers with a great deal at stake in making correct hiring decisions, students as study participants experience no comparable consequences for their judgments when they know the context of the study is for "research purposes only." And finally, despite our primary interest in the employment interview as a selection technique, many studies assess interviewer judgment in screening interviews, where recruitment and assessment of general applicant suitability is the primary purpose, not final selection of the best-qualified candidate. We actually know very little about the effects that each of these factors (i.e., simulated interview stimuli, student stand-ins for actual interviewers, interview purpose) has on understanding how a particular study's results generalize, but all three are potentially important.

Whether your interest is in conducting employment interview research, gaining insight from what has been learned about interviewing processes and outcomes, or incorporating promising innovations into your employment interview practices, it is our sincere hope that this handbook will become a valuable resource for you.

Acknowledgments

We would like to take this opportunity to acknowledge the many people who made this handbook possible. As lead editor, it was my good fortune to have Mike Harris join me as coeditor. Mike authored the last qualitative review of the employment interview published in *Personnel Psychology* in 1989 and brought a fresh perspective and complementary expertise to enrich this project. I am also thankful to Jerry Ferris, my coeditor on *The Employment Interview,* who agreed to be a contributing author and who extended his counsel in the development of this handbook.

A special thank-you goes to our contributing authors for the high-quality manuscripts they produced; they responded in a timely fashion and demonstrated a willingness to work with us in making their chapters even better. It was truly an honor and a pleasure to work with them. A personal note of gratitude goes to Astrid Virding and Judy Selhorst for their diligence in the final copyediting and production process, and especially to Marquita Flemming, our editor at Sage Publications, for her belief in this project and for providing the support necessary to help us deliver a high-quality product. The logistics of monitoring the progress of 21 manuscripts and 41 authors, keeping the correspondence and faxes flowing smoothly, and making what seemed to be an endless number of short deadlines would not have been possible without the help of the faculty support staffs in the School of Business Administration at both Portland State University and the University of Missouri–St. Louis. Finally, and in many respects most important, we would like to thank our families, who indulged us in this endeavor by putting up with our long hours at the office.

—Robert W. Eder
Portland

—Michael M. Harris
St. Louis

1

Employment Interview Research

Historical Update and Introduction

Robert W. Eder
Michael M. Harris

This introductory chapter sets the stage for the remainder of this handbook by presenting a brief historical review of the literature on the employment interview since 1915. The historical review highlights key events, findings, and shifts in research trends up through the 1990s and offers speculation about the future challenges and developments that await tomorrow's employment interview researcher. We conclude with an introduction to the contributed chapters that make up this handbook by placing each chapter's unique perspective within an integrated framework. This framework attempts to synthesize the diverse theoretical perspectives and complex causal relationships that exist between exogenous factors (e.g., preinterview impressions, interview context, interview content, and applicant strategies) and the endogenous factors of interpersonal dynamics and information processing as they combine to influence interviewer-applicant judgments and effective interview decision making. Before proceeding, we begin by defining what we mean by the term *employment interview.*

What Is the Employment Interview?

Guion (1997) recently noted, "There are many different interviewers, looking for many different things, and using many different methods" (p. 609). It is quite likely that each contributing author in this book assumes a connotation of the term *employment interview* that is slightly different from that assumed by his or her colleagues, in part because of the varied uses of the employment interview within work organizations' selection processes and the multifaceted nature of interviewer and applicant decisions. Dipboye (1994) has even argued that the interview has no unique content; it is simply a method of collecting information. Nevertheless, in order for research to proceed, we believe it is time to begin to develop a classification scheme for the employment interview. First, we offer a generic definition:

> The employment interview is defined as an interviewer-applicant exchange of information in which the interviewer(s) inquire(s) into the applicant's (a) work-related knowledge, skills, and abilities (KSAs); (b) motivations; (c) values; and (d) reliability, with the overall staffing goals of attracting, selecting, and retaining a highly competent and productive workforce.

As this definition suggests, the employment interview need not be restricted only to face-to-face meetings between one or more organizational representatives, or their designee, and the applicant. Employment interviews may include information exchanges that are achieved largely by electronic means—via phone, on-line "chat rooms," or even fax or e-mail technologies. However, the key word here is *exchange*—an *expectation* of give-and-take between the interviewer and the applicant. Perhaps it is the interviewer-applicant exchange that makes the interview more than just a method of obtaining information; it is the exchange itself that provides potentially unique information beyond what is ordinarily obtained from other methods. The line between an employment interview and an orally administered job knowledge test is probably crossed when the interviewer simply reads a list of prepared questions (and has no other interaction with the applicant) or the applicant responds to programmed questions given over the phone or on a computer screen. Another example would be when an applicant is requested to submit a video- or audiotape of his or her responses to interviewer questions. No doubt, these procedures can be used to assess job-relevant KSAs, but whether they should be called employment interviews, in our opinion, is more problematic.

The definition offered also gives primary meaning to the employment interview within the context of the employer's staffing process to attract, select, and retain competent and productive employees. First and foremost, the employment interview's raison d'être is the selection of an applicant who best "fits" the particular requirements believed to be associated with successful work performance. Complementary staffing objectives include attracting applicants who are interested in and willing to accept job offers, if selected, and providing applicants with realistic assessments of the work environment and the task demands they will face, to facilitate new employee socialization that enhances employee retention.

Beyond attraction, selection, and retention, interviewer judgment, as is true in virtually all human interaction, is subject to a variety of personal (e.g., likes the applicant on a personal level) and political (e.g., hires someone who will support the interviewer's positions within the organization) agendas. Further, one can study the employment interview from the perspective of the applicant's job/career search efforts, or as an important interpersonal communication event unto itself. However, the employment interview should be viewed primarily as a selection technique within a selection process designed to achieve the organization's staffing needs. Within the selection process, the employment interview may be used early as a recruitment and initial screening device to encourage applicant attraction, provide a realistic job preview, and determine whether the applicant is minimally qualified. Or the interview may take place during the later stages of the selection process, where more lengthy, in-depth discussions with coworkers and supervisors are conducted, often to determine who among the finalists for the job will be chosen. The selection process may include multiple interviews, each conducted by one or more interviewers.

Like other selection techniques (e.g., analysis of biographical data, pencil-and-paper tests, work samples), the employment interview provides the organization with the opportunity to infer whether the applicant possesses the critical knowledge, skills, abilities, and interests to be successful in the targeted position. Unlike other selection techniques, standardization in the analysis of applicant qualifications is made more difficult by the frequently informal, extemporaneous style of most interviewers and by interviewers' limited ability to determine the veracity of applicant self-reports of alleged competence. Clearly, the inherent information-processing limitations and non-job-relevant biases of the interviewer when engaged in information exchange with the applicant places the employment interview at a potential disadvantage compared with more standardized selection decision tools. The advent of structured interviewing in recent decades, as discussed throughout this handbook, appears to be a promising counteragent to the disadvantages and difficulties inherent in the interview. Further jeopardizing interviewer-applicant exchanges of accurate information are the dual but conflicting concerns each has over the mutual attraction and selection of one another. Both want complete and candid information, but often each is reluctant to risk candor that would diminish continuing interest by the other party.

In developing a categorization scheme, we argue that interviews can be classified on the basis of three dimensions: constructs assessed, types of questions asked, and degree of structure or standardization. Constructs assessed include applicant reliability, KSAs, values, and motivation. *Reliability* refers to the applicant's likelihood of adhering to the basic rules and policies of the job and organization, such as attendance, overtime, and travel requirements. *KSAs* are those knowledges (e.g., tax laws), skills (e.g., running a team meeting), and abilities (e.g., verbal reasoning) that are necessary to perform assigned tasks. *Values* are applicant preferences for aspects of the work environment (e.g., supervisory style) and organizational culture (e.g., teamwork) or applicant attitudes about work (e.g., possessing a strong customer service orientation) that the employer believes will drive both employee and firm performance. And finally, *motivation* refers to the applicant's inquiries into the different types of rewards he or she desires (e.g., salary expectations, promotion potential, opportunity to learn new skills, performance bonuses), which may have a significant impact on offer acceptance and employee retention.

Interviews can also be classified according to the types of questions asked, such as questions about training and experience, questions about willingness to work, and trait and behaviorally oriented questions. Training and experience questions include background questions designed to aid in the assessment of work experience, education, and training (see Campion, Palmer, & Campion, 1997), along with related questions intended to help in the assessment of applicant reliability (e.g., reasons for leaving last job, past attendance record). Willingness-to-work questions address the applicant's intentions to meet work schedules (e.g., to work required overtime, to work swing or graveyard shifts, to work scheduled weekends and holidays) and to work under potentially adverse (e.g., work alone, heavy travel schedule, work outdoors) or hazardous conditions (e.g., high noise, chemical exposure). For the most part, such questions are designed to aid in the assessment of applicant reliability and motivation.

Trait questions include a broad array of interviewer inquiries into applicant self-descriptions (e.g., What is your greatest strength or weakness?) and opinions (e.g., How do you feel about team meetings?). Often these questions are intended to tap any or all of the four constructs of applicant reliability, KSAs, values, and motivation. However, the relation of such inquiries to the prediction of work performance has not often been demonstrated. Over the past two decades considerable practitioner and researcher attention has been devoted to behaviorally oriented questions as a way to increase the job relatedness of interviewer judgments of applicant suitability. Behaviorally oriented questions include both situational interview (SI) questions (see Maurer, Sue-Chan, & Latham, Chapter 9, this volume), which focus on intentions or future behavior (e.g., What

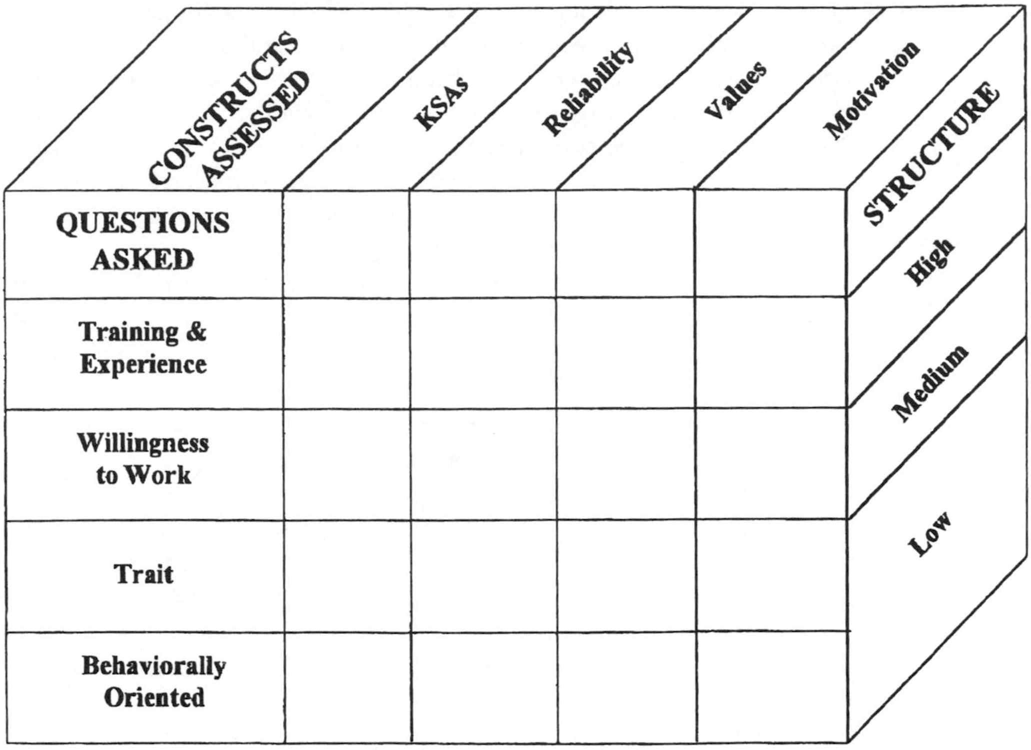

Figure 1.1. Taxonomy of Interviews

would you do?), and behavior description interview (BDI) questions (see Motowidlo, Chapter 10, this volume), which focus on past behavior (e.g., What did you do?). Both formats are based on an analysis of critical events on the job that must be performed and the preidentification of the desired behaviors to be exhibited in given situations. Often researchers have described structured interviewing as the use of either SI or BDI questions. However, it is also clear that there are other ways to provide structure in the interview.

On the third dimension of the categorization scheme depicted in Figure 1.1, there are many ways to increase the structure of the interview, including asking all applicants the same questions, using rating scales or scoring guidelines, and disallowing any questions from applicants (Campion et al., 1997). Although much of the writing on structured interviewing has made the implicit assumption that a dichotomy exists—an interview is either structured or not structured—it is clear that there are degrees or levels of structure. For example, Huffcutt and Arthur (1994) describe a scheme for examining the degree of structure in the employment interview based on the degree to which scoring is employed (three levels) and the degree to which questions are standardized (four levels). Due to the small number of studies in their meta-analytic analysis, they collapsed this 12-cell matrix into four combinations. However, the direction provided by Huffcutt and Arthur is an important first step in dimensionalizing what we mean when we refer to a *more structured* employment interview, and in understanding the effects of different levels and types of interview structure.

Questions of "constructs assessed," "interview content," and "structured interviewing" are at the core of much of the current research on the employment interview, and this is reflected across the chapters in this handbook. We believe the time has come to distinguish across levels of interview structure, types of interview content, and different constructs assessed to clarify advances in employment interview knowledge. Failure to do so will likely lead to continuing confusion among researchers and a limited ability for research to affect interview practice. We need to be clear with one another about what exactly the *interview* is, when it is most valid, and what conditions affect its validity. By using a common classification scheme, we can more readily agree about the conclusions inferred from research and advance employment interview knowledge in a meaningful manner.

What is not in debate is the continuing widespread use and reliance on the employment interview in the making of hiring decisions; the interview is used more often than any other selection technique. Despite continuing questions over the course of the 20th century about the interview's incremental contribution to the validity of employee selection, few individuals are hired without an interview. Perhaps because of this fundamental irony, few topics in the organizational sciences have received as much research activity as has the employment interview.

Employment Interview Research: History

In the past 50 years, 10 narrative reviews of the employment interview literature have been published (Arvey & Campion, 1982; Eder & Buckley, 1988; Hakel, 1982; Harris, 1989; Mayfield, 1964; Schmitt, 1976; Ulrich & Trumbo, 1965; Wagner, 1949; Webster, 1982; Wright, 1969).[1] Other noteworthy recent scholarly narratives of the interview literature include Robert Eder and Gerald Ferris's edited volume *The Employment Interview: Theory, Research, and Practice* (1989), Robert Dipboye's *Selection Interviews: Process Perspectives* (1992), and Michael Campion, David Palmer, and James Campion's 1997 review of structure in the selection interview in *Personnel Psychology*. There have also been seven quantitative meta-analytic reviews of employment interview validity studies, which collectively conclude that structured interviews are superior to unstructured interviews (Conway, Jako, & Goodman, 1995; Huffcutt & Arthur, 1994; Hunter & Hunter, 1984; Marchese & Muchinsky, 1993; McDaniel, Whetzel, Schmidt, & Maurer, 1994; Wiesner & Cronshaw, 1988; Wright, Lichtenfels, & Pursell, 1989). Of the 17 reviews mentioned, 10 were published in just the past decade (1988-1997), reflecting both renewed interest in the employment interview as a selection technique and in the widespread application of meta-analytic techniques where an abundance of empirical studies have been conducted (see Buckley & Russell, Chapter 2, this volume). In the following historical analysis, we identify significant trends that have emerged over the past 50 years, with particular emphasis on more recent developments and future trends.

This historical review of employment interview research is organized roughly by decades. Significant developments in the evolution of employment interview research, like the field of personnel psychology in general, were influenced by major historical events in the United States (e.g., World Wars I and II) and theoretical and methodological developments within the behavioral science research community (e.g., the advent of validity generalization and meta-analytic techniques in the 1980s). All of these developments are shown in Table 1.1, which displays a timeline that begins at 1915 and continues through the year 2005. The items listed in the second column of the table are the major research trends concerning the employment interview during given periods. The final column lists the major events that may have influenced the research endeavors of organizational scientists during each time period.

Early Work: 1915-1939

From 1915 to 1939, academic interest in the employment interview and guidelines for conducting scholarly research were just beginning to be established (e.g., *Journal of Applied Psychology*, 1917; *Personnel*, 1919; *Personnel Journal*, 1922). Division 14 of the American Psychological Association, which monitors the research of industrial and organizational psychologists, would not be founded until 1937. Consequently, most of the early literature on the employment interview offered simplistic laundry lists of dos and don'ts (Wagner, 1949). There were a few notable exceptions.

Scott (1915) was among the first to report research findings on the ability of the employment interview to distinguish adequately between potentially successful and unsuccessful applicants. Scott had 6 personnel managers rank 36 prospective employees for a sales job after an interview. There was little agreement among the personnel managers concerning the predicted success of these individuals. In fact, in approximately 77% of the cases, the managers could not even agree if the applicant should be ranked in the top or bottom half of the group. Follow-up studies supported Scott's initial finding that the interviewer's ability to identify successful

Table 1.1 A Historical Perspective on Interview Research

Year	Interview Research	Historical/Professional Developments
1915		Founding of *Journal of Applied Psychology, Personnel,* and *Personnel Journal*
1920		
1925	"How to" interviews	
1930		
1935		Founding of Division 14 APA
1940	Armed Services studies and introduction of new techniques	World War II
1945		Postwar economic expansion
1950		
		Interaction process analysis
1955	Partitioning the interview	Field theory
1960	Interviewer as decision maker	
		Civil Rights Act of 1964
1965		
1970	Interviewer as limited information processor	
		Equal Employment Opportunity Act of 1972
1975		
1980		Validity generalization/meta-analysis
	Structured interviewing (SI and BDI)	
1985		Global competition
	Meta-analytic studies	
1990	Americans with Disabilities Act	
1995	Further developments in interview structure	
		Evolution of computerized decision support software
2000		
2005	Construct, content, and incremental validity	

applicants was problematic (Scott, 1916; Scott, Bingham, & Whipple, 1916). Scott (1916) asked 13 executives to rate 12 men on their ability to sell. The average correlation of the executives was little better than chance. Scott et al. (1916) asked 20 sales managers and 3 personnel researchers to rank 24 applicants. Each applicant was to prepare a 5-minute sales speech, which the interviewer could listen to if he felt that doing so would be the best way to determine the applicant's ability to sell. Consequently, some applicants were not asked to deliver their speeches. The applicant who received the largest variation in rankings was rated 2nd by one rater and 24th by another. The applicant with the least variation in rankings was ranked 1st by one rater and 12th by another.

In a study that followed the same basic pattern as the Scott series, Hollingsworth (1922) asked 12 sales managers who were experienced in personnel selection to interview 57 applicants following any procedure they chose. After the interviews, each manager was asked to rank the applicants. On the whole, the results of the rankings showed great variability, although there was some agreement on the best and the worst candidates. According to Wagner (1949), this study was often cited as quite influential in undermining confidence in the employment interview process.

Moss (1931) asked interviewers to rate the scholastic ability of medical school applicants they had interviewed. He found that interview procedures could have detected 33% of the students who were admitted to medical school but who did not succeed. These results would have been encouraging if the interview procedure would not also have eliminated 23% of the students whose medical school performance earned an average of 85 or higher out of 100.

One of the few longitudinal studies performed on the interview during this period was reported by Kenagy and Yoakum (1925). These authors had an executive rate 34 newly hired salespersons based on information gathered in a half-hour interview. Two other executives were asked to rate the same 34 salespersons based on their daily 1-hour contacts with the individuals during a subsequent 2-week training program. After the sales personnel had been out in the field for 2 months, their sales performance was measured and then correlated with the ratings of each of the three executives. The correlations were .27 for the interviewing executive and .21 and .16 for the two interacting executives.

The War Years: 1940-1949

Much of the research reported during the 1940s continued to test the reliability and validity of the interview with large military samples. It is somewhat interesting to note that the first large-scale use of convenience samples in selection research involved not college sophomores but inductees of the armed services during World War II. One such study tested how successful the interview could be at predicting success at learning to fly an airplane. Dunlap and Wantman (1947) asked three interviewers, acting as a board, to study each applicant's Personal History Inventory (PHI) for 3 minutes prior to the applicant's entering the room for an interview. The PHI consisted of work, health, and personal history information completed by the applicant. At the conclusion of the 25-minute interview, each interviewer rated the applicant on nine different scales. The results showed that interrater agreement was high (.53 to .70) across all scales. However, when these predictions were compared with the results from flight school, overall prediction rates were little better than chance. Similar findings were reported 2 years later in a separate study by Newman, Bobbitt, and Cameron (1946).

Not only was the simple predictive validity of the interview questioned, but also the interview's incremental contribution to successful selection. Conrad and Satter (1946) conducted a study on the usefulness of the interview for the selection of 3,500 naval candidates into the Electricians' Mates School. Ratings were made based on test scores alone as well as based on test scores and information obtained in the interview. Results of the study indicated that test scores alone predicted better than tests scores combined with interview information. A more expansive study performed for the U.S. Navy by Bloom and Brundage was reported by Struit (1947). More than 37,800 cases of acceptance into technical schools were examined using a methodology similar to that used by Conrad and Satter (1946). The authors concluded that there was a relatively small gain in the ability to predict success when the interviewer's information was added to test scores.

On a more positive note, Putney (1947) conducted a study that suggested that the simple decision utility of the employment interview may be more impressive than predictive validity enhancement. In this study, men who were assigned to technical schools at random were compared with individuals who were assigned based on a classification interview. Results indicated that only 29% of the randomly selected applicants successfully completed the program, whereas 84% of the applicants selected through the interview were successful. To summarize, most of the empirical work on the employment interview during the first half of the 20th century directly assessed the interview's reliability and validity as a selection device. Based on a review of empirical results reported in only one-fourth of the 106 published articles during this period, Wagner (1949) found that the reliability of the interview ranged from .23 to .97 and overall validities ranged from −.20 to .85. In part, due to the early disappointing research results, the term *standardized interview* began to appear in the literature as a basic strategy for improving interview reliability. According to Wagner (1949), a standardized interview is one that is conducted according to an established pattern.

A second theme in this decade was the introduction of new techniques to be used in the interview. One novel approach was presented by Travers (1941), who suggested that applicants should be rated as they carry out a practical test (i.e., the interview as a work sample). A carpenter would be asked to build a small object, so that his work habits and techniques could be viewed and the finished object inspected for quality. Another innovative example was proposed by Brody (1947), who suggested that a group of 6 to 12 candidates participate in a discussion relevant to the position to be filled. Each candidate would also be asked to prepare a 3- to 5-minute talk on an assigned topic. While the candidates presented their speeches and participated in the discussion, the interviewers would observe the candidates' behavior and record their observations (i.e., mini-assessment center experience).

Partitioning the Interview: 1950-1959

During the 1950s, several procedures were presented for partitioning the interview into smaller pieces to standardize the interview so that it could become a viable research instrument, consistent with the advent of interaction process analysis (Bales, 1950) within social psychology. This procedure required observers to place segments of speech into 1 of 12 categories. The observations in each category were then analyzed to answer questions such as "Who is the leader?" and "What type of leadership style did they use?" Applying this analysis approach, Daniels and Otis (1950) were among the first to develop an unobtrusive methodology for observing and analyzing employment counseling interviews through the use of audiotaping. Interviews were electronically recorded in eight different employment offices, and a sample of 60 of these were examined. From these interviews, 26 categories were identified that could be used to analyze the content of the interview, including the total number of exchanges, time the interviewer spoke, time the applicant spoke, and number of questions asked by the applicant. Some of the more interesting findings included observations that interviewers had more control over the length of the interview and applicants had more control over the number of exchanges in the interview (probably due to the interviewer's counseling style). Another general partitioning procedure was introduced by Chappel and reported by Matarazzo, Suslow, and Matarazzo (1956). According to Matarazzo et al., Chappel devised a machine he called the Interaction Chronograph. The machine had keys that represented the interview participants. As each participant spoke, an observer would depress the key assigned to the speaking participant, and a line would be drawn on a constantly moving tape. When the participant stopped speaking, the observer released the key and the line stopped. By studying the line lengths, it was possible for a researcher to assign values to 10 variables, such as who talked most, who talked least, and the tempo of the conversation, which were then further examined.

Interviewer as Decision Maker: 1960-1969

During the 1960s, distinct "camps" or groups of researchers emerged, typically associated with particular geographic areas or institutions, each engaged in programmatic research on the interview. A series of studies was produced by Campbell and his colleagues (Brailey, Liske, Otis, and Prien), who represented one such camp at Case Western Reserve University. The main focus of their research was the examination of the interview as a predictor of performance ratings. In a review of these studies, Otis,

Campbell, and Prien (1962) suggested that even though the obtained validity coefficients had been modest, they were all positive, providing evidence that psychologists were able to predict success when the predictions were based on major sources of information. However, the interview alone produced valid predictions only for dimensions of interpersonal relations.

A second group of researchers consisted of Webster (1964) and his colleagues (Anderson, Crowell, Rowe, Springbett, and Sydiaha) at McGill University, who performed research on the decision-making process in the employment interview. One of the most frequently cited conclusions from these studies was the fact that interviewers developed a stereotype of an "ideal candidate" and then sought to match the candidates interviewed to that stereotype. Hakel, Hollman, and Dunnette (1970) would later replicate this finding, though London and Hakel (1974) found that the stereotypes used by the interviewer to judge an applicant diminished as the evaluation of the applicant continued. The results presented by the McGill team contributed to the development of another series of research studies conducted by Maier and his colleagues (see Maier & Thurber, 1968) and focused on honesty in interactions. Interviewers had considerable difficulty explaining their judgments of honesty or dishonesty in the interview. Maier and Thurber (1968) had undergraduates watch, listen to, or read a transcript of an interview concerning a student who may or may not have altered an exam before returning it for regrading. Results indicated that listeners and readers were better able to judge deception attempts than were watchers. A second frequently cited conclusion from the Webster group was that interviewer decisions were often made within the first 2 or 3 minutes of the interview. This assertion that interviewers routinely engage in "snap decisions" persists as part of our collective management lore, though Springbett's (1958) finding has never been replicated, and may in actual practice be more untrue than true (Buckley & Eder, 1988, 1989).

Carlson and Mayfield and their colleagues published a third group of studies that examined the employment interview in the insurance industry (Carlson, 1967a, 1967b, 1968; Mayfield, Brown, & Hamstra, 1980). In findings similar to the work of Webster (1964) and his colleagues, Carlson and Mayfield asked managers to make hire/no hire decisions and rate and then rank the favorability of each of eight hypothetical applicants. According to Wright (1969), the degree of information favorability was the most important variable in the decision-making process.

In their review of the literature since 1949, Ulrich and Trumbo (1965) argued that interviewers are all too frequently asked to do the impossible because of limitations on available time and information. Researchers of the 1950s and 1960s began to reveal the complex information exchanges and decision-making process dynamics within the interview event that may help to explain the interview's weak predictive validity as a selection technique. In fact, Ulrich and Trumbo went so far as to recommend that the interviewer's task be limited to a single trait or suitability rating for which acceptable validity might be possible—a recommendation that soon would be inconsistent with the documentation required to defend the employment interview from charges of unfair discrimination.

Interviewer as Limited Information Processor: 1970-1982

By the 1970s, it was rapidly becoming apparent that interviewer judgment is susceptible to a number of influences. Work continued to be published on the effects of verbal and visual cues, such as eye contact, smiling, posture, interpersonal distance, and body orientation (Imada & Hakel, 1977; Washburn & Hakel, 1973). However, the magnitude of these effects began to be challenged as being more experimenter induced than real (see London & Hakel, 1974). Although some researchers found significant influence in the order in which applicants were presented (i.e., contrast effects) (see also Wexley, Yukl, Kovacs, & Sanders, 1972), other researchers found nonsignificant or trivial effects when professional interviewers were used as research participants (Hakel, Dobmeyer, & Dunnette, 1970; Landy & Bates, 1973).

During this period, industrial/organizational psychologists began to incorporate into their research precepts from social cognitive psychology that human rationality is "bounded" (Simon, 1957), that people's cognitive capabilities are limited (Tversky & Kahneman, 1974), and that actuarial methods are consistently superior to clinical judgments such as the interview (Meehl, 1965). A cognitive information-processing theory assumes that information is attended to, categorized, and combined according to unique cognitive "schemata" (Taylor & Crocker, 1981; Wyer & Srull, 1981). The primary goal of this research is to study cognitive processing, from information acquisition and encoding to storage and memory retrieval (Ilgen & Feldman, 1983), and to delineate the variety of information-processing errors that undermine interview validity. Schmitt (1976) was the first to catalog the information-processing bias sources that limit interviewer accuracy. Subsequent scholarly reviews built upon this cognitive information-processing perspective with suggestions for interview practice, interviewer training, and future research (Arvey & Campion, 1982; Hakel, 1982; Webster, 1982).

Into the 1980s, work continued that was aimed at a better understanding of the interviewer's cognitively complex task and the frequent shortcuts the interviewer takes in arriving at an interview judgment (Motowidlo, 1986). Dipboye (1982) found that the cognitive schemata developed by the interviewer after a brief review of the candidate's résumé and application materials may likely guide the interview process and predetermine its outcome, raising fundamental questions about the incremental validity of the interview within the typical selection process. In support of Dipboye's perspective, Zedeck, Tziner, and Middlestadt (1983) found that in spite of training to the contrary, interviewers may use only a limited number of rating criteria to reach their decisions.

Though acknowledging the automated processes that limit human information processing, other researchers urged attention to aspects of the judgment process that may be responsive to external intervention. Dreher and Sackett (1983, pp. 323-332) suggested treating the interviewer as an active, rather than a passive, information seeker, focusing attention on the causal linkages in the interviewer's effort to seek, receive, and process information. Later in the decade, Eder and Buckley (1988) proposed an interactionist perspective to extend existing research to address more adequately the effects of interview context on interviewer information search efforts, placing a more equal emphasis on person and situation dimensions as they interact within the cognitive awareness of the interviewer. This interactionist perspective on interview research was employed as a framework by Eder and Ferris in their edited collection *The Employment Interview* (1989), which is a precursor to this handbook.

With passage of the Equal Employment Opportunity Act of 1972, vigorous enforcement of Title VII of the 1964 Civil Rights Act directed researcher attention to the interview's legal liability. Interview researchers had a new outcome variable to address beyond reliability and validity, namely, whether the employment interview gives unwarranted advantage to members of one group over another (i.e., concerns over disparate impact and differential validity, especially on the basis of race or gender). Perhaps due to the availability of data, research on gender bias was particularly plentiful.

Simas and McCarrey (1979) asked 84 personnel officers, both men and women, to evaluate videotaped recruitment interviews of male and female applicants. Each personnel officer was classified as possessing either a high or a low level of authoritarianism. Results indicated that high authoritarian personnel officers, regardless of their sex, rated the male applicants more favorably and indicated a higher likelihood of offering the male applicants a position. However, Rosen and Merich (1979) found no difference in the evaluations of males' and females' résumés by administrators who worked for companies with strong fair employment policies. Yet these same administrators recommended that female applicants be given lower starting salaries than their male counterparts.

Interest in gender bias extended to research on perceived attractiveness. Heilman and Saruwatari (1979) asked male and female college students to rate applicants, both male and female, who had been judged earlier to be attractive or unattractive. The type of position the applicant was applying for was either managerial or clerical. Although results indicated that attractiveness always helped the male candidates, it helped the female applicants only when the position was a clerical one. When a woman was considered for a managerial position, attractiveness worked against her. Using male interviewers as evaluators of job résumés, Dipboye, Fromkin, and Wiback (1975) found that unattractive candidates were discriminated against.

With the passage of the Vocational Rehabilitation Act of 1973, researchers also addressed whether disabled applicants were unfairly discriminated against in the employment interview. Kreftling and Brief (1977) found that more favorable evaluations were given to disabled individuals than actually were warranted. However, the finding was not consistent across all types of disabilities. For example, Nagi, McBroom, and Colletts (1972) reported that applicants with histories of mental illness were perceived more negatively when compared with applicants without such histories. Passage of the Americans With Disabilities Act of 1990 produced additional research on how disabled applicants are treated in the employment interview (see Roehling, Campion, & Arvey, Chapter 3, this volume) and how practitioners should adjust interviewing practices to be in compliance with the law (see Harris & Eder, Chapter 21, this volume).

After reviewing research on unfair discrimination in the employment interview, Arvey (1979) was able to conclude that available evidence left it unclear whether interviewers discriminated on the basis of race, age, or disability. It was clear that women may be at risk in the employment interview, receiving lower evaluations than men. However, Arvey was able to demonstrate that there was virtually no evidence, and little likelihood of ever finding such evidence, concerning the differential validity of the interview across these selected demographic groups. Although Arvey envisioned that litigation regarding unfair discrimination in the employment interview would escalate rapidly, at least up to the mid-1990s this has not come to pass, attesting perhaps to the widespread trust people have in the interview.

Structured Interviewing (SI and BDI): 1982-1989

On the economic front in the 1980s, U.S. firms faced the growing reality of accelerated global competition and the postindustrial economic transformation to an information- and service-based economy. Effective management of human resources became a more integral part of the firm's strategic effort to secure and maintain a competitive advantage in the marketplace, with increased attention on reducing labor costs and increasing worker productivity. One result of this changing economic reality was renewed interest in effective employee selection decisions and the relative predictive validity of different selection techniques (Hunter & Hunter, 1984; Reilly & Chao, 1982). This interest was fostered by the work of Hunter and Schmidt (1990) on meta-analytic literature review techniques and subsequent arguments for the validity generalization of cognitive and aptitude tests across diverse settings (Schmidt, Hunter, McKenzie, &

Muldrow, 1979). By the end of the decade, at least three large meta-analytic studies had been completed on the interview (McDaniel et al., 1994; Wiesner & Cronshaw, 1989; Wright et al., 1989). (Though McDaniel et al.'s study was not published until 1994, the primary work was completed in 1987 and widely distributed within the academic community.)

Most notable in the 1980s was the growing evidence that structured interviewing techniques like situational interviewing (Latham & Saari, 1984; Latham, Saari, Pursell, & Campion, 1980; Weekley & Gier, 1987) and behavior description interviewing (Janz, 1982; Janz, Hellervik, & Gilmore, 1986; Orpen, 1985) yielded more reliable and valid ratings of applicant suitability than did the unstructured interview. Perhaps the century-long quest for a more reliable, standardized interview form was reaching fruition. Still, questions remained about the incremental validity of these more structured techniques (see Dipboye, 1982), their practical use, and exactly how their "structure" modifies the interviewer's decision process in apparently positive ways (see Campion, Pursell, & Brown, 1988; Eder & Buckley, 1988; Harris, 1989).

Further Developments in Interview Structure: 1990-1998

As Harris (1989) concluded in his review, research conducted in the 1980s on structured interviewing provided a much more positive conclusion about the employment interview as a selection procedure. Subsequently, at least two distinct research streams emerged during the 1990s. First, research on interview structure increased significantly, with three tributaries. One tributary in this research stream addressed the realization that the term *structured interview* is far too broad to be meaningful. Specifically, interview "structure" was posed to be a multidimensional construct (Campion et al., 1997), with different levels or degrees of structure in the interviewer decision-making process (see Huffcutt & Arthur, 1994) and potential comparative performance differences across SI or BDI question formats (see Pulakos & Schmitt, 1995). This tributary continues to be active and is reflected in several chapters in this handbook.

A second tributary of this stream is research examining different levels of interview structure and different question formats as they relate to other constructs, such as cognitive ability (e.g., Huffcutt, Roth, & McDaniel, 1996). In part, this tributary attempts to address the incremental validity of the structured interview, to determine which forms of structured interviewing yield more unique contributions to the selection decision beyond what is available from other selection tests. Research has also examined the relationship between applicant race and different interview question formats (e.g., Lin, Dobbins, & Farh, 1992), with applied implications (e.g., Prewett-Livingston, Feild, Veres, & Lewis, 1996). Continued research along this tributary may provide further insight into what construct(s) the interview is measuring.

Investigations of various psychometric properties of different interviews (e.g., structured versus unstructured) constitute the third tributary.
For example, Conway et al. (1995) examined interrater and intrarater reliability and reported interesting implications for the number of questions
and use of multiple interviewers. Other possible psychometric properties
that may be worth exploring are factor structures, means, and variances as
they differ based on question format (e.g., SI versus BDI) and degree of
structure.

A second major stream of research during the 1990s, but one less
dominant than in the past, has focused on interviewer-applicant interaction
dynamics. One possible reason for the decline in relative interest here may
be that the structured interview heavily downplays the interaction between
interviewer and applicant. Nevertheless, significant contributions have
been made, largely driven by the expanding interest in impression management tactics (see Gilmore, Stevens, Harrell-Cook, & Ferris, Chapter 18,
this volume) and applicant reactions to selection procedures (see Gilliland
& Steiner, Chapter 4, this volume). For example, Stevens and Kristof
(1995) compared ratings of impression management behaviors made by
interviewers, applicants, and independent observers, and Powell (1991) and
Rynes, Bretz, and Gerhart (1991) examined applicant reactions to the
interview. In a related study within this research stream, Barber, Hollenbeck, Tower, and Phillips (1994) examined the effect of interview purpose
on applicants' processing of information.

With the exception of a few studies (e.g., Motowidlo & Burnett, 1995),
the study of interviewer-applicant communications (see Jablin, Miller, &
Sias, Chapter 17; and Kacmar & Young, Chapter 13, this volume) has not
been examined in the context of structured interviews. Therefore, considerable potential exists for research at the intersection of these two research
streams—the study of interview dynamics with structured interviews. This
observation also raises the fundamental question of whether researchers
should continue to study the unstructured interview.

The unstructured interview, where there are no constraints on the
questions asked of applicants and only a global assessment is made (i.e.,
Level I in Huffcutt and Arthur's [1994] framework), has been shown to
have scant validity as a selection technique. By analogy with the pharma-
ceutical field, one would probably not encourage drug companies to
continue to perform research on medications that have been shown to be
quite inferior to newer, more efficacious medications. However, we believe
that research on unstructured interviews may still be justified at this time.

First, most organizations continue to use the unstructured interview to
a large extent, and hence there is value to both the organization and the
applicant in scholarly studies of how these interview events affect important outcomes. Second, although unstructured interviews may have relatively low predictive validity as a traditional selection method, they may be
effective for related purposes of applicant attraction, new employee so-

cialization, and assessment of expanded notions of "fit" (e.g., person-organization). Third, unstructured interviews may be an appropriate context for researching a wide range of other interpersonal judgments, such as decision making, mood, and stereotyping. If the researcher's goal is to study nonselection aspects of the staffing process (e.g., how applicants perceive the organization) or other phenomena of interest (e.g., impression management tactics), then the use of unstructured interviews may be quite reasonable. However, if the researcher's intention is to refine and improve the interview as a valid selection device, then the study of unstructured interviews seems less justified.

Other Future Research Directions: The 21st Century and Beyond

Future research will continue to explore facets of structured interviewing, alternative questioning formats, and interviewer-applicant dynamics to increase our understanding of the incremental contribution the interview makes in effective staffing practices and the unique interpersonal dynamics of the interview event. Beyond the extension of these current research trends, there are several potential new streams that may emerge, some of which we discuss below (please keep in mind that our discussion is admittedly speculative).

One likely new stream of research will emerge from the rapid evolution and application of computerized decision support software, which assists the hiring manager in obtaining applicant information efficiently. Expanded use of information technologies may actually free the interviewer from having to use limited interview time to confirm factual information (e.g., documenting prior work experiences) or to probe into personally sensitive areas of inquiry (e.g., questions related to work attitudes, honesty, drug and alcohol use). The interviewer may have more time for focused, in-depth applicant-interviewer exchanges, which would enhance the value of the employment interview as a staffing tool.

As personal computer power and convenience grow in the workplace, traditional pencil-and-paper tests will be converted to computerized versions (this is already happening with most ability tests). This increase will lead to the development of new software packages tailored to the needs of hiring managers. Already on the market are software packages designed to screen résumés and applications. Today, an applicant waiting for an interview is often asked to sit at a personal computer and answer a variety of preinterview inquiries. The software program instantaneously transmits the applicant's responses on-line 24 hours a day, 7 days a week, for scoring and analysis. Within a few minutes an analysis is transmitted back to the interviewer that includes suggested areas for interviewer follow-up and even specific questions to ask during the face-to-face interview. The software may not only guide the manager in what to ask, it may also help the manager scrutinize the information collected and the likely truthfulness of the applicant's responses through a voice stress analyzer. Already the software applications are proceeding, far ahead of the research evidence needed before experts can advise their prudent use. In particular, research is needed to further our understanding of how best to design and use decision support software, and to determine what, if any, impacts it may have on interview outcomes of interest (e.g., enhancement of selection validity, improvement of applicant reactions, minimization of legal liability, more effective utilization of interviewer time).

Another likely stream of research on the horizon involves the assessment of expanded notions of applicant "fit," particularly person-organization fit (e.g., Bowen, Ledford, & Nathan, 1991; Cable & Judge, 1997; see also Parsons, Cable, & Liden, Chapter 7, this volume). Research on the assessment of person-organization fit is still in its infancy, but it has the potential to add incremental validity in the prediction of job success (e.g., both work performance and job survivability). Moreover, in light of rapidly changing organizations, tasks, and jobs, some experts have questioned the logic of making selection decisions based on specific, job-related KSAs and have recommended that selection decisions be based on broader considerations, such as the match between organizational values and needs and the applicant's values and preferences.

A third potential new stream of research involves cross-cultural considerations in employment interview research. What we know about the employment interview, as reflected in the many meta-analytic reviews of the literature, is essentially what we know about employment interviewing within the context of the unique social, economic, and cultural conditions that exist in the United States and Canada (see Boyacigiller & Adler, 1991). Hofstede (1994) has found national culture differences on dimensions of power distance, uncertainty avoidance, individualism, and masculinity—all dimensions that have the potential for influencing interviewer-applicant interactions and judgments. Recent research on performance feedback and assessment lends support to findings of cross-cultural differences in the interpretation of performance attributions and feedback reactions (Earley & Stubblebine, 1989; Farh, Dobbins, & Cheng, 1991). Yet only speculative and anecdotal information exists about how these cultural differences may alter employment interview processes and outcomes (Hui & Mobley, 1996; Shenkar, 1995).

Although widely adopted in North America, structured interviewing may meet considerable resistance in other countries where there is an absence of highly specific job descriptions and individual performance standards. Instead, unstructured interviewing is the norm in many countries; broad constructs and capabilities are assessed often in lengthy conversations that may focus as much on the applicant's family, childhood education, philosophy of life, and personal interests as on the applicant's work-related qualifications. The modest resistance reported in the current literature by both interviewers and applicants in North America toward structured interview content (e.g., SI and BDI questions) may be substantial in other cultures (see Gilliland & Steiner, Chapter 4, this volume).

Cross-cultural differences are likely to be even more important to our understanding of interviewer-applicant process dynamics. In North America, the employment interview has the element of a contest between the applicant and the interviewer. Interviewers often are confrontive and probing in their questioning; applicants are assertive, if not self-promoting. In contrast, the cultural expectations in many Asian countries, for example, are based on a collaborative style, personal modesty, and reluctance to speak about one's individual accomplishments in a comparative sense. Cross-cultural differences in the use of impression management tactics (see Gilmore et al., Chapter 18, this volume) would appear to be particularly prevalent. Cross-cultural research on the employment interview should, at the very least, assuage the Western ethnocentric bias that currently exists within the empirical literature and improve the prospects of advancing interview practice in an increasingly multicultural business world.

The Organizing Framework for This Book

The chapters that constitute this handbook are grouped into five parts in accordance with the integrative framework depicted in Figure 1.2. The authors' names and chapter numbers for the remaining 20 chapters in this volume are noted in the figure to provide the reader with a frame of reference. More introductory details are provided in the brief summary descriptions that precede each part of the book.

The chapters in Part I address interview outcomes of primary interest, namely, validity, fairness, and applicant reactions and attraction, which are depicted in Figure 1.2 as direct products of the interviewer's decision-making process and the interviewer-applicant dynamics that occur during the interview. Before exploring aspects of the decision-making process and interview dynamics, Part II broadens the traditional perspective on job-specific validity by examining expanded notions of applicant "fit" around personality assessment and person-organization fit. In particular, the chapters in Part II raise the fundamental question of what constructs the interview is attempting to measure, with particular attention to the ongoing discussion of what constitutes a structured interview and the latest thinking regarding both situational interviewing and behavior description interviewing.

Part III includes six chapters that address different research streams and perspectives on the interviewer's decision-making process. Key components of this process are the cognitive operations the interviewer employs to arrive at an evaluation of the applicant's suitability. These include

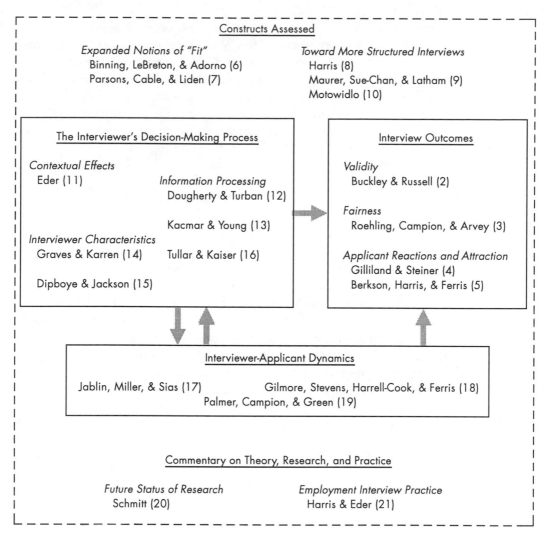

Figure 1.2. Organizing Framework for Integrating Current Research Streams on the Employment Interview

expectations the interviewer holds as a result of preinterview impressions, how the interviewer may process unfavorable information, and how multiple interviewer judgments may be synthesized effectively. Also addressed in Part III are the more exogenous factors of perceived interview context and the role of interviewer individual differences, particularly interviewer expertise and experience.

　Part IV consists of three chapters that address interviewer-applicant dynamics from both parties' perspectives. These differing perspectives may alter how the interview is conducted and the judgments made by interviewer and applicant. A review of the process dynamics, largely from the rich organizational communications literature, is provided, along with an update on the growing application of impression management tactics in the interview. The last chapter in Part IV discusses the state of interviewing training from the perspectives of both the interviewer and the applicant.

The final two chapters of this handbook (Part V) are commentaries by Neal Schmitt on employment interview research and by Michael Harris and Robert Eder on employment interview practice. These commentaries highlight the contributions to research and practice of the contributors to this book, take note of conflicting viewpoints, add ideas not previously raised, and suggest future directions for employment interview research and effective practice.

As with any effort to synthesize diverse research streams into a single organizational framework, parsimony has simplified but not completely captured the full complexity of the variable relationships addressed here. Nevertheless, our intent in offering this framework is to guide the reader through the remainder of this book and to place each chapter within a single perspective. One of the additional benefits of an integrative framework is the potential insight one may obtain by comparing and contrasting separate works that ostensibly address the same generic factor. Furthermore, the framework may encourage future researchers to conceptualize the interview in its totality, which may lead to a more systematic progression in employment interview research and the advancement of effective interviewing practices.

Note

1. This section expands upon the historical analysis provided by Eder, Kacmar, and Ferris (1989).

References

Arvey, R. D. (1979). Unfair discrimination in the employment interview: Legal and psychological aspects. *Psychological Bulletin, 86,* 736-765.

Arvey, R. D., & Campion, J. E. (1982). The employment interview: A summary and review of recent research. *Personnel Psychology, 35,* 281-322.

Bales, R. F. (1950). *Interaction process analysis.* Cambridge, MA: Addison-Wesley.

Barber, A. E., Hollenbeck, J. R., Tower, S. L., & Phillips, J. M. (1994). The effects of interview focus on recruitment effectiveness: A field experiment. *Journal of Applied Psychology, 79,* 886-896.

Bowen, D. E., Ledford, G. E., & Nathan, B. R. (1991). Hiring for the organization, not the job. *Academy of Management Executive, 5,* 35-51.

Boyacigiller, N. A., & Adler, N. J. (1991). The parochial dinosaur: Organization science in a global context. *Academy of Management Review, 16,* 262-290.

Brody, W. (1947). Judging candidates by observing them in unsupervised group discussion. *Personnel Journal, 26,* 170-173.

Buckley, M. R., & Eder, R. W. (1988). B. M. Springbett and the notion of the "snap decision" in the interview. *Journal of Management, 14,* 59-67.

Buckley, M. R., & Eder, R. W. (1989, May). The first impression. *Personnel Administrator,* pp. 72-74.

Cable, D. M., & Judge, T. A. (1997). Interviewers' perceptions of person-organization fit and organizational selection decisions. *Journal of Applied Psychology, 82,* 546-561.

Campion, M. A., Palmer, D. K., & Campion, J. E. (1997). A review of structure in the selection interview. *Personnel Psychology, 50,* 655-702.

Campion, M. A., Pursell, E. D., & Brown, B. K. (1988). Structured interviewing: Raising the psychometric properties of the employment interview. *Personnel Psychology, 41,* 25-42.

Carlson, R. E. (1967a). The relative influence of appearance and factual written information on an interviewer's final rating. *Journal of Applied Psychology, 51,* 461-468.

Carlson, R. E. (1967b). Selection interview decisions: The effect of interview experience, relative quota situation, and applicant sample on interview decisions. *Personnel Psychology, 20,* 259-280.

Carlson, R. E. (1968). Selection interview decisions: The effect of mode of applicant presentation on some outcome measures. *Personnel Psychology, 21,* 193-207.

Carlson, R. E., & Mayfield, E. C. (1967). Evaluating interview and employment application data. *Personnel Psychology, 20,* 441-460.

Conrad, H. S., & Satter, G. A. (1946). *The use of test scores and quality classification ratings in predicting success in Electricians' Mates School* (OSRD No. 133290). Washington, DC: U.S. Department of Commerce.

Conway, J. M., Jako, R. A., & Goodman, D. F. (1995). A meta-analysis of interrater and internal consistency reliability of selection interviews. *Journal of Applied Psychology, 80,* 565-579.

Daniels, H. W., & Otis, J. L. (1950). A method for analyzing employment interviews. *Personnel Psychology, 3,* 425-444.

Dipboye, R. L. (1982). Self-fulfilling prophecies in the selection interview. *Academy of Management Review, 7,* 579-586.

Dipboye, R. L. (1992). *Selection interviews: Process perspectives.* Cincinnati, OH: South-Western.

Dipboye, R. L. (1994). Structured and unstructured selection interviews: Beyond the job-fit model. In G. R. Ferris (Ed.), *Research in personnel and human resources management* (Vol. 12, pp. 79-123). Greenwich, CT: JAI.

Dipboye, R. L., Fromkin, H. L., & Wiback, K. (1975). Relative importance of applicant sex, attractiveness, and scholastic standing in evaluation of job applicant resumes. *Journal of Applied Psychology, 60,* 39-43.

Dreher, G. G., & Sackett, P. R. (1983). *Perspectives on employee staffing and selection.* Homewood, IL: AMACOM.

Dunlap, J. W., & Wantman, M. J. (1947). *An investigation of the interview as a technique for selecting aircraft pilots* (Report No. 50308). Washington, DC: U.S. Department of Commerce.

Earley, P. C., & Stubblebine, P. (1989). Intercultural assessment of performance feedback. *Group and Organization Studies, 14,* 161-181.

Eder, R. W., & Buckley, M. R. (1988). The employment interview: An interactionist perspective. In G. R. Ferris & K. M. Rowland (Eds.), *Research in personnel and human resources management* (Vol. 6, pp. 75-107). Greenwich, CT: JAI.

Eder, R. W., & Ferris, G. R. (Eds.). (1989). *The employment interview: Theory, research, and practice.* Newbury Park, CA: Sage.

Eder, R. W., Kacmar, K. M., & Ferris, G. R. (1989). Employment interview research: History and synthesis. In R. W. Eder & G. R. Ferris (Eds.), *The employment interview: Theory, research, and practice* (pp. 17-31). Newbury Park, CA: Sage.

Farh, J.-L., Dobbins, G. H., & Cheng, B.-S. (1991). Cultural relativity in action: A comparison of self-ratings made by Chinese and U.S. workers. *Personnel Psychology, 44,* 129-145.

Guion, R. (1997). *Assessment, measurement, and predictions for personnel decisions.* Mahwah, NJ: Lawrence Erlbaum.

Hakel, M. D. (1982). Employment interviewing. In K. M. Rowland & G. R. Ferris (Eds.), *Personnel management* (pp. 102-124). Boston: Allyn & Bacon.

Hakel, M. D., Dobmeyer, T. W., & Dunnette, M. D. (1970). Relative importance of three content dimensions in overall suitability ratings of job applicants' resumes. *Journal of Applied Psychology, 54,* 65-71.

Hakel, M. D., Hollman, T. D., & Dunnette, M. D. (1970). Accuracy of interviewers, certified public accountants, and students in identifying the interests of accountants. *Journal of Applied Psychology, 54,* 115-119.

Harris, M. M. (1989). Reconsidering the employment interview: A review of recent literature and suggestions for future research. *Personnel Psychology, 42,* 691-726.

Heilman, M. E., & Saruwatari, L. R. (1979). When beauty is beastly: The effects of appearance and sex on evaluations of job applicants for managerial and nonmanagerial jobs. *Organizational Behavior and Human Performance, 23,* 360-372.

Hofstede, G. (1994). Management scientists are human. *Management Science, 40,* 4-13.

Hollingsworth, H. L. (1922). *Judging human character.* New York: Appleton-Century-Crofts.

Huffcutt, A. I., & Arthur, W. (1994). Hunter and Hunter (1984) revisited: Interview validity for entry-level jobs. *Journal of Applied Psychology, 79,* 184-190.

Huffcutt, A. I., Roth, P. L., & McDaniel, M. A. (1996). A meta-analytic investigation of cognitive ability in employment interview evaluations: Moderating characteristics and implications for incremental validity. *Journal of Applied Psychology, 81,* 459-473.

Hui, C., & Mobley, W. H. (1996, April). *Employment interviewing in China and Hong Kong: Cultural moderators in a conceptual model of impression management.* Paper presented at the annual meeting of the Society for Industrial and Organizational Psychology.

Hunter, J. E., & Hunter, R. F. (1984). Validity and utility of alternative prediction of job performance. *Journal of Applied Psychology, 96,* 72-98.

Hunter, J. E., & Schmidt, F. L. (1990). *Methods of meta-analysis: Correcting error and bias in research findings.* Newbury Park, CA: Sage.

Ilgen, D. R., & Feldman, J. M. (1983). Performance appraisal: A process focus. In L. L. Cummings & B. M. Staw (Eds.), *Research in organizational behavior* (Vol. 5, pp. 141-197). Greenwich, CT: JAI.

Imada, A. S., & Hakel, M. D. (1977). Influence of nonverbal communication and rater proximity on impression and decisions in simulated employment interviews. *Journal of Applied Psychology, 62,* 295-300.

Janz, J. T. (1982). Initial comparisons of patterned behavior description interviews versus unstructured interviews. *Journal of Applied Psychology, 67,* 577-580.

Janz, J. T., Hellervik, L., & Gilmore, D. C. (1986). *Behavior description interviewing: New, accurate, cost effective.* Newton, MA: Allyn & Bacon.

Kenagy, H. G., & Yoakum, C. S. (1925). *The selection and training of salesmen.* New York: McGraw-Hill.

Kreftling, L. A., & Brief, A. P. (1977). The impact of applicant disability on evaluative judgments in the selection process. *Academy of Management Journal, 19,* 675-680.

Landy, F. J., & Bates, F. (1973). Another look at contrast effects in the employment interview. *Journal of Applied Psychology, 58,* 141-144.

Latham, G. P., & Saari, L. M. (1984). Do people do what they say? Further studies on the situational interview. *Journal of Applied Psychology, 69,* 569-573.

Latham, G. P., Saari, L. M., Pursell, E. D., & Campion, M. A. (1980). The situational interview. *Journal of Applied Psychology, 65,* 422-427.

Lin, T.-R., Dobbins, G. H., & Farh, J.-L. (1992). A field study of race and age similarity effects on interview ratings in conventional and situational interviews. *Journal of Applied Psychology, 77,* 363-371.

London, M., & Hakel, M. D. (1974). Effects of applicant stereotypes, order, and information on interview impressions. *Journal of Applied Psychology, 59,* 157-162.

Maier, N. R. F., & Thurber, J. A. (1968). Accuracy of judgments of deception when an interview is watched, heard, and read. *Personnel Psychology, 21,* 23-30.

Marchese, M. C., & Muchinsky, P. M. (1993). The validity of the employment interview: A meta-analysis. *International Journal of Selection and Assessment, 1,* 18-26.

Matarazzo, J. D., Suslow, G., & Matarazzo, R. G. (1956). The interaction chronograph as an instrument for objective measurement of interaction pattern during interviews. *Journal of Psychology, 41,* 347-367.

Mayfield, E. C. (1964). The selection interview: A re-evaluation of published research. *Personnel Psychology, 17,* 239-260.

Mayfield, E. C., Brown, S. H., & Hamstra, B. W. (1980). Selection interviewing in the life insurance industry: An update of research and practice. *Personnel Psychology, 33,* 41-55.

McDaniel, M. A., Whetzel, D. L., Schmidt, F. L., & Maurer, S. D. (1994). The validity of employment interviews: A comprehensive review and meta-analysis. *Journal of Applied Psychology, 79,* 599-616.

Meehl, P. E. (1965). Clinical versus statistical prediction. *Journal of Experimental Research in Personality, 63,* 81-97.

Moss, F. A. (1931). Scholastic aptitude tests for medical students. *Journal of the Association of American Medical Colleges, 6,* 1-16.

Motowidlo, S. J. (1986). Information processing in personnel decisions. In K. M. Rowland & G. R. Ferris (Eds.), *Research in personnel and human resources management* (Vol. 4, pp. 1-44). Greenwich, CT: JAI.

Motowidlo, S. J., & Burnett, J. R. (1995). Aural and visual sources of validity in structured employment interviews. *Organizational Behavior and Human Decision Processes, 61,* 239-249.

Nagi, S., McBroom, W. H., & Colletts, J. (1972). Work, employment and the disabled. *American Journal of Economics and Society, 31,* 20-34.

Newman, S. H., Bobbitt, J. M., & Cameron, D. C. (1946). The reliability of the interviewing method in an officer candidate evaluation program. *American Psychologist, 1,* 103-109.

Orpen, C. (1985). Patterned behavior description interviews versus unstructured interviews: A comparative validity study. *Journal of Applied Psychology, 70*, 774-776.

Otis, J. L., Campbell, J. H., & Prien, E. P. (1962). Assessment of higher-level personnel: VII. The nature of assessment. *Personnel Psychology, 15*, 441-446.

Powell, G. N. (1991). Applicant reactions to the initial employment interview: Exploring theoretical and methodological issues. *Personnel Psychology, 44*, 67-83.

Prewett-Livingston, A. J., Feild, H. S., Veres, J. G., III, & Lewis, P. M. (1996). Effects of race on interview ratings in a situational panel interview. *Journal of Applied Psychology, 81*, 178-186.

Pulakos, E. D., & Schmitt, N. (1995). Experience-based and situational interview questions: Studies of validity. *Personnel Psychology, 48*, 289-308.

Putney, R. W. (1947). Validity of the placement interview. *Personnel Journal, 26*, 144-145.

Reilly, R. R., & Chao, G. T. (1982). Validity and fairness of some alternative employee selection procedures. *Personnel Psychology, 35*, 1-62.

Rosen, B., & Merich, M. F. (1979). Influence of strong versus weak fair employment policies and applicants' sex on selection decisions and salary recommendations in management simulation. *Journal of Applied Psychology, 64*, 435-439.

Rynes, S. L., Bretz, R. D., & Gerhart, B. (1991). The importance of recruitment in job choice: A different way of looking. *Personnel Psychology, 44*, 487-521.

Schmidt, F. L., Hunter, J. E., McKenzie, R., & Muldrow, T. W. (1979). Impact of valid selection procedures on workforce productivity. *Journal of Applied Psychology, 64*, 609-626.

Schmitt, N. (1976). Social and situational determinants of interview decisions: Implications for the employment interview. *Personnel Psychology, 29*, 79-101.

Scott, W. D. (1915). Scientific selection of salesmen. *Advertising and Selling Magazine, 5*, 5-6ff.

Scott, W. D. (1916). Selection of employees by means of quantitative determinations. *Annals of the American Academy of Political and Social Science, 65*, 182-193.

Scott, W. D., Bingham, W. V., & Whipple, G. M. (1916). Scientific selection of salesmen. *Salesmanship, 4*, 106-108.

Shenkar, O. (1995). *Global perspectives of human resource management.* Englewood Cliffs, NJ: Prentice Hall.

Simas, K., & McCarrey, M. (1979). Impact of recruiter authoritarianism and applicant sex on evaluation and selection decisions in a recruitment interview analogue study. *Journal of Applied Psychology, 64*, 483-491.

Simon, H. A. (1957). *Models of man.* New York: John Wiley.

Springbett, B. M. (1958). Factors affecting the final decision in the employment interview. *Canadian Journal of Psychology, 12*, 13-22.

Stevens, C. K., & Kristof, A. L. (1995). Making the right impression: A field study of applicant impression management during job interviews. *Journal of Applied Psychology, 80*, 587-606.

Struit, D. (Ed.). (1947). *Personnel research and test development in the Bureau of Naval Personnel.* Princeton, NJ: Princeton University Press.

Taylor, S. E., & Crocker, J. (1981). Schematic bases of social information processing. In E. T. Higgins, C. P. Herman, & M. P. Zanna (Eds.), *Social cognitions: The Ontario Symposium on Personality and Social Psychology* (pp. 459-524). Hillsdale, NJ: Lawrence Erlbaum.

Travers, L. B. (1941). Improving practical tests. *Personnel Journal, 20*, 129-133.

Tversky, A., & Kahneman, D. (1974). Judgment under uncertainty: Heuristics and biases. *Science, 185,* 1124-1131.

Ulrich, L., & Trumbo, D. (1965). The selection interview since 1949. *Psychological Bulletin, 63,* 100-116.

Wagner, R. (1949). The employment interview: A critical review. *Personnel Psychology, 2,* 17-46.

Washburn, P. V., & Hakel, M. D. (1973). Visual cue and verbal content as influences on impressions after simulated employment interviews. *Journal of Applied Psychology, 58,* 137-140.

Webster, E. C. (1964). *Decision making in the employment interview.* Montreal: Eagle.

Webster, E. C. (1982). *The employment interview: A social judgment process.* Schomberg, ON: SIP.

Weekley, J. A., & Gier, J. A. (1987). Reliability and validity of the situational interview for a sales position. *Journal of Applied Psychology, 72,* 484-487.

Wexley, K. N., Yukl, G. A., Kovacs, S. Z., & Sanders, R. E. (1972). Importance of contrast effects in employment interviews. *Journal of Applied Psychology, 56,* 45-48.

Wiesner, W. H., & Cronshaw, S. F. (1988). A meta-analytic investigation of the impact of interview format and degree of structure on the validity of the employment interview. *Journal of Occupational Psychology, 61,* 275-290.

Wright, O. R. (1969). Summary of research on the selection interview since 1964. *Personnel Psychology, 22,* 391-413.

Wright, P. M., Lichtenfels, P. A., & Pursell, E. D. (1989). The structured interview: Additional studies and a meta-analysis. *Journal of Occupational Psychology, 62,* 191-199.

Wyer, R. S., & Srull, T. K. (1981). Category accessibility: Some theoretical and empirical issues concerning the processing of social information. In E. T. Higgins, C. P. Herman, & M. P. Zanna (Eds.), *Social cognitions: The Ontario Symposium on Personality and Social Psychology.* Hillsdale, NJ: Lawrence Erlbaum.

Zedeck, S., Tziner, A., & Middlestadt, S. E. (1983). Interviewer validity and reliability: An individual analysis approach. *Personnel Psychology, 36,* 355-370.

Part I

Interview Outcomes

Validity, Fairness, and Applicant Reactions and Attraction

The contributors to this section of the handbook address key interview outcomes, including validity, legality, and applicant reactions and attraction. In Chapter 2, Buckley and Russell focus on seven meta-analytic reviews of interview validity. As they note, these meta-analyses generally support the overall validity of the interview, particularly when it is relatively highly structured. In fact, as has been pointed out elsewhere, compared with the findings of meta-analyses for other selection devices (e.g., assessment centers, biodata), the interview appears to fare reasonably well in terms of validity. Furthermore, as Buckley and Russell observe, the major moderators of interview validity appear to be interview format and performance criterion. In light of these findings, the key question they pose is, What need, if any, is there to continue to do research on interview validity?

Buckley and Russell argue that despite the fact that a rather consistent set of results has been reported in the seven meta-analyses they examine (which, they correctly point out, are in several cases based on a common set of primary studies), there are several reasons to continue to do primary research on interview validity. First, meta-analysis may disguise true moderator effects as statistical artifacts. Second, evidence of a moderator does not indicate the causal mechanism that is operating. Third, research suggests that researcher motivation can affect the results that are found. Perhaps most important, Buckley and Russell argue, that insufficient attention has been paid to building a *theoretical* model for understanding why the interview is valid and understanding the various factors that contribute to its validity. They suggest, for example, that unstructured interviews may in fact reflect a much higher criterion-related validity in certain circumstances. They assert that primary studies, testing specific hypotheses, are needed to advance both applied and theoretical knowledge of interview validity. They conclude with a list of moderator variables (e.g., interview purpose, candidate quality) that deserve closer investigation.

We agree with Buckley and Russell's basic assertion that we don't know all there is to know about interview validity. Indeed, examination of two recent meta-analyses (Huffcutt & Arthur, 1994; McDaniel, Whetzel, Schmidt, & Maurer, 1994) reveals that even with moderator variables (e.g., interview structure) and elimination of statistical artifacts, considerable variance remains. In fact, Huffcutt and Arthur (1994) found a general increase in variance as the interview increased in structure, and they suggest a number of potential explanations. Based on these considerations, we conclude that meta-analysis has been very helpful in summarizing previous findings and providing new directions for researchers. However, we concur with Buckley and Russell that primary research should continue to investigate new hypotheses about interview validity.

In Chapter 3, Roehling, Campion, and Arvey address unfair discrimination in the employment interview. They begin with a brief overview of the three categories of employer practices that may constitute unfair discrimination (disparate treatment, disparate impact, and the failure to make reasonable accommodation), and then review selected court cases involving the employment interview. They identify four issues that are likely to sway court decisions: recruiting/prescreening tactics, subjective procedures, training of interviewers, and the nature of the interview questions. Next, they review the research literature on discrimination in the interview. They conclude that unfair bias appears to be highly affected by the specific context of the interview (e.g., the degree of sex bias depends on the nature of the job, the amount of information available, and the qualifications of the applicants). Moreover, the degree of bias may depend on who the interviewer is; applicants who are the same race as the interviewer may be rated higher than applicants who are of a different race. Roehling et al. therefore suggest that no simple conclusions can be drawn as to whether the interview creates unfair discrimination—the effect is too complex to predict. Moreover, they point out that most of the recent research on this topic has used highly structured interviews. Given that unstructured interviews are far more common in practice, generalizations from this body of research are even further limited. Roehling et al. conclude with a number of suggestions for future research, including the examination of process differences due to sex, race, disabilities, age, and other such factors.

We think that many of the research suggestions and needs that Roehling and his coauthors describe are worth further examination, and we will elaborate on a few of these areas. First, we recommend that researchers make use of our taxonomy of the interview in exploring unfair discrimination, especially in regard to the type of questions asked. To date, although many scholars have pointed out that there is no such thing as "the" interview, much of the literature has tended to examine unfair discrimination in "the" interview. As Roehling et al. correctly point out in their chapter, most of this research has involved highly structured interviews. Aside from one recent meta-analysis that compared race differences across interview structure, there has been little recognition that the presence of unfair discrimination may depend on the degree of interview structure. Alternatively, there may be certain types of questions that are more susceptible to unfair discrimination than others. For example, perhaps value questions are less susceptible to unfair discrimination than are trait questions. Just as there are different degrees of interview structure, different types of factors being measured in the interview, and different types of interview questions, there may be differences among *interviewers* with regard to unfair discrimination (for a discussion of interviewer differences, see Graves & Karren, Chapter 14, this volume). Although sufficiently large sample sizes would be necessary, a policy-capturing study might be helpful in this regard to examine the effects of candidate sex on interviewer ratings.

Second, we need more careful consideration of different models of unfair discrimination. Much (but not all) of the interview research has focused on mean differences in predictors. Research on cognitive ability testing, however, has shown that whereas minorities on average score lower than nonminorities, the difference in test scores is reflected in differences in job performance. Thus, interview ratings may vary by sex, race, and other protected categories, but we need to determine whether these differences are reflected in criteria. It is quite possible that there is no actual unfairness when psychometric models of bias are used.

Third, assuming that there are differences in interview ratings based on sex, race, and other protected categories, we need to develop and test theories that will help us understand these processes more fully. There are several basic reasons women may receive lower ratings than men, assuming equal job qualifications and behavior in the interview. One possibility is that women are asked different questions than are men, questions that in turn are more difficult for women to answer. A second possibility is that women are asked the same questions as men, but more difficult "scoring guides" are used, or perhaps even the same answers are evaluated differently (e.g., perhaps women are evaluated negatively when they express interest in rapid progression, whereas men are evaluated positively for giving the same answer). A third possibility is that nonverbal cues (e.g., smiling, head nodding) are treated differently for men and women; a nonverbal cue that is negatively perceived by the interviewer when demonstrated by women may be perceived as a neutral or positive cue when emitted by men. Finally, perhaps it is not specific questions that result in lower ratings for protected groups; instead, it may be intangible factors, such as perceived fit, that result in lower ratings for protected groups. Whatever the case, we need to go beyond examination of mere differences in interview ratings and focus more on specific sources that explain lower interview ratings for protected groups. After we gain a better understanding of the sources that lead to lower interview ratings for protected groups, the next step is for researchers to determine the causal mechanisms that are operating. For example, if men and women are being asked different questions, is this because interviewers are addressing different factors (e.g., KSAs, values) for men and women? If so, why? There is clearly a need for more research in this area, with practical implications for organizations wishing to reduce bias in the interview process.

In Chapter 4, Gilliland and Steiner address a newly emerging topic of interest in the selection area. Using research and theory on procedural and interactional justice, they develop hypotheses linking various features of interviews (e.g., use of standardized questions, number of interviewers) to applicant perceptions of procedural and interactional justice. A major theme of their chapter is that certain features that are associated with structured interviewing may have negative effects on applicant perceptions of the process. For example, use of standardized scoring procedures, which are practically synonymous with structured interviewing, is posited to be negatively related to applicant perceptions of feedback, two-way communication, and opportunity to perform.

One major contribution of Gilliland and Steiner's chapter is that it poses a challenge to the widely held enthusiasm scholars have for structured interviewing. Our own anecdotal evidence supports these authors' contention that structured interviewing is often not well regarded by job candidates. Gilliland and Steiner go a step further by providing specific hypotheses, thereby offering a framework for empirical investigation.

In addition, Gilliland and Steiner suggest that researchers consider a number of issues. First, further investigation is needed on the meaning of interviews for applicants. Specifically, whereas I/O psychologists focus on such aspects as whether questions are standardized, as Gilliland and Steiner note, we wonder whether applicants are generally aware of such practices. In other words, just how salient are such practices to applicants? It is noteworthy that of the three quotes presented at the beginning of their chapter, not one refers to question standardization, standardization of scoring, or other psychometrically recommended practice. To the contrary, the quote at the end of their chapter indicates that from the applicant's perspective, standardized questions (and presumably standardized scoring procedures) are a mere formality. In short, we believe that more exploratory work is needed with regard to the important dimensions of interview fairness.

Second, more work is needed on applicant expectations. As is noted elsewhere in this volume, the two basic purposes of the interview, from an employer's perspective, are recruitment and selection. Our assumption is that the applicant has certain expectations as to whether the interview will be more recruitment or more selection oriented. In the former case, the applicant is likely to perceive the interview process as more favorable ("This company seems really interested in hiring me") compared with the latter situation ("They must really be unsure if they are asking such tough questions"). If a job candidate is expecting a recruitment-oriented interview and instead perceives the interview to be more of a selection process, this may create a more negative perception. Conversely, if the job candidate expects a selection-oriented interview and perceives the actual interview to be recruitment oriented, he or she may leave with a relatively positive perception. Alternatively, some applicants will occasionally participate in interviews just to practice their interviewing skills. In such situations, a "good" interview may be regarded as one in which difficult questions were asked. A second determinant of expectations is the applicant's perception of his or her job qualifications. Applicants who feel more qualified and acceptable to the organization are likely to have more negative reactions to the interview process when they believe they were not successful in the interview. Conversely, applicants who felt that they had minimal chances for obtaining a job offer will have more positive reactions to the interview process even if they did only marginally well in the interview. This consideration is likely to be related to distributive justice perceptions. Whether candidates' expectations are met or not may have a great deal of influence over their perceptions of the fairness of the interview process.

Finally, much of the literature upon which Gilliland and Steiner's chapter is based comes from research comparing the interview to other selection techniques. We believe, however, that applicants view interviews as quite different from other selection techniques. First, the interview is (generally) conducted by members of the organization, and therefore is expected to provide information about specific organizational characteristics (e.g., the nature of the candidate's potential supervisor) and practices (e.g., work assignments). Second, as has been discussed in other places, both applicants and interviewers have "scripts" as to what should occur in the course of an interview. We assert that part of applicants' scripts is that the interview will provide an opportunity for them to describe their qualifications in the best light possible. Conversely, we posit that applicants view other selection techniques, such as personality tests, as hurdles that must be passed. In other words, job candidates view interviews as their chance to do their best (similar to Gilliland and Steiner's factor "opportunity to perform"), whereas they see other selection devices as simply an issue of passing. In sum, although we concur that procedural and interactional justice theories are applicable to the interview, we caution researchers about making simple comparisons between interviews and other selection techniques. The perceived roles of different selection techniques may be quite different.

The final chapter in this section addresses the employment interview as a recruitment device. Berkson, Harris, and Ferris develop a series of propositions regarding the use of the interview as a means of enhancing organizational reputation. Borrowing from research on the elaboration likelihood model and alpha-beta-gamma change, they argue that the recruitment interview can be useful for this purpose, particularly in the case of relatively inexperienced applicants. One of the major difficulties in this area is the lack of research or even conceptual thinking regarding the dimensionality of organizational reputation, how impressions of reputation are formed, and other basic considerations, such as the reliability with which this construct can be measured. Progress in this area is likely to move slowly until these basic issues are addressed.

Although not addressed by the authors of Chapter 5, another important question related to their discussion is the role of the interview in the context of new technology. For example, many more employers are putting information about their organizations and jobs on their Web sites. With information available from such sources, it is possible to argue that the role the interview plays in recruitment will diminish. Alternatively, perhaps the opportunity to meet face-to-face with a personable, interested representative of an organization will become scarcer in the future and thus will provide a competitive advantage for the organization. Relatedly, more research should examine the role of the recruitment interview as it is conducted over the Internet or via telephone or other media rather than in face-to-face meetings.

References

Huffcutt, A. I., & Arthur, W., Jr. (1994). Hunter and Hunter (1984) revisited: Interview validity for entry-level jobs. *Journal of Applied Psychology, 79*, 184-190.

McDaniel, M. A., Whetzel, D. L., Schmidt, F. L., & Maurer, S. D. (1994). The validity of employment interviews: A comprehensive review and meta-analysis. *Journal of Applied Psychology, 79*, 599-616.

2

Validity Evidence

M. Ronald Buckley
Craig J. Russell

Research on the interview process has been conducted for many years and by many sage researchers. In fact, few selection techniques have received the attention that has been afforded the interview process (Eder & Buckley, 1988). Qualitative literature reviews conducted starting with Wagner (1949) have consistently concluded that interviews yield unimpressive reliability and criterion-related validity relative to other selection techniques. In spite of this well-corroborated finding, Guion and Gibson (1988) report that criterion-related validation "research on interviewing continues, whether in desperation or hope" (p. 367). Management officials continue to treat the interview as an especially important component of selection systems, and it continues to be the most frequently used selection device. This has led Guion and Gibson to conclude that "repeatedly discouraging summaries of their reliabilities and validities [have not] deterred the use of interviews" (p. 367).

The thrust of literature reviews has changed considerably due to a qualitative review conducted by Harris (1989), who concludes that the interview is probably much more valid than previous reviewers had led us to believe. In addition, Harris suggests that "there is a strong need to develop and apply theories in order to attain greater understanding of the interview process and outcomes" (p. 720) and that meta-analysis should be used to summarize past research. Although the former has received scant attention, researchers have responded to the latter suggestion. During the past decade, seven reviews of interview criterion-related validity have appeared, all of which contain meta-analyses of the empirical literature. Our primary purpose in this chapter is to answer the question, What insight has been forthcoming from application of meta-analytic techniques to empirical interview research? Our secondary purpose is to explore directions for future research.

What Is Meta-Analysis, and What Does It Tell Us?

We first present a brief review of meta-analysis procedures and how they differ from qualitative reviews before we summarize findings reported in the seven meta-analyses reported in the literature.

What Is Meta-Analysis?

Meta-analysis is a family of procedures designed to examine statistical effects reported across independent primary research studies. Primary research is simply research conducted on the phenomena of interest (e.g., interviews), whereas secondary meta-analytic research is conducted on some statistic of interest generated by primary research studies. Meta-analyses generically seek (a) to derive the best point estimate of the statistic of interest (e.g., interview criterion-related validity estimates, ρ_{xy}); (b) to partition the observed variation in the statistic across studies into portions attributable to random sampling error, statistical artifacts, and so on; and (c) to derive the credibility interval of that statistic. The credibility interval is similar to confidence intervals, although the estimate of standard error has been corrected for sampling error.

For example, a meta-analyst may have 50 studies reporting the Pearson product-moment correlation between candidates' overall interview ratings and subsequent job performance ratings, capturing the strength of the linear relationship between the two (r_{xy}). Each study's r_{xy} represents the best estimate of the true population correlation ρ_{xy} *for that study*. However, if the studies were drawn from a single population (i.e., there is only one true value of ρ underlying each study's results), some combination of these 50 r_{xy}s should provide a more accurate estimate of ρ. Hunter and Schmidt (1990) derived an average r_{xy} weighted by sample size across studies such that

Caesar

$$\bar{r}_{xy} = \frac{\displaystyle\sum_{i=1}^{k} n_i r_i}{\displaystyle\sum_{i=1}^{k} n_i},$$

$$s_r^2 = \frac{\displaystyle\sum_{i=1}^{k} [n_i(r_i - r)^2]}{\displaystyle\sum_{i=1}^{k} n_i},$$

and k = the number of studies. Hunter and Schmidt also note that the expected variance in r_{xy} across studies due to random sampling error is

$$\sigma P_e^2 = \frac{(1 - \bar{r}^2)^2 \, k}{\displaystyle\sum_{i=1}^{k} n_i}.$$

Given that $\sigma^2_r = \sigma^2\rho + \sigma^2_e$, one can estimate the true variance in ρ by subtracting σ^2_e from both sides of the equation, or $\sigma^2\rho = \sigma^2_r - \sigma^2_e$. If in fact there is only one population value of ρ_{xy} underlying interview-criterion relationships in these k = 50 studies, then in the absence of other statistical artifacts, one would expect $\sigma^2_e = 0$. Note that if in fact one value of ρ does exist, random chance would dictate that 50% of the estimates of σ^2_e would be positive and 50% would be negative. Interpretations of the presence or absence of multiple ρ based on estimates of $\sigma^2\rho$ are sometimes referred to as the *residualization* approach. Corrections for other statistical artifacts (range restriction in the criterion, measurement error, and so on) may also be performed, though most influence $\bar{r}$ directly.

Differences From Qualitative Reviews

Qualitative literature reviews conducted on selection interview validities, like many qualitative reviews, can be plagued by a number of problems that are not found (or that are less severe) in meta-analysis. A sampling of these problems includes the following:

1. Qualitative literature reviews emphasize published research and typically do not sample unpublished research (this has been referred to as the "file drawer" problem; Glass, McGaw, & Smith, 1981). Second-order sampling

error may bias results to the extent that unpublished studies are characterized by very different results (i.e., estimates of population criterion-related validity, ρ) from those obtained in published studies. Further, contrary findings may be overlooked, especially if published in lower-tier or obscure journals.

2. Most qualitative reviews merely report results of research, absent any criticism of the research. All data may not have been collected in an appropriate, nonconfounded fashion that can lead to unambiguous interpretation. Some would argue that qualitative reviews inherently focus on the more seminal and higher-quality empirical work, and are thus adequate representations of the empirical research. We would argue that this assigns considerable latitude to the discretion of the qualitative reviewer—a relatively unpredictable phenomenon.

3. The link between research findings and researcher characteristics is frequently ignored. Evidence suggests that primary investigator decision processes are influenced by investigator values, attitudes, beliefs, knowledge, skills, ability, and so on (Russell et al., 1994; Sherwood & Nataupsky, 1968). Researchers conducting qualitative reviews are equally likely to make choices to ignore or include primary research in an unsystematic or biased fashion.

4. In data collected from actual interview situations, measures of both the predictor variable(s) and the criterion variable(s) have error associated with them. Further, relationships between predictor variables and criterion variables typically are influenced by the range restriction that occurs in concurrent validity designs—theoretically, candidates actually hired tend to receive higher ratings. It is difficult to qualitatively "add together" and synthesize diverse findings when studies are characterized by differing degrees of predictor/criterion unreliability and range restriction.

5. None of the qualitative literature reviews conducted thus far have examined whether differences in sample size account for variation in criterion-related validities reported across studies. Perplexing "mixed" results may in fact reflect variation in r_{xy} due to sampling error, which in turn influences the precision with which each study estimates ρ. Inferences drawn by qualitative reviews will be spurious to the extent that they fail to consider the possibility that mixed results are due to sampling error.

Meta-Analyses of Interview Criterion-Related Validities

In order to minimize the aforementioned problems, and heeding Harris's (1989) recommendation, seven teams of researchers have performed meta-analyses of interview criterion-related validities. These results contribute to our insight into interview-criterion relationships by circumventing the limitations associated with qualitative reviews, most notably,

Table 2.1 Meta-Analyses of Interview Criterion-Related Validities

Study	K	ΣN_i	$\bar{r}$	σ^2_r	σ^2_e	$\sigma^2\rho$	ρ
Marchese & Muchinsky (1993)							
Subjective criteria	23	2,290	.248	.025	.006	.036	.368
Objective criteria	12	1,875	.287	.024	.003	.034	.391
Wright et al. (1989)	13	827	.260	.028	.014	.014	.340
Huffcutt & Arthur (1994)							
Structure Level I	15	7,308	.200	—	—	.0064	—
Structure Level II	39	4,621	.350	—	—	.0324	—
Structure Level III	27	4,358	.560	—	—	.0400	—
Structure Level IV	33	2,365	.570	—	—	.0784	—
Hunter & Hunter (1984)							
Reanalysis of Dunnette (1966)	30	—	—	—	—	—	.160
Reanalysis of Reilly & Chao (1982)	11	—	—	—	—	—	.230
Hunter & Hunter (1984)							
Supervisor ratings	10	2,694	—	—	—	.0121	.140
Promotion	5	1,744	—	—	—	.0000	.080
Training success	9	3,544	—	—	—	.0049	.100
Tenure	3	1,925	—	—	—	.0000	.030
McDaniel et al. (1994)[a]							
Job performance criterion measures							
Structured	106	12,847	.240	.0324	—	—	.440
Test information available	9	1,031	.090	.0121	—	—	.160
Test information unavailable	36	4,865	.220	.0400	—	—	.400
Unstructured	39	9,330	.180	.0121	—	—	.330
Test information available	5	433	.180	.0036	—	—	.340
Test information unavailable	9	1,854	.32	.0144	—	—	.570
Training performance criterion measures							
Structured	26	3,576	.210	.0144	—	—	.340
Unstructured	30	47,576	.230	.0064	—	—	.360
Reilly & Chao (1982)[b]2	12	987	.190	—	—	—	—

NOTE: ρ = estimate of population criterion-related validity corrected for statistical artifacts (usually measurement reliability and range restriction); $\bar{r}$ = estimate of population criterion-related validity uncorrected for statistical artifacts.

a. All of McDaniel et al.'s (1994) results are not summarized here, as they also compiled meta-analytic results by type of criteria and interview content, structure, and purpose.

b. Based on Table 3 in Reilly and Chao (1982), most studies used structured or semistructured interviews.

sampling error's ability to obscure the true strength of latent predictor-criterion relationships.

Table 2.1 contains a summary of the meta-analytic results reported in the literature. Some of the meta-analyses overlap meaningfully in their sampling of primary studies. Choices of variables on which to subgroup studies in search of potential moderators do not appear to be theory driven. Most subgrouping variables seem to have been selected on the basis of convenience (i.e., the variable was noticed and subsequently coded when validities were "harvested" from the primary research studies) or some a priori methodological reason.

A number of patterns in ρ and $\bar{r}$ are of interest. First, note that, with the exception of a portion of Hunter and Hunter's (1984) results, all estimates of ρ and $\bar{r}$ are approximately .20 or higher. Hunter and Hunter's findings have been previously criticized by Roth and Campion (1992) for the researchers' failure to correct for range restriction and potential second-order sampling error (i.e., too few primary research studies). This suggests that interview evaluations are not the poor predictors they are made out to be in qualitative reviews. We would label this level of criterion-related validity *moderate* in comparison with meta-analytic estimates in the .30-.40 range reported for cognitive ability tests, biodata information inventories, and assessment centers (Gaugler, Rosenthal, Thornton, & Bentson, 1987; Russell & Kuhnert, 1992).

Second, the presence of "structure" in the interview appears to coincide with meaningful increases in interview criterion-related validity. Huffcutt (1992) defines structure as a reduction in procedural variability across applicants. Huffcutt and Arthur (1994) content analyzed structure in terms of scoring and question standardization and created four a priori levels. At one extreme, Level I structure is characterized by no constraints on question standardization and global assessment. In contrast, Level IV structure is characterized by the requirements that the exact same questions be asked, with no deviations or custom follow-up questions, and that each individual response be scored using preestablished answers.

Results summarized in Table 2.1 suggest validity increases from .20 to .57, a net gain of .37, in the use of Level I versus Level IV interview structure. These findings underscore and expand on the prior observation on absolute levels of interview criterion-related validities. The two most comprehensive meta-analyses, reported by Huffcutt and Arthur (1994) and McDaniel, Whetzel, Schmidt, and Maurer (1994), suggest criterion-related validities for structured selection interviews to be "large," that is, greater than .40.

Do Meta-Analytic Findings Suggest the Need for More Interview Research?

A number of authors have argued that meta-analytic results such as those reported in Table 2.1 resolve almost all ambiguity regarding criterion-related inferences one might wish to draw about a selection procedure (Schmidt, 1996). Hunter and Schmidt (1990) argue that when variance due to statistical artifacts constitutes a large portion of observed variance in criterion-related validities across studies (most notably variance due to random sampling error; i.e., $\sigma^2 \rho = \sigma^2_r - \sigma^2_e$), one can assume subjects in the studies were drawn from a single population characterized by one value of ρ. The common decision heuristic is to assume that "validity generalizes" if statistical artifacts (e.g., sampling error, range restriction, measurement error) explain at least 75% of the observed variance in effects sizes (note that no probability distribution of $\bar{r}$ is derived in this literature, so no probabilistic inferences about $\bar{r}$ can be drawn; Thomas, 1988). As mentioned above, this has come to be known as the residualization approach.

If one adopts this perspective, the results displayed in Table 2.1 permit at least three inferences. First, as noted above, structure in interview format is important, moderating average effect sizes obtained ($\bar{r}$). Second, when structured, interviews do yield validities comparable to estimates of $\bar{r}$ reported for cognitive ability tests, biographical information inventories, and assessment centers (Russell & Kuhnert, 1992). However, it is important to note that too few studies have simultaneously examined various interview formats and alternate selection technologies to estimate, for example, the interview's unique contribution to criterion-related validity in the presence of cognitive ability tests, scored biographical information inventories, or assessment center ratings. Third, with the exception of interview format and type of performance criterion (see McDaniel et al., 1994), all variation in observed criterion-related validities appears to be due to statistical artifacts (i.e., sampling error).

Again, adopting this residualized view of meta-analytic results, the results displayed in Table 2.1 yield implications for practice that deviate greatly from conclusions drawn by qualitative reviews. However, this implication will not *change* practice, as firms have happily continued to use interviews in spite of conclusions drawn from prior qualitative reviews (note that a number of primary researchers, such as Latham and colleagues, have made compelling arguments for structured interview formats for more than 15 years; see, e.g., Latham & Saari, 1984; Latham, Saari, Pursell, & Campion, 1980). More than 10 years ago, Guion and Gibson (1988) recommended a discontinuation of interview research due to low criterion-related validities. Should we draw the same conclusion on the basis of meta-analysis findings indicating generalizable high validities for structured interviews? Alternatively, have important questions gone unanswered?

We believe that neither individual primary research nor meta-analytic conclusions drawn from secondary analyses address a number of important issues. In the remainder of this chapter, we outline why suspension of primary research activities would be premature and present a programmatic guide to future research efforts.

Why Meta-Analytic Results Do Not Tell Us All We Need to Know

A lack of agreement is starting to emerge concerning conclusions drawn from the residualized view of meta-analytic results (i.e., where inferences are drawn from $\bar{r}$ and $\sigma^2 \rho$ *after* adjustments for statistical artifacts). James,

Demaree, Mulaik, and Ladd (1992) have demonstrated that meta-analysis systematically disguises true moderator effects when those moderators covary with statistical artifacts controlled for in the performance of the meta-analysis (see Burke, Rupinski, Dunlap, & Davison, 1996). Burke et al. (1996) tested James et al.'s notion and failed to find support for it. Unfortunately, Burke et al.'s test meta-analyzed relationships observed between measures of job satisfaction and job performance. Specifically, previous meta-analytic estimates of job satisfaction-job performance correlations are extremely low (e.g., Iaffaldano & Muchinsky, 1985, reported $\bar{r} = .05$ for pay satisfaction). If a true moderator is present, it would have to be of the strongest order, where a slight majority of moderator levels yield observations characterized by progressively stronger *positive* satisfaction-performance relationships, whereas the remaining moderator levels would yield observations characterized by progressively stronger *negative* relationships. Russell and Gilliland (1995) have demonstrated how meta-analytic evidence of moderator *presence* does not necessarily yield any insight into moderator *processes*. Just because the effect size covaries with some variable (e.g., degree of interview structure) does not mean *that* variable is the true cause of moderation.

Further, and perhaps most disturbing, are results suggesting that meaningful moderator effects can be present even when meta-analysis suggests that statistical artifacts account for all variance in effect sizes. This could mean, for example, that even though meta-analyses suggest that almost all variance in effect sizes for structured interviews is due to sampling error, some situational variable could cause wide swings in observed criterion-related validities. In this regard, one line of inquiry is of particular interest to inferences regarding interview criterion-related validity. Specifically, a number of literatures have shown that the purpose or source of motivation driving decision situations greatly influences both cognitive processes and decision outcomes. For example, Longenecker, Sims, and Gioia (1987), in a qualitative analysis, found that performance appraisal purpose was related to appraisal outcome. Using interview decision environments, Adkins, Russell, and Werbel (1994) found that congruence between recruiter and applicant work values was related to recruiter assessments of general employability and organizational "fit." Thus, prior findings suggest that interview motivation remains a prime moderator candidate of interview validities in spite of meta-analytic findings.

Perhaps most troublesome in light of the meta-analytic results reported above, empirical evidence suggests that key research decisions are influenced by researcher source of motivation in conducting the study to begin with. For example, Russell et al. (1994) found that characteristics of investigators publishing criterion-related studies in the *Journal of Applied Psychology* and *Personnel Psychology* between 1965 and 1992 predicted size of criterion-related validity reported (Russell et al. corrected for sampling error only while controlling for type of predictor, criterion, job type, and study design). It is very easy to become cynical about applied social science when Russell et al. report $\bar{r} = .218$ and $.331$, respectively, for investigators employed in academic settings attempting to test or develop some theory of performance prediction versus investigators employed in industry attempting to document compliance with equal employment opportunity guidelines. At this point, there is no reason to believe that researchers examining interview criterion-related validity are immune to these influences.

Russell et al. (1994) conclude that "if the universe of all criterion-related validity studies ever conducted were included, [meta-analytic] results can still be influenced by the capabilities and motivational agendas of the original investigators" (p. 169). They suggest that subtle aspects of investigator decision making are influenced by the investigators' capabilities and motivational agendas, resulting in enhanced or attenuated estimates of r. Wanous, Sullivan, and Malinak (1989) have made the same observation about judgment calls made by meta-analytic investigators using archival secondary data. In a similar vein, we find it curious that no mention has been made of Sherwood and Nataupsky's (1968) finding that demographic characteristics of primary *investigators* predicted differences in black-white intelligence test scores reported in published research, given recent attention to racial differences in cognitive ability (Herrnstein & Murray, 1996). Again, there is no reason to believe that either interviewers or researchers examining interview criterion-related validity are immune to these influences.

Additional Research Needs

Simply stated, meta-analysis cumulates its own set of shortcomings in addition to effect sizes. For example, consider the researcher facing hypothetical choices between expending resources needed to acquire information available from a single primary research effort with sample of size N versus information available from a meta-analysis of k studies where $Sn_i = N$. In the former circumstance, internal and external threats to validity of inferences drawn are well-known and documented (Cook & Campbell, 1979). Given a priori theory and/or a body of prior research findings, the investigator can estimate expected effect sizes and derive the probability of Type II error in any parametric statistical inferences. In the latter, meta-analytic circumstance,

1. internal and external threats to inference validity are cumulated across k studies (it is unlikely that these threats to validity are counterbalanced across studies in such a way that they sum to zero);
2. those threats to inference validity are likely not to be independent (reviewers and editors have a nagging tendency to require authors to demonstrate

how their research reflects and extends past research—we cannot think of any behavioral science literature in which large numbers of pure replications are conducted *or* published); and

3. errors occur due to the overzealous interpretation of meta-analytic results, such as those described above (see Schmidt, 1992, 1996). These include failure to detect true moderators due to confounding with statistical artifacts and failure to detect true moderators due to overinterpretation of the 75% "rule."

In contrast, "critical" tests of competing theoretical predictions in primary research can shed light without subsequent "sanction" of meta-analytic inferences (Greenwald, 1975). In the presence of prior research findings or strong theory, a priori estimation of expected effect sizes permits researchers to derive estimates of samples sizes (N) required for adequate statistical power for tests of research hypotheses. The specific directions for research outlined below constitute a programmatic effort to leverage existing knowledge to discover facets of interview content, context, or process influencing criterion-related validities. Although strong theories of work performance are not available to guide future primary research (Campbell, 1990), a programmatic effort at grounded theory building (Glaser & Strauss, 1967) should permit development of theories or models characterized by strong conceptual and operational definitions (Greenwald, 1975).

Clearly, we need a better understanding of how investigators' values, beliefs, and motivations influence outcomes of interview criterion-related validity research. Meta-analyses comparable to those reported by Russell et al. (1994) would be most useful for partitioning sources of variance in interview criterion-related validities. Once identified, investigator teams can be constructed to minimize or control for these influences, thus ensuring that any observed variation in future primary research results is due to characteristics of the interview, job, candidate, interviewer, and so on, and not some characteristic of the investigator. Latham, Erez, and Locke (1988) have demonstrated powerfully how investigator teams can be constructed to resolve, through primary research initiatives, critical key issues and create new knowledge (in the absence of a meta-analysis).

What Should We Do Next?

Meta-analytic results suggest that interviews are more valid than originally perceived by qualitative reviews of the literature and that structure is an important asset to an interview. In spite of this, we would suggest that the meta-analytic results should be examined with caution—it would be inappropriate to conclude that research on interview criterion-related validity and situational moderators should be discontinued. Using different combinations of variables for every situation, unstructured interviews may yield higher criterion-related validity in some selection contexts. Researchers should continue to examine situational moderators (and those moderators that may possibly influence research) in theory-based, programmatic efforts to understand the role that interview information plays in latent models of performance prediction.

We would like to suggest that the meta-analytic database developed to date has limited usefulness for helping us to understand why interviews yield higher criterion-related validities. Average interview criterion-related validities suggest that they are useful. Premature infatuation with meta-analytic interpretations may have contributed to a situation in which the field has relied too heavily on procedures and methods and too little on theory development. Bechtoldt (1959) once made an observation in a different measurement context that seems an appropriate response to those who believe that meta-analysis is the only means of advancing psychological theory (e.g., Schmidt, 1992): "To admit ignorance as an [*sic*] temporary state of science is one thing. To raise vagueness or lack of definition to the central status of a methodological principle is another" (p. 622). Similarly, in spite of its repeated nominations as a "methodological principle" poised to reveal previously unseen truth and beauty (Schmidt, 1992, 1996), meta-analysis has not advanced our understanding of why interviews work. As Marchese and Muchinsky (1993) admonish, "We should resist the temptation to produce singular coefficients with the accompanying appellation that they are estimates of the truth" (p. 25).

The next logical step toward enhancing our understanding of interview processes and how they might differ across situational contexts does not involve meta-analysis. What is needed is a return to a theory-driven sequence of empirical primary research efforts to incrementally (a) eliminate alternative explanations through "critical" tests (Greenwald, 1975) and (b) construct better models of human performance in organizations. Although meta-analysis has given us an idea of where interview research has been, it has not facilitated the development of any important theoretical insights concerning the directions in which this research should go.

Promising Moderator Candidates and Questions

We believe that there are a number of promising moderator variables and research questions. Although some moderator candidates have been included in previous meta-analyses, we believe that they require further investigation. Some of these variables are discussed at greater length in other chapters in this handbook; we have selected others on the basis of our qualitative assessment of the existing literatures in behavioral science. These include the following:

1. *Decision risk:* Decision risk comprises the costs, both positive and negative, associated with selection decisions. The reader need only consider the large literature on prospect theory (Tversky & Kahneman, 1981) for evidence that perceived likelihood of positive versus negative outcomes influences decision making in fundamentally different ways.

2. *Interview task clarity:* This is the degree to which the selection task is unambiguous and the interviewer is prepared for the selection task.

3. *Interview purpose/interviewer motivation:* This is the degree to which the purpose of the interview or the interviewer's motivation is related to the selection outcome.

4. *Candidate quality:* The true quality of the interviewees certainly influences the dynamics of the interview process. Again, the cognitive psychology literature provides models of circumstances in which cues and cue weights are not independent (Nisbett & Ross, 1980) that might guide research on this process in the interview context.

5. *Research study sample:* Real interviewers may well use judgment criteria that are different from the decision rules used by undergraduate students.

6. *Participant acceptability of the interview process:* The degree to which practicing managers believe the interview process is an effective methodology to use may influence criterion validities, as may candidates' perceptions of the interview.

7. *Incremental validity:* An interview is rarely the sole component of the selection process. Investigations of construct domain overlap with other selection technologies are needed.

There are many potential moderators of interview validity. Meta-analysis has shed little light on how interview processes influence interview outcomes. Moderators that have been examined within meta-analyses reflect where the field has been—ad hoc, atheoretical examinations of criterion-related validity. The meta-analytic results to date cause us to echo Harris's (1989) call for theory development, though the best means of doing so seems to be through programmatic primary research.

References

Adkins, C. L., Russell, C. J., & Werbel, J. D. (1994). Judgments of fit in the selection process: The role of work value congruence. *Personnel Psychology, 47,* 605-623.

Bechtoldt, P. (1959). Construct validity: A critique. *American Psychologist, 14,* 619-629.

Burke, M. J., Rupinski, M. T., Dunlap, W. P., & Davison, H. K. (1996). Do situational variables act as substantive causes of relationships between individual difference variables? Two large-scale tests of "common cause" models. *Personnel Psychology, 49,* 573-598.

Campbell, J. P. (1990). Modeling the performance prediction problem in industrial and organizational psychology. In M. D. Dunnette & L. M. Hough (Eds.), *Handbook of industrial and organizational psychology* (2nd ed., Vol. 1, pp. 687-732). Palo Alto, CA: Consulting Psychologists Press.

Cook, T. D., & Campbell, D. T. (1979). *Quasi-experimentation: Design and analysis issues for field settings.* Chicago: Rand McNally.

Dunnette, M. D. (1966). *Personnel selection and placement.* Belmont, CA: Wadsworth.

Eder, R. W., & Buckley, M. R. (1988). The employment interview: An interactionist perspective. In G. R. Ferris & K. M. Rowland (Eds.), *Research in personnel and human resources management* (Vol. 6, pp. 75-107). Greenwich, CT: JAI.

Gaugler, B. B., Rosenthal, D. B., Thornton, G. C., III, & Bentson, C. (1987). Meta-analysis of assessment center validity. *Journal of Applied Psychology, 72,* 493-511.

Glaser, B. G., & Strauss, A. L. (1967). *The discovery of grounded theory: Strategies for quali-tative research.* Chicago: Aldine.

Glass, G. V, McGaw, B., & Smith, M. L. (1981). *Meta-analysis in social research.* Beverly Hills, CA: Sage.

Greenwald, A. G. (1975). On the inconclusiveness of "crucial" cognitive tests of dissonance versus self-perception theories. *Journal of Experimental and Social Psychol-ogy, 11,* 490-499.

Guion, R. M., & Gibson, W. M. (1988). Personnel selection and placement. *Annual Review of Psychology, 39,* 349-374.

Harris, M. M. (1989). Reconsidering the employment interview: A review of recent literature and suggestions for future research. *Personnel Psychology, 42,* 691-726.

Herrnstein, R. J., & Murray, C. (1996). *The bell curve: Intelligence and class structure in Ameri-can life.* New York: Free Press.

Huffcutt, A. I. (1992). *An empirical investigation of the relationship between multidimensional degree of structure and the validity of the employment interview.* Unpublished doctoral dis-sertation, Texas A&M University.

Huffcutt, A. I., & Arthur, W., Jr. (1994). Hunter and Hunter (1984) revisited: Interview validity for entry-level jobs. *Journal of Applied Psychology, 79,* 184-190.

Hunter, J. E., & Hunter, R. F. (1984). Validity and utility of alternative prediction of job performance. *Journal of Applied Psychology, 96,* 72-98.

Hunter, J. E., & Schmidt, F. L. (1990). *Methods of meta-analysis: Correcting error and bias in research findings.* Newbury Park, CA: Sage.

Iaffaldano, M. T., & Muchinsky, P. M. (1985). Job satisfaction and job performance: A meta-analysis. *Psychological Bulletin, 97,* 251-273.

James, L. R., Demaree, R. G., Mulaik, S. A., & Ladd, R. T. (1992). Validity generaliza-tion in the context of situational models. *Journal of Applied Psychology, 77,* 3-14.

Latham, G. P., Erez, M., & Locke, E. A. (1988). Resolving scientific disputes by the joint design of crucial experiments by the antagonists: Application to the Erez-Latham dispute regarding participation in goal setting. *Journal of Applied Psychology, 73,* 753-772.

Latham, G. P., & Saari, L. M. (1984). Do people do what they say? Further studies on the situational interview. *Journal of Applied Psychology, 69,* 569-573.

Latham, G. P., Saari, L. M., Pursell, E. D., & Campion, M. A. (1980). The situational interview. *Journal of Applied Psychology, 65,* 422-427.

Longenecker, C. O., Sims, H. P., & Gioia, D. A. (1987). Behind the mask: The politics of employee appraisal. *Academy of Management Executive, 1,* 183-193.

Marchese, M. C., & Muchinsky, P. M. (1993). The validity of the employment inter-view: A meta-analysis. *International Journal of Selection and Assessment, 1,* 18-26.

McDaniel, M. A., Whetzel, D. L., Schmidt, F. L., & Maurer, S. D. (1994). The validity of employment interviews: A comprehensive review and meta-analysis. *Journal of Applied Psychology, 79,* 599-616.

Nisbett, R., & Ross, L. (1980). *Human inference: Strategies and shortcoming of social judgment.* Englewood Cliffs, NJ: Prentice Hall.

Reilly, R. R., & Chao, G. T. (1982). Validity and fairness of some alternative employee selection procedures. *Personnel Psychology, 35,* 1-62.

Roth, P. L., & Campion, J. E. (1992). An analysis of the predictive power of the panel interview and pre-employment tests. *Journal of Occupational and Organizational Psychology, 65,* 51-60.

Russell, C. J., & Gilliland, S. W. (1995). Why meta-analysis doesn't always tell you what the data really mean. *Journal of Management, 21,* 813-831.

Russell, C. J., & Kuhnert, K. W. (1992). New frontiers in management selection systems: Where measurement technologies and theory collide. *Leadership Quarterly, 3,* 109-135.

Russell, C. J., Settoon, R. P., McGrath, R. N., Blanton, A. E., Kidwell, R. E., Lohrke, F. T., Scifires, E. L., & Danforth, G. W. (1994). Investigator characteristics as moderators of personnel selection research: A meta-analysis. *Journal of Applied Psychology, 79,* 163-170.

Schmidt, F. L. (1992). What do the data really mean? Research findings, meta-analysis, and cumulative knowledge in psychology. *American Psychologist, 47,* 1173-1181.

Schmidt, F. L. (1996). Statistical significance testing and cumulative knowledge in psychology: Implications for training of researchers. *Psychological Methods, 1,* 115-129.

Sherwood, J. J., & Nataupsky, M. (1968). Predicting the conclusions of Negro-white intelligence research from biographical characteristics of the investigator. *Journal of Personality and Social Psychology, 8,* 53-58.

Thomas, H. (1988). What is the interpretation of the validity generalization estimate $Sp^2 = Sr^2 - Se^2$? *Journal of Applied Psychology, 73,* 679-682.

Tversky, A., & Kahneman, D. (1981). The framing of decisions and the psychology of choice. *Science, 211,* 453-458.

Wagner, R. (1949). The employment interview: A critical review. *Personnel Psychology, 2,* 17-46.

Wanous, J. P., Sullivan, S. E., & Malinak, J. (1989). The role of judgment calls in meta-analysis. *Journal of Applied Psychology, 74,* 259-264.

Wright, P. M., Lichtenfels, P. A., & Pursell, E. D. (1989). The structured interview: Additional studies and a meta-analysis. *Journal of Occupational Psychology, 62,* 191-199.

3

Unfair Discrimination Issues

Mark V. Roehling
James E. Campion
Richard D. Arvey

Arvey's (1979) review of the literature regarding unfair discrimination in the employment interview raised awareness regarding legal and psychological issues associated with the employment interview. It was suggested that interviewers may be biased against blacks, females, the disabled, and members of other protected classes, and hence highly vulnerable to legal attack. Arvey called for research that would contribute to the understanding of the factors producing unfair bias and of how the interview process could be designed to reduce unfair bias. In this chapter, we update Arvey's 1979 review and other reviews undertaken since that time (e.g., Arvey & Campion, 1982; Campion & Arvey, 1989) by summarizing legal developments and recent psychological research and by recommending guidelines for future practice and research.

Legal Aspects of Unfair Discrimination in the Interview

To prepare for this review, we examined federal and state court decisions that included the employment interview as a fair employment practice issue. Our primary source of reference materials was the Commerce Clearing House series titled Employment Decision Practices (1988-1996). We also examined relevant statutory developments and related administrative regulations, referenced below. We supplemented those searches with reviews of two publications that provide current information regarding developments in employment law to lawyers and other interested professionals: *Employment Coordinator* and *Personnel Management*.

We begin this section with an overview of the three general kinds of discriminatory behaviors about which interviewers and employers need to be concerned. Next, we present a summary of court cases in which we identify four areas that appear problematic for the interview. After illustrating some important issues using specific court cases, we link the courts' focus in dealing with these issues to the underlying theories of discrimination. We follow this discussion with some recommendations for practice.

Illegal Employment Discrimination

There are three categories of employer behavior or practice that may violate federal and state fair employment practice (FEP) laws: (a) disparate treatment, (b) the use of policies or practices having disparate impacts, and (c) the failure to make mandated "reasonable accommodations." A basic understanding of the elements of these three patterns of discriminatory behavior or practice is important to an understanding of the relationship between interview practices and legal defensibility.

Disparate Treatment

Disparate treatment discrimination occurs when an employer treats some less favorably than others because of their race, color, religion, sex, national origin, disability, or other protected characteristic. Proof of discriminatory motive is critical, although in some situations it can be inferred from the mere fact of differences in treatment (*International Brotherhood of Teamsters v. United States,* 1977). A prima facie case of disparate treatment can be established through the presentation of either "direct evidence" of discriminatory intent (e.g., actions or remarks of the employer that reflect a discriminatory intent) or circumstantial evidence. In cases in which plaintiffs attempt to prove discrimination claims through circumstantial evidence, the federal courts have uniformly adopted the three-step burden of proof framework initially set forth by the U.S. Supreme Court in *McDonnell Douglas Corporation v. Green* (1972). In the first step, the plaintiff must establish a prima facie case by establishing that he or she (a) is a member of a protected group, (b) applied for the position in question, (c) was qualified for the job, and (d) was rejected in favor of someone not a member of the protected group.

If the plaintiff succeeds in establishing a prima facie case, a presumption that the employer unlawfully discriminated against the employee is created. The burden then shifts to the employer to articulate a *legitimate nondiscriminatory* reason for the employee's rejection. This requires the employer to "clearly set forth," through the production of admissible evidence, the nondiscriminatory reasons for its rejection of the plaintiff (*Texas Department of Community Affairs v. Burdine*, 1981). Examples of the kinds of evidence that have been found to discharge the defendant's burden, taken from cases involving allegations of disparate treatment in the interview process, include evidence that the person who was hired was at least as qualified as the plaintiff (*Godlewski v. the Board of Education of the Utica City School District*, 1992) and evidence that the plaintiff was belligerent and offensive to multiple interviewers during the interview process (*Marlow v. Office of Court Administrator*, 1993).

If the employer satisfies its burden, it rebuts the presumption of discrimination raised by the plaintiff's prima facie case. The burden then shifts to the plaintiff to persuade the trier of fact that intentional discrimination occurred by proving that the employer's proffered reasons were untrue and given as a pretext for discrimination. Examples of the kinds of evidence that have helped plaintiffs discharge this burden include evidence that the employer failed to follow its own established interview procedures in its treatment of the plaintiff (*Roberts v. Houston*, 1993) and evidence that the plaintiff was "clearly better qualified" than the employees who were selected (*Odom v. Frank*, 1993).

Disparate Impact

Disparate impact discrimination involves the use of facially neutral tests, policies, selection criteria, or other practices that have an adverse impact on the employment opportunities of a protected group. The plaintiff can prevail in a disparate impact claim by showing that the employer's practices had a negative impact on a protected group; a showing of discriminatory intent is not required. An employer may defend such a case by attempting to rebut the plaintiff's evidence that the challenged practice resulted in a disparate impact. However, if it is established that the interview process does in fact have a disparate impact on a protected class, Title VII of the Civil Rights Act of 1991 requires that the employer justify its practice by showing that the process is "job related and consistent with business necessity" (42 U.C.S. § 2000e-2[k][1][A][iii]). Although there remains some uncertainty regarding the intended use of the two terms *business necessity* and *job related*, it would seem that the key concern is that the employer's hiring criteria provide an accurate measure of an applicant's actual ability to perform the job in question (Larson, 1996). This requires some kind of validation evidence, although courts are split in requiring the kind of empirical validation evidence contemplated by the *Uniform Guidelines on Employee Selection Procedures* (Equal Employment Opportunity Commission [EEOC], 1978). If the employer is able to demonstrate that the challenged practice is job related, the plaintiff's last resort is to demonstrate that there are other employment practices that would meet the employer's goals and have significantly less adverse impact.

Reasonable Accommodations

In addition to the usual ban on discrimination, when it comes to disabilities and religious beliefs and practices, the law requires employers to make "reasonable accommodations." In other words, it is not enough for an employer to refrain from discriminating against applicants or employees based on these characteristics; the employer must take affirmative steps to accommodate applicants' or employees' disabilities (or religious beliefs and practices), unless doing so would result in an undue hardship on the employer's business. In the interview context, the need to accommodate religious beliefs and practices is not likely to be an issue. However, most employers are likely to be called upon to fulfill their duty to make reasonable accommodations under the Americans With Disabilities Act of 1990 (ADA).

The ADA expressly prohibits preemployment inquiries into whether an applicant is an individual with a disability or as to the nature or severity of a disability prior to a conditional offer (discussed further below). In addition, the ADA requires that the employer provide reasonable accommodations, if needed, to enable an applicant with a disability to have an equal opportunity in the interview process. Required accommodations could include providing an accessible location for people with mobility impairments or varying the interview event itself to allow disabled applicants to participate on an equal basis (e.g., providing a sign language interpreter for people with hearing impairments, allowing breaks, increasing the time allowed for the interview; EEOC, 1995b).

How is an employer to know if there is a potential need for an accommodation in the interview process? Under recently revised guidelines (EEOC, 1995a), the employer may ask questions about an applicant's need for accommodations at the interview stage in three specific situations: (a) the employer reasonably believes an applicant will need reasonable accommodations because of an obvious disability, such as the use of a wheelchair or a severe visual impairment; (b) the employer reasonably believes an applicant will need accommodation because he or she voluntarily discloses a hidden disability; or (c) an applicant voluntarily discloses the need for accommodation during the interview, such as the need for periodic breaks to take medication.

In the abstract, it is not possible to specify the range of accommodations that will be deemed reasonable. It is clear, however, that once an employer is aware of a need for accommodation, unless the ability to participate in a typical interview is strongly linked to the performance of an essential job function (and no reasonable accommodation can be made on the job), the employer should be flexible and work with the disabled applicant to address the applicant's special needs in the interview process.

A Review of Selected Cases

Space limitations prevent us from providing a detailed discussion of each case that we read and analyzed in preparation for this review. Instead, we present a summary in which we identify and briefly discuss areas that appear problematic for the interview.

Preinterview Deterrence or Selection

An employer has no duty to interview all applicants for a job. However, denying an applicant an interview based on the applicant's membership in a protected group can constitute disparate treatment discrimination. Also, there are risks that the recruitment and prescreening of applicants may result in disparate impact discrimination. Potentially hazardous practices include not advertising for openings, using word-of-mouth recruiting, giving preferences to friends and relatives, discouraging applicants, and using unnecessary job experience requirements in selecting applicants to be interviewed.

The employer's recruiting and prescreening of pilots in *Garland v. U.S. Air* (1991) resulted in both forms of discrimination. In addition to U.S. Air's formal application and interview process, a "backdoor" hiring channel existed wherein relatives, friends, and applicants sponsored by influential persons bypassed established screening procedures and were referred directly to one of two senior officials. Every candidate hired through the alternative channel, including some who failed to meet objective written qualifications established by U.S. Air, was white. The court held that the alternative hiring channel resulted in a disparate impact against black applicants, and that the employer had failed to establish a business necessity that justified the alternative hiring channel. Further, the court's conclusion that U.S. Air applied a different, higher standard to black pilots in selecting applicants to be interviewed (no black applicant who failed to meet the written qualifications was given an interview) was among the facts the court relied upon in finding that the employer was also guilty of disparate treatment discrimination in its hiring of pilots.

Subjective Hiring Procedures

The problem of subjectivity is often raised in criticisms of the interview. The courts have articulated two concerns regarding the use of subjective hiring procedures. First, courts have recognized that subjective processes are susceptible to inappropriate biases, making them a ready mechanism for prohibited discrimination. Second, courts have expressed concern that highly subjective procedures may unfairly deny employees a reasonable opportunity to challenge and rebut the claimed basis for the employer's decision. This concern may be characterized as involving due process considerations.

Although subjective hiring procedures are not prohibited per se, courts have consistently held that the use of subjective procedures will be subject to close scrutiny. Generally, the more subjective a defendant's interview process, the more difficult will be the employer's task of meeting its burden of producing rebuttal evidence. For example, in *Bennett v. Veterans Administration Medical Center* (1988), the only white male among eight finalists for a position was selected based on his interview performance. There were no set procedures or guidelines for the interviews, none of the questions were in writing, and no notes were retained. The court noted that subjective interviews are not strictly prohibited, but found that the employer's action did not hold up under the higher scrutiny afforded subjective practices.

In *Reynolds v. Sheet Metal Workers Local 102* (1980), the court restrained the defendant from using scores obtained through its interview process to select applicants to an apprenticeship program because the court found that the interview had many of the subjective procedures that have been "condemned" by the courts, including "broad undefined criteria . . . no guidelines. . . . the interviewer's judgments are unreviewable . . . defendants have not attempted to validate any aspect of the interview" (p. 974). The court contrasted the defendant's practices with an interview process that withstood legal challenge in *EEOC v. E. I. duPont de Nemours et al.* (1978), which was based on written job descriptions, involved multiple interviewers, and provided review of interviewers' judgments.

In finding that the employer had failed to rebut prima facie cases of disparate treatment and disparate impact racial discrimination, the court in *Cook v. Billington* (1992) strongly criticized the employer's subjective interview practices, identifying a number of objectionable elements:

> Interviewing officials are free to ask questions they like, and are not even required to ask the same questions of all applicants for the same position. Interview officials may decide how much weight to accord each question, without any objective criteria to guide them. While interviewing officials are encouraged to take notes, they are not required to do so, nor are they required to keep any records of the questions asked during the interview. (p. 1013)

Selection and Training of Interviewers

The courts have viewed the race and/or gender makeup of interviewing teams as relevant to the question of whether unfair bias occurred in the interview process. Employers' reliance on all white interviewers has been treated as corroborating other evidence of discrimination in cases involving race discrimination (*Roberts v. Houston,* 1993), and the use of all male interviewers has been viewed as corroborating other evidence of discrimination in cases involving sex discrimination (*Stukey v. United States Air Force et al.,* 1992). The courts have been particularly concerned about the lack of race and gender diversity among interviewers when the facts of given cases indicate that there are other reasons to be concerned about the interviewers' ability to make objective judgments. For example, in *EEOC v. American Bank* (1979), the court criticized the bank's systematic rejection of black applicants because all officials involved in the decision-making process were white, none had received formal interview training, and only a few had previous hiring experience.

Court criticisms of inadequate interviewer training were also evident in *Green v. USX Corporation* (1988), wherein the court criticized the defendant in a race discrimination case for not providing formal instructions to interviewers and for the apparent lack of education or experience requirements in its selection of interviewers. Conversely, the fact that an interviewer had received interview training and was experienced has been cited in support of the court's finding of no disparate treatment discrimination in *United States v. City of Warren* (1992).

Interview Questions

Interview questioning practices frequently play a central role in discrimination cases involving employment interviews. There are several ways in which federal or state FEP law considerations constrain questioning practices. First, although very few questions are expressly prohibited under federal equal employment opportunity laws, the ADA and some state laws do make the asking of certain questions illegal. For example, the ADA expressly prohibits any inquiries into whether the applicant is an individual with a disability or as to the nature or severity of a disability prior to a conditional offer (for an in-depth discussion of prohibited questions, see EEOC, 1995a). Also, some state FEP laws expressly prohibit questions concerning the applicant's race, color, religion, sex, or national origin. Some state FEP laws have further prohibitions, making it illegal for employers to seek specific kinds of data that could indirectly reveal information about the applicant's race, color, and so on (e.g., place of birth, names of relatives, citizenship, color of eyes and hair).

Second, inconsistent or disparate asking of questions across groups of applicants may provide evidence of discriminatory intent. For example, in

Bruhn v. Foley (1993), a county board had interviewed candidates for the position of "weed superintendent" and subsequently hired a man. The board justified its decision, in part, by the fact that in response to the board's direct question, members had learned that the male hiree had a farming background. The fact the board did not ask the same question of the plaintiff, a female applicant who also had farming experience, was viewed as evidence of disparate treatment discrimination by the court.

Third, the content of some questions provides evidence of discriminatory intent. Although, as indicated above, very few questions are strictly prohibited under federal laws, the EEOC (1981) has made it clear that it looks with "extreme disfavor" on prehire questions that directly or indirectly disclose information regarding the applicant's race, national origin, religion, or other protected characteristics. Unless such questions are otherwise explained, courts have frequently viewed them as evidence of discriminatory intent.

Finally, the asking of certain questions that may seem neutral may actually involve the implementation of a selection standard that results in an adverse impact against a protected group. For example, in *Bailey v. Southeastern Area Joint Apprenticeship* (1983), a formally scored interview procedure that included questions about military service, work history, and education that were asked of all applicants resulted in a disparate impact against females. Noting that the interviewers were inexperienced and used ambivalent instructions in rating applicant performance, the court held that the defendant failed to demonstrate the business necessity of the questions, and therefore the interview process had resulted in sex discrimination.

Judicial Focus and Legal Theories of Discrimination

In evaluating interview cases, courts have focused on three related concerns: (a) the consistency of interview practices across protected groups, (b) job relatedness, and (c) objectivity. This focus can be conceptually linked to the theories of discrimination the courts are applying. The essence of any disparate treatment claim is that the aggrieved party was treated differently based on a protected characteristic. If all applicants are treated consistently, without regard for protected characteristics, disparate treatment discrimination cannot exist, almost by definition. Job relatedness is not essential to defending disparate treatment claims. An employer does not necessarily need to demonstrate that the interview process is job related in order to discharge its burden of articulating a legitimate, nondiscriminatory reason for the decision. However, increased job relatedness of the interview process will clearly increase the employer's ability to produce evidence of a legitimate nondiscriminatory reason.

There are two reasons why the objectivity or subjectivity of interview practices is often a focus of the courts' attention in disparate treatment cases. First, evidence of subjectivity is viewed as substantive evidence increasing the likelihood that unfair bias occurred. Second, once a plaintiff has established a prima facie case, the absence of objectivity decreases the employer's ability to discharge its burden of coming forward with admissible evidence that "clearly sets forth" a nondiscriminatory reason for its rejection of the plaintiff.

In contrast to disparate treatment claims, job relatedness is critical to rebutting a prima facie case of disparate impact discrimination. If the plaintiff establishes that an interview practice has had a disparate impact on a protected group, the defendant *must* persuade the trier of fact that the challenged practice is job related; merely articulating a legitimate, nondiscriminatory reason is not sufficient (*Griggs v. Duke Power,* 1971). The consistency of interview practices is not directly relevant to the defensibility of the interview process to disparate impact claims because such claims do not involve allegations of differential treatment. However, greater consistency and greater objectivity should improve the reliability of the interview process, which is a precondition for validity (i.e., psychometric job relatedness). Thus, consistency and objectivity are indirectly relevant to the defensibility of interviews to disparate impact claims.

In summary, in evaluating discrimination in interview cases, courts focus on the consistency, job relatedness, and objectivity of the employers' interviewing practices. This observation is consistent with the findings of Campion and Arvey's (1989) review. The most significant recent legal development affecting interviewing practices has been the passage of the ADA, which now prohibits employers from asking questions about applicants' disabilities and requires that employers make reasonable accommodations to enable applicants with disabilities to have equal opportunity in the interview process.

Research on Unfair Discrimination

Previous reviews by Arvey (1979), Arvey and Campion (1982), Campion and Arvey, (1989), and Harris (1989) have summarized the literature pertaining to sex, race, age, and disability bias in the employment interview. In this section, we note the trends and issues associated with this stream of research and summarize relevant recent research in order to illustrate salient points. We include studies that have examined bias in the interview based on the applicant's weight because discrimination based on weight is expressly prohibited by some state FEP laws and, depending on the circumstances, may also violate the ADA.

First, it appears that researchers have heeded previous criticism that the evaluations given to "paper people" are likely to differ from those given more fully described and portrayed stimulus people (Arvey, 1979). In a review of the relevant literature since 1989, we have identified only one study that did not use either videotaped stimulus material or a field setting. Researchers using videotaped stimulus materials have increasingly used subjects/raters who are employed and have at least some responsibility for interviewing at their places of work. Overall, there appears to be growing sensitivity to the threat of mono-operation bias associated with research designs that provide only one stimulus person for each experimental treatment. For example, Hitt and Barr (1989) provided subjects multiple targets for each experimental treatment, which involved physical characteristics of the applicants (e.g., 8 male and 8 female targets). Pingitore, Dugoni, Tindale, and Spring (1994) attempted to minimize potential confounding influences in their manipulation of applicant weight by having the same actors play the roles of both normal-weight and overweight applicants through the use of special effects and prostheses. Both studies utilized extensive pretesting of the stimulus material.

Second, a growing number of studies are examining information-processing variables. Gallois, Callan, and Palmer (1992) tested the similarity-attraction paradigm (Byrne, 1971) as part of their investigation of the influence of candidate and interviewer characteristics on hiring decisions. They had 56 personnel officers rate applicants based on videotaped interviews. Their findings indicate that female interviewers perceived female candidates to be more similar to themselves than male candidates, but male interviewers did not appear to differentiate between sexes in their assessment of candidates' similarity to themselves. Also, candidates of both sexes who had an assertive communication style were rated by all interviewers as more similar to themselves than candidates with aggressive or passive styles. Further analyses indicated that the effect of perceived similarity on hirability ratings was mediated by the candidate's likability, providing support for the similarity- attraction paradigm.

Several studies have investigated the role of inferences or attributions in mediating the effects of applicant characteristics on interview judgments. Pingitore et al. (1994) examined both the influence of applicant and rater characteristics on interview judgments and the expected mediating role of personality attributions. Videotaped interviews that manipulated applicant gender, applicant weight (normal versus 20% over normal), and job type were rated by 320 undergraduates. There was a strong bias against overweight applicants in participants' hire recommendations, especially for female applicants. Subjects made more negative personality attributions about overweight applicants, but the decision not to hire overweight applicants was only partially mediated by the negative personality attributions.

A study by Kleges et al. (1989) also provides evidence that applicant obesity may lead interviewers to make a number of negative inferences that are likely to affect interview outcomes. Undergraduates who viewed videotaped interviews rated overweight applicants as less qualified, having poorer work habits, and more likely to have absences. Further, on items assessing "emotional or personal problems," overweight applicants were rated as less likely to get along with others, lacking self-control discipline, lonely, depressed, and anxious. Only overweight applicants received these negative ratings, and their ratings were not affected by level of qualification for the job.

Kacmar, Wayne, and Ratcliff (1994) indirectly examined the influence of automatic versus controlled information processing on interview ratings by manipulating the amount of information available to undergraduate subjects prior to the subjects' viewing of videotaped interviews. Their findings yielded mixed support for the hypotheses that more prior information about minority applicants would reduce stereotyping and lead to higher minority applicant ratings.

Third, researchers continue to investigate contextual and other personal variables in combination with minority characteristics. Previous findings that males receive higher ratings for stereotypically masculine jobs and females receive higher ratings for stereotypically feminine jobs are further supported by the results of Van Vianen and Willemsen's (1992) field study. Interviewers who described their "ideal candidates" as having stereotypically male personality traits subsequently rated male applicants as having more stereotypically masculine personality traits and females applicants as having more feminine traits. Although there were no significant differences in nonpersonality qualifications (i.e., education and work experience), the interviewers rated a significantly higher percentage of the male candidates as acceptable.

Recent studies provide less evidence that other types of bias in the interview are moderated by job type. For example, Singer and Eder (1989) used videotaped stimulus material to investigate the effects of race on undergraduate interviewers' ratings of applicants. They found significant race main effects for four of seven criteria. Chinese applicants were rated higher than Maori applicants on fit, competence, likability, and self-assurance, and higher than Dutch applicants on likability and self-assurance. However, there were no race × job type (department manager, file clerk) interactions. Similarly, Pingitore et al.'s (1994) findings regarding the negative effects of applicant obesity on ratings, discussed above, did not vary as a function of job type (retail sales representative, systems analyst). Singer and Sewell's (1989) findings do suggest that the effect of applicant age on interview judgments might vary as a function of both the interviewer's age and the type of job in question, but Singer and Sewell did not specifically test that suggested effect.

Hitt and Barr (1989), whose work we mentioned briefly at the beginning of this section, used a policy-capturing approach to examine the influence of applicant demographic characteristics (age, race, gender) in combination with job-relevant variables (education, experience), rater demographic characteristics, and job type. They had 68 managers rate 16 applicants and make starting-salary recommendations based on the applicants' videotaped oral résumés. Although there was no evidence of age discrimination, Hitt and Barr's findings suggest that job-irrelevant variables may be more important than job-relevant variables in explaining favorability ratings of applicants. Blacks were rated lower than whites, and females lower than males. Managers' demographic characteristics also influenced both favorability ratings and recommended starting salaries. Numerous significant interactions, primarily among job-irrelevant variables, suggest that managerial selection decision models are complex and involve configural cue processing.

Christman and Branson (1990) studied the influence of applicant's attire and disability on interview judgments. They had 180 employed individuals with some interviewing responsibility rate videotaped interviews of a female applicant that manipulated physical condition (able-bodied, on crutches, in a wheelchair) and the appropriateness of the applicant's attire. Based on pretesting, the applicant in the most appropriate dress condition wore a dark jacket and skirt; the applicant in the least appropriate dress condition wore a light-colored sweater, tank top, and slacks. Disabled applicants were rated higher; however, the overall magnitude of the disability effect across five criteria was low in comparison to the attire effect. Using a similar approach, Forsythe (1990) looked at the extent to which the masculinity of female applicants' attire influenced male and female raters' perceptions of management characteristics and their decision to hire. Increased masculinity of applicant attire (e.g., masculine dark tailored suit versus feminine soft beige dress) resulted in more favorable perceptions of management characteristics and more favorable hiring recommendations, regardless of the rater's gender.

Fourth, researchers have begun to investigate whether "format" features affect interview bias. Lin, Dobbins, and Farh (1992) conducted a field study that examined the effects of interviewer and applicant race and age similarity on interview outcomes under two different formats: a conventional structured panel interview and a situational panel interview. Two-person panels that were varied by race and age interviewed 2,805 applicants for the position of custodian. The results showed evidence of a same-race bias for black and Hispanic interviewers. The same-race effect appeared stronger in the conventional structured interviews than in the situational interviews. Lin et al. interpret the latter finding as suggesting that adding structure to interviews may minimize same-race bias. Further, the same-race bias was avoided when mixed-race panels were used. No age similarity effects were detected with either interview procedure.

Further support for the use of racially mixed panels to minimize unfair bias has been provided by Prewett-Livingston, Feild, Veres, and Lewis (1996). In their recent field study, which used a structured, situational interview format, four-member interview panels that were varied by racial composition (primarily white, primarily black, balanced) interviewed 153 police officers applying for promotion to a supervisory position. Results showed a same-race rating effect for black and white interviewers on racially balanced panels and a majority-race rating effect for black and white interviewers on primarily white panels. The rating patterns for black and white interviewers on racially unbalanced panels suggested that candidates who were racially similar to the majority race of interviewers (e.g., white candidates interviewed by a primarily white panel) received higher ratings from both black raters and white raters.

Fifth, recent research suggests that the risk of adverse impact associated with interviews may be less than that associated with traditional cognitive tests. Huffcutt and Roth (1996) conducted a meta-analysis of 14 interview studies with a total sample size of 3,685 and found that, across different levels of interview structure, mean interview scores for black applicants were on average .24 standard deviations less than those for white applicants. This amount is only one-fourth of the one standard deviation difference between black and white subgroup means that is typically associated with cognitive ability tests. Mean interview scores for whites and Hispanics were essentially the same. In their field study, Pulakos and Schmitt (1995) found only small differences in subgroup performance (white, black, Hispanic, male, and female) on an experience-based interview, and the interview was equally valid for all subgroups. Interview questions were based on a thorough job analysis and appeared to tap a broad range of job-relevant skills and abilities, and the interviews were conducted by three-person panels that included at least one minority and one female "when possible."

Finally, although there have been calls for research that investigates bias by looking at what actually occurs in the interview, we were able to identify only one such recent study. In a field study, Kacmar and Hochwarter (1995) looked at whether gender and race affected interview communication patterns and interview outcomes (i.e., ratings and referrals). Twenty interviewers who had just completed extensive interview training interviewed job seekers recruited from a college placement office. A total of 32 interviews were videotaped, and interviewer-applicant communication patterns were content analyzed. Results indicated that race and gender did not affect communication patterns or interview outcomes.

Conclusions Regarding
Research Evidence on Bias

There is a continuing need to be tentative with regard to drawing conclusions about bias in the employment interview. We base this statement on two primary observations. First, existing empirical research has almost exclusively involved relatively highly structured interviews. However, research suggesting that adding structure can reduce bias (e.g., Lin et al., 1992) and a review of the kinds of interview practices typically associated with court cases involving illegal discrimination provide reason to expect that bias is much more likely to be associated with the kind of subjective interview practices more commonly found in the workplace than with the highly structured practices upon which current empirical findings are based. As a result, although the focus on highly structured interviews has allowed the kind of experimental control that is useful in the investigation of a number of important issues, it has severely restricted our ability to make inferences about the pervasiveness of discrimination in the employment interview based on the current literature.

Second, even if generalizations are limited to relatively highly structured interview practices, existing evidence suggests that most forms of unfair bias are affected by contextual and situational variables, making it difficult to conclude simply that bias of a particular kind does or does not exist. For example, when gender bias is found, it appears to be a function of the type of job, amount of information available to the interviewer, and the qualifications of the applicants. Similar considerations and evidence that findings are influenced by research methodologies make it difficult to draw firm conclusions regarding bias against applicants with disabilities, age bias, or racial bias in interviewer judgment.

With the foregoing caveat, we can note that evidence from recent research provides reason to be concerned about bias in the interview. For example, both recent studies that investigated race bias in field settings, taking into account the potential interaction of rater and applicant race, found evidence of same-race bias, despite the fact that the interviewers were trained and a highly structured format was used (Lin et al., 1992; Prewett-Livingston et al., 1996). Also, both recent studies that looked at bias against overweight applicants found evidence of a strong bias against significantly overweight applicants. In one study, applicant weight explained 34% of the variance in raters' hiring recommendations (Pingitore et al., 1994), and in the other study, raters made numerous negative inferences about the overweight applicant that were not affected by the level of the applicant's qualifications (Kleges et al., 1989). Again, because of the considerations identified earlier, these findings cannot be broadly generalized with a high degree of confidence.

Future Research on Unfair Discrimination in the Interview

Additional research is needed in a number of areas. Several of these have been identified in previous reviews, but we reiterate them here because the need for additional research remains.

First, research is needed that investigates bias in traditional, highly subjective interviews. Although such interview practices may not be recommended, they are still widely used. Information about the nature and amount of bias in traditional interviews may provide a "baseline" that will be useful to employers assessing the utility of interventions and to judges and policy makers addressing issues related to discrimination in the employment interview. Compared with highly structured interviews, there is likely to be more variance in information-processing variables and micro-level behaviors in subjective interviews. By providing richer data, the study of traditional interviews may lead to insights that will improve the understanding of bias in interviewing, suggesting further improvements that can be made in structured approaches.

Second, greater attention needs to be paid to the examination of interaction effects among the factors thought to influence rater bias, as demonstrated by Hitt and Barr's (1989) work. Evidence of "similar to me" biases suggests that when there is relevant heterogeneity among raters and applicants/targets, the interaction of rater characteristics with applicant characteristics should be examined.

Third, greater effort should be made to understand micro-level behavioral processes that might be involved in interview situations and their covariation with bias. For example, court cases involving disparate treatment discrimination provide evidence of not-so-subtle differences in how some male interviewers treat female applicants versus male applicants. Perhaps there are also subtle behavioral differences that emerge when males interview females, females interview females, and so forth, that could account for differential evaluations. With few exceptions, researchers fail to collect and analyze such data systematically in interview contexts.

Fourth, researchers should investigate whether or not training can reduce bias. The courts have accepted that interviewer training reduces the likelihood of discrimination, and there is reason to expect that bias may be reduced through the training of interviewers to base decisions only on job-relevant information, to follow standardized procedures, and to avoid stereotyping. However, there is very little empirical evidence regarding whether interview bias can actually be reduced or eliminated through training procedures.

Fifth, research examining the effects of format features on interview bias should be extended. For example, does increased interviewer accountability reduce differential evaluations? In discussing their findings that the consensus ratings from an interview panel had higher validities than the panel members' averaged individual ratings, Pulakos, Schmitt, Whitney, and Smith (1996) suggest that consensus ratings increase interviewer accountability, leading to increased accuracy of ratings. Are there other interview policies or practices that will increase interviewer accountability and reduce bias? Increased accountability may be a key to reducing intentional discrimination in the interview.

Sixth, research is needed to establish further whether interview judgments are biased against overweight applicants. Relatively little research has been conducted on this issue, but recent findings based on simulated interviews indicate a strong bias against the overweight. Would those findings be replicated in field settings?

Seventh, greater consideration should be given to the potential trade-offs associated with efforts to minimize unfair discrimination through strict structuring of interview content. Are there boundary conditions beyond which additional structure has little or no benefit but added costs? The use of fixed interview questions with no opportunity for follow-up should reduce the opportunity for disparate treatment discrimination, but could *well-trained* interviewers get better insights using careful, in-depth, job-related probing of standard questions? Is there some point at which increased structure negatively affects applicants' evaluations of the organization or their perceptions of the fairness of the process?

Eighth, as sufficient numbers of studies accumulate, meta-analyses should be utilized to summarize past research and identify moderating factors that might explain some of the results that appear to be inconsistent.

Finally, there is an obvious need for more field research to assess the actual extent of bias and disparate treatment associated with different interview practices. Finding organizations willing to host the needed studies, however, may be the greatest challenge that researchers in this area face.

Increasing the Defensibility of Interview Practices: Recommendations

The above review suggests several actions that can be expected to enhance the legal defensibility of the employment interview by improving its consistency, job relatedness, and objectivity. Although implementation of all the following steps may be unnecessary or impractical for many jobs, generally, employers concerned about the legal defensibility of their interview processes should at least consider each step.

■ *Develop job descriptions:* Often the courts have criticized the lack of job descriptions to guide interviewers. The availability and use of job descriptions for developing interview objectives, questioning strategies, and evaluation standards should enhance the consistency and job relatedness of interview practices.

■ *Examine question content and techniques:* Questioning practices are frequently offered as evidence of discrimination, and they are carefully examined by the courts. Employers should check relevant state FEP laws to identify any preemployment inquiries that are expressly prohibited. Questions should be prepared in advance, job relevant, and uniformly asked of all applicants.

■ *Select and train interviewers:* The race and sex makeup of the members of the interviewing team, their training, and their background have been viewed by the courts as relevant to the question of whether discrimination occurred. Incorporating diversity where possible and providing interviewer training should minimize exposure.

■ *Introduce review:* Usually, the interviewer alone decides on the objectives, question strategy, and evaluation standards. Anything that can be done to introduce additional review of these elements would counter subjectivity arguments (e.g., the use of multiple interviewers, panel interview, and/or management committees to review interviewer recommendations).

■ *Keep accurate, relevant records:* A serious problem for some organizations in defending their practices has been a lack of information that would have allowed them to document the job relatedness of their selection procedures. Undocumented, after-the-fact reconstructions are not given much credence. Job-relevant note taking and a system for recording and storing this information for several years would be useful in defending lawsuits.

■ *Monitor for disparate impact:* Monitoring interviewer decisions would appear to be a prudent and preventive step. Based on the present review, approximately 54% of disparate impact claims have been decided in favor of the defendants. The most successful defense has been to show that the interview did not have a disparate impact on a protected class. When an organization is able to present evidence that it monitored its practices for disparate impact and took specific actions to try to assure fairness, the employer's defense is bolstered.

Conclusion

Unfair interviewer bias can undermine an employer's ability to select the best-qualified employees and can leave the company open to costly and timely charges of employment discrimination. Thus, employers and interviewers must be sensitive to the subtleties of discrimination against females, minorities, the disabled, and other protected classes. When it comes to addressing unfair discrimination in the employment interview process, there is substantial convergence between recommendations based on review of relevant legal authority and recommendations based on empirical research. Courts have emphasized the importance of consistent practices across protected groups, job relatedness, and objectivity in the interview process. Recent research indicates that the structuring of the interview can reduce subjectivity and improve job relatedness. More research is needed to improve our understanding of the process and contextual factors that produce unfair bias and to determine how interviews can be designed to diminish bias. Research in these areas and related interventions should not only increase interview fairness and defensibility, but also benefit employee productivity and morale.

References

Americans With Disabilities Act of 1990, 42 U.S.C.A. § 12101 *et seq.* (West 1993).

Arvey, R. D. (1979). Unfair discrimination in the employment interview: Legal and psychological aspects. *Psychological Bulletin, 86,* 736-765.

Arvey, R. D., & Campion, J. E. (1982). The employment interview: A summary and review of recent research. *Personnel Psychology, 35,* 281-322.

Bailey v. Southeastern Area Joint Apprenticeship, 51 F. Supp. 895 (1983).

Bennett v. Veterans Administration Medical Center, 721 F. Supp. 723 (1988).

Bruhn v. Foley, 824 F. Supp. 1345 (1993).

Byrne, D. (1971). *The attraction paradigm.* New York: Academic Press.

Campion, J. E., & Arvey, R. D. (1989). Unfair discrimination in the employment interview. In R. W. Eder & G. R. Ferris (Eds.), *The employment interview: Theory, research, and practice* (pp. 61-73). Newbury Park, CA: Sage.

Christman, L. A., & Branson, D. H. (1990). Influence of physical disability and dress of female job applicants on interviewers. *Clothing and Textiles Research Journal, 8,* 51-57.

Cook v. Billington, 59 F.E.P. 1010 (1992).

Equal Employment Opportunity Commission (EEOC). (1978). *Uniform guidelines on employee selection procedures.* Washington, DC: Author.

Equal Employment Opportunity Commission (EEOC). (1981). *Pre-employment inquiries and equal employment opportunity.* Washington, DC: Author.

Equal Employment Opportunity Commission (EEOC). (1995a). *ADA enforcement guidance: Preemployment disability-related questions and medical examinations.* Washington, DC: Author.

Equal Employment Opportunity Commission (EEOC). (1995b). *Disability discrimination.* Washington, DC: Author.

EEOC v. American Bank, 652 F.2d 1176 (1979).

EEOC v. E. I. duPont de Nemours et al., 445 F. Supp. 223 (1978).

Forsythe, S. M. (1990). Effect of applicant's clothing on interviewer's decision to hire. *Journal of Applied Social Psychology, 20,* 1579-1595.

Gallois, C., Callan, V. J., & Palmer, J. M. (1992). The influence of applicant communication style and interviewer characteristics on hiring decisions. *Journal of Applied Social Psychology, 22,* 1041-1060.

Garland v. U.S. Air, 767 F. Supp. 715 (1991).

Godlewski v. the Board of Education of the Utica City School District, 62 E.P.D. 42434 (1992).

Green v. USX Corporation, 843 F.2d 1511 (3d Cir. 1988).

Griggs v. Duke Power, 401 U.S. 432 (1971).

Harris, M. M. (1989). Reconsidering the employment interview: A review of recent literature and suggestions for future research. *Personnel Psychology, 42,* 691-726.

Hitt, M. A., & Barr, S. H. (1989). Managerial selection decision models: Examination of configural clue processing. *Journal of Applied Psychology, 74,* 53-61.

Huffcutt, A. I., & Roth, P. L. (1996, April). *A meta-analysis of adverse impact on the employment interview.* Paper presented at the annual meeting of the Society for Industrial and Organizational Psychology, San Diego, CA.

International Brotherhood of Teamsters v. United States, 431 U.S. 324 (1977).

Kacmar, K. M., & Hochwarter, W. A. (1995). The interview as a communication event: A field examination of demographic effects on interview outcomes. *Journal of Business Communication, 32,* 207-232.

Kacmar, K. M., Wayne, S. J., & Ratcliff, S. H. (1994). An examination of automatic vs. controlled information processing in the employment interview: The case of minority applicants. *Sex Roles, 30,* 809-828.

Kleges, R. C., Klem, M. L., Hanson, C. L., Eck, L. H., Ernst, J., O'Laughlin, D., Garrot, A., & Rife, R. (1989). The effects of applicant's health status and qualifications on simulated hiring decisions. *Journal of Obesity, 14,* 527-535.

Larson, L. K. (1996). *Employment discrimination.* New York: Matthew Bender.

Lin, T.-R., Dobbins, G. H., & Farh, J.-L. (1992). A field study of race and age similarity effects on interview ratings in conventional and situational interviews. *Journal of Applied Psychology, 77,* 363-371.

Marlow v. Office of Court Administrator, 69 F.E.P. 389 (1993).

McDonnell Douglas Corporation v. Green, 411 U.S. 792 (1972).

Odom v. Frank, 3 F.3d 839 (1993).

Pingitore, R., Dugoni, B. L., Tindale, R. S., & Spring, B. (1994). Bias against overweight job applicants in a simulated employment interview. *Journal of Applied Psychology, 79,* 909-917.

Pulakos, E. D., & Schmitt, N. (1995). Experience-based and situational interview questions: Studies of validity. *Personnel Psychology, 48,* 289-308.

Pulakos, E. D., Schmitt, N., Whitney, D., & Smith, M. (1996). Individual differences in interviewer ratings: The impact of standardization, consensus discussion, and sampling error on the validity of a structured interview. *Personnel Psychology, 49,* 85-102.

Prewett-Livingston, A. J., Feild, H. S., Veres, J. G., III, & Lewis, P. M. (1996). Effects of race on interview ratings in a situational panel interview. *Journal of Applied Psychology, 81,* 178-186.

Reynolds v. Sheet Metal Workers Local 102, 498 F. Supp. 952 (1980).

Roberts v. Houston, 819 F. Supp. 1019 (1993).

Singer, M. S., & Eder, G. S. (1989). Effects of ethnicity, accent, and job status on selection decisions. *International Journal of Psychology, 24,* 13-34.

Singer, M. S., & Sewell, C. (1989). Applicant age and selection interview decisions: Effect of information exposure on age discrimination in personnel selection. *Journal of Applied Social Psychology, 42,* 133-154.

Stukey v. United States Air Force et al., 809 F. Supp. 513 (1992).

Texas Department of Community Affairs v. Burdine, 450 U.S. 258 (1981).

United States v. City of Warren, 759 F. Supp. 368 (1992).

Van Vianen, A. F. M., & Willemsen, T. M. (1992). The employment interview: The role of sex stereotypes in the evaluation of male and female job applicants in the Netherlands. *Journal of Applied Social Psychology, 22,* 471-491.

4

Applicant Reactions

Stephen W. Gilliland
Dirk D. Steiner

The interview was a discussion, rather than a question and answer session. It was very casual. I was able to give them a real idea of who I was and why I was qualified.

The interviewer showed his excitement and enthusiasm when I gave my answers, which made me excited to continue the interview. I knew I was doing a good job and he offered me the job on the spot.

I was interviewed by five people at the same time. Only two of the people asked me questions; the others just sat there looking bored. I inferred that they had no input, but were forced to be there anyway. A female interviewer asked me an easy question that I answered confidently. She then burst out laughing at me. I left [the interview] very sure I did not want the job.

Interview researchers have long acknowledged the importance of applicants' reactions to interviews in terms of their impact on job acceptance decisions (e.g., Schmitt & Coyle, 1976). Reactions to interviews may be particularly important given that interviews serve as the cornerstones (at least in the applicants' eyes) of many selection systems, and interviews also give applicants the opportunity to gather information. Applicant reactions to interviews have been related to perceptions of the attractiveness of the organization and to job choice intentions (Schmitt & Coyle, 1976; Taylor & Bergmann, 1987). Intentions to recommend a job to others are also related to applicant reactions (e.g., Smither, Reilly, Millsap, Pearlman, & Stoffey, 1993). Therefore, treatment of applicants during interviews may affect an organization's ability to recruit and hire highly qualified applicants. There is also some evidence of a spillover of applicant reactions into job-related attitudes and behaviors (Gilliland, 1994; Gilliland & Troth, 1996) and even customer purchase intentions (Macan, Avedon, Paese, & Smith, 1994). Clearly, as human resource functions adopt more of a total quality or customer service orientation (Bowen & Lawler, 1992), applicant reactions represent important criteria for evaluating interview procedures.

Comparisons of interviews with other selection procedures indicate that employment interviews are seen as fair and appropriate by applicants (e.g., Smither et al., 1993; Steiner & Gilliland, 1996). Of course, there is variation across interviews in terms of interview content and interviewer behavior, and considerable research indicates that variation in interviewer behavior is related to applicants' attitudes toward the interview (Rynes, 1991). Less research has examined the impact of interview content on applicant reactions, but available evidence suggests that the types of questions asked, particularly if questions are seen as inappropriate, can affect applicant reactions to the interview (e.g., Bies & Moag, 1986).

A number of conceptual frameworks have been proposed for examining applicant reactions to interviews (e.g., Rynes, 1989). One framework that is theoretically grounded and has received considerable recent support is provided by organizational justice theory. Gilliland (1993) has proposed an organizational justice framework for studying applicant reactions to the selection process and alternative selection methods. Applying this model to interviews suggests that applicant reactions are based upon formal characteristics of the interview (procedural justice) and the way the interview is implemented (interactional justice). For example, in our previous work, we found that the interview was perceived more favorably than other selection methods in terms of the opportunity it provides applicants to demonstrate their abilities (procedural justice) and in terms of interpersonal warmth (interactional justice) (Steiner & Gilliland, 1996). Additionally, Kravitz, Stinson, and Chavez (1996) found that interviews were perceived among selection procedures to be the least invasive of personal privacy. Although the concepts of procedural and interactional justice may not capture the entire range of reactions to interviews (see Schmitt & Coyle, 1976), they clearly represent important concepts in terms of predicting attitudes and outcomes that are of organizational importance (Gilliland, 1993). In this chapter we examine applicant reactions to different characteristics of interviews along organizational justice dimensions related to procedural and interactional justice.

Interview researchers have devoted considerable attention to the development of new technologies designed to improve the reliability and validity of interviews (see Dipboye, 1994). Structured interview questions and responses, situational questions, and panels of interviewers are some of the changes that have been proposed to improve the psychometric characteristics of interviews. Although these changes have improved the psychometric properties of interviews (Harris, 1989), they have rarely been examined from the applicants' perspective. A few studies have compared structured and unstructured interviews using scenarios or brief descriptions of different interview methods. Smither et al. (1993) compared unstructured interviews that focused on interests and background with structured, situational interviews and found that they did not differ in terms of perceived predictive validity or face validity. It is worth noting that all of Smither et al.'s participants had recently experienced both types of interviews. Rynes and Connerley (1993) found that situational interview scenarios were perceived more positively than generic unstructured interview scenarios in terms of faith in the accuracy of evaluation and perceptions of the company's need to know the kind of information collected. In contrast, Schuler (1993) found that applicants perceived greater fairness with unstructured interviews than with structured interviews. Similarly, Latham and Finnegan (1993) found that students perceived greater fairness and opportunity to present one's abilities in unstructured interviews than in situational interviews. Clearly, many of these results are at odds with one another. Efforts to understand how applicants react to different interview methods must carefully define the type of interview and the dimensions along which reactions are being collected. In this chapter we address each of these issues and develop hypotheses based on the interview and justice literatures.

Recent Interview Technology

A number of terms have been used to describe different interview methods, including *structured, situational, structured behavioral, patterned behavioral,* and *simulation.* Even within the category of structured interviews, considerable variation exists in terms of the operationalization and dimensions of structure (see Dipboye, 1994; Huffcutt & Arthur, 1994). Rather than examine specific "types" of interviews, we will present a number of dimensions along which structured interviews can differ and consider the potential justice reactions related to these dimensions. It would potentially be useful to use the different dimensions of structure that we identify when conducting validity studies as well, to clarify which dimensions, alone or in combination, produce the highest validity coefficients. It is necessary to note as well that our discussion is limited to dimensions of structure. There are other important dimensions along which interviews differ, such as characteristics of the interviewer, that also affect applicant reactions to interviews. Our purpose here is not to be exhaustive, but rather to focus on the structuring aspect of interview design.

The first two dimensions of interview structure are the degrees of standardization in the questions and in their scoring (Huffcutt & Arthur, 1994). For standardization of interview questions, all applicants are asked the same questions. Standardization of scoring involves the establishment of clear criteria for evaluating the responses to the questions. From an applicant's perspective, both of these aspects of standardization may or may not be readily observable. Applicants are more likely to perceive the standardization of questions through the way questions are presented or the way they are asked to respond. On the other hand, applicants may rarely see the interview scoring process, although an explanation of it could be provided during the interview, or the applicant may sometimes observe the interviewer scoring responses on a form. For the purposes of our presentation, we will assume that these two aspects of interview structure are at least somewhat transparent to applicants. In some cases, organizations may find it useful to clarify to candidates that they will all be asked the same questions and evaluated according to the same standards.

Another aspect of interview technology that has received considerable attention is the use of situational and behavioral questions. Situational questions (Latham, Saari, Pursell, & Campion, 1980) are future-oriented, hypothetical questions (e.g., "what would you do . . . ?") and are based on research from goal-setting theory, which suggests that intentions are related to actual behavior. The situations are developed from critical incidents identified through job analyses, and so are directly related to job requirements. On the other hand, behavioral questions ("What did you do . . . ?") are based on the belief that past behavior is the best predictor of future behavior (Janz, 1989); they are used to assess how applicants responded to various situations in the past. As in situational questions, the situations used in behavioral questions are job related and are based on a job analysis. Both situational and behavioral questions have demonstrated improved validity over traditional unstructured interviews (Harris, 1989).

A fifth dimension characterizing interview questions is the degree to which they relate to job requirements as determined by a job analysis (Dipboye, 1994). Designing questions based on a job analysis would presumably be perceived as face validity by the applicant. This dimension is distinct from the prior dimensions in that face-valid questions can take a variety of forms, from structured situational questions to unstructured, open-ended questions. Interviews also vary in the degree to which they use ancillary information (see Dipboye, 1994), such as test scores or application blanks. The use of such information may be apparent to applicants when interviewers make direct reference to test scores or information on a résumé, for example, and ask the applicant to expand or comment on this information.

The number of interviewers involved in an interview is another aspect of interview design that will be readily noticed by applicants. Panel interviews use a number of interviewers and are designed to reduce the impact of idiosyncratic biases on interview decisions. Although it has been suggested that panel interviews may improve interview validity (Campion, Pursell, & Brown, 1988), recent meta-analyses have not confirmed this relationship (Marchese & Muchinsky, 1993).

A final dimension of interview structure might be the amount of time allowed for applicants to ask questions to get information about the job, the organization, or the selection process. Some interviews may allow no questions from the applicant at all; others may give the applicant free rein to request as much information as desired.

In summary, we will consider applicant reactions to interviews as a function of question standardization, scoring standardization, situational questions, behavioral questions, question face validity, use of ancillary information, number of interviewers, and opportunity for applicant questions.

Dimensions of Procedural and Interactional Justice

Applicant reactions to interviews may also be examined along several dimensions. Gilliland (1993) has discussed the justice of personnel selection procedures in terms of a number of underlying justice dimensions. The dimensions relevant to our examination of the interview can be classified as procedural dimensions, which involve the procedures followed in the interview, and interactional dimensions, which involve the interpersonal treatment perceived during the interview. First, considering the procedural dimensions, those that are relevant in the interview context are applicant perceptions of (a) job relatedness or the perceived face validity of interview questions, (b) propriety of questions (i.e., the degree to which inappropriate or invasive questions are asked), (c) opportunity to perform and demonstrate one's abilities, and (d) consistency of treatment. The interactional dimensions are applicant perceptions of (a) feedback regarding one's performance in the interview, (b) opportunity for two-way communication, and (c) interpersonal treatment on the part of the interviewer. These dimensions are all related to the perceived justice or fairness of selection procedures such that when applicants perceive these dimensions to be satisfied, they also believe that they have been treated fairly in the selection process.

Initial research in which applicants' descriptions of fair and unfair interviews were content coded suggests (a) that these seven dimension are all salient to applicants, (b) that they capture most of the variation in applicant reactions, and (c) that interpersonal treatment may be the most important dimension (Gilliland, 1995). In addition to replicating these results with different research methods, further research is needed to determine whether the importance of a dimension varies systematically across different interview methods. It may also be possible to collapse the seven dimensions into three or four more global dimensions, as some researchers have done (e.g., Latham & Finnegan, 1993; Rynes & Connerley, 1993). Nonetheless, we will consider all seven justice dimensions here, as they represent a theoretically grounded and analytically useful framework for discussion.

Justice of Recent Interview Technology

In Table 4.1, we present hypotheses about the nature of the relationships between the interview dimensions and the justice dimensions. Research is somewhat instructive with regard to these relationships, but no systematic research has been conducted to date to address the various components of interviews as they relate to applicant reactions toward the interview. Given this lack of research, each of the relationships proposed in Table 4.1 represents a hypothesis that should be tested in subsequent research.

Beginning with standardized questions, we expect a direct, positive link to the perception of administration consistency. It is likely that applicants will be aware that they are asked a standard set of questions, and that this will be perceived positively, as they know that all candidates are treated the same. On the other hand, the standardized questions may cause applicants to feel that they have not been given the opportunity to display their own unique characteristics—other questions should have been asked of them—so that opportunity to perform would be affected negatively. Similarly, the standardization of questions may limit the conversational nature of the interview and thus may have a negative impact on two-way communication.

The interview dimension of standardized scoring is expected to have a direct, positive impact on administration consistency. Candidates who are aware of a standardized scoring procedure may also feel that it limits their opportunity to perform. They may perceive that only a limited number of their qualities can affect the score, and that other characteristics that they view to be important will be overlooked in the scoring procedure. The way in which standardized scoring is administered may also affect perceptions of feedback and two-way communication. If the interviewer simply takes notes during the interview and scores the applicant's responses following the interview, there may be limited opportunity for feedback and two-way communication. In this way, standardization of scoring may have a negative impact on these interactional justice dimensions.

Table 4.1 Hypothesized Impact of Interview Technology on Dimensions of Procedural and Interactional Justice

	Procedural				Interactional		
	Job Relatedness	Question Propriety	Opportunity to Perform	Administration Consistency	Feedback	Two-Way Communication	Interpersonal Treatment
Standardized questions			neg	pos	neg	neg	
Standardized scoring			neg	pos	neg	neg	
Situational questions	pos	pos	neg	pos		neg	
Behavioral questions	pos	pos	pos	pos		neg	
Face validity	pos	pos	pos				
Ancillary information	pos		pos	pos			
Number of interviewers			curv		curv	neg	curv
Opportunity for questions	pos		pos	neg	pos	pos	pos

NOTE: pos = positive relationship; neg = negative relationship; curv = curvilinear relationship.

Situational interview questions (e.g., Latham et al., 1980) have a future-oriented time frame ("What would you do in a given situation?"), and situations are often taken from job analysis. As such, they are likely to have positive impacts on perceptions of job relatedness, question propriety, and administration consistency. However, applicants may feel that they were not allowed to discuss their past experiences and accomplishments; therefore, they may feel that their opportunity to perform was limited. They may also feel that the question format does not lend itself to a highly interactive discussion, so these questions may have negative repercussions for the two-way communication dimension of interactional justice.

Behavioral questions (Janz, 1989) have a past-oriented time frame and focus on what applicants have already done in various job-related situations. Applicants are therefore likely to perceive these questions to be job related, high on propriety, and, in contrast to future-oriented questions, high on opportunity to perform, as they are able to discuss their past experiences to a greater degree. Behavioral questions, like the situational ones, should have positive impact on administration consistency and negative impact on two-way communication. If research confirms that behavioral questions are perceived more positively by applicants on the dimension of opportunity to perform, and if we also consider that recent research has demonstrated higher validities for experience-based behavioral interview questions than for situational questions (Pulakos & Schmitt, 1995), there may be a compelling argument for the adoption of behavioral interview questions as opposed to situational questions.

Face validity as an interview dimension involves the asking of questions that appear relevant to the job. Face-valid questions are hypothesized in Table 4.1 to have only positive impacts on justice dimensions. Notably, we postulate that face validity will affect perceptions of job relatedness, question propriety, and opportunity to perform.

It is unclear how the use of ancillary information might affect interview validity, as this information can create initial impressions that may aid information gathering but bias decision making (Harris, 1989). However, the use of ancillary information in an interview is likely to improve perceptions of job relatedness and opportunity to perform as candidates perceive that other aspects of the selection process are connected to the interview and are considered as part of the selection process. Applicants may also feel that referring to ancillary information in the interview allows them the chance to explain and elaborate on this information, thus further creating an opportunity to perform. Ancillary information is also likely to add to the perception that all candidates are treated similarly (consistency of administration) because candidates are likely to feel that the same information is sought and included for all candidates.

The number of interviewers present for a single interview may possibly have a curvilinear relationship with opportunity to perform, but we expect that the direction changes quite rapidly. That is, going from one to two interviewers is likely to be perceived as giving candidates the opportunity to show their abilities to a wider audience; however, beyond two or three interviewers, candidates are likely to feel that there is too much pressure, and that this added pressure limits their ability to perform at their best. A similar curvilinear relationship is hypothesized for feedback and inter-personal treatment as candidates initially appreciate the opportunity to interact with more organizational representatives and receive more feedback, but may feel overwhelmed by the use of an excessive number of interviewers. The optimal interaction involving two-way communication may occur with a single interviewer, and with more interviewers candidates may feel that they have limited opportunity to have an interactive dialogue during the interview.

Opportunity for questions is the final interview dimension that we treat in Table 4.1. This dimension allows candidates time to ask questions of the interviewers or to present other information that they believe to be relevant and important for consideration by the interviewers. Greater opportunity for questions is likely to have many positive impacts on applicant perceptions of justice in the interview. Applicants are likely to perceive the interview as job related and as giving them more opportunity to demonstrate their abilities and motivation. Opportunity for questions likely will have its greatest impact on improving the interactional justice dimensions of applicant reactions, including perceptions of feedback, two-way communication, and interpersonal treatment. The only negative relationship we postulate is for consistency of administration, but this impact is likely to be slight on the overall justice perceived in the interview process, particularly if all candidates are given the same opportunity for questions.

Integration

The above discussion of interview dimensions and justice dimensions proposes that many advances in interview technology may have positive impacts on some justice dimensions and negative impacts on others. For example, situational questions are suggested to be positive in terms of job relatedness, question propriety, and consistency, but negative in terms of opportunity to perform and two-way communication. Given these suggestions, it is unclear whether applicants would perceive situational questions to be fair or unfair overall. Clearly, applicants' overall reactions will be influenced by the importance or salience of each justice dimension. Gilliland (1993) suggests that the relative importance of different justice dimensions is influenced by a number of factors, including the types of selection procedures experienced. For example, Gilliland (1995) found that the justice dimension most frequently cited by applicants considering interview fairness was interpersonal treatment, whereas with written ability tests and work sample tests, job relatedness was the most commonly mentioned determinant of fairness. It is not clear which aspects of selection procedure experiences influence the salience or importance of different justice dimensions; however, different evaluation contexts likely create different expectations regarding treatment, and these expectations influence justice dimension importance. This is clearly a direction for future research.

Gilliland (1993) suggests that interpersonal treatment, two-way communication, and opportunity to perform are the most salient justice dimensions of the interview. Supporting this suggestion, Latham and Finnegan (1993) found that applicants did not feel it was particularly important that interviewers ask job-related questions or that the same questions be asked of all applicants. Rather, applicants felt that the important issues were their being given the chance to say everything they wanted to say, being able to demonstrate their abilities and motivation, and having an interview that allowed them to relax; these dimensions can be interpreted as two-way communication, opportunity to perform, and interpersonal treatment, respectively. If these are indeed the salient justice dimensions for most applicants, we would expect applicants to react negatively toward situational questions, which is what Latham and Finnegan found. Future research should examine the importance of different justice dimensions in determining applicants' reactions toward interviews and should examine whether importance varies as a function of the type of interview.

In addition to future research examining the importance of different justice dimensions, it should be emphasized that many of the relationships hypothesized in Table 4.1 do not have supporting research and should be investigated more directly. Given that researchers are examining many of the interview dimensions in terms of validity (e.g., Pulakos & Schmitt, 1995), it would often be possible and desirable for them to include examination of applicants' reactions in their research efforts. We hope that future research will clearly distinguish dimensions of interviewing and dimensions of justice as we have in this chapter, such that a consistent set of results can emerge. If situational questions are not distinguished from behavioral questions, or perceptions of job relatedness are not distinguished from perceptions of opportunity to perform, conflicting results will likely be observed. Evidence of this possibility can be found in the research summarized earlier that compared applicants' reactions to structure and unstructured interviews. Some researchers have found that structured interviews were preferred, some have found that unstructured were preferred, and some have found no differences.

We must also emphasize that Table 4.1 is not comprehensive in terms of either dimensions of interview technology or dimensions of potential justice reactions. For example, characteristics of the interviewer are like to be as important aspects to consider as are dimensions of interview technology. The interviewer's role in the organization, such as being supervisor of the position in question as opposed to being a member of the human resources department, is likely to influence perceptions of justice. Other procedural justice dimensions might also be relevant to interviews. For example, the perception that answers to certain types of interview questions are more easily faked than others may be an important dimension of procedural justice. In addition, we have not addressed an important dimension of organizational justice, namely, distributive justice. *Distributive justice* refers to the fairness of the evaluation or decision that results from an interview. Some of the interview dimensions we have discussed may actually influence perceptions of distributive justice. For example, applicants may feel they are given more opportunity to ask questions because they have done well in the interview and are going to get the job. In addition to examining the hypotheses presented in Table 4.1, future research should also include some of these additional interview and justice dimensions.

Practical Implications

Our analysis of the impact of interview technology on dimensions of procedural and interactional justice suggests that many of the interview innovations designed to improve the reliability and validity of interviews may have negative impacts on some dimensions of applicant reactions if used alone or in the absence of some of the other positive aspects of interview design. Research needs to address the relative importance of different justice dimensions and the extent to which each dimension must be present for applicants to perceive that justice has been fulfilled. Three methods often discussed in human resource management textbooks as ways to improve interviews include standardization, situational questions, and multiple interviewers (e.g., Noe, Hollenbeck, Gerhart, & Wright, 1996). As discussed, all three of these methods may result in negative applicant reactions, particularly along dimensions of opportunity to perform and two-way communication, unless the interview also includes ample opportunity for questions. We have argued in this chapter that applicants' reactions are important to consider in the interviewing context, but the degree of importance assigned to applicants' reactions relative to interview validity may depend on the extent to which the interview is designed to serve recruiting versus screening functions.

One approach to improving both interview validity and applicants' reactions may be to emphasize those interview dimensions that contribute to both validity and positive reactions. For example, we hypothesize that behavioral questions may be more acceptable to applicants than situational questions. Some research also suggests that behavioral questions may produce higher validities than do situational questions (Pulakos & Schmitt, 1995). If both of these advantages of behavioral questions are confirmed in subsequent research, interview questions should focus on experience-oriented behaviors rather than on future intentions. Additionally, face-valid or job-related questions are hypothesized to be evaluated positively by applicants and should also be associated with higher content and criterion-related validity. It is important to note, however, that many behavioral and job-related questions can be used only with experienced applicants. On the other hand, future-oriented questions can be used with both experienced and inexperienced applicants. It is possible that future-oriented situational questions may also be preferred by inexperienced applicants or applicants for entry-level positions. We need to understand more clearly if and when behavioral questions are preferred over situational questions.

A second approach to improving both validity and applicants' reactions may be to combine some of the interview technology dimensions that have positive impacts on applicants' reactions with those that have negative impacts but offer substantial psychometric advantages. For example, applicants may find some situational and standardized questions acceptable if they are also offered the opportunity to ask a lot of questions or to demonstrate their competency in a less structured portion of the interview. Part of the interview could be used for selection decision making and the other part to satisfy applicants' perceptions of fairness. Systematic research is needed to examine more thoroughly the psychometric and social effectiveness of this composite interview. Schuler (1993) refers to the composite approach as a "multimodal interview" and suggests that considerable anecdotal evidence supports the positive impact such an interview has on applicants' reactions. Consider the words of one of our own M.B.A. students, who was asked to describe his best interviewing experience:

> The interviewer and I talked openly about the job and industry. This relieved all the pressure from the interview and made it a very relaxed atmosphere. At the end of the interview, the interviewer had not asked but a few standard questions and felt obligated to ask more. He finished the interview with half a dozen standard questions.

References

Bies, R. J., & Moag, J. S. (1986). Interactional justice: Communication criteria of fairness. *Research on Negotiation in Organizations, 1,* 43-55.

Bowen, D. E., & Lawler, E. E. (1992). Total quality human resource management. *Organizational Dynamics, 20*(4), 29-41.

Campion, M. A., Pursell, E. D., & Brown, B. K. (1988). Structured interviewing: Raising the psychometric properties of the employment interview. *Personnel Psychology, 41,* 25-42.

Dipboye, R. L. (1994). Structured and unstructured selection interviews: Beyond the job-fit model. In G. R. Ferris (Ed.), *Research in personnel and human resources management* (Vol. 12, pp. 79-123). Greenwich, CT: JAI.

Gilliland, S. W. (1993). The perceived fairness of selection systems: An organizational justice perspective. *Academy of Management Review, 18,* 694-734.

Gilliland, S. W. (1994). Effects of procedural and distributive justice on reactions to a selection system. *Journal of Applied Psychology, 79,* 691-701.

Gilliland, S. W. (1995). Fairness from the applicant's perspective: Reactions to employee selection procedures. *International Journal of Selection and Assessment, 3,* 11-19.

Gilliland, S. W., & Troth, M. A. (1996). *Consequences of employee selection system justice.* Manuscript under review.

Harris, M. M. (1989). Reconsidering the employment interview: A review of recent literature and suggestions for future research. *Personnel Psychology, 42,* 691-726.

Huffcutt, A. I., & Arthur, W., Jr. (1994). Hunter and Hunter (1984) revisited: Interview validity for entry-level jobs. *Journal of Applied Psychology, 79,* 184-190.

Janz, J. T. (1989). The patterned behavior description interview: The best prophet of the future is the past. In R. W. Eder & G. R. Ferris (Eds.), *The employment interview: Theory, research, and practice* (pp. 158-168). Newbury Park, CA: Sage.

Kravitz, D. A., Stinson, V., & Chavez, T. L. (1996). Evaluations of tests used for making selection and promotion decisions. *International Journal of Selection and Assessment, 4,* 24-34.

Latham, G. P., & Finnegan, B. J. (1993). Perceived practicality of unstructured, patterned, and situational interviews. In H. Schuler, J. L. Farr, & M. Smith (Eds.), *Personnel selection and assessment: Individual and organizational perspectives* (pp. 41-55). Hillsdale, NJ: Lawrence Erlbaum.

Latham, G. P., Saari, L. M., Pursell, E. D., & Campion, M. A. (1980). The situational interview. *Journal of Applied Psychology, 65,* 422-427.

Macan, T. H., Avedon, M. J., Paese, M., & Smith, D. E. (1994). The effects of applicants' reactions to cognitive ability tests and an assessment center. *Personnel Psychology, 47,* 715-738.

Marchese, M. C., & Muchinsky, P. M. (1993). The validity of the employment interview: A meta-analysis. *International Journal of Selection and Assessment, 1,* 18-26.

Noe, R. A., Hollenbeck, J. R., Gerhart, B., & Wright, P. M. (1996). *Human resource management: Gaining a competitive advantage* (2nd ed.). Chicago: Irwin.

Pulakos, E. D., & Schmitt, N. (1995). Experience-based and situational interview questions: Studies of validity. *Personnel Psychology, 48,* 289-308.

Rynes, S. L. (1989). The employment interview as a recruitment device. In R. W. Eder & G. R. Ferris (Eds.), *The employment interview: Theory, research, and practice* (pp. 127-141). Newbury Park, CA: Sage.

Rynes, S. L. (1991). Recruitment, job choice, and post-hire consequences: A call for new research directions. In M. D. Dunnette & L. M. Hough (Eds.), *Handbook of industrial and organizational psychology* (2nd ed., Vol. 2, pp. 399-444). Palo Alto, CA: Consulting Psychologists Press.

Rynes, S. L., & Connerley, M. L. (1993). Applicants reactions to alternative selection procedures. *Journal of Business and Psychology, 7,* 261-272.

Schmitt, N., & Coyle, B. W. (1976). Applicant decisions in the employment interview. *Journal of Applied Psychology, 61,* 184-192.

Schuler, H. (1993). Is there a dilemma between validity and acceptance in the employment interview? In B. Nevo & R. S. Jager (Eds.), *Educational and psychological testing: The test taker's outlook* (pp. 239-250). Toronto: Hogrefe & Huber.

Smither, J. W., Reilly, R. R., Millsap, R. E., Pearlman, K., & Stoffey, R. W. (1993). Applicant reactions to selection procedures. *Personnel Psychology, 46,* 49-76.

Steiner, D. D., & Gilliland, S. W. (1996). Fairness reactions to personnel selection techniques in France and the United States. *Journal of Applied Psychology, 81,* 134-141.

Taylor, M. S., & Bergmann, T. J. (1987). Organizational recruitment activities and applicants' reactions to different stages of the recruitment process. *Personnel Psychology, 40,* 261-285.

5

Enhancing Organizational Reputation to Attract Applicants

Howard M. Berkson
Michael M. Harris
Gerald R. Ferris

The employment interview may serve a number of different purposes. In most cases, however, the purpose of the employment interview is the selection or recruitment of the best applicants for the organization. In other words, interviews are conducted to assess applicants to determine if they will meet the job requirements or to encourage applicants to join the organization. Of course, the interviewer may also have both purposes in mind, or the interviewer may switch from one purpose to the other during the course of an interview. This chapter focuses on the employment interview as a means of encouraging applicants to join the organization. Specifically, we address the question of whether the interview can be used to enhance organizational reputation in order to improve applicant attraction. Toward that end, we first briefly review the factors that affect applicant attraction. We then discuss the construct of organizational reputation and whether organizational reputation affects applicant attraction. Following this, we introduce a model of persuasive communication and a model of change and use them to illustrate how the employment interview can enhance organizational reputation. We conclude with a series of questions regarding the links among organizational reputation, the interview, and applicant attraction.

Factors Affecting Applicant Attraction

In order to discuss applicant attraction, it is necessary first to define the term. As Barber (1998) observes, there are different phases in the recruitment process, and it is possible that different factors are important during the various phases (see also Taylor & Bergmann, 1987). For example, recruiter behaviors may be far more important in the early stages of the recruitment process and relatively unimportant in later stages. For present purposes, however, we will consider job choice, or the stage at which an applicant must decide whether or not to accept a job offer, as the central focus. Barber (1998) organizes factors posited to affect job choice into three categories: objective factors (i.e., job attributes), subjective factors (e.g., "fit"), and recruitment practices (e.g., nature of the recruiters). With regard to job attributes (e.g., pay), although they clearly play an important role in an applicant's decision to accept a job offer, questions remain as to the relative importance of different factors and whether the importance placed on them by applicants differs depending on certain variables, such as age. Research on subjective factors has focused on fit, but organizational reputation may also fall into this category. Barber concludes that fit is clearly a major consideration in applicants' job choices, but that considerable research remains to be done before we can completely understand the construct and before we can determine which aspects of fit are most important. Finally, there is some debate as to the effect of recruitment practices (e.g., recruiter warmth) on job choice, although the evidence in regard to earlier stages of recruitment is relatively strong.

Taken as a whole, then, there is a large body of research concerning the factors that affect job choice as well as other stages in the recruitment process, such as the decision to apply for a job. Nonetheless, there are large gaps in our knowledge of the recruitment field. One issue that has been largely underresearched concerns the role that organizational reputation plays in job choice. In the next section we define *reputation* and discuss the research linking this variable to applicant attraction.

Organizational Reputation

A Definition

The terms *organizational image* and *corporate reputation* have been used interchangeably in the literature. Barber (1998) suggests that the most comprehensive definition of organizational image is "the way people perceive an organization . . . [in terms of] knowledge, beliefs and feelings" (p. 32). Gatewood, Gowan, and Lautenschlager (1993) define corporate image as a general reaction to the organization's name." In a more general context, Fombrun (1996) defines corporate reputation as "the 'net' affective or emotional reaction . . . to the company's name" (p. 37). These very similar definitions suggest that *image* and *reputation* are different names for the same construct (Gatewood et al., 1993). For the purposes of this chapter, we use the term *reputation* because it appears to be more widely used than *image* in the general management literature. We also adopt the prevailing definition of reputation—namely, people's general reaction to the organization as a whole.

Construct Validity of Organizational Reputation

To date, there has been a paucity of research on organizational reputation as a construct. For the most part, the literature has assumed that organizational reputation is a unidimensional construct. For example, Fombrun and Shanley (1990) used a composite index from *Fortune* magazine's annual survey of companies as a measure of reputation. The survey included eight attributes (e.g., financial soundness, quality of products or services) that were rated by business experts. Aside from reporting a measure of internal reliability, Fombrun and Shanley provide no construct validity information.

Fryxell and Wang (1994) examined the dimensionality of the *Fortune* survey using confirmatory factor analysis. They conclude that one dominant factor, which they label *financial performance,* explains most of the item variance. In other words, "it seems unlikely that Fortune's expert raters adequately discriminated between financial and nonfinancial aspects of a firm's reputation" (p. 11). Thus, the *Fortune* survey of organizational reputation appears to reflect financial performance more than any other construct.

Gatewood et al. (1993) performed some analyses that related to construct validity concerns. They found that reputation ratings from the 1990 *Fortune* magazine survey correlated only .25 with students' ratings of the same attributes. Moreover, the correlation between student ratings of corporate image and recruitment image (which students rated based on company recruitment ads in the *College Placement Council Annual*) was "nonsignificant" (Gatewood et al. do not report the actual correlation). Furthermore, Gatewood et al. examined the dimensionality of recruitment image using multidimensional scaling (MDS). Their results indicate that recruitment image was based on amount of information regarding job attributes and job information, emphasis on telecommunications and technology, and general information about the company. Gatewood et al.'s results, then, suggest that different parties may perceive organizational reputation differently. Furthermore, the context in which organizational reputation is measured (e.g., general reputation versus recruitment reputation) may lead to different results.

Some caveats should also be observed in regard to Gatewood et al.'s findings. First, as Barber (1998) notes, Gatewood et al. had students rate only the organizations with which they were familiar. Second, recruitment reputation was based on students' examinations of specific recruiting advertisements from the *College Placement Council Annual.* It is therefore unclear whether these students would have made different ratings if they were exposed to different pieces of information (e.g., meetings with a recruiter) or to no specific information at all. Third, based on the MDS results, it appears that job attributes and organizational reputation may be somewhat confounded in this study.

In sum, we know very little regarding the construct validity of organizational reputation. It seems quite possible that different individuals will have different definitions of what "organizational reputation" is, and different factors may differentially affect ratings of corporate reputation. Reputation may be perceived differently depending on the context of the question. That is, it seems possible that an organization may have one reputation as an employer and a different reputation as a product/service provider. Clearly, there is a need for more research. For present purposes, however, we will assume that *organizational reputation* refers to an overall impression of the organization that is held by a job seeker and that this impression is conceptually and empirically distinct from job attributes. Furthermore, we believe that the development and promotion of organizational reputation is a proactive process involving multiple media of communication techniques, the content of which is conveyed by numerous sources. The communications reflect recruiters' attempts to convey a consistent and high-quality image. We turn now to consideration of the next question: Does organizational reputation affect applicant attraction to the organization?

Does Organizational Reputation Affect Applicant Attraction?

Two studies have examined organizational reputation and applicant attraction. Gatewood et al. (1993) examined the relationship between two measures of reputation (overall reputation and recruitment reputation, both based on student ratings) and applicant attraction. They found that overall reputation was significantly related to two indices of applicant attraction; recruitment reputation was related to only one of these (the probability of responding to a job advertisement). As noted above, however, Gatewood et al. did not control for job attributes, and that may have led to some confounding of reputation and job attributes.

Turban, Forret, and Hendrickson (1998) examined organizational reputation in the context of recruiter interviews. Reputation was measured prior to the interview, and applicant attraction to the organization was measured both prior to and after the interview. Turban et al. found that organizational reputation had a positive effect on postinterview measures of job and organizational attributes as well as a positive effect on perceptions of recruiter behaviors. Although these findings support the argument that a positive reputation helps improve organizational attractiveness, Turban et al. note an alternative explanation for the findings—namely, that organizations with superior reputations may also provide better jobs and have more effective recruiters.

In sum, although there is support for the proposition that organizational reputation is related to applicant attraction, the causal direction is unknown. And, even more important, these findings do not offer any evidence as to whether the employment interview can enhance organizational reputation. We consider this issue in more detail next.

Can the Recruitment Interview Affect Organizational Reputation?

Barber (1998) questions whether organizational reputation can be enhanced in the broader context of the recruitment process and concludes that change is more likely to occur for relatively inexperienced job applicants (e.g., new college graduates) compared with more experienced job applicants (e.g., senior executives). This assertion is supported elsewhere. First, Fryxell and Wang (1994) found that *Fortune* magazine's expert ratings of corporate reputation were dominated by financial considerations, and Gatewood et al. report that students' ratings of corporate reputation had a low correlation with these expert ratings. Hence, relatively inexperienced job seekers' (e.g., students) ratings may not be tapping a financial factor, which therefore could make those perceptions more amenable to influence by a recruiter. Conversely, experts' ratings, which appear to have a strong financial basis, may be far more difficult for recruiters to influence. Second, Turban and Greening (1997) found that students were unfamiliar with a large number of companies, suggesting that many inexperienced job seekers do not have predetermined perceptions of organizational reputations. Accordingly, we make the following proposition:

■ *Proposition 1:* Relatively inexperienced job seekers will be more susceptible to attempts to influence their perceptions of corporate reputation during the interview than will experienced job seekers.

In sum, we expect that the interview can be used to enhance organizational reputation. We turn next to a discussion of the recruitment interview as a form of persuasive communication.

The Recruitment Interview as Persuasive Communication: Using the ELM Approach

In order to illustrate how the recruitment interview can affect applicants' perceptions of organizational reputation, we introduce in this section the elaboration likelihood model (ELM), a theory of persuasive communication that has been applied elsewhere to the employment interview (Harris, 1989; Powell, 1991). Following a brief review of this theory, we develop a series of propositions linking ELM to enhancement of organizational reputation in the employment interview.

Central Versus Peripheral Processing

According to Petty and Cacioppo (1986), individuals who are the recipients of persuasive communication may process this information in a highly deliberate fashion (i.e., using central processing) or in a cursory fashion (i.e., using peripheral processing). Which route the recipient uses depends on two basic factors: (a) the recipient's *ability* to process the information and (b) the recipient's *motivation* to process the information. (Note that although we describe the manner of processing in terms of a dichotomy, in reality the type of processing actually forms a continuum.)

Research in social psychology has focused on a few key variables that, for the most part, are likely to affect *motivation* to process information, including personal relevance of the information (e.g., a decision is being made that will/will not affect the recipient) and involvement of the recipient (e.g., the recipient is personally responsible for a decision or is working as part of a large group). In the present context, for example, an applicant may not be motivated to process information if he or she is merely using the interview for practice. Degree of distraction is an example of a variable that has been examined in terms of *ability* to process information. In the present context, applicants may have limited ability to process information because they are fatigued. According to ELM, only when both motivation and ability are high will the recipient use central processing. Otherwise, the recipient will use peripheral processing.

Effects of Central Versus Peripheral Processing

Which type of processing the recipient uses has several consequences. One of the most important results is the effectiveness of persuasive communication. That is, if a person is using central processing, then he or she is more likely to be swayed by highly convincing information. Under peripheral processing, the same individual will be less swayed. On the other hand, the reverse is true for relatively unpersuasive communication. As an example, assume that the recruiter for NewBrand, Inc., informs the applicant that a recent study conducted on campus by NewBrand revealed that the organization was rated in the top 10% of companies recruiting on campus. For the sake of the example, assume that this is a relatively weak support for organizational reputation, because the study was performed by the organization itself. According to ELM, this information should be more persuasive to an individual using peripheral processing than to an individual using central processing. The underlying explanation for this difference is that the latter individual will examine this information more carefully and therefore is more likely to realize that the same company conducted the study and to conclude that the study is not quite so credible. Conversely, the individual who is using peripheral processing is paying only cursory attention and is less likely to attend to the fact that the organization performed the study.

Aside from the relative impact of the persuasive attempts, there are some other important differences between information that is received via central versus peripheral processing. Two important differences are the stability and predictability of behavior that results from the influence attempts. Compared with recipients who use peripheral processing, recipients who use central processing are influenced for longer periods of time by the communication and are more resistant to counterpersuasion, and their attitudes are more predictive of behavior.

Peripheral Cues

Another major feature of ELM is the role of peripheral cues. A peripheral cue affects a recipient's reaction to the persuasive information, but it does not constitute actual information. For example, in the field of advertising, the celebrity status of a product endorser (e.g., Mark McGwire appearing in an ad for automobiles) may serve as a peripheral cue (note that if McGwire were to appear in an ad for baseball bats, his presence would probably constitute actual information, because he would be considered an expert source on this matter; his presence would probably not be a peripheral cue). There are two kinds of peripheral cues. As indicated in the example of Mark McGwire appearing in an automobile ad, the *source* of the information may be a peripheral cue. In the recruitment context, the rank of the recruiter may constitute a peripheral cue (e.g., whether the recruiter is the CEO or an entry-level manager; Harris, 1989). A *feature* of the information may also constitute a peripheral cue. The total number of pieces of information, for example, may be a peripheral cue. According to ELM, peripheral cues have the least influence when the recipient uses central processing; they have the greatest influence when the recipient uses peripheral processing. Thus, if you are using peripheral processing, someone who presents 10 different reasons for you to change your opinion should be more influential than someone who presents 2 reasons, all else being equal.

ELM and Organizational Reputation

We turn now to a consideration of how ELM can be applied to the enhancement of organizational reputation in the recruitment interview. This section is divided into two parts. First, we offer a proposition regarding information content. Second, we present factors that are likely to affect the type of processing used by the applicant in a recruitment interview addressing organizational reputation. We should point out here that we do not assume that central processing is always the preferred applicant mode from the point of view of interviewers who are attempting to enhance organizational reputation. Indeed, as we will discuss later, there may be situations in which it is to the interviewer's advantage for the applicant to be using peripheral processing.

Information Content

In applying ELM to the issue of enhancing organizational reputation, it is instructive first to consider the nature of the information that is being conveyed. As noted above, there is a paucity of research on how reputation is formed on the part of applicants. One factor discussed by Barber (1998), however, is the role of familiarity. Based on existing research, Barber proposes that familiarity is a major determinant of reputation for relatively inexperienced job seekers, such that familiarity is positively related to perceptions of reputation. The role of familiarity appears to be much like that of the total number of pieces of information, which, as noted above, constitutes a peripheral cue. In any case, if familiarity is indeed a determinant of reputation, it would seem that the more familiar the recruiter can make the organization appear, the more positive will be the applicant's perceptions of reputation. For example, the recruiter might point out examples of organizational products or services the applicant may have used (e.g., consumer products), offer brochures and reports describing the organization, mention cases the applicant may have used in class as a student, and name alumni from the applicant's university who are now working in the organization. Thus, we offer the following proposition:

■ *Proposition 2:* The greater the degree to which the recruiter can make the organization appear familiar to the applicant, the more positive the applicant's perceptions of the organizational reputation will be.

Ability and Motivation to Process Information

Recall that an applicant will process information using central or peripheral processing. We now discuss three kinds of variables that will affect the nature of the processing used by the applicant: interview variables, applicant variables, and recruiter variables.

Interview Variables

There are two variables pertaining to the interview that will affect the applicant's ability and motivation to process information. The first is the purpose of the interview (Eder, 1989). Barber, Hollenbeck, Tower, and Phillips (1994) found that interviews that had a dual purpose (i.e., both recruiting and selection) were more distracting for applicants and therefore the applicants were less able to process information. Second, Harris (1989) cites research indicating that applicants experience more anxiety when faced with structured interviews. Kohn and Dipboye (1998) found that applicants perceived the job, organization, and interviewer more negatively when highly structured interviews were used. Together, these findings suggest that less structured interviews, compared with more structured interviews, will increase applicants' ability and motivation to process information. This is not inconsistent with Dipboye's (1992, 1994) perspective on the many roles and functions of the interview and the flexibility provided for achieving multiple objectives (including promoting reputation) through the use of relatively unstructured interviews. Thus, we offer the following proposition:

▓ *Proposition 3:* Sole-purpose and relatively unstructured interviews will be more likely to lead to central processing than will dual-purpose and highly structured interviews.

Applicant Variables

Harris (1989) suggests several applicant variables that may affect ability and motivation to process information. First, extensive research on individual differences in anxiety suggests that some applicants experience greater anxiety than others (Heimberg, Keller, & Peca-Baker, 1986). Although moderate amounts of anxiety probably serve to engage the applicant, dysfunctional amounts of anxiety (i.e., too little or too much) are likely to limit the applicant's motivation and/or ability to process information. Second, Harris postulates that applicants who perceive they have more job opportunities will be more motivated to process information offered during the interview because they will be concerned about choosing the best job offer. Alternatively, applicants who perceive they have few job opportunities will be less concerned about processing information and more concerned about impressing the interviewer. Thus, we expect that applicants with more job opportunities will have greater ability to process information compared with applicants with fewer job opportunities. On this basis, we offer the following proposition:

■ *Proposition 4:* Applicants who experience moderate amounts of anxiety and have more perceived job opportunities will be more likely to use central processing compared with applicants who experience too little or too much anxiety and have fewer job opportunities.

Recruiter Variables

We predict that recruiters can also affect applicants' ability and motivation to process information. First, recruiters can try to reduce high levels of anxiety by using rapport-building techniques. These techniques may include making some initial casual conversation, indicating interest in what the applicant has to say, and using effective nonverbal behaviors (e.g., smiling). In turn, such rapport-building tactics should increase applicants' ability to process information. Second, there are certain other verbal and nonverbal behaviors that recruiters can use to increase applicants' motivation to process information. For example, a recruiter may be effective in convincing an applicant that the interview offers additional, useful information about organizational reputation by presenting results of confidential industry surveys. Third, Ferris and his colleagues have argued that the perception and subjective experience of events in organizations is the result of active efforts by individuals to manage shared meaning (MSM; Ferris, Bhawuk, Fedor, & Judge, 1995; Ferris, King, Judge, & Kacmar, 1991). Because of the ambiguity and subjectivity of many organizational phenomena, meaning can be shaped by active efforts to promote and manage images. Indeed, organizational reputation is not an objective reality, but a socially constructed one. It is therefore susceptible to such shaping and meaning management. It is reasonable to expect that a recruiter who is high on MSM will be more capable of producing higher levels of motivation to process information than will a recruiter who is low on MSM. Based on the above discussion, we offer the following proposition:

■ *Proposition 5:* Applicants are more likely to use central processing when they are interviewed by recruiters who use more rapport-building techniques, induce a perception that the interview is a valuable means of learning more about reputation, and have greater capacity for MSM.

The Recruitment Interview as a Change Process: Using the Alpha-Beta-Gamma Model

A second model that may be useful here is the alpha-beta-gamma change model. A concept originally developed in the organizational development literature, *alpha-beta-gamma change* refers to three different kinds of change that may occur in an individual's understanding of a particular phenomenon (Golembiewski, Billingsley, & Yeager, 1976). *Alpha change* refers to what we normally think about change: the level of a variable measured on a stable scale has been altered (e.g., the level goes up or down). For example, whereas an applicant may perceive that the organization has only an average reputation, the recruiter may state that the organization has one of the best reputations in the industry. Alpha change in this context represents a direct approach to enhancing organizational reputation.

Beta change refers to a change in the calibration, or scale, of a variable. For instance, an applicant may have heard that the organization has been investigated for environmental safety problems (which we will assume is true). He or she may therefore have concluded that this company has a poor reputation. The recruiter might then state that many large companies are regularly investigated for environmental safety problems, which in turn changes the job seeker's scale (i.e., given that most companies have been investigated at least a few times, an organization that has been investigated only once appears to have a better-than-average record). In turn, this should positively enhance the applicant's perception of this particular organization's reputation.

Gamma change refers to a "redefinition or reconceptualization of some domain, a major change in the perspective or frame of reference within which phenomena are perceived and classified" (Golembiewski et al., 1976, p. 135). We propose that effective recruiters will be able to induce gamma change in perceptions of organizational reputation, particularly for relatively inexperienced job seekers. For instance, suppose a recruiter is talking with an applicant and realizes that the applicant perceives that reputation is based on its record of EEOC charges and investigations of safety violations. The recruiter may be able to persuade this applicant that a much more important component of reputation is the organization's degree of new product development. Thus, the recruiter may be able to change the applicant's perception of organizational reputation by creating a completely different understanding of this construct.

It should be noted that both beta and gamma change represent indirect ways to change organizational reputation. Because these two ways of inducing change are less direct, they seem less likely to lead to the applicant's questioning the credibility of the recruiter. On that basis, we offer the following proposition:

■ *Proposition 6:* Recruiters who use beta or gamma change tactics to enhance organizational reputation will be more effective in attracting applicants than will recruiters who rely on alpha change tactics.

Enhancing Organizational Reputation: A Contingency Approach

So far, we have presented a series of propositions regarding the conditions under which applicants will use central versus peripheral processing and the types of change strategies that recruiters might use to enhance organizational reputation. Next, we combine these two models by presenting some considerations as to what might be the preferred tactics for recruiters to use to enhance organizational reputation, depending on the applicant's perceptions of that reputation. Our suggestions in this section are admittedly tentative, but we believe that they constitute a useful first step toward advancing the research on organizational reputation.

Consider first the situation in which the organizational reputation is positive. In this situation, the goal of the recruiter should be to enhance the applicant's perceptions of the organization. The best way to do this would be for the recruiter to transmit information that the applicant will receive using central processing; this should lead to long-lasting, strong effects. The applicant's use of central processing is particularly important if the applicant's perceptions of the organizational reputation are not as positive as they could be given the actual reputation of the company.

Now, consider the case in which the applicant has a neutral opinion of the organizational reputation. Let us assume that, indeed, the organization has about an average reputation in all aspects compared with other organizations that are competing for the applicant. In this case, the best strategy for the recruiter may be to elicit the applicant's peripheral processing of reputational information that will lead to enhanced perceptions through multiple pieces of information, highly credible sources (e.g., encouraging top executives to participate in recruiting), and other peripheral cues. If, however, the applicant uses central processing, he or she might perceive relatively neutral information as less positive. Hence, in this case, it may be more desirable for the applicant to use peripheral processing in considering information about organizational reputation. We would like to point out, however, that this strategy requires careful thinking, because discouraging recruiters from using such things as rapport-building behavior (e.g., see Proposition 5) could have negative effects in other areas. Rather, techniques such as the dual-purpose interview might attain the same effect, without negative side effects.

Finally, consider the third case, in which the applicant has a negative perception of the organizational reputation. Again, let us assume that this reflects the actual state of affairs. Furthermore, assume that this is a well-known fact and that the recruiter's arguing to the contrary will only serve to undermine his or her reputation. In this situation, the recruiter has two basic choices. One is to downplay the importance of organizational reputation and explain to the applicant why this factor is not important in choosing a job (e.g., stating that "a job in our organization will provide many learning opportunities because we are going through many changes and doing many new things"). Alternatively, the recruiter might try to change the applicant's understanding of what reputation is (i.e., gamma change) by trying to redefine reputation. For example, the recruiter might emphasize the organization's record on recycling, diversity efforts, or other factors that might reflect an aspect of reputation that the applicant has not considered.

In sum, we offer the following, albeit tentative, propositions:

■ *Proposition 7:* The best approach for the recruiter to use in enhancing reputation will differ depending on the applicant's perception of the organizational reputation.

■ *Proposition 7a:* When the organizational reputation is positive, the recruiter should encourage central processing of positive information.

■ *Proposition 7b:* When the organizational reputation is neutral, the recruiter should encourage peripheral processing and use peripheral cues.

■ *Proposition 7c:* When the organizational reputation is negative, the recruiter should attempt to induce gamma change.

Organizational Reputation, Recruitment Interviews, and Applicant Attraction: Additional Issues

We have offered a number of testable propositions regarding the employment interview as a means of enhancing organizational reputation. There are, however, two key issues for which any offer of propositions would be premature. We address these issues below, but refrain from stating any specific predictions.

To What Degree Do Organizations Use Reputation to Attract Applicants?

Although there is much talk in the popular press about organizational reputation, there has been little rigorous research on this topic. We can think of two factors that may determine the degree to which organizations use reputation to attract applicants. One factor is the organization's business and human resource strategy. Specifically, it is possible that organizations that emphasize innovation or quality enhancement may leverage reputation as a competitive advantage in their recruitment strategies. Organizational reputation may also be emphasized when there is a tight labor market or severe labor shortages. More research should be performed linking organization-level variables to use of reputation as a recruitment strategy.

What Factors Affect Applicants' Attention to Organizational Reputation?

A largely unaddressed issue concerns the degree to which applicants consider organizational reputation in the recruitment process. A related question is, At what point in the recruitment process are applicants most open to persuasive efforts regarding organizational reputation? Does reputation have different effects on applicants in different stages of the recruitment process? Are there various factors that affect the role of reputation on applicants? For example, it seems possible that reputation may have a greater effect on higher-level employees than on lower-level employees. Alternatively, higher-level employees may base their judgments of reputation on a completely different set of factors than that used by lower-level employees. Another factor that may play a role in judgments of reputation is area of expertise. That is, it seems likely that a marketing professional would be more familiar with and knowledgeable in judging an organization's marketing reputation, whereas a human resource professional would be more familiar with and knowledgeable in judging an organization's human resource reputation. Another question we have not addressed here is how best to radically change an applicant's perceptions of organizational reputation. If, for example, an applicant has a negative perception of an organization's reputation, despite the fact that the organization is considered to have a very positive reputation, what is the best way to change that perception? Finally, we know little about the relationship between job attributes and organizational reputation. Do applicants perceive these as completely independent factors? Or could there be an interaction such that a poor reputation negatively affects perceptions of job attributes?

Summary

To date, there is a paucity of literature concerning applicant attraction and organizational reputation, particularly in regard to how the recruitment interview may play a major role in linking these two constructs. From a practical perspective, in light of the labor shortages in many areas and the need to keep a tight rein on costs, organizations must leverage all of their resources to both attract and retain qualified employees. Organizational reputation is increasingly being viewed as a necessary ingredient in building and maintaining an effective workforce. Both scholars and practitioners would therefore benefit from continued investigation of the interview as a means of enhancing organizational reputation.

References

Barber, A. (1998). *Recruiting employees: Individual and organizational perspectives.* Thousand Oaks, CA: Sage.

Barber, A., Hollenbeck, J., Tower, S., & Phillips, J. (1994). The effects of interview focus on recruitment effectiveness: A field experiment. *Journal of Applied Psychology, 79,* 886-896.

Dipboye, R. L. (1992). *Selection interviews: Process perspectives.* Cincinnati, OH: South-Western.

Dipboye, R. L. (1994). Structured and unstructured selection interviews: Beyond the job-fit model. In G. R. Ferris (Ed.), *Research in personnel and human resources management* (Vol. 12, pp. 79-123). Greenwich, CT: JAI.

Eder, R. W. (1989). Contextual effects on interview decisions. In R. W. Eder & G. R. Ferris (Eds.), *The employment interview: Theory, research, and practice* (pp. 113-126). Newbury Park, CA: Sage.

Ferris, G. R., Bhawuk, D. P. S., Fedor, D. B., & Judge, T. A. (1995). Organizational politics and citizenship: Attributions of intentionality and construct definition. In M. J. Martinko (Ed.), *Advances in attribution theory: An organizational perspective* (pp. 231-252). Delray Beach, FL: St. Lucie.

Ferris, G. R., King, T. R., Judge, T. A., & Kacmar, K. M. (1991). The management of shared meaning in organizations: Opportunism in the reflection of attitudes, beliefs, and values. In R. A. Giacalone & P. Rosenfeld (Eds.), *Applied impression management.* Hillsdale, NJ: Lawrence Erlbaum.

Fombrun, C. J. (1996). *Reputation: Realizing value from the corporate image.* Boston: Harvard Business School Press.

Fombrun, C. J., & Shanley, M. (1990). What's in a name? Reputation building and corporate strategy. *Academy of Management Journal, 33,* 233-258.

Fryxell, G., & Wang, J. (1994). The *Fortune* corporate "reputation" index: Reputation for what? *Journal of Management, 20,* 1-14.

Gatewood, R., Gowan, M., & Lautenschlager, G. (1993). Corporate image, recruitment image, and initial job choice decisions. *Academy of Management Journal, 36,* 414-427.

Golembiewski, R. T., Billingsley, K., & Yeager, S. (1976). Measuring change and persistence in human affairs: Types of change generated by OD designs. *Journal of Applied Behavioral Science, 12,* 133-157.

Harris, M. (1989). The recruitment interview as persuasive communication: Applying the elaboration likelihood model. In J. Breaugh, M. Harris, & M. S. Taylor (Chairs), *Organizational recruitment research: Taking stock and setting future directions.* Symposium conducted at the annual meeting of the Academy of Management, Washington, DC.

Heimberg, R. G., Keller, K. E., & Peca-Baker, T. (1986). Cognitive assessment of social-evaluative anxiety in the job interview: Job interview self-statement schedule. *Journal of Counseling Psychology, 33,* 190-195.

Kohn, L. S., & Dipboye, R. L. (1998). The effects of interview structure on recruiting outcomes. *Journal of Applied Social Psychology, 28,* 821-843.

Petty, R. E., & Cacioppo, J. T. (1986). *Communication and persuasion: Central and peripheral routes to attitude change.* New York: Springer-Verlag.

Powell, G. N. (1991). Applicant reactions to the initial employment interview: Exploring theoretical and methodological issues. *Personnel Psychology, 44,* 67-83.

Taylor, M. S., & Bergmann, T. J. (1987). Organizational recruitment activities and applicants' reactions at different stages of the recruitment process. *Personnel Psychology, 40,* 261-285.

Turban, D., Forret, M., & Hendrickson, C. (1998). Applicant attraction to firms: Influences of organization reputation, job and organizational attributes, and recruiter behaviors. *Journal of Vocational Behavior, 52,* 24-44.

Turban, D., & Greening, D. (1997). Corporate social performance and organizational attractiveness to prospective employees. *Academy of Management Journal, 40,* 658-672.

Part II

Constructs Assessed

Expanded Notions of "Fit"

The contributions to this section of the handbook examine the nature of the constructs measured in the interview. Chapter 6, by Binning, LeBreton, and Adorno, is based on the premise that the interview can be an effective tool for measuring job-related personality constructs. The authors provide a number of reasons the interview has advantages over other selection procedures in this regard, including the opportunity the interview provides to assess both candidates' self-reports and their actual behaviors. As Binning et al. acknowledge, however, a personality-oriented interview can also be so poorly designed or conducted that it may provide little or no relevant information.

Binning and his colleagues use various theoretical frameworks to develop their thesis. For example, they describe four factors that affect the accuracy of personality judgments, including the quality of the interviewer and the predictability of the candidate. They then offer a number of potentially interesting uses of a personality-based interview, such as the measurement of problem traits that are generally not assessed with traditional personality measures and a means of reconciling contradictory information regarding a particular candidate. Finally, Binning et al. recommend that the interview be used to examine how applicants felt about and perceived various aspects of important situations, rather than how they behaved in those circumstances. These authors argue that information about how applicants understood and felt about particular situations may be just as important as information regarding the behaviors they demonstrated in those situations.

Binning et al. capitalize on two significant trends that have occurred in the selection research over the past decade: the reconsideration of the validity of the employment interview and the rethinking of the role of personality measures. By combining the strengths of these two selection procedures, they offer some new possibilities for interviewing. From a practical standpoint, there may be much interest in this approach. First, organizations seem particularly interested in measuring "problem personality" characteristics in light of concerns over violence in the workplace, the emphasis on teamwork, and a need for employees to adapt to continuous change. Second, given that different predictors often have little or no intercorrelation, discrepancies between different selection tools are likely to occur with some regularity. The interview may be a means of understanding such discrepancies. Finally, as technology and jobs experience rapid changes, organizations appear to be placing less emphasis on specific knowledge, skills, and abilities (KSAs) and more emphasis on general "competencies." The personality-based approach appears to be more in keeping with this staffing trend.

At the same time, the personality-based interview is not without problems. First, it may be much more susceptible to subjectivity and biases, particularly compared with the structured interview. Second, the personality-oriented interview may come close to assessing disabilities (note that Binning et al. make reference to the American Psychiatric Association's *Diagnostic and Statistical Manual of Mental Disorders,* an important guide concerning psychological disorders). Managers using this approach may be more likely to violate provisions of the Americans With Disabilities Act. Finally, there are practically no empirical data addressing the personality-based approach, whereas there is a large database affirming the validity of structured interviews and objective personality measures. Careful study is needed before we can replace well-regarded, carefully studied techniques with new, as yet untested procedures.

In Chapter 7, Parsons, Cable, and Liden address the interview from two perspectives. First, they consider the interview as a means of assessing the fit between the applicant's values and the organization's values. Second, they examine the interview as a communication device that provides information about organizational values and perhaps even serves to alter the applicant's values. They provide a number of research suggestions in this regard.

Parsons et al. address a growing literature on person-organization fit, a topic that has stimulated considerable interest in the past 5 to 10 years.

Although there has been a great deal of research supporting the link between P-O fit and various criteria, such as job satisfaction, relatively few studies have investigated the determinants of P-O fit. This is particularly problematic in the case of the interview, because we need to know how interviewers arrive at such judgments. Are there certain questions, for example, that are particularly effective for measuring P-O fit? What about the issue of social desirability and applicants' ability to tell interviewers what they think they want to hear? Is background information (e.g., extracurricular activities or courses taken) used in making P-O fit judgments? If the interview is used to measure P-O fit in any systematic, valid way, a theoretical framework should be developed that describes these linkages.

In the second part of their chapter, Parsons et al. address the communication of values during the interview. The communication aspects of the interview received a great deal of attention in the 1980s, but there has been a decline in such research in the past few years. We attribute part of this decline to the increasing attention to the selection aspects of the interview, based on meta-analytic evidence that interviews are more valid than originally thought. At the same time, research conducted over the past 10 years casts doubt on the effect the initial interview has on applicant perceptions of the job and organization. By framing the communication component of the interview as an examination of values, Parsons et al. provide a variety of potentially interesting hypotheses that may produce renewed interest in this area. First, to what degree do applicants view the interview as an opportunity to learn about the organization's values? How does the interview compare with other possible sources (e.g., Web pages, newspaper articles) of information regarding values? What cues and questions do applicants use to learn more about the organization's values? Which organizational members (e.g., human resource manager, supervisor, peers) do applicants rely upon most for information about organizational values? Parsons et al. point out that the interview may even be used to alter applicants' values. If so, are there some communication techniques that are particularly effective for promoting changes in values? Clearly, this chapter raises a variety of interesting and important issues for future investigation.

Toward More Structured Interviews

In Chapter 8, Harris explores the constructs that are being measured in the structured (i.e., BDI/SI) interview. He proposes four possible constructs that the structured interview may be measuring: cognitive ability, practical intelligence, traditional KSAs, and P-O fit. He offers explanations as to why the structured interview may be measuring each of these and makes some suggestions for possible future research. A recent meta-analysis appears to rebut the assertion that structured interviews measure cognitive ability. A traditional KSA perspective has limited support, but there is more support for a "situation" or exercise effect (i.e., the interview measures how well a candidate functions in a one-on-one situation), similar to research demonstrating exercise, not dimension, factors in assessment centers. Harris also points out the need for a clearer definition of what "values" are, particularly concerning how they differ from other constructs, such as "intentions."

One of the central issues that Harris addresses, and one that Schmitt comments on later in this volume as well (Chapter 20), is that the interview is a "method" of selection, but its content may vary widely. Therefore, just as we maintain there is no such thing as "the" interview, any discussion of what interviews may be attempting to measure must be prefaced by some description of the type of interview and the questions used. Even so, it seems possible that two interviewers using the same questions and format may have different purposes in mind, and the interviews may therefore measure different constructs.

A secondary theme in Harris's chapter is a comparison between the situational interview (SI) and the behavior description interview (BDI). Although Harris argues that both are likely to be measuring the same basic construct, he does offer some findings indicating that the SI and BDI may differ. Further comparisons between the SI and BDI are highlighted in Chapter 9, by Maurer, Sue-Chan, and Latham, and in Chapter 10, by Motowidlo. Maurer et al. offer a summary of recent research on the SI, including criterion-related validity findings, construct validation work, reliability coefficients, findings regarding fairness, and investigations of the practicality of the SI. Despite a preponderance of evidence that the SI is a valid, fair, cost-effective, and well-regarded interview approach, its use does not appear to be widespread. Maurer et al. conclude with some general suggestions about how to address this issue.

Motowidlo discusses the putative basis for why the SI and BDI are valid measures of job performance. He asserts that BDI questions are valid because they reflect consistent patterns of choices made by the candidate in situations likely to happen on the job. SI questions are valid because they measure candidates' intentions, which in turn are precursors of workplace behaviors. Motowidlo proceeds to offer various factors, such as degree of control over one's behavior, that may affect the relationship between intentions and behavior. He also asserts that under certain conditions, SI and BDI questions may provide the same information and therefore should be equally valid; under other conditions, however, questions about behavior in actual past situations (i.e., BDI questions) would be more valid.

Taken together, Chapters 9 and 10 provide some interesting directions for future research. First, as articulated by Maurer and his colleagues, there is a need to examine structured interviewing from both the applicant's and the interviewer's perspectives. One heretofore unaddressed question, for example, is, To what degree does the interviewer's perception of the interview format affect the applicant's reactions? Given that there may be wide variation in interviewers' perceptions of the same interview, it seems quite reasonable to expect that the same interview may be perceived quite differently by different job candidates.

Second, given that several studies have compared the BDI and SI, it is now time to go beyond simple comparisons of their validity and fairness. We need to design specific hypotheses in terms of how and why they differ, incorporating a broader list of variables. In terms of validity, for example, Motowidlo suggests that when behavior is under less than complete volitional control by the employee, intentions will be less predictive of future behavior than will past behavior. A study could compare either dimensions or organizations that differ in amount of volitional control to see if indeed SI questions are less valid for performance dimensions or organizations that provide less discretion to employees.

6

Assessing Personality

John F. Binning
James M. LeBreton
Anthony J. Adorno

Theory and assessment of human personality engender both interest and trepidation for many research-oriented and applied human resource professionals. In fact, few other areas of psychological assessment are generally considered so wide-ranging, complex, and controversial. It is clear that the prominence of personality assessment in the general human resource management literature as well as the literature specific to employment interviewing has been stifled in the past 30 or so years due to a confluence of legal, social, conceptual, and practical issues (Hough & Schneider, 1996). For example, out of 637 references in Eder and Ferris's 1989 edited collection *The Employment Interview*, the word *personality* appeared in the titles of only eight (1.3%) articles. In the past decade, however, personality theory and assessment have had a public rebirth that has invigorated considerable discussion. Recent empirical evidence demonstrates unequivocally that well-constructed personality assessment systems are valid predictors of job performance and that they can enhance fairness in the employment process (Funder, 1995; Hogan, Hogan, & Roberts, 1996;

Sackett & Wanek, 1996). Yet little systematic research has been conducted on how the employment interview can enhance personality assessment. In this chapter we explore how the employment interview may uniquely contribute to personality assessment and thus enhance human resources decision making.

Personnel selection specialists sample job candidates' past and present behavior as a basis for predicting these individuals' future behavior. Because a variety of behavior sampling methods are available, one important consideration in the design of a selection system is the proper combination of specific methods. With regard to personality assessment, structured inventories have been the assessment method of choice for most selection specialists. We would like to call particular attention to the fact that, compared with structured inventories, the employment interview is a unique behavior sampling method because it combines direct observation of candidates' behavior with the potential for asking probing questions about candidates' overt behavior outside the interview as well as covert emotional and cognitive processes. In light of the fact that there are limitations on personality assessment through self-report inventories (Mount, Barrick, & Strauss, 1994; Ozer & Reise, 1994), it is our contention that the interview's methodological uniqueness can be capitalized upon to make it a valuable tool for assessing job-relevant personality differences. This may contribute significant incremental validity for personnel selection decisions.

As we intimated earlier, the interview's potential contribution to personality assessment may largely be attributed to its uniqueness as a behavior sampling method. In personnel selection contexts, a predictor can be viewed as a set of stimulus conditions that elicits a sample of behavioral information from which one may draw inferences about future behavior. Behavioral information can vary along at least five distinct dimensions: source, temporal locus, construct domain sampled, observability, and specificity. *Source* refers to whether the behavioral evidence derives from self-reports, other reports, or direct observations of candidate behavior. *Temporal locus* refers to the time that has elapsed between when the behavior was exhibited and when the information is gathered. Direct observations of candidate behavior minimize this time lapse, whereas biographical information can be temporally quite distant from the assessment process. With reference to the third dimension, any predictor can be developed to sample either (or both) a *job performance domain* or a *psychological construct domain*. This is schematically represented in Figure 6.1. It is in this sense that Binning and Barrett (1989) refer to content-related and construct-related predictor sampling strategies. A predictor can be designed to sample directly the content of a specific performance domain. Alternatively, a predictor can be designed to sample specific psychological construct domains previously determined to underlie job performance. *Observability* refers to the fact that behavioral information can take the form of overt

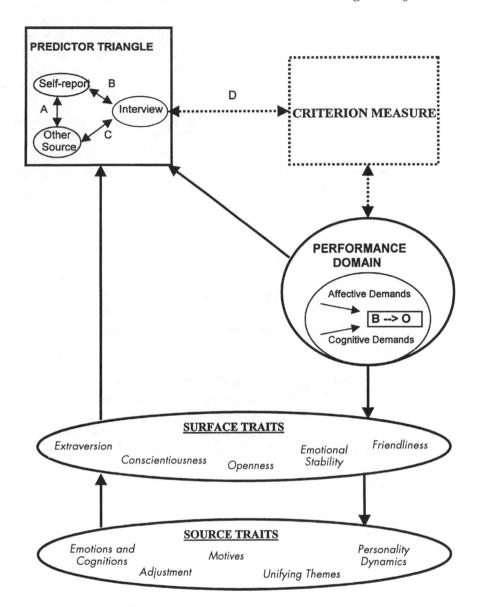

Figure 6.1. A Modified Framework Illustrating the Conceptual and Empirical Inferences in the Interview Development Process
SOURCE: Adapted from Binning and Barrett (1989, fig. 3).

activities or more covert forms, such as emotional and cognitive activities. Finally, *specificity* refers to whether the behavioral information is specific to a very clearly delineated set of situational conditions or is a more general summary of behavior in broader classes of situations (e.g., job-specific situations versus general life situations).

A face-to-face interview is a unique predictor sampling method in that it can span these dimensions more broadly than can any other single predictor method. A given interview can generate candidate self-reports and interviewers' direct observations of behavior. It can gather behavioral information from the distant past, the recent past, and the present. It can gather information relevant to both job performance domains and psychological construct domains, and, while doing so, it can gather information about overt behaviors as well as covert emotional and cognitive processes. Finally, it can gather behavioral information about a specific job situation and more general life situations. To summarize, the employment interview can be a uniquely fertile source of behavioral information from which to draw inferences about job candidates' personality functioning. Of course, this uniqueness can be both a strength and a weakness. Poorly designed interviews may gather such a smattering of behavioral information that they do not allow effective assessment of any meaningful psychological variables. The challenge is to design interviews that are coherent behavior samples from which to draw valid, job-related inferences.

When considering whether personality can or should be assessed based on an employment interview, a crucial first question is whether there is any evidence that employment interviewers could, under any circumstances, be expected to provide accurate assessments of applicant personality. The answer is a qualified, but emphatic, yes. Considerable research in social and personality psychology indicates that under certain circumstances, observers' perceptions of personality achieve a reasonable degree of accuracy (Funder, 1995). The second important question therefore becomes whether these "accuracy-conducive" conditions can be attained in the employment interview setting. A brief review of these conditions follows.

Interview Conditions Conducive to Accurate Personality Assessment

Funder's (1995) realistic accuracy model (RAM) is a simplified characterization of the way personality judgment happens in real life and is used to explain the conditions in which personality judgments can be accurate. According to the RAM, interviewers' personality judgments can be accurate if behavioral information that is (a) *available for observation* is (b) *relevant to target traits* and the interviewers can (c) *manage to detect* and (d) *correctly use* the information. Therefore, in an employment interview where job candidates exhibit trait-driven behaviors, it is likely that only a subset of those behaviors will be manifestations of job-related traits and only some of those behaviors are available to the interviewer.

For example, a candidate who throws a lit cigarette into a restroom trash can during an assessment break may be exhibiting a very relevant conscientiousness-related behavior, but the interviewer cannot incorporate it into a trait judgment unless it is observed. Of course, the interviewer can ask the candidate whether he or she has ever thrown a lit cigarette into a public trash can, but the candidate may deny ever having done so. Conversely, the candidate may exhibit behaviors in the interviewer's presence that are irrelevant to job-related traits. An example would be a candidate for a telemarketing position who maintains poor eye contact during an interview.

A third condition for accuracy requires that the interviewer be able to detect trait-relevant and available behaviors. Both situational and personal variables may contribute to the interviewer's inattentiveness, distractions, and unperceptiveness, which may lead to otherwise available behaviors' going unobserved. An interviewer's poor auditory selective attention ability could interact with frequent interruptions (e.g., ringing telephones, outside sirens) to undermine significantly the effective use of available behavioral information. Finally, the interviewer must make correct use of the relevant, available, and detected behaviors to make appropriate inferences. An interviewer's personality traits, implicit theories, or idiosyncratic conceptual schemata may lead him or her to believe that a behavior is diagnostic of one trait when actually it is more diagnostic of another. For example, an interviewer low in self-esteem may view a candidate's self-confidence as a sign of narcissism or aggressiveness.

In addition to the conditions mentioned above, there are four broad categories of variables that may moderate the accuracy of personality judgments: (a) quality of the interviewer, (b) judgeability of the candidate, (c) judgeability of the target trait or behavior, and (d) quality of the behavioral information (Funder, 1995). Differences between accurate and inaccurate interviewers would result from differential detection or use of behavioral cues. For example, interviewers may differ in their knowledge of personality dynamics, in their specific cognitive abilities, in their motivation to form accurate judgments, or in their distortion proneness (e.g., defensiveness, lack of humor, narcissism). Graves and Karren (1992) found that effective interviewers were more disciplined and focused more on interpersonal skills than did their less effective counterparts. There is also evidence that an individual's personality may predispose him or her to infer trait explanations versus situational explanations from observations of others' behavior (Krull & Erickson, 1995). Despite potential managerial resistance to the notion, there clearly is a need for more research on individual differences that might be associated with the accuracy of interviewers' judgments.

Job candidates also will differ in the ease with which their general behavior patterns and personality can be judged correctly based on relatively limited observations. Some job candidates will provide more behavioral cues, some will adjust their behaviors to the situation more sensitively (e.g., high self-monitors), and some will behave more consistently across situations. Some candidates are more "nonjudgeable" because their actions and thoughts cannot readily be predicted from observations of what they say or do, resulting from either fragmentation and incoherence of personality functioning or deliberate attempts at deception or concealment (e.g., Hogan's [1995] "hollow core syndrome" or Gustafson & Ritzer's [1995] "aberrant self-promoter").

Just as candidates vary in their judgeability, traits vary in judgeability. As we explain in more detail below, surface traits are more judgeable than source traits, and some surface traits are more judgeable than others due to the differential availability and relevance of behavior cues (Funder, 1995). For example, sociability is more readily judgeable than ego strength or parental attachment. In addition, the open expression of some traits is more socially desirable than the expression of others, and the quality of behavioral information can vary.

The diagnostic value of the information is also important. Funder and Sneed (1993) investigated which behaviors affected judges' perceptions of specific traits and found that certain behaviors were more "diagnostic" than others. This line of research could be expanded to determine the types of candidate work behaviors that are most diagnostic of specific Big Five traits. Differences in the judgeability of Big Five traits could also be studied. To extend this idea, an applicant's discussions of his or her thoughts and feelings associated with past experiences may be more diagnostic of personality functioning than having that same applicant describe only behaviors and outcomes associated with critical incidents (e.g., "emotion description interviews" versus "behavior description interviews"). Research on how different types of interview information can be effectively elicited and used to form accurate personality judgments is clearly warranted. With the RAM as a conceptual backdrop, we now turn to a discussion of several issues that must be addressed in the design of employment interviews to assess personality.

Designing Employment Interviews to Assess Personality

To delimit the conceptual boundaries of personality theory and to make more manageable a discussion of how the employment interview can enhance personality assessment, we offer the following characterization. *Personality* can refer to behavioral functioning at either of two nomological levels, and therefore assessment can focus on either (a) observable (and largely interpersonal) behavior or (b) systems of internal emotional and cognitive processing that explain the regularities in observable behavior (Hogan, 1991). Observable behavior regularities, or surface (phenotypic) traits, are more publicly verifiable, whereas the nomologically deeper regularities called source (genotypic) traits are more private and require greater inferential effort and insight on the interviewer's part to discover and understand. Regardless of whether surface or source traits are the object of study, there is general agreement that personality assessment is a process of discovering the general coherence, unifying themes, and characteristic adaptations of an individual's affective, cognitive, and behavioral functioning in various spheres of life (see Bandura, 1986; Buss & Finn, 1987; Epstein, 1994; Funder, 1991; Hogan, 1991; Mischel & Shoda, 1995; Ozer & Reise, 1994; Paulhus & Martin, 1987; Wiggins & Pincus, 1992).

Regardless of which nomological level is being assessed, a thorough job analysis should be conducted to determine which profile of traits is necessary for successful job performance. In the following discussion, we address issues associated with analyzing jobs to determine personality requirements as a precursor to proper interview design.

Job Analysis for Personality Requirements

There is evidence that professional interviewers and student judges can make meaningful discriminations of incumbents' modal personality characteristics (Paunonen & Jackson, 1987). Although it is encouraging to note that these macro-level judgments of job-related personality characteristics can be made, they are not specifically tied to organizationally valued performance outcomes. Therefore, we believe that the rigor provided by thorough job and organization analysis is necessary to match personality requirements optimally with job demands. Different organizations require different patterns of typical and maximal goal-oriented and interpersonal behavior (Schneider, 1987, 1996). Similarly, at a micro level, different jobs require different patterns of behavior (Hogan & Blake, 1996; Hough & Schneider, 1996; Lowman, 1991). For example, jobs can differ in terms of how much autonomy is afforded the incumbent, and these "strong" versus "weak" situations have been shown to moderate the predictive validity of personality constructs (Mount & Barrick, 1995). Therefore, as an initial determination, the "strength" of a job situation could be characterized by job analysis.

Evidence is beginning to emerge that different combinations of Big Five personality traits are relevant for different jobs and job families (Gottfredson, Jones, & Holland, 1993; Hogan & Blake, 1996). For example, considerable evidence exists that behaviors associated with conscientiousness are positively correlated with performance in some job situations and unrelated to or negatively correlated with performance in others (Hogan & Blake, 1996). Similarly, both qualitative and quantitative meta-analyses suggest that there are different personality-performance relationships across various jobs (Hogan & Blake, 1996; Hough & Schneider, 1996; Mount & Barrick, 1995). To summarize this point, job analysis should provide a coherent description of job-related behavioral regularities, embedded in a social environment, that are required to achieve valuable organizational outcomes. Underlying these important behavioral regularities in the performance domain are the psychological constructs associated with a particular job in a particular organization. The relationships among the performance domain, surface and source trait domains, and the employment interview are depicted in Figure 6.1.

Several existing job analysis systems could be adapted for determining personality requirements. These include threshold traits analysis (Lopez, Kesselman, & Lopez, 1981) and adjective checklists to translate job demands into relevant personality traits (Hogan & Arneson, 1987). There also could be considerable merit in adapting Q-sort ratings of personality requirements for job analysis. Drawing from the person-job fit paradigm described by Caldwell and O'Reilly (1990), overt behavioral indicators of personality traits could be Q-sorted to describe job performance requirements. Another framework that may have great utility for linking job demands and personality requirements is described by Hogan et al. (1996). They call their framework the 5×6 model because it integrates the Big Five personality factors with Holland's six occupational groups. Finally, perhaps the most ambitious work in this area has resulted in the development of a structured job analysis questionnaire designed to identify the Big Five personality requirements of jobs (Raymark, Schmit, & Guion, 1997).

Assessing Surface Versus Source Traits in the Employment Interview

Personality research and practice in personnel selection contexts is dominated by rather static, surface trait models, with less emphasis on dynamic theories of emotional and cognitive functioning involving source traits. Identification of a job candidate's surface trait profile can provide valuable descriptive and predictive information, but research and theorizing at both nomological levels is ultimately desirable for scientific understanding.

There is considerable evidence that people can reliably and validly provide personality descriptions of others' interpersonal behaviors based upon surprisingly limited direct interaction (Albright, Kenny, & Malloy, 1988; Ambady & Rosenthal, 1992; Jackson, Peacock, & Smith, 1980; James, Campbell, & Lovegrove, 1984; Mount et al., 1994; Paunonen, Jackson, & Oberman, 1987) and that people are intuitively knowledgeable about the traits that they can judge with more or less agreement (Funder, 1995). Viewed pragmatically if not optimistically, this indicates that a reasonably competent interviewer could be expected to provide some valuable information about a job candidate's Big Five status subsequent to an adequately conducted interview. Other aspects of interpersonal functioning also could be captured, such as functional flexibility or basic social skills (Paulhus & Martin, 1988; Riggio, 1986), along with possible situational moderators of such behavior. This would constitute personality description at the surface trait level as depicted in Figure 6.1.

An alternative use of the interview would be to probe more deeply for information at the emotional and cognitive level of source traits. Specific theoretical formulations would guide interview design. For example, an interview could be designed to probe for information about actions, cognitions, and emotions associated with avoiding anxiety and maintaining self-esteem. Wiggins (1973) has reviewed how psychoanalytic, interpersonal, transactional, cognitive, multivariate, and social learning models of personality can guide assessment, with myriad implications for specific assessment processes. The important issue is that interview validity is likely to be dependent upon the extent to which its design is tied to a coherent model of personality functioning.

Assessing the Dark Side of Personality in the Interview

The discussion of personality assessment at both levels described above has focused on the normal or "bright" side of personality. It is also possible to assess candidates' "dark" side personality characteristics and behavioral predispositions (Baumeister & Scher, 1988; Costa & McCrae, 1992a; Gustafson & Ritzer, 1995; Hogan, 1990; Hogan, Curphy, & Hogan, 1994; Hogan, Raskin, & Fazzini, 1990; Lowman, 1996; Widiger, Mangine, Corbitt, Ellis, & Thomas, 1995). Individuals who have a truly pathological dark side are less likely even to seek employment (Lowman, 1996), but many personality tendencies may not qualify as clinically significant and yet be particularly disruptive to interpersonal functioning on the job (Gustafson & Ritzer, 1995; Hogan, 1994; Hogan et al., 1994; Kagan, 1990; Lowman, 1996). Assessing these individuals with "subclinical" personality tendencies may be a useful focus of the interview (e.g., using the Hogan Development Survey [HDS; Hogan, 1995], the Inventory of Interpersonal Problems [IIP; Horowitz, Rosenberg, Baer, Ureno, & Villasenor, 1988], or the Narcissistic Personality Inventory [NPI; Raskin & Hall, 1981]).

Take, for example, an individual who has a narcissistic predisposition. Traditional personality assessments that are designed to tap the brighter side of personality (e.g., the NEO Personality Inventory [NEO PI; Costa & McCrae, 1992b], the California Psychological Inventory [CPI; Gough, 1987], or the Hogan Personality Inventory [HPI; Hogan & Hogan, 1995]) would reveal this person to be assertive, self-confident, outgoing, motivated, socially competent, and energetic. It is only when one assesses the darker side of this individual's personality that one would find him or her to be self-centered, manipulative, arrogant, insensitive, and competitive (Kagan, 1990; Hogan, 1994; Hogan et al., 1994). Hogan et al. (1994) make the point that these "irritating tendencies" are very difficult to detect in typical assessment situations because they tend to covary with ostensibly positive traits. Gustafson and Ritzer (1995) describe their attempts to assess "aberrant self-promoters" (ASPs). ASPs represent a nonclinical population of individuals who engage in dysfunctional behavior that may be counterproductive to many organizational goals. Gustafson and Ritzer define aberrant self-promotion as "a subclinical pattern of characteristics that [is] functionally analogous to psychopathy, the difference being one of degree, not kind" (p. 175). They have used various structured inventories and interviews to identify this personality type, which may represent a dangerous "employment risk." ASPs are viewed as bad employees because they engage in narcissistic and antisocial behavior. Trying to assess narcissistic patterns of behavior associated with either the narcissistic manager (Hogan et al., 1994; Kagan, 1990) or the ASP (Gustafson & Ritzer, 1995) is an unconventional assessment task, and it may require an unconventional method of assessment. Personality inventories and traditional employment interviews may not be able to pick up on the more subtle cues given off by such persons (Kagan, 1990).

An employment interview could be organized around the results of a structured inventory specifically designed to assess the dark side of personality (e.g., the HDS or the NPI). For example, an interviewer could structure questions to tap those "dysfunctional dispositions" identified by the HDS that may be particularly problematic in a specific workplace. For example, if on the HDS a prospective manager scores particularly high on the Excitable Scale (i.e., borderline tendencies), the interviewer could probe further; for example, he or she might ask the candidate to describe the persons from his or her past experience with whom he or she most and least enjoyed working. Candidates with borderline tendencies are unusually emotionally volatile and are more likely than other candidates to idealize those with whom they get along and dramatically devalue others. Lanyon and Goodstein (1997) point out that the interview provides a unique opportunity for assessment of not only the *content* of the candidate's response, but also the *style* of the response. The style of the response could provide additional evidence of interpersonal "red flags" (Kagan, 1990). Furthermore, both the content and style of responses could be subjected to a structured scoring procedure.

Relatedly, Hogan and Hogan (1995) discuss various "syndromes" that are characterized by different configurations of Big Five traits. For example, a person who evidences the hollow core syndrome is someone who is publicly cheerful but privately doubting and unhappy (e.g., low emotional stability). Hogan and Hogan suggest that these people likely will have performance difficulties, and they note that this syndrome is particularly difficult to identify from a typical employment interview. Another potential approach would involve the interviewer's questioning candidates about their characteristic coping styles. An appendix to the fourth edition of the American Psychiatric Association's *Diagnostic and Statistical Manual of Mental Disorders* (1994) proposes a defensive functioning scale that describes the different adaptive values of 27 strategies for coping with emotional conflict and external stressors. For example, job candidates who are prone to anxiety (i.e., high neuroticism scores on a structured inventory) could be questioned about their characteristic ways of dealing with stressful life and work events. Certain maladaptive coping styles would be particularly likely to lead to performance difficulties in certain jobs (e.g., habitual devaluation of coworkers or avoidance of conflict). Discovering these very important work-related, albeit negative, personality characteristics poses a unique challenge to selection specialists. This challenge may be addressed in the context of a multiple-source assessment model anchored by the employment interview, which we describe below.

The Interview as Part of an
Integrated Predictor Triangle

We believe that a significant psychometric synergy may be realized through the strategic combination of the employment interview with other sources of behavioral information and the use of this combination to probe for inconsistencies among the sources. Of course, the notion of combining structured assessment with interviewing is not entirely novel (e.g., First, Spitzer, Gibbon, & Williams, 1995; Hogan & Hogan, 1995; Weitzul, 1992). However, we are unaware of any conceptual or empirical work in industrial and organizational psychology or human resources management that focuses on the design of a personality assessment system in which the complementary roles of the interview and other assessment methods are built upon current theory and explicitly delineated. Instead of using structured personality assessment as an independent component or first-stage screening device, we are advocating the use of a "localized" version of Cronbach and Meehl's (1955) nomological network-based construct validation paradigm grounded in psychometric triangulation. The use of an integrated, multiple-source *predictor triangle* is also consistent with the model of judgmental accuracy (i.e., RAM) discussed earlier.

Most important, such an integrated predictor triangle would identify discrepancies among data sources that may be as informative as convergences (Funder, 1995). For example, if a candidate's self-reports on a structured inventory suggest moderate to high conscientiousness, although the descriptions of a third party (e.g., previous employer, coworker, or close acquaintance) indicate otherwise, this could be the basis for a hypothesis to explore the origin of the candidate's differential trait status. Given the factorial fuzziness of the conscientiousness dimension (Hough & Schneider, 1996; Mount & Barrick, 1995), this discrepancy could derive from the candidate's behaving dependably versus having achievement strivings. Perhaps a "theory of discrepancies" could be developed to structure and enhance the probative value of the interview process. The interview would be designed explicitly to probe for information specifically relevant to reconciling any discrepancies and refining a personality portrait of the job candidate.

Recall the candidate whose self-report indicates high conscientiousness but the third-party report does not. If the job being considered is in accounting, the self-report data would represent a good job match and the third-party report would indicate a poor match. Clarifying this discrepancy could enhance the validity of a hiring decision. To illustrate further, we had occasion to administer a vocational interest inventory and a personality inventory to a group of candidates for a career development program. The interest inventory placed a particular candidate in the 62nd percentile on the Work Style scale, suggesting that she enjoyed working with others in teams, was talkative, and was expressive. Her Sociability score was at the 4th percentile, indicating that "she was unusually quiet, reserved, perhaps shy," and enjoyed working with technology, data, or equipment. Clearly these portrayals are discrepant. In trying to understand this discrepancy, we might hypothesize that she is outgoing at work, but does not socialize in her private life. This hypothesis could be explored in an interview. It is not so much an issue that one of the data sources is "right" and the other is "wrong," but rather that the discrepancy may result from situational differences that may be important to clarify.

Interview Structure and Personality Assessment

The employment interview's reputation for validity has experienced a recent turnaround. After decades of empirical embarrassment, recent meta-analytic research supports the belief that respectable levels of validity can be attained through responsible use of more structured interviews (see Huffcutt & Arthur, 1994). It is somewhat ironic, therefore, to propose that, for personality assessment, a moderate rather than high level of interview structure might be optimal. To the extent that an interviewer is probing for or following up on inconsistencies, some flexibility in questioning may be necessary. Similarly, viewing the interview as an interpersonal behavior sample, Lanyon and Goodstein (1997) suggest that the interview should possess a relaxed structure. They state, "Less structured interviews, which offer subjects few or no clear directions and permit great latitude in the areas to be covered, clearly provide interpersonal behavior samples" (p. 160).

In fact, the meta-analytic research on interview validity may support this recommendation. Huffcutt and Arthur (1994) found that Level III structured interviews (i.e., not fully structured) are as valid as Level IV structured interviews (i.e., completely structured). We are suggesting that there may be some optimal level of structure that enhances the validity of personality assessment in the employment interview. Realizing that interview structure involves both questioning and response scoring, an optimal interview design for assessing personality might consist of relatively unstructured questioning combined with structured scoring schemes built from coherent personality theory. An additional consideration is that practicing managers are likely to find this type of interview more acceptable than the highly structured interview (Church, 1996; Dipboye, 1994). Research is sorely needed to determine how interview design affects the construct validity of personality judgments.

If the employment interview is semistructured, it is important to consider how preinterview hypotheses will affect the subsequent interview. There has been considerable research on how preinterview impressions can affect interviewers' conduct of the interview as well as their postinterview decisions (Dipboye, 1989) by inducing confirmatory and disconfirmatory questioning patterns. Although the effects of preinterview impressions on unstructured questioning strategies generally are not large, there is evidence that they do replicate. However, existing research on preinterview impression effects has focused on structural or semantic characteristics of interview questions (e.g., Macan & Dipboye, 1988) or the general positivity/negativity of questions (e.g., Binning, Goldstein, Garcia, Harding, & Scattaregia, 1988) rather than on the specific psychological constructs being tapped (Huffcutt, Roth, & McDaniel, 1996). Properly structured interviews, designed to focus on specific constructs and probe for diagnostic inconsistencies, may exhibit greater construct and criterion-related validity. Borkenau and Muller (1992) found that personality judgments actually reflect both confirming and disconfirming evidence. Huffcutt et al. (1996) found that more structured interviews were least saturated with cognitive ability, suggesting that other constructs were being assessed and that general impressions of intelligence were minimized. Based upon a review of the human judgment literature, Faust (1986) advocates the use of disconfirmatory strategies as a "corrective measure" to improve clinical judgment. Semistructured interviews may be particularly suited to allowing interviewers to draw the "clinical" inferences needed to assess adequately the personality dynamics, emotional functioning, and cognitive interpretations that affect typical day-to-day behavioral regularities. This contrasts starkly with drawing KSA inferences about behavioral regularities associated with maximum performance conditions (Widiger et al., 1995). Research is needed to clarify the roles that specific questioning strategies play in interviewers' forming of judgments about job candidates.

Question development processes and taxonomic efforts to isolate critical question characteristics are very important (e.g., Graesser, Lang, & Horgan, 1988). Huffcutt et al. (1996) discovered that interviews comprising situational questions (i.e., hypothetical job-related situations) were more saturated with cognitive ability than were interviews comprising behavior description questions (i.e., descriptions of relevant past situations). Andersen (1984) demonstrated that listening to a person talk about his or her thoughts and feelings resulted in more accurate personality judgments than did listening to that same person talk about his or her activities and hobbies. One implication is that certain types of structured questioning may better isolate and tap affective constructs compared with cognitive or other ability constructs.

A variation of the critical incident technique or behavior description interview format may be particularly useful. Traditional questioning about critical incidents starts with the identification of notably good or poor performance *outcomes* in some task situation. The goal is to elicit situational, cognitive, and behavioral precursors to valued organizational outcomes. An alternative questioning paradigm might be called the personal incident technique, in which the candidate describes particularly memorable, emotional, or personally meaningful events and experiences. The emphasis would be on how the candidate felt and perceived aspects of the situations described. One goal of questioning could be to identify distinctive "if . . . then . . ." situation-behavior relations that characterize the underlying invariance that may be an important signature of personality. As Mischel and Shoda (1995) note, "To discover the potentially predictable patterns of behavior variability that characterize individuals, a first step is to identify those features of situations that are meaningful to and that engage their important psychological qualities" (p. 250).

The interviewer could probe for "SERPA" units, in that there will be information about the circumstances (situation → emotional reactions → perceptions → actions) associated with each incident. Depending upon the interviewer's theoretical predilections, the focus may be on typical perceptions and cognitive framing of work-related situations or on the emotional and cognitive determinants of actions taken. SERPA units could also be elicited in the examination of "daily-life events" (Cantor & Harlow, 1994; Ozer & Reise, 1994). This molecular account of the "little experiences" of daily life could focus on (a) everyday events and associated mood, affect, and well-being; (b) the relations between life events and the job candidate's goals, plans, and intentions; and (c) associations between life events and previously measured personality traits. The typical collection of daily-life event data is very labor-intensive, however, and may be feasible only for current employees who are being considered for promotion.

Alternatively, the interviewer might probe for what Wiggins (1973) calls problematic situations. The focus here is on the adequacy with which a candidate responds to various problem situations. Interestingly, Wiggins describes how problematic situations can be compiled and standard responses scaled for effectiveness. In essence, a situational interview could be developed around such a compilation. Russell (1990) describes interviews designed to tap specific accomplishments, disappointments, obstacles, conflicts, and learning that took place in previous job situations. Bernardin (1987) describes the development of a structured instrument to measure job candidates' likelihood of experiencing job-related discomfort associated with common job demands. An interviewer could probe to better understand the responses to this structured inventory.

This brief review highlights the fact that many questioning variations exist for eliciting information about candidates' behavioral, emotional, and cognitive functioning as it relates to personality. Regardless of the specific theory guiding the interview, the interview would be a semistructured search for patterns of personality coherence relevant to specific job demands.

Conclusion

In this chapter we have discussed how one of the most commonly used human resource selection procedures can be used to assess psychological characteristics that underlie all aspects of human functioning. Put this way, it is perhaps even more surprising to realize that there is clearly a dearth of research on personality assessment in the employment interview. Therefore, this chapter can be viewed as a call for systematic research on how the employment interview process can contribute to personality assessment, and we have attempted to describe several issues that must be addressed in a research program.

We would like to conclude by reiterating that Funder's (1995) realistic accuracy model may provide a useful guide for future interview research. The RAM is philosophically founded on the assumption that accuracy of personality judgments can be determined only through systematic comparisons among multiple sources of data. Furthermore, discrepancies between data sources are considered to be as informative as convergences. In addition to this fundamental reliance on triangulation of data sources, the RAM also assumes that personality judgment should be studied using real people in real settings, as opposed to "paper people" in socially and emotionally impoverished research settings. Applied human resource decision makers therefore have a great deal to offer through their access to field research opportunities. The RAM also maintains that the accuracy of personality judgments should be based upon the three criteria of interobserver agreement, candidate-other agreement, and behavior prediction. Thus, a predictor triangle combined with criterion-related validity research would represent an operationalization of these accuracy criteria (these criteria are portrayed as A, B, C, and D in Figure 6.1). We conclude by noting that, given the resurgence of interest in personality-based human resource decisions, the time has come for systematic research on personality assessment in the employment interview to provide valuable guidance to this burgeoning area of scientific and applied psychology.

References

Albright, L., Kenny, D. A., & Malloy, T. E. (1988). Consensus in personality judgments at zero acquaintance. *Journal of Personality and Social Psychology, 55,* 387-395.

Ambady, N., & Rosenthal, R. (1992). Thin slices of expressive behavior as predictors of interpersonal consequences: A meta-analysis. *Psychological Bulletin, 111,* 256-274.

American Psychiatric Association. (1994). *Diagnostic and statistical manual of mental disorders* (4th ed.). Washington, DC: Author.

Andersen, S. M. (1984). Self-knowledge and social inference: II. The diagnosticity of cognitive/affective and behavioral data. *Journal of Personality and Social Psychology, 46,* 294-307.

Bandura, A. (1986). *Social foundations for thought and action: A social cognitive theory.* Englewood Cliffs, NJ: Prentice Hall.

Baumeister, R. F., & Scher, S. J. (1988). Self-defeating behavior patterns among normal individuals: Review and analysis of common self-destructive tendencies. *Psychological Bulletin, 104,* 3-22.

Bernardin, H. J. (1987). Development and validation of a forced choice scale to measure job-related discomfort among customer service representatives. *Academy of Management Journal, 30,* 162-173.

Binning, J. F., & Barrett, G. V. (1989). Validity of personnel decisions: A conceptual analysis of the inferential and evidential bases. *Journal of Applied Psychology, 74,* 478-494.

Binning, J. F., Goldstein, M. A., Garcia, M. F., Harding, J. L., & Scattaregia, J. H. (1988). Effects of preinterview impressions on questioning strategies in same- and opposite-sex employment interviews. *Journal of Applied Psychology, 73,* 30-37.

Borkenau, P., & Muller, B. (1992). Inferring act frequencies and traits from behavior observations. *Journal of Personality, 60,* 553-573.

Buss, A. H., & Finn, S. E. (1987). Classification of personality traits. *Journal of Personality and Social Psychology, 52,* 432-444.

Caldwell, D. F., & O'Reilly, C. A. (1990). Measuring person-job fit with a profile comparison process. *Journal of Applied Psychology, 75,* 648-657.

Cantor, N., & Harlow, R. E. (1994). Personality, strategic behavior, and daily-life problem solving. *Current Directions in Psychological Science, 3,* 169-172.

Church, A. H. (1996). From both sides now: The employee interview—the Great Pretender. *Industrial-Organizational Psychologist, 34,* 108-117.

Costa, P. T., Jr., & McCrae, R. R. (1992a). The five-factor model of personality and its relevance to personality disorders. *Journal of Personality Disorders, 6,* 343-359.

Costa, P. T., Jr., & McCrae, R. R. (1992b). *NEO PI-R: Professional manual.* Odessa, FL: Psychological Assessment Resources.

Cronbach, L. J., & Meehl, P. E. (1955). Construct validity in psychological tests. *Psychological Bulletin, 52,* 281-302.

Dipboye, R. L. (1989). Threats to the incremental validity of interviewer judgments. In R. W. Eder & G. R. Ferris (Eds.), *The employment interview: Theory, research, and practice* (pp. 45-60). Newbury Park, CA: Sage.

Dipboye, R. L. (1994). Structured and unstructured selection interviews: Beyond the job-fit model. In G. R. Ferris (Ed.), *Research in personnel and human resources management* (Vol. 12, pp. 79-123). Greenwich, CT: JAI.

Eder, R. W., & Ferris, G. R. (Eds.). (1989). *The employment interview: Theory, research, and practice*. Newbury Park, CA: Sage.

Epstein, S. (1994). Integration of the cognitive and psychodynamic unconscious. *American Psychologist, 49,* 709-724.

Faust, D. (1986). Research on human judgment and its application to clinical practice. *Professional Psychology: Research and Practice, 17,* 420-430.

First, M. B., Spitzer, R. L., Gibbon, M., & Williams, J. B. W. (1995). The structured clinical interview for DSM-III-R personality disorders (SCID-II): Part I. Description. *Journal of Personality Disorders, 9,* 83-91.

Funder, D. C. (1991). Global traits: A neo-Allportian approach to personality. *Psychological Science, 2,* 31-39.

Funder, D. C. (1995). On the accuracy of personality judgment: A realistic approach. *Psychological Review, 102,* 652-670.

Funder, D. C., & Sneed, C. D. (1993). Behavioral manifestations of personality: An ecological approach to judgmental accuracy. *Journal of Personality and Social Psychology, 64,* 479-490.

Gottfredson, G. D., Jones, E. M., & Holland, J. L. (1993). Personality and vocational interests: The relation of Holland's six interest dimensions to five robust dimensions of personality. *Journal of Counseling Psychology, 40,* 518-524.

Gough, H. G. (1987). *California Psychological Inventory administrator's guide*. Palo Alto, CA: Consulting Psychologists Press.

Graesser, A. C., Lang, K., & Horgan, D. (1988). A taxonomy for question generation. *Question Exchange, 2,* 3-15.

Graves, L. M., & Karren, R. J. (1992). Interviewer decision processes and effectiveness: An experimental policy-capturing investigation. *Personnel Psychology, 45,* 313-340.

Gustafson, S. B., & Ritzer, D. R. (1995). The dark side of normal: A psychopathy-linked pattern called aberrant self-promotion. *European Journal of Personality, 9,* 147-183.

Hogan, J., & Arneson, S. (1987, April). *Using the "Big Five" personality dimensions in job analysis*. Paper presented at the annual meeting of the Society for Industrial and Organizational Psychology, Atlanta, GA.

Hogan, R. (1991). Personality and personality measurement. In M. D. Dunnette & L. M. Hough (Eds.), *Handbook of industrial and organizational psychology* (2nd ed., Vol. 2, pp. 873-919). Palo Alto, CA: Consulting Psychologists Press.

Hogan, R. (1994). Trouble at the top: Causes and consequences of managerial incompetence. *Consulting Psychology Journal, 46,* 9-15.

Hogan, R. (1995). *Hogan Development Survey*. Tulsa, OK: Hogan Assessment Systems.

Hogan, R., & Blake, R. J. (1996). Vocational interests: Matching self-concept with the work environment. In K. R. Murphy (Ed.), *Individual differences and behavior in organizations*. San Francisco: Jossey-Bass.

Hogan, R., Curphy, G. J., & Hogan, J. (1994). What we know about leadership: Effectiveness and personality. *American Psychologist, 49,* 493-504.

Hogan, R., & Hogan, J. (1995). *Hogan Personality Inventory manual* (2nd ed.). Tulsa, OK: Hogan Assessment Systems.

Hogan, R., Hogan, J., & Roberts, B. W. (1996). Personality measurement and employment decisions: Questions and answers. *American Psychologist, 51,* 469-477.

Hogan, R., Raskin, R., & Fazzini, D. (1990). The dark side of charisma. In K. E. Clark & M. B. Clark (Eds.), *Measures of leadership*. West Orange, NJ: Leadership Library of America.

Horowitz, L. M., Rosenberg, S. E., Baer, B. A., Ureno, G., & Villasenor, V. S. (1988). Inventory of Interpersonal Problems: Psychometric properties and clinical applications. *Journal of Consulting and Clinical Psychology, 56*, 885-892.

Hough, L. M., & Schneider, R. J. (1996). Personality traits, taxonomies, and applications in organizations. In K. R. Murphy (Ed.), *Individual differences and behavior in organizations*. San Francisco: Jossey-Bass.

Huffcutt, A. I., & Arthur, W., Jr. (1994). Hunter and Hunter (1984) revisited: Interviewer validity for entry-level jobs. *Journal of Applied Psychology, 79*, 184-190.

Huffcutt, A. I., Roth, P. L., & McDaniel, M. A. (1996). A meta-analytic investigation of cognitive ability in employment interview evaluations: Moderating characteristics and implications for incremental validity. *Journal of Applied Psychology, 81*, 459-473.

Jackson, D. N., Peacock, A. C., & Smith, J. P. (1980). Impressions of personality in the employment interview. *Journal of Personality and Social Psychology, 39*, 294-307.

James, S. P., Campbell, I. M., & Lovegrove, S. A. (1984). Personality differentiation in a police-selection interview. *Journal of Applied Psychology, 69*, 129-134.

Kagan, D. (1990, May 21). Unmasking incompetent managers. *Insight*, pp. 42-44.

Krull, D. S., & Erickson, D. J. (1995). Inferential hopscotch: How people draw social inferences from behavior. *Current Directions in Psychological Science, 4*, 35-38.

Lanyon, R. I., & Goodstein, L. D. (1997). *Personality assessment* (3rd ed.). New York: John Wiley.

Lopez, F. M., Kesselman, G. A., & Lopez, F. E. (1981). An empirical test of a trait-oriented job analysis technique. *Personnel Psychology, 34*, 479-502.

Lowman, R. L. (1991). *The clinical practice of career assessment: Interests, abilities, and personality*. Washington, DC: American Psychological Association.

Lowman, R. L. (1996). Work dysfunctions and mental disorders. In K. R. Murphy (Ed.), *Individual differences and behavior in organizations*. San Francisco: Jossey-Bass.

Macan, T. H., & Dipboye, R. L. (1988). The effects of interviewers' initial impression on information gathering. *Organizational Behavior and Human Decision Processes, 42*, 364-387.

Mischel, W., & Shoda, Y. (1995). A cognitive-affective system theory of personality: Reconceptualizing situations, dispositions, dynamics, and invariance in personality structure. *Psychological Review, 102*, 246-268.

Mount, M. K., & Barrick, M. R. (1995). The Big Five personality dimensions: Implications for research and practice in human resource management. In G. R. Ferris (Ed.), *Research in personnel and human resources management* (Vol. 13, pp. 153-200). Greenwich, CT: JAI.

Mount, M. K., Barrick, M. R., & Strauss, J. P. (1994). Validity of observer ratings of the Big Five personality factors. *Journal of Applied Psychology, 79*, 272-280.

Ozer, D. J., & Reise, S. P. (1994). Personality assessment. *Annual Review of Psychology, 45*, 357-388.

Paulhus, D. L., & Martin, C. L. (1987). The structure of personality capabilities. *Journal of Personality and Social Psychology, 52*, 354-365.

Paulhus, D. L., & Martin, C. L. (1988). Functional flexibility: A new conception of interpersonal flexibility. *Journal of Personality and Social Psychology, 55*, 88-101.

Paunonen, S. V., & Jackson, D. N. (1987). Accuracy of interviewers and students in identifying the personality characteristics of personnel managers and computer programmers. *Journal of Vocational Behavior, 31,* 26-36.

Paunonen, S. V., Jackson, D. N., & Oberman, S. M. (1987). Personnel selection decisions: Effects of applicant personality and the letter of reference. *Organizational Behavior and Human Decision Processes, 40,* 96-114.

Raskin, R., & Hall, C. S. (1981). The Narcissistic Personality Inventory: Alternative form reliability and further evidence of construct validity. *Journal of Personality Assessment, 53,* 66-80.

Raymark, P. H., Schmit, M. J., & Guion, R. M. (1997). Identifying potentially useful personality constructs for employee selection. *Personnel Psychology, 50,* 723-736.

Riggio, R. E. (1986). Assessment of basic social skills. *Journal of Personality and Social Psychology, 51,* 649-660.

Russell, C. J. (1990). Selecting top corporate leaders: An example of biographical information. *Journal of Management, 16,* 73-86.

Sackett, P. R., & Wanek, J. E. (1996). New developments in the use of honesty, integrity, conscientiousness, dependability, trustworthiness, and reliability for personnel selection. *Personnel Psychology, 49,* 787-830.

Schneider, B. (1987). The people make the place. *Personnel Psychology, 40,* 437-453.

Schneider, B. (1996). When individual differences aren't. In K. R. Murphy (Ed.), *Individual differences and behavior in organizations.* San Francisco: Jossey-Bass.

Weitzul, J. B. (1992). *Evaluating interpersonal skills in the job interview: A guide for human resource professionals.* New York: Quorum.

Widiger, T. A., Mangine, S., Corbitt, E. M., Ellis, C. G., & Thomas, G. V. (1995). *Personality Disorder Interview IV.* Odessa, FL: Psychological Assessment Resources.

Wiggins, J. S. (1973). *Personality and prediction: Principles of personality assessment.* Menlo Park, CA: Addison-Wesley.

Wiggins, J. S., & Pincus, A. L. (1992). Personality: Structure and assessment. *Annual Review of Psychology, 43,* 473-504.

7

Establishing Person-Organization Fit

Charles K. Parsons
Daniel M. Cable
Robert C. Liden

Individuals and organizations appear to be most effective when their respective values, goals, and interests are aligned (Govindarajan, 1989; O'Reilly, Chatman, & Caldwell, 1991; Sheridan, 1992). Presumably, similar attributes between individuals and groups lead to improved communication and liking, which in turn affect job attitudes and organizational outcomes (Cable & Judge, 1996). Furthermore, theory suggests that firms can sustain a competitive advantage by creating better "match quality" between employees and organizations, because person-organization (P-O) fit appears to be a unique, valuable resource that is difficult to imitate (Barney, 1991). In light of these positive outcomes, researchers have suggested that organizations proactively hire employees based on their fit with the characteristics of the organization rather than just the requirements of a particular job (Bowen, Ledford, & Nathan, 1991).

The employment interview may play a critical role in establishing P-O fit in organizations (Cable & Judge, 1997; Judge & Ferris, 1992; Rynes & Gerhart, 1990). As one of the few interpersonal methods of employee selection, the interview enables organizational representatives and job seekers to interact, offering the opportunity for both parties to determine their level of fit with the other. As discussed later in this chapter, the interpersonal nature of the interview also may allow interviewers to socialize applicants, or to change their P-O fit.

Although some past research has suggested that P-O fit may be established during interviews, little research has considered the underlying processes that enable the interview to inculcate fit. For example, little research has examined interviewers' abilities to assess applicants' P-O fit. Furthermore, no research to date has examined the role of the employment interview as a socialization mechanism that may help establish P-O fit. Consistent with the work of Jablin (1987) and Chatman (1991), job seekers' initial interactions with organizational representatives represent one form of "anticipatory socialization." Because interviewers often are job seekers' first direct exposure to an organization, and because subsequent interviews often involve job seekers' future supervisors and peers, the employment interview may represent an initial and important socialization mechanism.

Figure 7.1 depicts the processes through which the employment interview may facilitate the development of P-O fit, and therefore guides the discussion in this chapter. The upper part of the framework emphasizes interviewers' perceptions and judgments (e.g., selection), and the lower part of the framework emphasizes the effect of the interview on applicant values (e.g., socialization). Following the layout of this framework, we first examine P-O fit from the organizational perspective, focusing on the hypothesis that the interview is a selection device that allows organizations to evaluate applicants based on P-O fit. We delineate the assumptions inherent in this approach, review relevant past research, and present possible research directions on this topic.

Consistent with the lower part of the figure, we next examine the interview as an anticipatory socialization device that shapes applicant and supervisor perceptions and expectations, thus helping establish P-O fit early in the organizational entry process. Accordingly, we address P-O fit and the interview from the *applicant* perspective. Specifically, we review relevant research on socialization and leader-member exchange, highlighting the processes through which the employment interview may function as a socialization mechanism. Importantly, this section suggests a number of new directions for interview research by highlighting the importance of postcampus, or "site visit," interviews on subsequent P-O fit.

What Is P-O Fit?

Past P-O fit research has examined congruence among a diverse collection of attributes. Job seekers' goals, values, needs, interests, and personalities

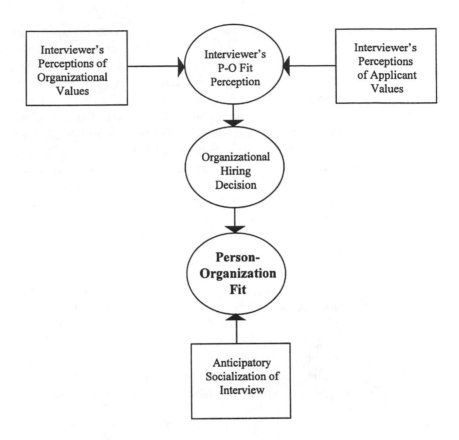

Figure 7.1 The Role of the Employment Interview in Establishing P-O Fit

have been compared with organizations' cultures, pay systems, size, structure, and values (Judge & Cable, 1997; Kristof, 1996). However, two recent advances in the P-O fit research literature have been a focus on the definition of person-organization fit on similarity in terms of *values* (Chatman, 1989, 1991; Dawis, 1990) and the development of value typologies that are *commensurate* to both individuals and organizations (Chatman, 1989; Dawis, 1990; Meglino, Ravlin, & Adkins, 1989; O'Reilly et al., 1991). Values are enduring beliefs that a specific mode of conduct or end state is preferable to its opposite, therefore guiding individuals' attitudes, judgments, and behaviors (Chatman, 1989, 1991; Rokeach, 1973). Accordingly, while recognizing the multitude of applicant and organizational characteristics that might be compared, we define P-O fit as the congruence between applicants' and organizations' values. For example, P-O fit might take the form of similarity between an organization that values individualism, aggressiveness, and results orientation and the degree to which a job seeker values these same attributes.

There are three primary methods of calculating and assessing P-O fit. Much past research has relied on "profile comparisons," in which an array of organizational characteristics is compared with an array of person characteristics, resulting in difference scores or correlation coefficients. Although profile comparisons are consistent with theoretical conceptualizations of P-O fit, and therefore have been recommended and used by P-O fit researchers (Chatman, 1989, 1991; Rynes & Gerhart, 1990), they also have been criticized (Edwards, 1993). Accordingly, other researchers have suggested a polynomial regression approach to assessing P-O fit, which requires nomothetic (instead of ipsative, or forced ranking) measurement and large sample sizes to accommodate multiple interaction variables and higher-order terms. Finally, researchers also have begun to measure P-O fit *perceptions* by assessing people's "subjective" interpretations of P-O fit (Kristof, 1996). Clearly, this "direct assessment" approach represents a departure from the statistical approaches discussed above, and may be more susceptible to common method bias. On the other hand, individuals generally respond to people and situations based on their perceptions rather than some objective standard (Cable & Judge, 1997), indicating that examining subjective impressions of P-O fit may be a meaningful approach. Because there are benefits and drawbacks to all measurement approaches, P-O fit researchers must balance their research needs against the trade-offs inherent in either approach to P-O fit measurement.

Interviewers' P-O Fit Perceptions

P-O fit is a separate construct from "general employability" (Adkins, Russell, & Werbel, 1994; Rynes & Gerhart, 1990), and interviewers' P-O fit judgments appear to influence hiring decisions and actual job offers (Cable & Judge, 1997). These cumulative results suggest that the employment interview can initiate P-O fit during selection, at least to the extent that interviewers' P-O fit judgments are accurate. Accurate P-O fit judgments are reliant on interviewers' recognition of similarity between their organizational values and applicants' values. Thus, as suggested by Figure 7.1, interviewer accuracy requires P-O fit perceptions based on accurate beliefs about the organizational culture and applicants' values. These assumptions are examined in turn below.

Interviewers' Perceptions of Their Organizational Values

If applicants are offered and denied jobs based, in part, on the similarity between their personal values and an organization's culture, the values congruence of the organization's workforce will increase over time

(Schneider, 1987). Thus, an interviewer can help establish P-O fit by evaluating applicants based on the organization's culture. However, interviewers may base their P-O fit evaluations on three sources of comparison that do not accurately represent their organizations' values.

First, interviewers may compare job applicants' values to some generalized notion of an "ideal applicant." Thus, an interviewer may compare job applicants' attributes with a generic ideal that would be valuable in any organization (e.g., motivated, trustworthy) rather than with the organization's idiosyncratic set of values (Adkins et al., 1994; Rynes & Gerhart, 1990). To the extent that interviewers' P-O fit judgments are based on global positive attributes, the interview does not establish P-O fit so much as it promotes the "general employability" of new hires. Although valuable, this process does not necessarily culminate in organizational values congruence.

Second, interviewers may base their P-O fit judgments on their own personal values rather than on those of their organizational cultures. As Gilmore and Ferris (1989) note, managers may prefer to hire individuals who are similar to themselves, because this allows them to build political coalitions and contributes to their personal power base. Furthermore, most interviewers probably consider themselves to be successful organizational members, and therefore may assume that their personal attributes provide an exemplary template for evaluating job applicants (Ferris & Judge, 1991). Although some degree of similarity may exist between an interviewer's values and those of his or her organization, there is less likelihood that P-O fit will be established during interviews when fit evaluations are based on personal, rather than organizational, values (Ferris & Judge, 1991).

Finally, interviewers simply may compare applicants' values to an incorrect image of the organization. Past research has suggested that interviewers from the same organization vary widely in their interpretations of specific information and the goals of the interview (Rynes & Gerhart, 1990; Valenzi & Andrews, 1973), and organizational culture is a relatively subjective criterion. Furthermore, research suggests that most interviewers receive little to no training (Rynes & Boudreau, 1986), suggesting that each interviewer derives his or her perceptions of organizational values from personal inferences about idiosyncratic organizational experiences. Thus, interviewers may compare applicants' attributes to their perceptions of their organization, but the resulting P-O fit evaluations may be misguided if their inferences about the organization are incorrect. Furthermore, because reliability sets the upper bound for validity, unreliable culture perceptions across multiple interviewers constrain the cumulative validity of their P-O fit perceptions and the success of promoting P-O fit.

Despite these sources of potential error in interviewers' perceptions of their organizations, some evidence exists that interviewers base their P-O fit judgments on their organizations' specific sets of values. Rynes and Gerhart (1990) found that when multiple interviewers from the same firm evaluated applicants' P-O fit, interrater reliability was greater (.49) than for interviewers from different organizations (.20). These researchers also reviewed similar findings reported by Bass (1951) indicating that consistency across evaluations of job seekers was highest when raters were from the same organization. As Rynes and Gerhart note, these results indicate some (albeit low) level of consistency in interviewers' beliefs about their organizations' values and suggest that there is some degree of organizational specificity to interviewers' P-O fit judgments.

Unfortunately, no research to date has examined the *validity* of interviewers' perceptions of their organizations' values systems. Although it is appropriate to examine interviewers' subjective perceptions of their organizational values when the outcome variable is interviewers' personal evaluations and decisions, the *accuracy* of interviewers' organizational perceptions becomes critical when one is examining whether the employment interview represents a valid method for organizations to use in establishing P-O fit. Accordingly, future research should determine the degree to which interviewers' organizational perceptions are accurate by comparing the agreement between interviewers and multiple organizational members.

Future research also should examine the degree to which interviewer training can improve the accuracy of interviewers' organizational perceptions. It may be advantageous for organizations to conduct "image analyses" with knowledgeable employees in order to codify and formalize their organizational culture (e.g., Chatman, 1989; Garbett, 1988). Results from image analyses could be used to train interviewers using "cognitive script methods," which help organizational representatives develop sophisticated knowledge structures and help them remember and apply organizational information (Leigh & McGraw, 1989). This combination of image analysis and interviewer training should help align multiple recruiters' perceptual maps of their organizational images and standardize the process of comparing organizational images to job seekers' attributes. The results of this process should be more reliable and accurate interviewer judgments of applicants' P-O fit and improved interviewer abilities to establish P-O fit in organizations.

Having discussed interviewers' perceptions of their organizational cultures and the need for accurate organizational perceptions on the part of interviewers making P-O fit judgments, we turn now to the subject of interviewers' perceptions of applicants and the processes through which interviewers may make accurate evaluations of applicants' values and P-O fit.

Interviewers' Perceptions of Applicant Values

One assumption underlying the P-O fit literature is that job seekers have relatively stable values that determine their fit with particular organizations. Ostensibly, interviewers make inferences about applicants' values that influence their evaluations of applicants' fit and subsequent hiring decisions (Cable & Judge, 1997). Thus, as suggested above, interviewers will make more accurate P-O fit assessments to the extent that their inferences about applicants' values are accurate.

To date, surprisingly little interview research has examined the accuracy of interviewers' assessments of applicants' values. Fortunately, it is possible to draw on the substantial psychological research literature on person perception, which has examined observers' perceptual accuracy. Although this literature has focused primarily on personality traits (not values), results generally have indicated that observers' ratings and self-ratings of personality traits converge significantly (e.g., Bernieri, Zuckerman, Koestner, & Rosenthal, 1994). In fact, even when only minimal information regarding a target person is exchanged, there is agreement between observers regarding the target, as well as agreement between the observers with the target, on personality traits and intelligence (Borkenau & Liebler, 1993; Kenny, Horner, Kashy, & Chu, 1992; Watson, 1989). The term "consensus at zero acquaintance" was coined by Albright, Kenny, and Malloy (1988) to describe this phenomenon of interpersonal assessment accuracy, which may arise from the target person's dress, appearance, and nonverbal behaviors. Levesque and Kenny (1993) confirmed these results with behavioral ratings of target personality traits, and Ambady and Rosenthal (1993) found that inferences based on 10-, 5-, and even 2-second video clips of teacher on-the-job behavior were significantly correlated with student ratings and supervisor ratings of teacher effectiveness.

Because the consensus at zero acquaintance and person perception research has focused on the Big Five framework of personality traits, extending these findings to work values requires further research. Specifically, what is the degree to which interviewers and applicants agree on the applicant's work values following an interview? Cable and Judge (1997) suggest that a significant, though small, relationship exists between interviewers' and applicants' assessments of applicant values. Although this is encouraging, it would be helpful for additional research to confirm and extend these findings. For example, future research could examine inter-rater agreement in controlled laboratory studies in which raters view a standardized videotape of an interview and rate the applicant on several work value measures. Also, future field research could examine agreement among multiple interviewers regarding an applicant's work values; this would appear to be particularly relevant to on-site interviews in which applicants meet with multiple organizational representatives (Taylor & Bergmann, 1987).

Of even greater importance than agreement levels between applicants and interviewers is understanding *how* interviewers try to assess applicant work values. Anecdotal evidence suggests that some interviewers intentionally focus on work values by asking applicants about their innovativeness, interest in teamwork, and so on. Interviewers may also develop these questions by asking applicants for specific examples from their work histories that demonstrate these values or characteristics. This direct approach to assessing work values can be contrasted to a more passive approach whereby interviewers simply make inferences about applicant values based on appearance and nonverbal communication.

It appears likely that significant advances could be made in this research domain through the adaptation of methods from traditional interviewing research. For example, patterned description interviews and situational interviews both have been shown to improve predictive validity for job performance (Campion, Pursell, & Brown, 1988; McDaniel, Whetzel, Schmidt, & Maurer, 1994). Extending this research to P-O fit may suggest methods for structuring the interview to better assess applicant work values (Cable & Judge, 1997). One fruitful approach might be to utilize a critical incidents methodology that focuses on the fit of employees in the organization's culture. Thus, employees who are familiar with their organization's culture could be asked to describe specific situations in which it was apparent that a new employee did not fit in with the company culture. Multiple critical incidents from multiple employees could be sorted into work value categories, transformed into hypothetical situations, and used in the interview to assess applicant values and P-O fit. It may even be possible to code applicants' responses according to the extent to which they exemplify work values that are relevant to an organization's culture.

In addition to developing the assessment of work values by extending the psychometrics of interview methods, future research also should consider how interviewers' motivations influence their assessments of applicants' work values. For example, Parsons, Cable, and Wilkerson (in press) demonstrated that interviewers' perceptual accuracy was higher under conditions of explicit instructions to focus on work values than when there were no explicit instructions regarding values. Thus, it may be possible to "train" interviewers to assess applicant values and P-O fit with greater accuracy. Parsons et al. also found that perceptual accuracy was greater when the work values were relevant to the recruiter's organizational culture, indicating that "functional relevance" may operate in the assessment of applicant values and P-O fit (Gangestad, Simpson, Digeronimo, & Biek, 1992).

Other Factors Related to the Assessment of Applicant Work Values

The traditional employment interviewing literature provides other interesting research directions in the context of P-O fit. Due to space constraints, we briefly examine only two here. First, there has been extensive research regarding interviewers' *first impressions* and their effects on interviewer behavior and judgments about applicant behavior (e.g., Dougherty, Turban, & Callender, 1994). Because work values are hypothetical constructs with uncertain behavioral cues, interviewers' implicit theories of applicant work values may explain a large percentage of their subsequent judgments of applicants' work values. For example, an applicant's arriving early for the interview may influence the interviewer's judgment about the applicant's values. Future research is needed to help us understand the degree to which first impressions affect interviewers' final assessments of applicant work values and P-O fit.

Decision-making process research, which has examined how interviewers or raters "weight" various informational cues about applicants, also has implications for P-O fit in the interview context. For example, Dunn, Mount, Barrick, and Ones (1995) found that general mental ability and conscientiousness influenced judgments about job suitability for a wide variety of jobs, whereas other Big Five personality traits were influential in limited job categories. Kinicki, Lockwood, Hom, and Griffeth (1990) found that interviewer inferences of applicant "attitude," "job interest," and "appearance" had the largest effects on hiring decisions and also were predictive of future job satisfaction and organizational commitment. This line of interview research suggests that interviewers' judgments about applicant work values may be studied as a function of multiple applicant cues, including appearance, verbal and nonverbal responses during the interview, and other applicant attributes (e.g., demographics, test scores, grades).

In summary, much research is needed if we are to understand how interviewers make judgments about applicant work values and P-O fit, and how these judgments may be improved. Recent person perception research on self-observer agreement suggests that there is potential for the assessment of work values during an employment interview. It also appears that much of the contemporary research on traditional job interviewing can be adapted to improve the assessment of work values. In the next section, we turn our attention to how employment interviews may affect P-O fit through their impact on applicants' work values and choices.

The Interview as an Anticipatory Socialization Device

Thus far we have examined how interviewers perceive their organizations and applicants for the purpose of selecting those applicants with better P-O fit. In this section we take a different perspective, examining how employment interviews might change the employment relationship and P-O fit by altering employees' expectations, especially in the context of supervisory relationships. We also extend traditional interview research in this section by focusing not on campus interviews, but on second interviews, or site visits. This focus appears appropriate given that site visits typically involve multiple interviews and are more intensive than campus interviews (Taylor & Bergmann, 1987), thus offering greater opportunities for anticipatory socialization.

Anticipatory socialization involves the process in which the applicant learns about the organization and job prior to entering the organization (Feldman, 1981). It is during the anticipatory stage that newcomers form expectations about the organization and other employees. The more accurate the information that newcomers receive prior to joining an organization, the more likely it is that their expectations will be met (Wanous, 1977) and that they will encounter fewer surprises upon entry into the organization (Louis, 1980).

One critical source of information during the anticipatory socialization period is the employment interview. However, most interview research has focused on campus recruitment interviews; second or site-visit interviews—which provide much richer information about the organization—have been ignored (Jablin, 1987). For example, it is during site-visit interviews that potential newcomers are likely to be interviewed by their potential supervisors. Given that the immediate supervisor has been shown to play a significant role in the socialization of a newcomer after entry (Green, 1991; Major, Kozlowski, Chao, & Gardner, 1995), it is probable that the supervisor also may be influential during the anticipatory socialization period. In fact, site-visit interviews may provide the initial interaction during which supervisors and newcomers develop expectations about one another. These expectations, in turn, help determine the relationship that forms upon the organizational entry of the newcomer (Liden, Wayne, & Stilwell, 1993), as well as subsequent outcomes, such as values congruence, commitment, turnover intentions, and satisfaction (Major et al., 1995).

Perceptions Formed During the Interview

Research on leader-member exchange has shown that the nature of the relationship between supervisor and subordinate is established very quickly, typically within the first 2 weeks after the two begin working together (Bauer & Green, 1996; Liden et al., 1993). Furthermore, supervisor and subordinate expectations of one another measured during the first 5 days on the job have been shown to be positively related to the nature of the relationship 6 months later (Liden et al., 1993). These results suggest that leader-member exchange development may actually begin prior to the time when the two begin to work together.

During the series of site-visit interviews, supervisors and prospective subordinates form expectations concerning the relationship that will develop between them. Expectations may be influenced by interpersonal attraction and liking of, or perceived similarity with, the other person (Graves & Powell, 1995; Stilwell, 1992). Adding complexity to this initial encounter, both supervisor and subordinate may engage in impression management behaviors in an attempt to influence the other's perceptions and resulting expectations (Baron, 1989; Gilmore & Ferris, 1989; Stevens & Kristof, 1995; Wayne, Liden, & Sparrowe, 1994). In essence, before newcomers begin their first day on a job, their expectations concerning their relationships with supervisors may already have been formed, or at least are in the process of being developed.

Also, the realistic job preview literature demonstrates that when accurate information about both negative and positive aspects of the job is provided to applicants or newcomers prior to their starting work in an organization, their expectations are more likely to be met and satisfaction and job performance are often higher and turnover lower than when such information is not provided (Premack & Wanous, 1985; Wanous & Colella, 1989). We anticipate that a similar process operates at the level of the organization. Realistic expectations of organizational culture, structure, and policies may also lead to greater P-O fit due to applicant self-selection (Rynes, Bretz, & Gerhart, 1991; Schneider, 1987), resulting in higher values congruence and organizational commitment as well as lower turnover.

Furthermore, it is likely that applicants do more than passively absorb information provided in site-visit interviews. Rather, applicants may be proactive in seeking information. Recent research has demonstrated that upon organizational entry, newcomers, as a way of promoting their own socialization process, may be very active in seeking information that will enhance their assimilation into the organization (Ashford & Black, 1996; Bauer & Green, 1994; Miller & Jablin, 1991; Morrison, 1993). Interestingly, applicants' proactive information seeking has not been explored during the anticipatory socialization phase that occurs prior to organizational entry. For example, applicants may actively seek information that will assist them in making a job offer acceptance decision as well as in preparing for the new job. Research has shown proactive information seeking during the organizational entry phase of socialization to enhance acculturation, social integration, commitment, performance, and satisfaction (Ashford & Black, 1996; Bauer & Green, 1994; Morrison, 1993). We contend that information seeking during the anticipatory socialization phase provides benefits to newcomers. In particular, information seeking prior to organizational entry, such as in site-visit interviews, may be positively related to ease of entry into the organization.

A final possibility that has received no research attention is that applicants' values and aspirations are actually *altered* or socialized through the course of the interviewing process. Specifically, by exposing applicants to an organization's culture and goals, organizational representatives (and potential supervisors) may influence applicants' beliefs about the ideal organizational culture or lifestyle. It also is possible that an intensive series of site-visit interviews may expose applicants to new and attractive opportunities that they previously had not considered. For example, a job applicant with no previous aspirations for a foreign assignment may be convinced during a site interview with a potential supervisor of the value and excitement of taking an overseas position. Thus, the organization may, in effect, change or reveal applicants' beliefs about lifestyles, goals, and ideal organizational culture. This intriguing possibility appears particularly relevant in the case of college graduates who have had little previous exposure to the real opportunities and experiences available in different organizations. This sample of applicants also appears particularly important to hiring organizations, because college graduates now constitute a substantial percentage of new job entrants (Bishop & Carter, 1991).

In summary, we propose integrating the employment interview and socialization research literatures. Of particular importance is the link between site-visit interviews and the anticipatory socialization period. We contend that relationships between supervisors and subordinates may begin their development during this period, and that applicants may be proactive in seeking information about organizational culture.

The integration of the employment interview and socialization literatures suggests several areas that are ripe for empirical research. First, the development of leader-member exchange probably commences during the anticipatory socialization period, prior to the beginning of a relationship between a supervisor and a future subordinate. An interesting research approach would be to utilize a longitudinal design and undertake data collection prior to and immediately after the first interview. At these times, preinterview impressions of both the supervisor and subordinate could be assessed as well as impressions and expectations formed as a result of the interview. The second data collection would occur subsequent to site-visit interviews, and the data could be used to assess the impact on the applicant of this more extensive and visible contact with the organization and the possible interaction between the supervisor and subordinate. A third data collection would be appropriate immediately after the subordinate enters the organization, and the final data collection might take place 6 months following entry. Such a design would enable researchers to test hypotheses concerning the effects of impressions generated during the preinterview and initial screening interview on the supervisor-subordinate relationship at subsequent time periods. Similarly, the interaction between supervisor and potential subordinate during site-visit interviews could be examined for its influence on expectations and the quality of the relationship that exists at subsequent time periods. Such research may indicate, for example, that in many cases leader-member exchanges may be partially formed before a true "working relationship" develops.

Second, research is needed to elucidate applicants' proactive information-seeking behaviors during employment interviews, especially during site-visit interviews. Much research has been conducted on formal organizational programs, such as realistic job previews, designed to provide applicants with information about the job. However, research is needed on the extent to which individuals seek organization-level information and the effects of such proactive behaviors on P-O fit, ease of assimilation upon entry, and traditional outcome variables such as organizational commitment, turnover, and performance.

Applications

Based on the literature reviewed above, we have hypothesized that the conduct of employment interviews affects P-O fit through the decision processes of the interviewer and the mutual adjustment of expectations between interviewers and applicants. Should these hypothesized relationships be substantiated empirically, clear implications exist for practice.

First, the veridicality of interviewer P-O fit judgments is increased when interviewers have accurate perceptions of their organization, which may be enhanced through training. Likewise, organizations can influence the P-O fit judgment process by ensuring that interviewers focus on the appropriate applicant values. Facilitating P-O fit through anticipatory socialization requires presenting more accurate and meaningful information about the organization's culture to job applicants. Accordingly, extending the logic of the realistic job preview to the realistic organization preview is intuitively appealing. Finally, it is possible that the goals of selecting for P-O fit may be at odds with the anticipatory socialization function. Interviews that focus on applicant assessment would tend to be oriented toward having applicants disclose information about themselves. Anticipatory socialization, on the other hand, requires the interviewer to disclose information about the organization and him- or herself (if the interviewer is likely to be the applicant's supervisor). The trade-offs between these two goals merit further investigation.

One caveat in closing: Although one of our underlying goals for this chapter is the development of research and theory on how organizations can establish better P-O fit, we should note that negative outcomes may result from "interviewing for fit." First, to the extent that values are related to demographics, *P-O fit* may be a euphemism for *discrimination*. However, research indicates that values congruence need not constrain demographic diversity, because there appears to be little relationship between demographics and work values within specific target markets of job seekers (Byrne, 1969; Chatman, 1991; O'Reilly et al., 1991). Other researchers have proposed negative effects of fit for organizational effectiveness. For example, Argyris (1976) and Schneider (1987) assert that as organizations become full of similar employees, they have increasing difficulty in adapting to environmental changes. Perhaps due to the difficulty in studying such a proposition empirically, research has not documented the negative effects of P-O fit on organizational effectiveness or survival. However, the possibility of "too much fit" appears unlikely, given organizations' tendencies to become differentiated by function as well as the different types of training and experience required for different jobs. Finally, to the extent that an organization's values are undergoing change, hiring for fit becomes particularly difficult. Should interviewers attempt to match the "old" culture or the "new" culture, and what are the short- and long-term consequences of each approach? Clearly, further research is needed to establish the optimal level of P-O fit in organizations.

References

Adkins, C. L., Russell, C. J., & Werbel, J. D. (1994). Judgments of fit in the selection process: The role of work value congruence. *Personnel Psychology, 47,* 605-623.

Albright, L., Kenny, D. A., & Malloy, T. E. (1988). Consensus in personality judgments at zero acquaintance. *Journal of Personality and Social Psychology, 55,* 387-395.

Ambady, N., & Rosenthal, R., (1993). Half a minute: Predicting teacher evaluations from thin slices of nonverbal behavior and physical attractiveness. *Journal of Personality and Social Psychology, 64,* 431-441.

Argyris, C. (1976). Problems and new directions for industrial psychology. In M. D. Dunnette (Ed.), *Handbook of industrial and organizational psychology.* Chicago: Rand McNally.

Ashford, S. J., & Black, J. S. (1996). Proactivity during organizational entry: The role of desire for control. *Journal of Applied Psychology, 81,* 199-214.

Barney, J. (1991). Firm resources and sustained competitive advantage. *Journal of Management, 17,* 99-120.

Baron, R. A. (1989). Impression management by applicants during employment interviews: The "too much of a good thing" effect. In R. W. Eder & G. R. Ferris (Eds.), *The employment interview: Theory, research, and practice* (pp. 204-215). Newbury Park, CA: Sage.

Bass, B. M. (1951). Situational tests: Individual interviews compared with leaderless group discussions. *Educational and Psychological Measurement, 11,* 67-75.

Bauer, T. N., & Green, S. G. (1994). Effect of newcomer involvement in work-related activities: A longitudinal study of socialization. *Journal of Applied Psychology, 79,* 211-223.

Bauer, T. N., & Green, S. G. (1996). The development of leader-member exchange: A longitudinal test. *Academy of Management Journal, 39,* 1538-1567.

Bernieri, F. J., Zuckerman, M., Koestner, R., & Rosenthal, R. (1994). Measuring person perception accuracy: Another look at self-other agreement. *Personality and Social Psychology Bulletin, 20,* 367-378.

Borkenau, P., & Liebler, A. (1993). Convergence of stranger ratings of personality and intelligence with self-ratings, partner ratings, and measured intelligence. *Journal of Personality and Social Psychology, 65,* 546-553.

Bowen, D. E., Ledford, G. E., & Nathan, B. R. (1991). Hiring for the organization, not the job. *Academy of Management Executive, 5,* 35-51.

Bishop, J. H., & Carter, S. (1991). The worsening shortage of college-graduate workers. *Educational Evaluation and Policy Analysis, 13,* 221-246.

Byrne, D. (1969). Attitudes and attraction. In L. Berkowitz (Ed.), *Advances in experimental social psychology* (Vol. 4, pp. 35-89). New York: Academic Press.

Cable, D. M., & Judge, T. A. (1996). Person-organization fit, job choice decisions, and organizational entry. *Organizational Behavior and Human Decision Processes, 67,* 294-311.

Cable, D. M., & Judge, T. A. (1997). Interviewers' perceptions of person-organization fit and organizational selection decisions. *Journal of Applied Psychology, 82,* 546-561.

Campion, M. A., Pursell, E. D., & Brown, B. K. (1988). Structured interviewing: Raising the psychometric properties of the employment interview. *Personnel Psychology, 41,* 25-42.

Chatman, J. (1989). Improving interactional organizational research: A model of person-organization fit. *Academy of Management Review, 14,* 333-349.

Chatman, J. (1991). Matching people and organizations: Selection and socialization in public accounting firms. *Administrative Science Quarterly, 36,* 459-484.

Dawis, R. V. (1990). Vocational interests, values, and preferences. In M. D. Dunnette & L. M. Hough (Eds.), *Handbook of industrial and organizational psychology* (2nd ed., Vol. 1, pp. 833-871). Palo Alto, CA: Consulting Psychologists Press.

Dougherty, T. W., Turban, D. B., & Callender, J. C. (1994). Confirming first impressions in the employment interview: A field study of interviewer behavior. *Journal of Applied Psychology, 79,* 659-665.

Dunn, W. S., Mount, M. K., Barrick, M. R., & Ones, D. S. (1995). Relative importance of personality and general mental ability in managers' judgments of applicant qualifications. *Journal of Applied Psychology, 80,* 500-509.

Edwards, J. F. (1993). Problems with the use of profile similarity indices in the study of congruence in organizational research. *Personnel Psychology, 46,* 641-665.

Feldman, D. C. (1981). The multiple socialization of organizational members. *Academy of Management Review, 6,* 309-318.

Ferris, G. R., & Judge, T. A. (1991). Personnel/human resource management: A political influence perspective. *Journal of Management, 17,* 447-488.

Gangestad, S. W., Simpson, J. A., Digeronimo, K., & Biek, M. (1992). Differential accuracy in person perception across traits: Examination of a functional hypothesis. *Journal of Personality and Social Psychology, 62,* 688-698.

Garbett, T. (1988). *How to build a corporation's identity and project its image.* Lexington, MA: Lexington Books.

Gilmore, D. C., & Ferris, G. R. (1989). The effects of applicant impression management tactics on interviewer judgments. *Journal of Management, 15,* 557-564.

Govindarajan, V. (1989). Implementing competitive strategies at the business unit level: Implications of matching managers to strategies. *Strategic Management Journal, 27,* 25-41.

Graves, L. M., & Powell, G. N. (1995). The effect of sex similarity on recruiters' evaluations of actual applicants: A test of the similarity-attraction paradigm. *Personnel Psychology, 48,* 85-98.

Green, S. G. (1991). Professional entry and the adviser relationship: Socialization, commitment, and productivity. *Group & Organization Studies, 16,* 387-407.

Jablin, F. M. (1987). Organizational entry, assimilation, and exit. In F. M. Jablin, L. L. Putnam, K. H. Roberts, & L. W. Porter (Eds.), *Handbook of organizational communication* (pp. 679-740). Newbury Park, CA: Sage.

Judge, T. A., & Cable, D. M. (1997). Applicant personality, organizational culture, and job choice decisions. *Personnel Psychology, 50,* 359-394.

Judge, T. A., & Ferris, G. R. (1992). The elusive criterion of fit in human resource staffing decisions. *Human Resource Planning, 15,* 47-67.

Kenny, D. A., Horner, C., Kashy, D. A., & Chu, L. (1992). Consensus at zero acquaintance: Replication, behavioral cues, and stability. *Journal of Personality and Social Psychology, 62,* 88-97.

Kinicki, A. J., Lockwood, C. A., Hom, P. W., & Griffeth, R. W. (1990). Interviewer predictions of applicant qualifications and interviewer validity: Aggregate and individual analysis. *Journal of Applied Psychology, 75,* 477-486.

Kristof, A. L. (1996). Person-organization fit: An integrative review of its conceptualizations, measurement, and implications. *Personnel Psychology, 49,* 1-49.

Leigh, T. W., & McGraw, P. F. (1989). Mapping the procedural knowledge of industrial sales personnel: A script-theoretic investigation. *Journal of Marketing, 53,* 16-34.

Levesque, J. J., & Kenny, D. A. (1993). Accuracy of behavioral predictions at zero acquaintance: A social relations analysis. *Journal of Personality and Social Psychology, 65,* 1178-1187.

Liden, R. C., Wayne, S. J., & Stilwell, D. (1993). A longitudinal study on the early development of leader-member exchanges. *Journal of Applied Psychology, 78,* 662-674.

Louis, M. R. (1980). Surprise and sense making: What newcomers experience in entering unfamiliar organizational settings. *Administrative Science Quarterly, 25,* 226-251.

Major, D. A., Kozlowski, S. W., Chao, G. T., & Gardner, P. D. (1995). A longitudinal investigation of newcomer expectations, early socialization outcomes, and the moderating effects of role development factors. *Journal of Applied Psychology, 80,* 418-431.

McDaniel, M. A., Whetzel, D. L., Schmidt, F. L., & Maurer, S. D. (1994). The validity of employment interviews: A comprehensive review and meta analysis. *Journal of Applied Psychology, 79,* 599-616.

Meglino, B. M, Ravlin, E. C., & Adkins, C. L. (1989). A work values approach to corporate culture: A field test of the value congruence process and its relationship to individual outcomes. *Journal of Applied Psychology, 74,* 424-432.

Miller, V. D., & Jablin, F. M. (1991). Information seeking during organizational entry: Influences, tactics and a model of the process. *Academy of Management Review, 16,* 92-120.

Morrison, E. W. (1993). Longitudinal study of the effects of information seeking on newcomer socialization. *Journal of Applied Psychology, 78,* 173-183.

O'Reilly, C. A., Chatman, J., & Caldwell, D. F. (1991). People and organizational culture: A profile comparison approach to assessing person-organization fit. *Academy of Management Journal, 34,* 487-516.

Parsons, C. K., Cable, D., & Wilkerson, J. M. (in press). Assessment of applicant work values through interviews: The impact of focus and functional relevance. *Journal of Occupational and Organizational Psychology.*

Premack, S. L., & Wanous, J. P. (1985). A meta-analysis of realistic job preview experiments. *Journal of Applied Psychology, 70,* 706-719.

Rokeach, M. (1973). *The nature of human values.* New York: Free Press.

Rynes, S. L., & Boudreau, J. W. (1986). College recruiting in large organizations: Practice, evaluation, and research implications. *Personnel Psychology, 39,* 729-757.

Rynes, S. L., Bretz, R. D., & Gerhart, B. (1991). The importance of recruitment in job choice: A different way of looking. *Personnel Psychology, 44,* 487-521.

Rynes, S. L., & Gerhart, B. (1990). Interviewer assessments of applicant "fit": An exploratory investigation. *Personnel Psychology, 43,* 13-35.

Schneider, B. (1987). The people make the place. *Personnel Psychology, 40,* 437-453.

Sheridan, J. E. (1992). Organizational culture and employee retention. *Academy of Management Journal, 35,* 1036-1056.

Stevens, C. K., & Kristof, A. L. (1995). Making the right impression: A field study of applicant impression management during job interviews. *Journal of Applied Psychology, 80,* 587-606.

Stilwell, C. D. (1992). *Initial performance expectations, strength of those expectations, and social interaction behavior of subordinates: Their effect on the development process in leader-member exchange theory.* Unpublished doctoral dissertation, Georgia Institute of Technology.

Taylor, M. S., & Bergmann, T. J. (1987). Organizational recruitment activities and applicants' reactions at different stages of the recruitment process. *Personnel Psychology, 40,* 261-285.

Valenzi, E., & Andrews, I. R. (1973). Individual differences in the decision process of employment interviewers. *Journal of Applied Psychology, 58,* 49-63.

Wanous, J. P. (1977). Organizational entry: Newcomers moving from outside to inside. *Psychological Bulletin, 84,* 601-618.

Wanous, J. P., & Colella, A. (1989). Organizational entry research: Current status and future directions. *Research in Personnel and Human Resource Management, 7,* 59-120.

Watson, D. (1989). Strangers' ratings of the five robust personality factors: Evidence of a surprising convergence with self-report. *Journal of Personality and Social Psychology, 57,* 120-128.

Wayne, S. J., Liden, R. C., & Sparrowe, R. T. (1994). Developing leader-member exchanges: The influence of gender and ingratiation. *American Behavioral Scientist, 37,* 697-714.

8

What Is Being Measured?

Michael M. Harris

Now that it has been well established that the structured interview has relatively high criterion-related validity (Harris, 1989; Huffcutt & Arthur, 1994; Wiesner & Cronshaw, 1988), some scholars have asserted that the next major challenge is to examine the nomological network of this selection technique (McDaniel, Whetzel, Schmidt, & Maurer, 1994). The purpose of this chapter, then, is to consider what construct(s) the structured interview might be measuring. First, I discuss what I mean by *the structured interview*. I then review four possible constructs that the structured interview may be measuring and suggest future research to examine those possibilities.

There are two reasons why I concentrate here only on the structured interview. First, because structured interviews appear to have greater validity than do unstructured interviews, further understanding of structured interviews would seem to have a greater payoff in terms of practice. Second, unstructured interviews may differ greatly from study to study in terms of the questions asked. It is therefore not possible to describe precisely what "the" unstructured interview is. There is far more agreement among scholars as to what a structured interview entails. Even here, however, there are different possibilities in terms of the questions asked. I explore this issue in greater detail in the following section.

What Is the Structured Interview?

In addition to a certain degree of standardization, in both which questions may be asked and the way in which responses are scored (Huffcutt & Arthur, 1994), the term *structured interview* is generally associated with a particular *type* of question. There are two primary types of questions used in structured interviews (Harris, 1989): situational interview (SI) questions, which ask applicants what they would do or say in various hypothetical situations (Latham, 1989); and behavior description interview (BDI) questions, which ask applicants how they actually have behaved in past circumstances (Janz, Hellervik, & Gilmore, 1986). In a meta-analysis, Huffcutt, Roth, and McDaniel (1996) found that the majority of structured interviews used either SI or BDI questions. Of the 22 high-structure interviews located by Huffcutt et al., 10 involved SI questions and 7 involved BDI questions. Thus, the majority of structured interviews examined in the research literature have involved the use of either SI or BDI questions.

For two reasons, I consider here only structured interviews involving SI or BDI questions. First, as indicated above, these appear to be the most common types of structured interviews in the research literature. Second, failure to circumscribe the type of interview questions asked could lead to an argument that the interview simply measures any construct that one designs it to measure. As described by Dipboye (1992), unlike other selection techniques, "selection interviews possess no unique content" (p. 3). Furthermore, Dipboye asserts that an employment interview is simply "a dialogue initiated by one or more persons to gather information and evaluate the qualifications of an applicant for employment" (p. 3). For example, based on Dipboye's definition, both an orally presented cognitive ability test and an orally presented personality test would qualify as "interviews"—in which case any attempt to pinpoint what the "structured interview" is measuring becomes rather vacuous. Therefore, I limit discussion in this chapter to the consideration of what constructs are being measured by structured interviews using SI and BDI questions.

BDI and SI Questions: An Overview

BDI (e.g., Janz, 1982) and SI (e.g., Latham, Saari, Pursell, & Campion, 1980) questions have been discussed in the research literature for more than 15 years. Whereas their proponents have emphasized the differences between the two approaches (e.g., Latham, 1989), others have suggested that BDI and SI questions may be more similar than not (e.g., Campion,

Campion, & Hudson, 1994). I present below brief descriptions of BDI and SI questions.

The BDI

According to Janz et al. (1986), the BDI does not examine achievements (e.g., size of budget managed), technical knowledge, experience, or self-evaluations. Rather, the BDI evaluates actual past behavior in job-related situations. According to advocates of this approach, BDI questions may be used to assess a range of abilities, such as interpersonal relations, judgment, negotiation tactics, and quality performance (Janz et al., 1986). Pulakos and Schmitt (1995), for example, created BDI questions to assess seven abilities, including adapting to changing situations, demonstrating initiative and motivation, and planning/organizing/prioritizing. A BDI question developed by Campion et al. (1994) was: "What is the biggest difference of opinion you ever had with a coworker? How did it get resolved?" The scoring guide indicates that an excellent answer would include such points as the applicant and his or her coworkers examined the situation, discovered the cause of the problem, and resolved the differences in an open way. A marginal answer would be that the supervisor was asked to resolve the problem or that the applicant never had such a problem.

The SI

The SI is based on the critical incident technique. Questions are developed that pose hypothetical situations to the applicant, so that the applicant can demonstrate his or her intentions or future behavior. A scoring guide is developed for each question (Latham, 1989). Latham and Saari (1984) have designed SI questions to assess such dimensions as initiative/motivation. A sample SI question from Latham (1989) asks the applicant to decide between loaning a truck to another manager or keeping the truck and probably winning an award for profitability. Thus, the applicant must choose between two goals: profits and peer cooperation. A poor answer would focus on profitability, and a good answer would involve cooperating with the peer.

SI and BDI Questions: Are They Measuring the Same Constructs?

At least on the surface, both SI and BDI questions seem to be useful for assessing similar constructs, such as initiative/motivation. Campion et al. (1994), as well as others, have conducted studies to compare these question types directly. Indeed, when they standardized format (e.g., to eliminate differences in use of a scoring key and follow-up probes),

Campion et al. (1994) found a correlation of .73 (without correcting for unreliability) between BDI and SI questions. For the most part, then, in the remainder of this chapter I will assume that the SI and BDI can be discussed interchangeably; I will note possible differences where relevant.

I turn now to a discussion of the possible constructs that the structured interview may be measuring. Specifically, I offer cognitive ability, tacit knowledge, assessment center dimensions, and person-organization (P-O) fit as potential candidates for the construct being measured by the structured interview.

The Structured Interview: Is It Measuring Cognitive Ability?

Some have argued that the structured interview is simply measuring cognitive ability (Hunter & Hirsch, 1987). One of the most frequently cited studies in support of this assertion was conducted by Campion, Pursell, and Brown (1988), who found an uncorrected multiple correlation of .59 and a corrected (for range restriction) multiple correlation of .75 between the structured interview and four cognitive ability tests (mathematical aptitude, mechanical aptitude, oral instructions, and reading). Of the four possible reasons that Huffcutt et al. (1996) present as to why interview ratings may be correlated with cognitive ability test scores, the one that seems particularly relevant here is that applicants with higher cognitive ability would be more capable of thinking in complex ways and would be able to call upon a greater body of knowledge than would applicants with lower cognitive ability.

Huffcutt et al. (1996) meta-analyzed the relationship between interview ratings and cognitive ability scores and found an *overall* corrected correlation between these two variables of .40. They report a corrected correlation of .32 between SI interviews and cognitive ability scores, and a corrected correlation of .18 between BDI interviews and cognitive ability scores. On that basis, they conclude that there was a "fairly low-ability saturation for most of the situational interviews . . . and even less for the behavior description interviews" (p. 369). Thus, the relationship between structured interviews and cognitive ability scores is quite modest.

Although both SI and, particularly, BDI questions measure something other than cognitive ability, this meta-analysis suggests that SI and BDI questions demonstrate different relationships, which conflicts with my earlier suggestion that they are measuring the same construct. At least two explanations may be offered for these results. First, the SI seems more amenable to job knowledge questions, which applicants with greater cognitive ability are likely to be more successful in answering than are applicants with less cognitive ability (Borman, White, & Dorsey, 1995).

Conversely, the BDI questions seem less likely to involve job knowledge (e.g., Janz et al., 1986), instead focusing more on interpersonal relations and self-management themes, which might not be affected by cognitive ability. Thus, differences in dimensions typically assessed by the SI compared with the BDI may explain differences in their relationship with cognitive ability. Second, SI questions might be more closely related to cognitive ability because applicants with higher cognitive ability may be better at guessing the right answers than are applicants with lower cognitive ability. Conversely, because the BDI requires the applicant to report actual situations, cognitive ability may have less of an effect. Research is needed to test these alternative explanations, using equivalent versions of the SI and BDI questions.

Finally, in light of the rather high multiple correlation between interview ratings and cognitive ability tests reported by Campion et al. (1988), Huffcutt et al.'s (1996) results may seem surprising. One potential explanation (aside from the possibility of sampling error) is that Campion et al.'s interview was neither a BDI nor an SI approach; rather, it was based on a mix of job knowledge, simulation, situational, and worker willingness questions. More important, the sample job knowledge question that Campion et al. provide in their article assessed mechanical comprehension; the sample simulation question asked applicants to read aloud a 90-word instructional paragraph. These two questions suggest that their interview contained oral miniversions of the mechanical aptitude and reading tests. It is possible, then, that the unusually high correlation that Campion et al. report is due to conceptual overlap between the interview and the tests. In support of this explanation, it is noteworthy that the mechanical aptitude test and reading test correlated much higher with the structured interview ($r = .54$ and $r = .50$ for the mechanical aptitude and reading tests, respectively) than did either the mathematical aptitude test ($r = .27$) or the oral instructions test ($r = .37$).

In sum, it has been suggested that the structured interview is measuring cognitive ability. Results from Huffcutt et al. (1996) indicate that the relationship between cognitive ability and SI and BDI questions is, at best, quite modest. It appears that the structured interview is not tapping cognitive ability to any meaningful degree.

The Structured Interview: Is It Measuring Tacit Knowledge?

I have suggested in previous work that the BDI and SI may measure practical intelligence or tacit knowledge (Harris, 1989). As defined by Sternberg, Wagner, Williams, and Horvath (1995), tacit knowledge has three basic features:

1. It is procedural in nature; that is, tacit knowledge involves *how* to do things, rather than basic facts about things. For example, an item tapping academic knowledge might ask about the physics of how a pulley works. An item tapping tacit knowledge might ask how best to use a pulley in a given situation.

2. It involves information that is useful in attaining valued outcomes. In the work context, tacit knowledge would presumably comprise job-related information that affects performance.

3. It is learned with little or no environmental intervention; that is, tacit knowledge is generally learned through one's own efforts because it comprises information that is "unspoken, underemphasized, or poorly conveyed relative to its importance" (Sternberg et al., 1995, p. 917). In the work setting, this may refer to information "learned on the job."

To measure tacit knowledge, Wagner and Sternberg (1985) and Wagner (1987) developed paper-and-pencil questionnaires that ask respondents how they would handle different situations involving self-management, task management, and interactions with others. Experts' ratings of alternative courses of action were used to create a scoring guide for each question. Thus, on a superficial level at least, tacit knowledge measures appear quite similar to SI questions.

Conceptually, there are also some parallels between SI and BDI interviews and tacit knowledge measures. In terms of the first characteristic of tacit knowledge, a focus on how to do things, SI and BDI questions also focus on how the applicant would or did perform in specific situations. In terms of the second characteristic, given that some type of job analysis is used to create the SI and BDI questions, these questions are likely to represent knowledge useful in attaining important outcomes. It is not possible to assess whether the third characteristic—that the information being assessed is learned with little or no environmental intervention (e.g., formal training)—is a common feature of SI and BDI questions.

The limited empirical research on tacit knowledge has produced some results of potential relevance here. First, researchers have reported very low correlations with traditional measures of cognitive ability; Wagner (1987), for instance, found a correlation of −.12 between tacit knowledge and verbal reasoning ability. As observed above, Huffcutt et al.'s (1996) meta-analysis of interview ratings and cognitive ability test scores indicates low to modest correlations with SI and BDI questions. Second, tacit knowledge measures have demonstrated little relationship with sex and race (Sternberg et al., 1995); research on structured interviews has shown relatively small sex and race differences (e.g., Pulakos & Schmitt, 1995). Huffcutt and Roth (1997) report that African Americans, compared with whites, are rated only slightly lower (i.e., one-fifth of a standard deviation and one-tenth of a standard deviation lower on the SI and BDI, respectively) on structured interviews. Finally, Wagner (1987) found evidence that a single factor accounted for his tacit knowledge items, which meshes with what Pulakos and Schmitt (1995) report for their interview questions. Thus, there are both conceptual and empirical parallels between measures of tacit knowledge and structured interviews.

In sum, there is sufficient reason to pursue further research regarding the relationship between tacit knowledge and structured interviews. In this vein, I offer three suggestions. First, I would encourage researchers to examine the Tacit Knowledge Inventory for Managers (Sternberg et al., 1995) in relationship to SI and BDI questions. High correlations between this inventory and structured interview scores would support the notion that BDI and SI questions are measuring tacit knowledge. Second, I would encourage researchers to assess more precisely what type of knowledge is being assessed by BDI and SI questions. Recall that one of the features of tacit knowledge is that it involves information that is learned with little or no help from the environment. Whether this is true for BDI and SI questions should be investigated. One way to examine this would be to have subject matter experts indicate how the relevant information is learned (e.g., formal or informal training; Goldstein, 1991).

Third, given that tacit knowledge measures have focused on self-management, interactions with others, and task management, it seems likely that a measure of this construct may be particularly helpful in predicting contextual performance. As defined by Motowidlo and Van Scotter (1994), contextual performance involves activities that pertain to the organization's broader environment and goals. For example, among the items Motowidlo and Van Scotter used to measure contextual behavior were "cooperate with others in the team," "look for a challenging assignment," and "take the initiative to solve a problem" (p. 477). Some of the dimensions measured by SI and BDI questions that were described earlier, such as initiative, mesh closely with these items. Further research, along the lines of that conducted by Latham and Skarlicki (1995), is needed to determine whether structured interviews and tacit knowledge measures exhibit similar relationships with contextual performance. If such results are found, this would support the notion that the structured interview is measuring tacit knowledge. In general, examination of the comparative validity of tacit knowledge tests and structured interviews using a variety of criteria, such as organizational citizenship behavior, would be valuable for furthering our understanding of these constructs.

The Structured Interview: Is It Measuring Assessment Center Dimensions?

As I have noted in previous work, the factors measured in structured interviews, such as interpersonal ability, seem similar to dimensions measured in assessment centers (Harris, 1989). Granted that the assessment center considers how applicants *actually* behave in various exercises (i.e., a high-fidelity situation), whereas the structured interview considers how applicants *say they would* (SI) or *say they did* (BDI) behave (i.e., a low-fidelity situation), on the surface at least, there is a close parallel between the constructs measured in the assessment center and the constructs measured in the structured interview. Thus, one would expect a relatively high correlation between assessment center dimension ratings and structured interview scores.

There is, however, much research indicating that assessment center ratings reflect *exercise*, not dimension, factors (e.g., Bycio, Alvares, & Hahn, 1987; Sackett & Dreher, 1982). The precise reason for this finding is not known, but one explanation is that behavior differs from situation to situation (Harris, Becker, & Smith, 1993). If indeed behavior differs from situation to situation, one would expect that, all things being equal, dimension ratings in situations that are similar to one another would show a higher correlation than dimension ratings in situations that are not similar to one another. Based on this line of reasoning, then, one would expect structured interview ratings to correlate higher with assessment center exercises involving a one-on-one information exchange than with other kinds of assessment center exercises.

To compare "dimension" versus "exercise" explanations for structured interview ratings, I used assessment center ratings and structured interview ratings from applicants ($N = 28$) for a technical job at a *Fortune* 500 company. The same 10 dimensions (e.g., oral communication, tolerance for stress) were assessed in both the assessment center and the structured interview. Briefly, the assessment center consisted of four exercises: a scheduling exercise, a leaderless group discussion (LGD), and two one-on-one role-plays with a "customer." Assessors used a consensus process to arrive at overall dimension ratings as well as dimension ratings in each exercise. The structured interview, which each applicant had to pass in order to proceed to the assessment center, was based on BDI questions. For example, a question to assess "behavioral flexibility" was: "Can you remember a situation in which you had to change your course of action or strategy because of another individual's opinion? How did you handle it?"

The correlation between the average assessment center dimension rating and the average interview rating was .33, which is *smaller* than one would expect if the two selection procedures are measuring the same constructs. However, the notion that the interview would correlate most highly with assessment center exercises involving one-on-one situations was supported. Whereas the average rating for the exercise involving selling a product to a customer correlated .40 with the average interview rating, the scheduling exercise rating correlated −.06 with the average interview rating. The exercise involving dealing with a customer refund correlated .30 with the interview; the LGD exercise correlated .20 with the interview. These results suggest limited support for the notion that the structured interview is measuring the same construct as the assessment center. These results do, however, support the notion that the interview is measuring ability to function effectively in certain situations.

Accordingly, as has been suggested for the assessment center (Sackett & Harris, 1988), more attention should be devoted to understanding the *context* of the interview. Perhaps the interview should be designed to reflect, at least to some degree, important job situations. For instance, if the job involves dealing with rude customers, perhaps the interview should simulate this setting (e.g., the interviewer should interrupt the candidate from time to time). This leads to a number of interesting research questions about the interview context. First, does the administrative process (e.g., having a telephone interview, computer-based interview, or face-to-face interview) affect candidate responses to and the validity of the interview? Second, does the pleasantness of the interview situation affect validity? That is, for a stressful job, will an interview that is designed to make applicants nervous be more valid than an interview that provides a relaxed setting? Third, will a panel interview be more valid than an individual interview for jobs involving much interaction with groups? To date, there has been no research linking the interview context with the job context.

A critic might challenge this perspective by arguing that it runs counter to the underlying premise of the structured interview and recent meta-analytic findings, namely, that the key to a valid interview is appropriate questions, with answers scored using a proper scoring guide. By implication, the context should have no effect, and extraneous cues (e.g., nonverbal information) should be irrelevant. In response to that criticism, I would point to a recent study by Motowidlo and Burnett (1995) in which subjects rated videotaped BDI and SI interviews based on visual information only (i.e., subjects saw the applicant but did not hear the applicant's actual answers to questions), aural information only (i.e., subjects heard the applicant's answers to questions but did not see the applicant), or visual and aural information (i.e., subjects both saw and heard the applicant). Motowidlo and Burnett found that the most valid assessments were made when subjects had access to both visual and aural information. This study supports an argument that valid information can be obtained not only from *what* the applicant says, but also from *how* the applicant says it. Thus, factors other than content may constitute valid cues.

In light of the above discussion, it is apparent that more research is needed to examine the relationship between assessment center dimension and exercise ratings and structured interview scores. First, given the very small sample size reported here, a replication study using a larger sample is clearly needed. Second, a comparison of both BDI and SI questions with assessment center dimension and exercise ratings would be valuable. Third, it would be quite helpful to determine whether both the interview and the assessment center dimension and exercise ratings account for *independent* amounts of variance in job performance. Fourth, Highhouse and Harris (1993) applied Bem's technique for measuring situation similarity in an assessment center context. Researchers might adapt this technique to compare work contexts and interview contexts. Finally, more research is needed regarding the types of cues interviewers use in making their ratings in a structured interview and whether nonverbal cues increase, decrease, or have no effect on validity.

In sum, the structured interview may be measuring how candidates would behave in certain situations. This is clearly a possibility in need of careful research, which may also extend our understanding of assessment center constructs.

The Structured Interview: Is It Measuring Person-Organization Fit?

Person-organization fit is a construct that has been the center of a great deal of scholarly attention for the past 10 years. Although P-O fit has been examined from both the organization's perspective (e.g., selection of effective employees) and the employee's perspective (e.g., work attitudes), in this chapter I address only the perspective of the interviewer. In the following discussion, therefore, I consider P-O fit from the organization's, not the applicant's, perspective.

In an integrative review of the P-O fit literature, Kristof (1996) distinguished between two conceptualizations of this construct: complementary fit and supplementary fit. According to Kristof, the former approach defines fit in terms of the degree to which the applicant will be able to supply the knowledge, skills, and abilities (task and interpersonal) and resources (e.g., time, effort) that the organization needs. Thus, the complementary fit approach meshes with the perspective that the structured interview is measuring assessment center ratings or tacit knowledge.

Supplementary fit, according to Kristof (1996), represents "the relationship between the fundamental characteristics of an organization and a person" (p. 3). Fundamental characteristics of an organization include "culture, climate, values, goals, and norms" (p. 3); for an applicant, fundamental characteristics include "values, goals, personality, and attitudes" (pp. 3-4). Although there are a number of fundamental characteristics, Kristof asserts that the most commonly examined one is values. Moreover, some empirical studies have examined values in the context of employment interviews (Adkins, Russell, & Werbel, 1994; Cable & Judge, 1997). Thus, I will address P-O fit only in terms of *value* congruence.

In considering value congruence and whether that is what the structured interview is measuring, it is important first to understand the definition of *values*. Nicholson (1995) defines values as "a set of core beliefs held by individuals concerning how they should or ought to behave over broad ranges of situations" (p. 598). Cable and Judge (1997) define values as "enduring beliefs that a specific mode of conduct or end-state is preferable to its opposite" (p. 547). These beliefs are considered to be deeply held by individuals and to have much influence over their behavior. Values, then, are highly influential beliefs about how one should behave.

In terms of empirical research, Adkins et al. (1994) used the Comparative Emphasis Scale, developed by Ravlin and Meglino (1987), to assess organizational (i.e., interviewers' perceptions of their organization), interviewer (i.e., interviewers' ratings of themselves), universal (i.e., cross-organizational), and applicant (i.e., applicants' perceptions of themselves) values. The Comparative Emphasis Scale assesses four key work values: achievement, fairness, honesty, and helping/concern for others. Applicant-organizational work value congruence (i.e., the match between interviewers' ratings of organizational values and applicants' ratings of their own values) was *not* significantly related to recruiter ratings of a 4-item employability index (e.g., "How likely do you think this candidate is to receive other job offers?") or to a 6-item general P-O fit measure (e.g., "Given your overall impression of this candidate, how good a 'fit' do you think there is between the candidate and your organization?"). Applicant-organizational work value congruence was *not* related to the applicant's receiving a second interview. However, applicant-*interviewer* work value congruence and applicant-universal congruence were significantly related to the employability index and the general P-O fit measure.

Cable and Judge (1997) used a 40-item version (e.g., "risk taking," "fairness") of the Organizational Culture Profile, designed by O'Reilly, Chatman, and Caldwell (1991). Interviewers made ratings for each applicant and for their organization. Applicants made self-ratings using the same set of items. Cable and Judge found a statistically significant relationship between interviewers' *perceived* value congruence (i.e., the match between interviewers' ratings of applicants' values and interviewers' ratings of their organization's values) and subsequent hiring decisions. However, there was only a small correlation ($r = .23$) between *actual* value congruence (i.e., the match between interviewers' ratings of their organization's values and applicants' ratings of their own values) and *perceived* value congruence. Actual value congruence also exhibited a very small relationship with subsequent hiring decisions. On the basis of their findings, Cable and Judge conclude that value congruence plays an important role in the hiring process and suggest that "the interview may have its greatest utility as a P-O fit assessment device" (p. 34), rather than as a measure of abilities.

I find it noteworthy that both of these studies found little or no relationship between actual value congruence and *employment* outcomes. Although both sets of researchers conclude that value congruence is important in selection decisions, it should be noted that it was the interviewer's idiosyncratic and subjective judgment of value congruence, not *actual* applicant-organizational value congruence, that was found to be most highly related to employment decisions. Even more important, neither study addressed the structured interview as a measure of P-O fit. Hence, although these two studies contribute important information toward our understanding of P-O fit as measured in an interview context, future research must address several issues. First, these studies indicate that interviewer judgments of P-O fit are not highly accurate. Many irrelevant factors appear to enter in when interviewers make P-O fit ratings. Therefore, researchers must examine what information interviewers use in making ratings of perceived value congruence. Are there certain questions, for example, that interviewers do (or should) ask that will enable them to make more accurate judgments of applicant values? It seems reasonable to hypothesize that certain BDI and SI questions would be helpful in assessing applicant values. Alternatively, are there certain nonverbal cues that interviewers use in rating applicant values? This is clearly an important issue if we are to understand interviewers' judgment processes in making P-O fit ratings. Second, neither study attempted to ascertain the *validity* of these judgments in predicting job success. There is no evidence, then, that P-O fit is a valid predictor of job performance.

Third, we need more careful consideration of the definitions of *values, intentions,* and *assessment center dimensions* to determine if these actually represent conceptually different constructs. Recall that values have been described as a set of core beliefs about how one should behave in a wide set of circumstances. Now consider the example of an SI question from Latham (1989) provided earlier, which involved a situation in which the applicant had to decide between two competing organizational goals—cost savings and peer cooperation. Given the definition provided above, it would be reasonable to suggest that this sample question may measure the *value* an applicant places on profits versus cooperation. Or consider this sample SI question from Campion et al. (1994): "Suppose you had an idea for a change in work procedure to enhance quality, but there was a problem in that some members of your work team were against any type of change. What would you do in this situation?" (p. 999). The scoring guide indicates that an excellent answer includes explaining the change, showing the benefits of change, and discussing the issues openly in a meeting; "tell the supervisor" would constitute a marginal answer. Compare that question and scoring guide with the following items from the values scale used by Cable and Judge: "confronting conflict directly," "taking individual responsibility," "being team oriented," and "sharing information freely." Based on these examples, the distinctions among values, intentions, and assessment center dimensions seems less clear than one might initially think. In other words, it is possible that P-O fit is quite similar to intentions and assessment center dimensions as those terms are used in the literature. Finally, research is needed to compare the structured interview and measures of P-O fit to determine their statistical relationship. To my knowledge, no empirical study has examined these variables together.

In sum, there is reason to believe that the structured interview may be measuring P-O fit. One critical suggestion is that researchers be far more careful in defining what they mean by *values,* compared to *assessment center dimensions* and *intentions,* as measured in the structured interview. Second, far more research is needed to compare the incremental validity of P-O fit measures and structured interview scores in predicting job performance. Third, researchers need to investigate how interviewers assess P-O fit and whether use of structured interviews can produce accurate assessments of P-O fit.

Conclusion

In this chapter I have discussed four possible constructs that the structured interview may be measuring. Although there is little reason to believe that the structured interview is measuring cognitive ability, the structured interview may be measuring tacit knowledge, assessment center dimensions, or P-O fit. It is even possible that the structured interview is measuring two or three of these constructs at the same time. A greater understanding of the constructs assessed by the structured interview would be useful for both practical and theoretical purposes.

References

Adkins, C. L., Russell, C. J., & Werbel, J. D. (1994). Judgments of fit in the selection process: The role of work value congruence. *Personnel Psychology, 47,* 605-623.

Borman, W. C., White, L., & Dorsey, D. (1995). Effects of ratee task performance and interpersonal factors on supervisor and peer performance ratings. *Journal of Applied Psychology, 80,* 168-177.

Bycio, P., Alvares, K., & Hahn, J. (1987). Situational specificity in assessment center ratings: A confirmatory factor analysis. *Journal of Applied Psychology, 72,* 463-474.

Cable, D. M., & Judge, T. A. (1997). Interviewers' perceptions of person-organization fit and organizational selection decisions. *Journal of Applied Psychology, 82,* 546-561.

Campion, M. A., Campion, J. E., & Hudson, J. P. (1994). Structured interviewing: A note on incremental validity and alternative question types. *Journal of Applied Psychology, 79,* 998-1002.

Campion, M. A., Pursell, E. D., & Brown, B. K. (1988). Structured interviewing: Raising the psychometric properties of the employment interview. *Personnel Psychology, 41,* 25-42.

Dipboye, R. L. (1992). *Selection interviews: Process perspectives.* Cincinnati, OH: South-Western.

Goldstein, I. L. (1991). Training in organizations. In M. D. Dunnette & L. M. Hough (Eds.), *Handbook of industrial and organizational psychology* (2nd ed., Vol. 2, pp. 507-619). Palo Alto, CA: Consulting Psychologists Press.

Harris, M. M. (1989). Reconsidering the employment interview: A review of recent literature and suggestions for future research. *Personnel Psychology, 42,* 691-726.

Harris, M. M., Becker, A., & Smith, D. (1993). Does the assessment center scoring method affect the cross-situational consistency of ratings? *Journal of Applied Psychology, 78,* 675-678.

Highhouse, S., & Harris, M. M. (1993). The measurement of assessment center situations: Bem's template matching technique for examining exercise similarity. *Journal of Applied Social Psychology, 23,* 140-155.

Huffcutt, A. I., & Arthur, W., Jr. (1994). Hunter and Hunter (1984) revisited: Interview validity for entry-level jobs. *Journal of Applied Psychology, 79,* 184-190.

Huffcutt, A. I., & Roth, P. L. (1997, April). *Racial group differences in employment interview evaluations.* Paper presented at the annual meeting of the Society for Industrial and Organizational Psychology, St. Louis, MO.

Huffcutt, A. I., Roth, P. L., & McDaniel, M. A. (1996). A meta-analytic investigation of cognitive ability in employment interview evaluations: Moderating characteristics and implications for incremental validity. *Journal of Applied Psychology, 81,* 459-473.

Hunter, J. E., & Hirsch, H. R. (1987). Application of meta-analysis. In C. L. Cooper & I. T. Robertson (Eds.), *International review of industrial and organizational psychology* (pp. 321-357). Chichester: John Wiley.

Janz, J. T. (1982). Initial comparisons of patterned behavior description interviews versus unstructured interviews. *Journal of Applied Psychology, 67,* 577-580.

Janz, J. T., Hellervik, L., & Gilmore, D. C. (1986). *Behavior description interviewing: New, accurate, cost effective.* Newton, MA: Allyn & Bacon.

Kristof, A. L. (1996). Person-organization fit: An integrative review of its conceptualizations, measurement, and implications. *Personnel Psychology, 49,* 1-49.

Latham, G. P. (1989). The reliability, validity, and practicality of the situational interview. In R. W. Eder & G. R. Ferris (Eds.), *The employment interview: Theory, research, and practice* (pp. 169-182). Newbury Park, CA: Sage.

Latham, G. P., & Saari, L. M. (1984). Do people do what they say? Further studies on the situational interview. *Journal of Applied Psychology, 69,* 569-573.

Latham, G. P., Saari, L. M., Pursell, E. D., & Campion, M. A. (1980). The situational interview. *Journal of Applied Psychology, 65,* 422-427.

Latham, G. P., & Skarlicki, D. (1995). Criterion-related validity of the situational and patterned behavior description interviews with organizational citizenship behavior. *Human Performance, 8,* 67-80.

McDaniel, M. A., Whetzel, D. L., Schmidt, F. L., & Maurer, S. D. (1994). The validity of employment interviews: A comprehensive review and meta-analysis. *Journal of Applied Psychology, 79,* 599-616.

Motowidlo, S. J., & Burnett, J. R. (1995). Aural and visual sources of validity in structured employment interviews. *Organizational Behavior and Human Decision Processes, 61,* 239-249.

Motowidlo, S. J., & Van Scotter, J. (1994). Evidence that task performance should be distinguished from contextual performance. *Journal of Applied Psychology, 79,* 475-480.

Nicholson, N. (1995). *The Blackwell encyclopedic dictionary of organizational behavior.* Cambridge, MA: Blackwell.

O'Reilly, C. A., Chatman, J., & Caldwell, D. F. (1991). People and organizational culture: A profile comparison approach to assessing person-organization fit. *Academy of Management Journal, 34,* 487-516.

Pulakos, E. D., & Schmitt, N. (1995). Experience-based and situational interview questions: Studies of validity. *Personnel Psychology, 48,* 289-308.

Ravlin, E. C., & Meglino, B. M. (1987). Effects of values on perception and decision-making: A study of alternative work value measures. *Journal of Applied Psychology, 72,* 666-673.

Sackett, P. R., & Dreher, G. W. (1982). Constructs and assessment center dimensions: Some troubling empirical findings. *Journal of Applied Psychology, 67,* 401-410.

Sackett, P. R., & Harris, M. M. (1988). A further examination of the constructs underlying assessment center ratings. *Journal of Business and Psychology, 3,* 214-229.

Sternberg, R. J., Wagner, R. K., Williams, W. M., & Horvath, J. A. (1995). Testing common sense. *American Psychologist, 50,* 912-917.

Wagner, R. K. (1987). Tacit knowledge in everyday intelligent behavior. *Journal of Personality and Social Psychology, 52,* 1236-1247.

Wagner, R. K., & Sternberg, R. J. (1985). Practical intelligence in real-world pursuits: The role of tacit knowledge. *Journal of Personality and Social Psychology, 49,* 436-458.

Wiesner, W. H., & Cronshaw, S. F. (1988). A meta-analytic investigation of the impact of interview format and degree of structure on the validity of the employment interview. *Journal of Occupational Psychology, 61,* 275-290.

9

The Situational Interview

Steven D. Maurer
Christina Sue-Chan
Gary P. Latham

In the past two decades, much has been written about the benefits of the situational interview (SI; see, e.g., Latham, Saari, Pursell, & Campion, 1980). Among these writings is a 1989 chapter by Latham in which he recounted SI research to that point in time. Despite the fact that much of the proposed research agenda in that chapter has been addressed in the years since its publication, our encounters with consultants and practitioners conversant with the SI have revealed several issues that have yet to be addressed. Our purposes in this chapter are to provide a review of extant research and to present some proposals for future inquiry. Our intent is to respond to the human resource manager's need to decide the usefulness of any selection method according to its psychometric, operational, and economic properties. Hence, we focus here on practitioner concerns with four factors: validity, reliability, legality, and practicality. We argue that extant empirical data regarding these factors provide a basis for future studies that should yield functionally meaningful answers to these key issues.

AUTHORS' NOTE: This chapter is based on a paper funded by an ASSHRC grant to the third author.

SI Characteristics

Because some practitiionrs assert that they are already "doing" situational interviews because they include an occasional situational question into an otherwise loosely structured and past-oriented (i.e., "conventional") interviewing strategy, we begin our description of the SI's main elements by distinguishing it from other interview methods. First, in contrast to the conventional assumption that past behavior is predictive of future behavior, the SI is based on the theory that intentions predict behavior (Latham et al., 1980). This premise, derived from goal-setting theory (Locke & Latham, 1990), has been specifically supported by experimental research (e.g., Latham & Saari, 1984; Latham & Skarlicki, 1995). This theoretical premise differentiates the SI from nonbehavioral methods as well as from past-oriented behavioral interviews (Janz, 1982).

Second, rather than making general inquiries regarding events and self-perceptions, the SI poses job-related dilemmas that are designed to "force" applicants to state what they truly believe they would do in given situations. The purpose of the dilemma is to minimize social desirability responses that can be learned and rehearsed in relation to more general, past-oriented inquiries.

Finally, in the SI, a highly structured behaviorally anchored scoring guide is used to evaluate the answer to each question as it is given in terms of what constitutes an excellent, acceptable, or unacceptable answer in a particular organizational setting. This scoring guide, typically absent from conventional interviews, reflects the culture or values of the organization, because an acceptable answer in one organization might be unacceptable in another (Latham & Sue-Chan, 1996).

Validity

In the decade since the publication of Eder and Ferris's *The Employment Interview* (1989), confidence in the criterion-related validity of the SI has increased as a result of three meta-analyses. McDaniel, Whetzel, Schmidt, and Maurer (1994) examined 143 validity coefficients, 16 of which came from SI studies. They found that the corrected mean validity of the SI (.50) was greater than that of all other job-related interviews (.29). Similarly, Huffcutt and Arthur (1994) meta-analyzed 33 validity coefficients from interviews that were conducted and scored in the same way as the SI. They computed a corrected mean validity of .57, a level that they note is "essentially the same validity as ability tests" (p. 188). Most recently, Latham and Sue-Chan (1999) conducted a meta-analysis of 16 validity coefficients, 7 of which were not included in the McDaniel et al. (1994)

study, and found a mean corrected validity of .50. Together, these three analyses suggest that practitioners can confidently conclude that the corrected population validity of the SI is approximately .50.

The question of whether these results can be generalized to a variety of job settings and performance criteria has also been addressed. With regard to job settings, McDaniel et al. (1994) found that evidence indicated the generalizability of the SI method. This conclusion is supported by the variety of samples and jobs from which the validity coefficients were derived. The samples include office clerical employees (e.g., Latham & Saari, 1984), clerical/administrative employees in the financial services industry (e.g., Robertson, Gratton, & Rout, 1990), school custodians (e.g., Lin et al., 1994), school cafeteria managers (e.g., Lin & Adrian, 1993), bank clerks (Schuler & Funke, 1989), sawmill workers (Latham et al., 1980), pulpmill workers (Latham et al., 1980), newsprint employees (Latham et al., 1980), retail sales personnel (Weekley & Gier, 1987), factory service technicians (Delery, Wright, McArthur, & Anderson, 1994), frontline supervisors (Latham & Saari, 1984), public health supervisors and managers (Maurer & Fay, 1988), student nurses (Sue-Chan, Latham, & Evans, 1995), managers (Latham & Skarlicki, 1995), and university faculty (Latham & Skarlicki, 1995). With regard to performance criteria, SI studies have shown that, in addition to predicting supervisor evaluations of job performance, the SI is a valid predictor of peer assessments of organizational citizenship behavior (Latham & Skarlicki, 1995), sales volume (Weekley & Gier, 1987), and university grades (Sue-Chan et al., 1995).

Despite these encouraging indicators of the SI's validity, several issues have yet to be addressed regarding the SI's effectiveness as a predictor. Perhaps the most basic issue to be addressed is the relative effectiveness of the SI in comparison with other, more traditional, interview procedures. One method for examining this issue is to use a design similar to that used by Latham and Skarlicki (1995), who examined the validity of the SI as a predictor of university faculty organizational citizenship behavior. Results of interviews based on both SI and patterned behavior description interview (PBDI) questions revealed that only the SI had criterion-related validity. However, a scoring guide was not used with the PBDI.

There is a need to go beyond evidence on validity issues to understand more fully exactly *why* the SI works. Robertson et al. (1990) have noted that "as far as situational interviews are concerned, the questions of how and why they work are unresolved" (p. 74). In light of this observation, we present preliminary evidence and future research ideas based on the belief that the SI works because it (a) provides a highly structured questioning and scoring method, (b) poses job-related situational dilemmas, (c) promotes accurate encoding and scoring of interview information, and (d) measures psychological constructs that are key dimensions of job performance.

Questioning Structure and Scoring Method

Huffcutt and Arthur (1994) provide meta-analytic evidence that supports the contention offered by some authors that the validity of the SI is due, in part, to the high degree of structure in both the questioning and scoring procedures (see Hunter & Hirsch, 1987; Maurer & Fay, 1988). This assertion is also supported by Motowidlo et al. (1992), who examined the degree to which the validity of a behavioral interview format is due to its behaviorally structured protocol. They noted that "the interview's structured behavioral format, which stipulates the kinds of situations about which the interviewer should ask and the behavioral dimensions along which they should evaluate interviewees, is probably responsible for its validity" (p. 582). Further, Motowidlo et al. argue that interviewers who ask questions using the structured behavioral format are able to gain more job-relevant information and that "more accurate judgments . . . can be made when interviewers elicit more relevant information" (p. 582).

The assertion that the criterion-related validity of the SI is due to its high level of consistency in its questioning structure is in accord with studies that show that interview validity is enhanced through the consistent asking of highly structured questions (see Arvey & Campion, 1982; Wright, 1969). However, contribution of the behavioral scoring scale to validity is less certain. Latham and Saari (1984) found that when interviewers ignored the scoring guide for the SI, the criterion-related validity for the SI was only .14. When the scoring guide was used, the validity coefficient was .40.

One strategy for assessing the contribution of the scoring scale would be to conduct a validity study based on two or more independent sets of SI-based ratings. In this design, one set of ratings could be gathered using a scoring guide developed for the SI, and the other set would be based on ratings developed without the help of the scoring guide. If these ratings were gathered from pairs of raters, the contribution of the SI scale to both the validity and the interrater reliability of the ratings could be assessed.

Situational Dilemmas

Latham and Sue-Chan (1996) argue that the SI's criterion-related validity is due in part to the situational "dilemma," which they define as two or more equally desirable or undesirable courses of action. The purpose of the dilemma is to minimize socially desirable responses. Preliminary evidence concerning the importance of this trait to SI questions has been illustrated by Campion, Campion, and Hudson (1994). Using what they call a future intentions (FI) format, the researchers obtained significant validity coefficients with questions that did not contain dilemmas; however, they obtained incremental validity for PBDI questions but not for FI items. The reverse might have occurred if the FI items had contained dilemmas and were, hence, SI items.

A simple approach to testing the importance of the dilemma to criterion-related validity would be to prepare two sets of questions, one containing questions with dilemmas and the other without dilemmas. Using the same scoring guide, the questions could then be presented to applicants. The validity coefficients obtained from the ratings of the applicants' responses to the two sets of questions could then be compared to see if they differ significantly.

Evaluations of Interview Information

Research suggesting that the SI facilitates accurate judgments of applicant information has been conducted by Maurer and Lee (in press). They found that interviewers exhibited a high level of accuracy in rating applicants who appeared in various interview sequences and who offered information indicating several different levels of applicant ability. Further, they found that the ability to evaluate information accurately was not adversely affected by contrast or assimilation effects.

One strategy for examining the relationship between SI rating accuracy and criterion-related validity would begin with the videotaping of actual job interviews to be used in a classical validity study. Panels of experts could then view the tapes and use the same SI scale used by the interviewer to determine the "true" quality of the answers provided by each applicant. Using procedures similar to those employed by Maurer and Lee (in press), the researcher could then determine differential accuracy scores for each interview (by comparing ratings to true scores). These scores could then be correlated with the criterion measure and/or used in tests designed to determine the covariance between rating accuracy and validity of interviewer ratings.

Measurement of Key Constructs

One of the more recent developments in SI research is the attention being given to the definition of job-related psychological constructs measured by this method. Tentative results indicate that the SI taps key constructs that are at least conceptually related to actual job performance. An example of this line of inquiry is a study by Sue-Chan et al. (1995), who examined three psychological correlates of the SI: cognitive ability, practical intelligence, and self-efficacy. They hypothesized that cognitive ability is a psychological correlate of the SI because both Hunter and Hirsch (1987) and Schmidt (1988) have argued that the interview is essentially an orally administered intelligence test. Sue-Chan et al. also investigated practical intelligence as a correlate of the SI because both Harris (1989) and Motowidlo, Dunnette, and Carter (1990) have suggested that the SI may be measuring what Wagner (1987) and Wagner and Sternberg (1985, 1986) label *practical intelligence* or *tacit knowledge*. This is because the critical incident technique (CIT) that is used to develop the SI may be identifying practical intelligence about ways of performing effectively in an organization. Finally, because the SI identifies intentions or goals for future performance (Locke & Latham, 1990) and empirical evidence indicates that self-efficacy directly and indirectly affects performance through goal commitment and goal choice (Bandura, 1986; Latham & Locke, 1991; Locke & Latham, 1990), Sue-Chan et al. argue that the SI measures not only the candidate's intentions or goals for future job performance, but also confidence or self-efficacy in committing to and implementing these intentions.

With regard to the issue of cognitive ability, Sue-Chan et al. (1995) found that the SI does not measure this element in job applicants. This result is consistent with a similar conclusion by Delery et al. (1994) and the meta-analytic findings of Huffcutt, Roth, and McDaniel (1996), which suggest that structured interviews are less effective for assessing cognitive ability. At the same time, Sue-Chan et al. found that the SI correlated significantly with self-efficacy ($r = .59$); they conclude that the criterion-related validity of the SI may be a result of measuring the candidate's intentions or goals for future job performance and confidence or self-efficacy in committing to and implementing these intentions. Together, these results are consistent with Huffcutt et al.'s (1996) assertion that a "generalized motivation factor" (p. 470) rather than cognitive ability may explain the criterion-related validity of structured interviews.

In considering the ability of the SI to assess practical intelligence, Sue-Chan et al. (1995) found initially that the correlation between the SI and this factor was not significant. However, because the sample size was reduced due to missing values on the practical intelligence measure, they used regression imputation (Darlington, 1990; Roth & Switzer, 1995) to estimate those missing values. When this was done, they found a significant correlation between SI and practical intelligence ($r = .34$); they conclude that further investigation of practical intelligence as a construct underlying the SI appears to be warranted.

These preliminary findings need to be replicated and extended if we are to get a clearer picture of why the SI predicts job performance. In this regard, future research could focus on constructs measured by the SI and the extent to which those constructs covary with the Big Five personality dimensions (Barrick & Mount, 1991). One possibility has been suggested by Gellatly (1996), who found that personal goals mediate the relationship between conscientiousness and task performance. This finding indicates that conscientiousness is a determinant of one's goals or intentions toward task performance and that, thus, the SI may be tapping the applicant's conscientiousness through its focus on applicant intentions. The possibility that the SI's ability to measure conscientiousness is a key factor in its ability to predict job performance is suggested by Barrick and Mount (1991), who provide meta-analytic evidence that conscientiousness predicts job performance in a variety of situations.

Further studies of the construct validity of the SI might employ at least two methods. First, researchers might use the multitrait, multimethod approach recommended by Lawler (1967). Second, they might conduct a series of correlational studies in which the SI is correlated with psychological construct(s) that it, in theory, measures. A meta-analysis, similar to Huffcutt et al.'s (1996), combined with structural equation modeling (Viswesvaran & Ones, 1995), could then be conducted to determine the mean correlation between the SI and the psychological construct(s) and the nomological net to which it belongs.

Reliability

Interrater reliability of SI ratings is important to SI research because reliability places an upper bound on validity (see Cascio, 1978) and responds to the practitioner's responsibility for the quality of hiring decisions (Eder, 1989) by providing evidence of consistency across interviewers. Further, rating reliability is "politically" important to practitioners because inconsistency among interviewers may erode confidence in the hiring process and in the human resource practitioners involved with it.

Research evidence shows that the SI yields high levels of agreement (i.e., interrater reliability) across interviewers. Latham et al. (1980) obtained interrater reliability coefficients that ranged from .76 to .87 in the hiring of workers in the wood products industry. In an enumerative review of the literature, Latham (1989) found interobserver reliabilities that ranged from .81 to .96. Recent studies have yielded interrater reliabilities for the SI that range from .88 (Sue-Chan et al., 1995) to .90 (Latham & Skarlicki, 1995). Further, in a specific attempt to compare rater agreement using conventional structured interviews with that achieved using the SI, Maurer and Fay (1988) found that even without any training, agreement in ratings among managers who used the SI was significantly greater than that for managers who used a traditional structured interview after having received 2 days of workshop instruction on how to develop and use these interviews. Moreover, McDaniel et al. (1994) found that the reliability of the structured interview, which includes the SI, is .84 ($SD = .15$). This is a higher value than the mean interobserver reliability of .68 ($SD = .25$) for job-related unstructured interviews.

There are at least four reasons for the higher interrater reliability of the SI. First, SI questions are developed from a job analysis. Second, answers to the SI questions are rated on a question-by-question basis. Third, it is expected that an interview panel, rather than a single rater, should be used to evaluate candidate responses in the SI. Finally, a scoring guide specific to each SI question is used. Conway, Jako, and Goodman (1995), in their meta-analysis of the interrater reliability of selection interviews, found that these four factors contribute to high levels of interrater reliability in structured interviews.

A reliability issue deserving of further attention is the need to determine whether ratings of interviewers acting individually are as reliable as those of interviewers participating as members of interviewing boards. This information would be useful for the comparison of research results derived from SI panels (e.g. Latham et al., 1980; Lin, Dobbins, & Fahr, 1992) to those based on independent observations (e.g. Maurer & Lee, 1994, in press). Meta-analytic evidence that panel interviews are generally more valid than individual interviews (Wiesner & Cronshaw, 1988) suggests that the structure and/or questioning processes of panel interviews may also contribute to greater interrater reliability. From a practitioner's perspective, research dedicated to quantifying the actual differences, if any, in the rating reliability of panelists and individual interviewers could be important for decision making concerning whether to incur the expense and inconvenience of conducting panel interviews. Because several panel studies have been performed that have employed panels consisting of two or more raters (Latham et al., 1980; Lin et al., 1992; Motowidlo et al., 1992), a direct approach to this issue would be to replicate these studies using controls to assure that ratings are individually determined and then compare reliabilities of individual ratings to those reported by interview panelists.

Legality

Conformity to legal standards and avoidance of discriminatory biases in interviewer decisions are certainly among the operational requirements of any interviewing method. As it turns out, there is growing evidence that responsiveness to these legal concerns is one of the strengths of the SI. To begin with, the SI is based on a job analysis, namely, the critical incident technique (Flanagan, 1954). The CIT is highly consistent with the job analysis principles described in *Uniform Guidelines on Employee Selection Procedures* (Equal Employment Opportunity Commission, 1978) and has been cited as an acceptable job analysis method in court rulings (see Thompson & Thompson, 1982). Further, the CIT conforms with court and guidelines expectations that job analysis procedures include job incumbents in the collection of information regarding the identification of critical dimensions of job performance (Thompson & Thompson, 1982).

In addition to such arguments concerning the SI's basic conformity to legal requirements, research evidence gathered from legal experts and experimental tests of the SI's resistance to various forms of bias suggest its legal merits. With regard to the evidence gained from experts, Latham and Finnegan (1993) surveyed 41 attorneys who specialize in Title VII litigation to gain perceptions of their relative ability to defend hiring decisions based on SIs, patterned interviews (i.e., structured conventional interviews), and unstructured interviews. Results showed that hiring decisions based on the SI were perceived to be significantly easier to defend than those based on other interview techniques. Moreover, attorneys perceived the SI to be significantly superior to the alternative methods in terms of the job analysis procedures used to create the interview, job representativeness of the interview questions, consistency in the questions asked of applicants, and freedom from interviewer bias.

Empirical evidence also shows that the SI is relatively free from interviewer biases. For instance, in an investigation of age and race bias, Lin et al. (1992) compared panel ratings based on SIs to those based on structured conventional interviews. They found that neither interview exhibited bias due to age similarity. Bias due to race similarity, however, was detected in conventional interview evaluations of both white and Hispanic applicants, whereas no such bias was found when the SI was used. Results also showed that African American applicants were more favorably evaluated by African American panelists regardless of interview method, but, in contrast to conventional interview ratings, no difference was found in SI assessments of African American applicants by Hispanic, white, or mixed-race panels. These results are consistent with the findings of other studies that have shown that SI ratings minimize bias against African American applicants (Latham et al., 1980) and may, in fact, yield slight overprediction (i.e., a positive bias) of their abilities (Campion, Pursell, & Brown, 1988).

Besides demonstrating resistance to race and age bias, the SI has been shown to be free of gender bias in its predictive validity in the hiring of hourly workers (Latham et al., 1980) and test fairness in the hiring of mill workers into male-dominated jobs (Campion et al., 1988). Further, Maurer and Fair (1988) found no differences among health care managers in the rating reliability of male and female applicants, thus indicating an absence of gender effect in ratings across interviewers. In yet another setting, Maurer and Lee (1994) observed no differences in the accuracy of SI ratings of male and female applicants for historically male-dominated police sergeant and lieutenant jobs by an all-male group of experienced sergeants and lieutenants. Similarly, Kataoka, Latham, and Whyte (1997) found that the SI was more resistant to anchoring effects than a patterned behavior interview or a conventional structured interview. Latham and Skarlicki (1995) showed that French-Canadian managers in the province of Quebec were biased in favor of francophones when a conventional structured interview was used, but that this decision-making bias was eliminated when SI questions were given.

Despite these encouraging results, further work is needed to explore additional areas of legal concern. One such possibility is the examination of the SI in terms of its potential for avoiding discrimination in hiring persons with disabilities. Because the Americans With Disabilities Act of 1990 (ADA) states that employers may ask applicants with disabilities how they would perform (with or without accommodation) essential job functions associated with work situations, it seems logical to explore the SI as a vehicle for posing highly job-related scenarios and a behavioral scoring device that would, in accordance with the ADA, focus on the individual's abilities rather than his or her disabilities. In this regard, it would also be useful to compare the SI to other interview methods in terms of issues such as its effect on applicant perceptions of fairness, its ability to detect unseen disabilities that might require accommodation, and its relative ability to predict factors of specific concern to employers in hiring persons with disabilities, such as job performance, longevity, and absenteeism. Such an inquiry would also be useful in regard to Canadian laws, because the Canadian Charter of Rights and Freedoms, as well as various federal and provincial Human Rights Acts, provide similar protections for persons with disabilities.

Practicality

In general, research conducted in the past 10 years suggests that the SI does what it purports to do: provide a valid, reliable, and legal assessment of job candidates. This suggests that a failure by practitioners to adopt this method may be grounded in three possibilities: (a) The SI remains too new to be widely used, (b) the evidence noted here is not known to practitioners because it has been published primarily in academic journals, and/or (c) practical reservations remain concerning its use. In this section we turn our attention to the last of these explanations and consider interviewer/applicant reactions and economic factors as inhibiting factors preventing the use of the SI.

Interviewer Reactions

Preliminary evidence concerning interviewer reactions to the SI are generally positive. For instance, Latham and Finnegan (1993) addressed this issue in a survey of interviewers who had experience with situational interviews as well as interviewers who had never used this procedure. Both groups rated the SI as more practical than either the patterned (i.e., structured conventional) or the unstructured interview. Moreover, although both groups evaluated the SI to be more difficult to prepare than the other methods, they rated it significantly superior to the alternatives in terms of perceived legality, objectivity, job relatedness, and assessment accuracy.

However, despite these favorable overall responses to the SI, research is needed to consider the effects of providing greater flexibility in the rating procedures and/or the range of questioning allowed interviewers. Such investigations are necessary to consider potential objections to the structural constraints of the SI and interviewers' inability to seek additional information regarding the answers given.

With regard to rating procedures, recall that Latham and his colleagues have stipulated that the SI is conducted by rating one answer at a time as it is given. Although this approach tends to facilitate the accuracy of each rating (Maurer & Lee, 1997) and enhances the validity of the process (see Jako & Murphy, 1990), it also can become tedious. These factors suggest a need to consider how response scoring affects rating outcomes. Related to this issue is a study conducted by Pulakos and Schmitt (1995), who computed validity of an SI in which dimensional ratings were gathered on two or three items for each dimension and then averaged at the completion of each interview. Results of this study underscore the importance of rating each answer as it is given, because the dimensional rating strategy produced one of the few SI-related studies that yielded a validity coefficient that was not significantly different from zero.

The possibility of expanding the scope of the SI's inquiry process to allow interviewer probing of applicant answers has already received some attention. Evidence that follow-up probing may cause psychometric problems was found by Latham and Skarlicki (1995), who compared the SI to the PBDI (Janz, 1982), a behavioral interview that specifically requires the use of probing questions. Results revealed that the PBDI was less valid and reliable than the SI, thus suggesting that probing may have sensitized applicants to socially desirable responses.

Notwithstanding this dissuasive initial finding, the effect of allowing interviewers to probe responses to each situational item, as is done with the PBDI, needs to be investigated. Such probing may provide valuable supplemental information regarding the knowledge that underlies the applicant's initial responses, as well as the assumptions made by the candidate that need to be explicated if the interviewer is to evaluate the applicant's responses accurately. It also may tap into insights gained from past experiences similar to the situations posed that may be useful for understanding the applicant's responses. An interesting possibility in this line of inquiry might be to compare the SI with a PBDI that includes a scoring guide in order to either support or refute Huffcutt and Arthur's (1994) argument that it is time orientation (future intentions versus past behavior) as well as structure that accounts for the validity of structured interviews.

A final research area suggested by potential objections to the constraints of the SI's structure is to consider combining SI inquiries with questions based on methods used to evaluate other dimensions of applicant suitability. Schuler and Funke (1989) have offered a strategy for combining methods. They have developed a "multimodal interview" that combines 45 SI questions with biographical questions, behavioral scales for evaluating self-presentation questions, and vocational interest and choice questions. Item analysis followed by cross-validation could be used to determine the most appropriate questions (Cureton, 1950).

Applicant Reactions

In the only known study conducted on this issue to date, Latham and Finnegan (1993) examined applicant reactions to the SI from the viewpoint of students who had never experienced an SI and that of employees who were actually hired using this method and had also been exposed to both patterned and unstructured interviews. Those hired through the SI reported no significant differences in the advantages of any of the three interview methods. Students, however, perceived the SI to be more consistent in administration, more likely to foster interrater reliability, and more likely to render objective assessments of their capabilities than alternative interview methods. However, these same students rated the SI lower than an unstructured interview in terms of the degree to which the SI allowed them the ability to say what they wanted to say, feel relaxed, demonstrate their motivation, and earn an evaluation based on their own abilities rather than the interviewer's skills. Based on the students' generally negative reactions to the controls posed by the SI, Latham and Finnegan speculate that the students may have disliked the SI because it limited their ability to control the interview process and inhibited their impression management skills.

One inference of Latham and Finnegan's findings is that the SI may frustrate less qualified applicants who wish to seize control of the interview in order to impress the interviewer with well-rehearsed answers to commonly asked questions regarding their past accomplishments and future goals. Evidence in support of this attribution is offered by Robertson, Iles, Gratton, and Sharpley (1991), who examined the perceptions of managers in a U.K. financial institution who were evaluated for promotion using the SI, biodata questionnaires, and an assessment center. Employees who failed the SI held significantly lower beliefs about its adequacy (i.e., its fairness, accuracy in assessing important qualities, and appropriateness for use in making selection decisions) than those who passed. The negative response by applicants who had been rejected may reflect frustration over their inability to manipulate the SI's results. This explanation is supported by the finding that the mean adequacy rating by applicants who passed the SI ($M = 3.48$, $SD = .71$; 5-point scale) was quite similar to the mean adequacy rating assigned by those who passed each of the employer's two assessment centers ($M = 3.56$, $SD = 1.05$, and $M = 4.02$, $SD = .58$).

Future research on applicant reactions could consider reactions to the SI and other interview techniques from a procedural justice perspective. In particular, researchers could consider the extent to which applicants perceive that the SI and other interview methods conform to four procedural justice rules asserted by Gilliland (1994) and Steiner and Gilliland (1996) to be applicable to selection methods: (a) perceived job relatedness, (b) opportunity to demonstrate ability, (c) interpersonal treatment, and (d) propriety of questions. Such research would be of practical importance because there is evidence that these procedural justice factors influence fairness perceptions (Gilliland, 1994). Further, perceptions of fairness may also influence applicant comments to others about the employer and/or the likelihood that rejected applicants may pursue "discriminatory rejection" legal action.

Economic Considerations

One of the most important practitioner concerns with any method is whether it is economically "worthwhile." This concern elicits perhaps the greatest perceived barrier to the use of the SI and clearly dictates a need for future investigations of the SI's costs and benefits.

With regard to the issue of costs, there is a need to document actual development and user costs. In particular, research is needed to respond to two prominent misconceptions associated with the SI. The first of these pertains to the actual expenditures required to develop the SI scales. Some of the misconception regarding actual costs has arisen from a misinterpretation of the literature by Green, Alter, and Carr (1993), who state that "in a typical SI, the cost of developing anchors for each interview may be prohibitive, exceeding $1000 per question" (p. 205) and that "a typical SI might require $20,000 to $30,000 to develop" (p. 204). These authors cite Campion et al. (1988) as the source for this conclusion. However, Campion et al. (1988) actually state, "Precise development costs were unknown, but they would be small compared with this gain in utility (e.g., $20,000 to $30,000 in salaries)" (p. 34).

A second misconception that may prevent managers from using the SI is the amount of time they believe is required to develop a behavioral scoring guide. The misconception is that the scoring guide essentially is a behaviorally anchored rating scale for each interview question, and that Smith and Kendall's (1963) retranslation process is therefore required. However, all that is required for developing a scoring guide is for subject matter experts (SMEs) in the organization to obtain consensus regarding excellent, average, and poor answers to each SI question (Latham, 1989; Latham & Sue-Chan, 1996). This generally takes no longer than a few minutes per question. SMEs are simply asked to think of the best, the average, and the poorest employees, and to speculate what each of them would say in response to each interview question. The 5, 3, and 1 behavioral benchmarks reflect consensus among the SMEs.

To respond to these misconceptions, future work is needed to specify precisely the amount of time and actual economic expenditures required to develop an SI. Such research should use precise methods such as those associated with time and motion studies to document the procedures involved, the number of employee hours required, and the full range of economic expenditures (downtime, consultant/coordinator costs, and so on) associated with the development of the SI instrument. In addition to such specific inquiries, researchers should develop the convention of routinely reporting such factors in their descriptions of procedures associated with the development of SI scales and other forms of structured interviews constructed for other research purposes. As this information accumulates, practitioners can make informed comparisons between the development costs of the SI and other "competing" interview forms.

One cost concern associated with the SI is the time it takes to do a job analysis using the CIT to identify key behaviors and performance situations. Although there is no one best way to do a job analysis (Levine, Ash, & Bennett, 1980), the developers of the SI (Latham et al., 1980) suggest the use of the critical incident technique because it is a "cornerstone of behavior-based performance measurement systems" (Latham & Wexley, 1994, p. 62). However, research has yet to consider viable alternatives to this method as a means of developing situational scenarios. To examine this issue, job analysis techniques such as functional job analysis (FJA) could be used to generate the SI questions. FJA- and CIT-generated questions could be posed to separate sets of applicants. The researcher could then determine the criterion-related validity of the questions based on the different job analyses to see if there is a significant difference between the coefficients.

Research to date has focused primarily on the SI's decision-making benefits and has left decision makers to speculate about the economic advantages to be gained from using this interviewing approach. To address the potential economic advantages of the SI, researchers might begin by considering factors such as specific and readily identifiable cost savings in interviewer training. Such work might extend that started by Maurer and Fay (1988), who found that even without training, managers using SIs were able to produce ratings more reliable than those achieved by managers trained in the use of conventional interviews. Further studies are needed to determine the amount and form of interviewer training, if any, required to maximize the effectiveness of SI processes. Such work might draw on research concerning interviewing factors important to job candidates (Maurer, Howe, & Lee, 1992) and differences between professional human resource representatives and line managers (Maurer & Howe, 1995) to determine how practitioners might minimize training expenditures and develop training strategies that maximize both the recruiting and the selection potential of the SI.

Studies of economic issues could also consider the savings associated with employers' ability to prevent and defend potential discrimination suits. In order to determine indirect costs in terms of discrimination suits to organizations of not using the SI, researchers could conduct a survey of U.S. EEO/Canadian Human Rights Act settlements broken down by organizational characteristics, such as number of employees and industry, and of organizations that have lost U.S. EEO/Canadian Human Rights

Act cases. The results of such a survey could be used in a loss-prevention/risk-analysis approach to economic assessment.

Finally, research on the economic benefits of SIs should go beyond a focus on traditional job performance behaviors. For example, studies are still needed in response to Latham's (1989) suggestion that the SI constitutes a realistic job preview (Wanous, 1973). In keeping with the research on realistic job previews, efforts might focus on whether (or the degree to which) the SI may reduce voluntary turnover relative to alternative interview techniques, affect job acceptance and subsequent citizenship behavior of newly hired employees, and influence perceived justice by applicants who are rejected. Examination of these questions will require follow-up on hires who have been interviewed using an SI versus another interview technique, and on those individuals who have been rejected. Thus, for example, the effect on the above dependent variables of an SI can be compared with the effects of a PBDI, a conventionally structured interview, and an unstructured interview.

Conclusion

Our purposes in this chapter have been to present the existing research on the SI and to pose an agenda for future study. In offering this agenda, we conclude with three general observations concerning future SI research.

First, it is essential that researchers attend closely to the interests of managers to determine the factors of true importance in deciding the merits of any human resource method/practice. Research concerning the SI has shown a fairly broad attempt to respond to this imperative. However, if future work regarding this method is to have any meaning to those who must decide its fate, researchers must be vigilant in their attention to factors of "real" importance to human resource decision makers.

Second, it is necessary that researchers realize that adoption of industrial/organizational psychology innovation by managers is based on imitation as well as technical merit. This suggests that, as Johns (1993) cogently argues, there is a strong need to publish in practitioner journals the names of organizations where SI studies have been conducted. This is because imitation rather than technical merit often determines whether industrial/organizational psychology innovations are adopted by organizations. As well, the SI should be brought to the attention of decision makers in large, rather than small, organizations, because large organizations tend to be the first to adopt innovations (Johns, 1993).

Third, researchers should look for unique political or crisis opportunities to introduce and examine the SI. As a case in point, the SI itself was developed at the Weyerhaeuser Company in response to two crises: an urgent need for a "quick and dirty" way to identify the employees to be retained after the company purchased a sawmill and a need to respond to changes in Equal Employment Opportunity Commission documentation requirements. In another setting, Scott Paper Company, the SI was introduced and used throughout the company to respond to a need for a method that would get decision makers, prior to hiring applicants, to agree on the behaviors indicative of the organization's values. Thus, in the Weyerhaeuser Company the SI was used successfully to respond to environmental threats, and in the Scott Paper Company the political influence of decision makers led to its implementation throughout the firm. Researchers should continually explore such circumstances for their potential as sources for extending both the richness and the relevance of SI research.

References

Americans with Disabilities Act of 1990, 42 U.S.C.A. § 12101 *et seq.* (West 1993).

Arvey, R. D., & Campion, J. E. (1982). The employment interview: A summary and review of recent research. *Personnel Psychology, 35,* 281-322.

Bandura, A. (1986). *Social foundations of thought and action: A social cognitive theory.* Englewood Cliffs, NJ: Prentice Hall.

Barrick, M. R., & Mount, M. K. (1991). The Big Five personality dimensions and job performance. *Journal of Applied Psychology, 78,* 111-118.

Campion, M. A., Campion, J. E., & Hudson, J. P. (1994). Structured interviewing: A note on incremental validity and alternative question types. *Journal of Applied Psychology, 79,* 998-1002.

Campion, M. A., Pursell, E. D., & Brown, B. K. (1988). Structured interviewing: Raising the psychometric properties of the employment interview. *Personnel Psychology, 41,* 25-42.

Cascio, W. F. (1978). *Applied psychology in personnel management.* Reston, VA: Reston.

Conway, J. M., Jako, R. A., & Goodman, D. F. (1995). A meta-analysis of interrater and internal consistency reliability of selection interviews. *Journal of Applied Psychology, 80,* 565-579.

Cureton, E. E. (1950). Validity, reliability, and baloney. *Educational and Psychological Measurement, 10,* 94-96.

Darlington, R. B. (1990). *Regression and linear models.* New York: McGraw-Hill.

Delery, J. E., Wright, P. M., McArthur, K., & Anderson, D. C. (1994). Cognitive ability tests and the situational interview: A test of incremental validity. *International Journal of Selection and Assessment, 2,* 53-58.

Eder, R. W. (1989). Contextual effects on interview decisions. In R. W. Eder & G. R. Ferris (Eds.), *The employment interview: Theory, research, and practice* (pp. 113-126). Newbury Park, CA: Sage.

Equal Employment Opportunity Commission. (1978). *Uniform guidelines on employee selection procedures.* Washington, DC: Author.

Flanagan, J. C. (1954). The critical incident technique. *Psychological Bulletin, 51,* 327-358.

Gellatly, I. R. (1996). Conscientiousness and past performance: Test of a cognitive process. *Journal of Applied Psychology, 81,* 474-482.

Gilliland, S. W. (1994). Effects of procedural and distributive justice on reactions to a selection system. *Journal of Applied Psychology, 79*, 691-701.

Green, P. C., Alter, P., & Carr, A. F. (1993). Development of standard anchors for scoring generic past-behavior questions in structured interviews. *International Journal of Selection and Assessment, 1*, 203-212.

Harris, M. M. (1989). Reconsidering the employment interview: A review of recent literature and suggestions for future research. *Personnel Psychology, 42*, 691-726.

Huffcutt, A. I., & Arthur, W., Jr. (1994). Hunter and Hunter (1984) revisited: Interview validity for entry-level jobs. *Journal of Applied Psychology, 79*, 184-190.

Huffcutt, A. I., Roth, P. L., & McDaniel, M. A. (1996). A meta-analytic investigation of cognitive ability in employment interview evaluations: Moderating characteristics and implications for incremental validity. *Journal of Applied Psychology, 81*, 459-473.

Hunter, J. E., & Hirsch, H. R. (1987). Application of meta-analysis. In C. L. Cooper & I. T. Robertson (Eds.), *International review of industrial and organizational psychology* (pp. 321-357). Chichester: John Wiley.

Jako, R. A., & Murphy, K. R. (1990). Distributional ratings, judgment decomposition, and their impact on interrater agreement and rating accuracy. *Journal of Applied Psychology, 75*, 500-505.

Janz, J. T. (1982). Initial comparisons of patterned behavior description interviews versus unstructured interviews. *Journal of Applied Psychology, 67*, 577-580.

Johns, G. (1993). Constraints on the adoption of psychology-based personnel practices: Lessons from organizational innovation. *Personnel Psychology, 46*, 569-592.

Kataoka, H. C., Latham, G. P., & Whyte, G. R. (1997). The relative resistance of the situational, patterned behavior, and conventionally structured interviews to anchoring effects. *Human Performance, 10*, 47-63.

Latham, G. P. (1989). The reliability, validity, and practicality of the situational interview. In R. W. Eder & G. R. Ferris (Eds.), *The employment interview: Theory, research, and practice* (pp. 169-182). Newbury Park, CA: Sage.

Latham, G. P., & Finnegan, B. J. (1993). Perceived practicality of unstructured, patterned, and situational interviews. In H. Schuler, J. L. Farr, & M. Smith (Eds.), *Personnel selection and assessment: Individual and organizational perspectives* (pp. 41-55). Hillsdale, NJ: Lawrence Erlbaum.

Latham, G. P., & Locke, E. A. (1991). Self-regulation through goal setting. *Organizational Behavior and Human Decision Processes, 50*, 212-247.

Latham, G. P., & Saari, L. M. (1984). Do people do what they say? Further studies on the situational interview. *Journal of Applied Psychology, 69*, 569-573.

Latham, G. P., Saari, L. M., Pursell, E. D., & Campion, M. A. (1980). The situational interview. *Journal of Applied Psychology, 65*, 422-427.

Latham, G. P., & Skarlicki, D. (1995). Criterion-related validity of the situational and patterned behavior description interviews with organizational citizenship behavior. *Human Performance, 8*, 67-80.

Latham, G. P., & Sue-Chan, C. (1996). A legally defensible interview for selecting the best. In R. S. Barrett (Ed.), *Fair employment strategies in human resource management* (pp. 134-143). New York: Quorum.

Latham, G. P., & Sue-Chan, C. (1999). A meta-analysis of the situational interview: An enumerative review of reasons for its validity. *Canadian Psychology, 40*, 56-67.

Latham, G. P., & Wexley, K. N. (1994). *Increasing productivity through performance appraisal* (2nd ed.). Reading, MA: Addison-Wesley.

Lawler, E. E. (1967). The multitrait-multirater approach to measuring managerial job performance. *Journal of Applied Psychology, 51,* 369-381.

Levine, E. L., Ash, R. A., & Bennett, N. (1980). Exploratory comparative study of four job analysis methods. *Journal of Applied Psychology, 65,* 524-535.

Lin, T.-R., & Adrian, N. (1993, May). *Multi-method multi-dimension structure interviewing: A field study.* Paper presented at the annual meeting of the Society for Industrial and Organizational Psychology, San Francisco.

Lin, T.-R., Dobbins, G. H., & Farh, J.-L. (1992). A field study of race and age similarity effects on interview ratings in conventional and situational interviews. *Journal of Applied Psychology, 77,* 363-371.

Lin, T.-R., Dobbins, G. H., Farh, J.-L., Martin, L., Hrowal, H., & Regev, R. (1994, August). *Effects of gender, race, and age similarity on interview ratings in a one-rater-panel situational interview.* Paper presented at the annual meeting of the American Psychological Association, Los Angeles.

Locke, E. A., & Latham, G. P. (1990). *A theory of goal setting and task performance.* Englewood Cliffs, NJ: Prentice Hall.

Maurer, S. D., & Fair, B. L. (1988). Examination of rating agreement and rater error in the use of situational interviews. In *Proceedings of the 1988 meetings of the Southern Management Association.*

Maurer, S. D., & Fay, C. (1988). Effects of situational interviews, conventional structured interviews, and training on interview rating agreement: An experimental analysis. *Personnel Psychology, 41,* 329-344.

Maurer, S. D., & Howe, V. (1995). Comparing personnel representatives and line managers/engineers as engineering recruiters: An application of the elaboration likelihood model of persuasive communication. *Journal of High Technology Management Research, 6,* 243-259.

Maurer, S. D., Howe, V., & Lee, T. W. (1992). Organizational recruiting as marketing management: An interdisciplinary study of engineering graduates. *Personnel Psychology, 45,* 807-833.

Maurer, S. D., & Lee, T. W. (1994). Toward a resolution of contrast error in the employment interview: A test of the situational interview. In D. P. Moore (Ed.), *Best papers proceedings: Academy of Management* (pp. 132-136). Madison, WI: Omnipress.

Maurer, S. D., & Lee, T. W. (1997). Situational interview accuracy in a multiple rating context. In L. N. Dosier & J. B. Keys (Eds.), *Academy of Management: Best paper proceedings* (pp. 149-153). Statesboro: Georgia Southern University, College of Business Administration, Office of Publications and Faculty Research.

Maurer, S. D., & Lee, T. W. (in press). Accuracy of the situational interview in rating multiple job candidates. *Journal of Business and Psychology.*

McDaniel, M. A., Whetzel, D. L., Schmidt, F. L., & Maurer, S. D. (1994). The validity of employment interviews: A comprehensive review and meta-analysis. *Journal of Applied Psychology, 79,* 599-616.

Motowidlo, S. J., Carter, G. W., Dunnette, M. D., Tippins, N., Werner, S., Burnett, J. R., & Vaughan, M. J. (1992). Studies of the structured behavioral interview. *Journal of Applied Psychology, 77,* 571-587.

Motowidlo, S. J., Dunnette, M. D., & Carter, G. W. (1990). An alternative selection procedure: The low-fidelity simulation. *Journal of Applied Psychology, 75,* 640-647.

Pulakos, E. D., & Schmitt, N. (1995). Experience-based and situational interview questions: Studies of validity. *Personnel Psychology, 48,* 289-308.

Robertson, I. T., Gratton, L., & Rout, U. (1990). The validity of situational interviews for administrative jobs. *Journal of Organizational Behavior, 11,* 69-76.

Robertson, I. T., Iles, P. A., Gratton, L., & Sharpley, D. (1991). The impact of personnel selection and assessment methods on candidates. *Human Relations, 44,* 963-982.

Roth, P. L., & Switzer, F. S. (1995). A Monte Carlo analysis of missing data techniques in an HRM setting. *Journal of Management, 21,* 1003-1023.

Schmidt, F. L. (1988). The problem of group differences in ability test scores in employment selection. *Journal of Vocational Behavior, 33,* 272-292.

Schuler, H., & Funke, U. (1989). The interview as a multimodal procedure. In R. W. Eder & G. R. Ferris (Eds.), *The employment interview: Theory, research, and practice* (pp. 183-192). Newbury Park, CA: Sage.

Smith, P. C., & Kendall, L. M. (1963). Retranslation of expectations: An approach to the construction of unambiguous anchors for rating scales. *Journal of Applied Psychology, 47,* 149-155.

Steiner, D. D., & Gilliland, S. W. (1996). Fairness reactions to personnel selection techniques in France and the United States. *Journal of Applied Psychology, 81,* 134-141.

Sue-Chan, C., Latham, G. P., & Evans, M. G. (1995, June). *The construct validity of the situational and patterned behavior description interviews: Cognitive ability, tacit knowledge, and self-efficacy as correlates.* Poster session presented at the annual meeting of the Canadian Psychological Association, Charlottetown, Prince Edward Island.

Thompson, D. E., & Thompson, T. A. (1982). Court standards for job analysis in test validation. *Personnel Psychology, 35,* 865-874.

Viswesvaran, C., & Ones, D. S. (1995). Theory testing: Combining psychometric meta-analysis and structural equations modeling. *Personnel Psychology, 48,* 865-883.

Wagner, R. K. (1987). Tacit knowledge in everyday intelligent behavior. *Journal of Personality and Social Psychology, 52,* 1236-1247.

Wagner, R. K., & Sternberg, R. J. (1985). Practical intelligence in real-world pursuits: The role of tacit knowledge. *Journal of Personality and Social Psychology, 49,* 436-458.

Wagner, R. K., & Sternberg, R. J. (1986). Tacit knowledge and intelligence in the everyday world. In R. J. Sternberg & R. K. Wagner (Eds.), *Practical intelligence: Nature and origins of competence in the everyday world* (pp. 51-83). Cambridge: Cambridge University Press.

Wanous, J. P. (1973). Effects of a realistic job preview on job acceptance, job attitudes, and job survival. *Journal of Applied Psychology, 51,* 327-332.

Weekley, J. A., & Gier, J. A. (1987). Reliability and validity of the situational interview for a sales position. *Journal of Applied Psychology, 72,* 484-487.

Wiesner, W. H., & Cronshaw, S. F. (1988). A meta-analytic investigation of the impact of interview format and degree of structure on the validity of the employment interview. *Journal of Occupational Psychology, 61,* 275-290.

Wright, O. R. (1969). Summary of research on the selection interview since 1964. *Personnel Psychology, 22,* 391-413.

10

Asking About Past Behavior Versus Hypothetical Behavior

Stephan J. Motowidlo

Results of many studies confirm that structured interviews are usefully valid. In a meta-analysis, Wiesner and Cronshaw (1988) found mean, uncorrected validity estimates of .35 for structured, individual interviews, based on 32 coefficients and 7,873 cases. In another meta-analysis, McDaniel, Whetzel, Schmidt, and Maurer (1994) found mean, uncorrected validity estimates of .25 for structured, individual interviews, based on 61 coefficients and 8,944 cases. And, of course, validity estimates can be much higher when adjusted for estimates of reliability and range restriction.

Although the validity of structured interviews in general is empirically well established, the reasons such interviews are valid are not fully understood. One possibility is that structured interviews are empirically valid because they measure constructs causally linked to job performance through questions that are job related and behaviorally focused (Hakel, 1989). If this is true, we need to know more about what constructs structured interviews measure that might explain their predictive validity (Huffcutt, Roth, & McDaniel, 1996; Latham, 1989; Schuler & Funke,

1989). This chapter examines the potential of two widely used forms of structured interview questions for assessing constructs that are thought to be related to performance.

Questions About the Past and About the Future

One well-known type of structured questioning format focuses on applicants' past behavior. Past-oriented questions make up the patterned behavior interview format (Janz, 1982, 1989) and the structured behavioral interview format (Motowidlo et al., 1992). They ask applicants to describe what they did in past situations that resemble situations that might happen on the job. Here is an example of an interview question designed to tap leadership potential by asking about behavior in a past situation (Motowidlo & Burnett, 1995):

> I'd like you to think of a time when you were working with other people, either on a special project or on an everyday task, when there was some type of crisis and it was necessary for someone to take charge. What was your role in this situation?

Another well-known type of structured questioning format focuses on applicants' hypothetical future behavior. Future-oriented questions characterize the situational interview format (Latham, 1989; Latham, Saari, Pursell, & Campion, 1980). A form of low-fidelity simulation (Motowidlo, Dunnette, & Carter, 1990; Motowidlo, Hanson, & Crafts, in press; Motowidlo & Tippins, 1993), it presents situations that might happen on the job and asks applicants what they would do if they were in those situations. Here is an example of an interview question designed to tap leadership potential by asking about behavior in a hypothetical future situation (Motowidlo & Burnett, 1995):

> I'd like you to imagine that your supervisor has asked you to join an established task force to fill a vacancy left by another manager who recently resigned. You have an interest in the project they were working on and you agree to at least sit in on a meeting this afternoon. Thirty minutes into the meeting, you feel that the program the task force is ready to implement is inadequate and will have many problems. What would you do?

Questions in both formats are usually developed from results of job analyses, and both types are typically scored according to the degree to which answers describe effective actions in either the hypothetical or actual situations posed in the questions. Other types of structured question formats have also been developed and have been shown to be predictively useful (e.g., Campion, Pursell, & Brown, 1988), but in this chapter I restrict attention to these two because they focus more specifically and exclusively on behavior and because differences between them point to implications for differences in the constructs they measure.

Habitual, Intentional Behavior in Answers to Questions About the Past

Janz (1989) argues that the reason answers to interview questions about behavior in actual past situations can predict job performance is basically that past behavior predicts future behavior. Answers to such interview questions "reveal specific choices applicants have made in the past" (p. 159), and "the more long-standing the applicant's behavior pattern in the past, the more likely it will predict behavior in the future" (pp. 159-160).

Two elements of this argument bear special attention. First, behaviors described in applicants' answers are presumed to be deliberate choices, not mindless, reflex actions performed without consideration for their consequences. If they are choices, they are driven by factors that affect motivation to behave in one way but not in other ways, to behave more or less energetically, and for some period of time; they are shaped by goals and intentions. Second, the more consistent the behaviors are over a number of occasions in the past, the better they are presumed to be able to predict job performance. When behavior patterns have been consistent across occasions in the past, they can be expected to continue to be consistent in similar situations in the future. Thus, when people find themselves in similar situations on the job, they should make similar choices, form similar intentions, and consequently behave in a manner similar to the way they say they behaved in their answers to interview questions. According to this argument, therefore, answers to questions about past behavior predict job performance because they describe habitual patterns of intentional behavior that applicants perform in situations that are like situations that happen on the job.

This argument assumes that applicants give truthful answers to these interview questions. However, people in job interviews are probably highly motivated to make favorable impressions on their interviewers (Baron, 1989) and would be understandably eager to put their best foot forward and tempted to exaggerate their strong points while downplaying their weaknesses. It is not clear how easy it is for applicants to answer interview questions by fabricating past experiences that they think will create a favorable impression, especially if skilled interviewers probe extensively for details about the actions and circumstances surrounding those experiences. At the very least, however, applicants might say that they cannot think of a time when they were in a situation like the one described in the interview question if they cannot remember a time when they performed effectively in such a situation. Or they might choose simply to relate less detailed information about past actions that they think are not especially flattering.

The argument also assumes that situations described in interview questions are similar to situations that happen on the job. One implication of this is that questions about past behavior might become less valid if job situations become less stable and less predictable. Speculations that organizations are being forced to adapt to increasingly turbulent and unpredictable environmental pressures by developing flexible work structures based on ever-changing team assignments instead of rigidly defined, individual jobs (e.g., Motowidlo & Schmit, in press) suggest that it might become more difficult to anticipate the kinds of job situations that will confront incumbents with enough precision to represent their essential psychological features in interview questions. This implies that the usefulness of past behavior for predicting future job behavior might be diminished if the situational influences that govern future behavior cannot be anticipated under more organic and flexible organizational forms of the future.

Habitual, Intentional Behavior in Answers to Questions About the Future

Latham (1989) argues that the reason answers to questions about behavior in hypothetical future situations can predict job performance is that they measure intentions. This argument derives from a basic principle of goal-setting theory (Locke, 1968; Locke & Latham, 1990), that the most immediate antecedent of behavior is intention or goal. The idea is that if interviewers present applicants with problem situations that might happen on the job and ask them what they would do if they were in those situations, the applicants will reveal their intended actions for those situations. Then, when similar situations occur on the job, people transform their intentions into actions and behave according to the intended behavior they described in their answers to the interview questions when they were applicants.

There is a great deal of empirical support for predictions made by goal-setting theory about effects of goals on performance level (Locke & Latham, 1990). There is also a great deal of empirical evidence that, under certain conditions, behavior can be predicted from intention quite accurately (Ajzen, 1991). And there is a great deal of empirical support for the validity of interviews that use structured questions about behavior in hypothetical future situations (McDaniel et al., 1994). However, this still leaves open the question of whether such interview questions measure intentions and are valid because they measure intentions.

The argument that intentions explain the validity of questions about hypothetical behavior in future situations rests on two assumptions. First is the assumption that the questions do measure intentions, that what people say they would do in hypothetical situations accurately represents their true intentions for action in such situations. Second is the assumption that the intentions people have when applying for a job and answering interview questions predict what they actually do later when they are on the job and confronted with those situations.

The first assumption is vulnerable to the chance that applicants might be inclined to try to deceive recruiters by telling them what they think will create a favorable impression (Baron, 1989). Latham (1989) recognizes this possibility in his admonition that interview questions about behavior in hypothetical future situations should not be so obvious that applicants can tell what the correct answers are. He recommends that interview questions be pilot tested, and that any question that is answered correctly by everyone in the pilot test should be discarded. Although this is sound advice and should help to avoid problems of socially desirable responding and outright dissimulation, it does not guarantee that applicants will answer questions by describing their true intentions for action in the situations posed. If applicants answer questions with something other than their true intentions and the interview is predictively valid anyway, it must be valid for some other reason.

The second assumption concerns the predictive potential of intentions. As mentioned, there is a great deal of evidence that intentions predict behavior quite accurately—under certain conditions (Ajzen, 1991). According to Ajzen (1985), "Intentions can be expected to predict behavior only when two conditions are met. First, the measure of intention available to the investigator must reflect respondents' intentions as they exist just prior to performance of the behavior; and, second, the behavior must be under volitional control" (p. 18).

With respect to the first condition, Ajzen (1985) mentions several factors that could change intentions between the time they are measured and the time the behavior is to be performed. One is the salience of beliefs. According to the principle that a goal's avoidance gradient changes more quickly with decreasing psychological distance than does its approach gradient, if people believe that a behavior they intend to perform has both advantages and some disadvantages, their beliefs about its disadvantages should become more salient as the time for actually performing the behavior draws near. Conceivably, therefore, by the time the occasion for performing the behavior arrives, beliefs about its negative features could outweigh beliefs about its positive features, and the intention to perform it would change accordingly. Another factor is new information. After forming an intention to perform a particular behavior, but before actually performing it, people might learn new information that alters their beliefs about its advantages or disadvantages and change their intentions for that reason. Both factors operate to destabilize intentions over time. Thus, the longer the time interval between measuring an intention and the occasion for performing the intended behavior, the more opportunity these two factors have to change the intention.

With respect to the second condition, Ajzen (1991) argues that when a particular behavior is under someone's volitional control, intention alone can predict it quite accurately. However, to the degree that the performance of a behavior depends on factors that are not under someone's control, another variable besides intention must also be taken into account: perceived behavioral control. Tubbs and Ekeberg (1991) make a similar point by including a variable they call action control as a moderator of the relation between intention and action in their model of intentional work behavior. However, they argue that the theoretically important variable is how much control people actually have over an action, not how much control they perceive.

Intentions measured in selection interviews are about behaviors that would be performed on the job. Months or even years could pass before someone on the job has an opportunity to perform behaviors described in answers to interview questions. If this is ample time for belief salience and new information to affect intentions expressed in a job interview, they could not be expected to predict the behavior someone actually performs months or years later on the job. Even if they are good measures of intentions that are stable over time, unless they ask about behaviors that are predominantly under a person's volitional control, they are unlikely to be good predictors of behavior on the job. If people do not have the abilities or skills needed to perform an intended behavior, if external resources needed to perform the behavior turn out to be unavailable, or if unexpected situational constraints emerge to interfere with the performance of the behavior, their intentions as job applicants will not accurately predict their behavior as job incumbents.

In sum, the assertion that questions about behavior in hypothetical future situations predict job performance because they measure applicants' intentions assumes that the intentions are stable over time and that they involve behaviors that are under job incumbents' volitional control. Now, if intentions are stable over time, their stability must extend to the past as well as to the future. That is, intentions that applicants express in a job interview about behavior in a particular situation should be the same as the intentions they hold when those situations actually occur on the job and should also be the same as the intentions they held when similar situations occurred in the past before they were applicants. In addition, if the intended behavior is consistently under volitional control, the intention should be a very good predictor of the behavior in all the situations in which it is engaged.

Therefore, if intentions are stable and if intended behaviors are under volitional control, the intended behavior will closely resemble the actual behavior in all past and future occurrences of the specified situation. Under these conditions, information about actual behavior in a situation that occurred in the past is identical to information about intended behavior if that situation were hypothetically to occur in the future. This means that if questions about behavior in hypothetical future situations predict job performance because they measure intentions, they are valid for the same reason that answers to questions about behavior in actual past situations are valid—answers to both types of questions describe habitual patterns of intentional behavior that applicants perform in situations similar to situations that are likely to occur on the job.

This analysis points to three sets of factors that make it unlikely that the reason questions about behavior in hypothetical future situations predict job performance is that they measure intentions. The factors are, first, pressures on applicants to create a favorable impression in the interview; second, possible changes in intentions over time; and third, possible lack of volitional control over intended behaviors. Furthermore, if questions about behavior in future situations are designed in such a way that they are immune to effects of these factors, the information they provide is the same as information that questions about behavior in actual past situations are presumed to provide because actual behavior in the past situation is the same as intended behavior in the same hypothetical future situation under these conditions.

Ajzen (1991) argues that the correlation between past behavior and future behavior is essentially their reliability or stability and represents the maximum degree to which the future behavior can be predicted. Therefore, if intention is the only immediate determinant of future behavior, as it would be if the intention is perfectly stable and the intended behavior is perfectly under volitional control, the correlation between intention and future behavior should be the same as the correlation between past behavior and future behavior; intention and past behavior should predict future behavior with equal accuracy. If the behavior is not perfectly under volitional control, Ajzen's theory of planned behavior predicts that in addition to intention, perceived behavioral control is another determinant of future behavior. In this case, the correlation between intention and future behavior should be less than the correlation between past behavior and future behavior, assuming that perceived behavioral control is stable and affected past behavior in the same way that it will affect future behavior.

Consequently, if questions about behavior in hypothetical future situations do measure stable intentions about behaviors that are under volitional control, they should predict job performance as accurately as questions about behavior in actual past situations. However, if the intentions they measure are not stable or if they involve behaviors that are not under volitional control, questions about behavior in hypothetical future situations should predict job performance less accurately than questions about behavior in actual past situations. This might explain results of several recent studies that directly compared the validity of questions about past behavior with the validity of questions about future behavior and found that questions about future behavior were more valid (Bosshardt, 1992; Campion, Campion, & Hudson, 1994; Motowidlo & Burnett, 1995; Pulakos & Schmitt, 1995).

Job Knowledge in Answers to Questions About the Future

If people do not give truthful answers to questions about hypothetical future behavior, if they give truthful answers but their intentions are unstable, or if they do not have volitional control over their intended actions, that question format cannot attribute its predictive validity to constructs that reflect habitual patterns of intentional behavior. It might be possible to control socially desirable answers and outright dissimulation to some degree through careful questioning, but issues related to the stability of intentions over time and volitional control over intended behaviors are less tractable. They pose serious obstacles to the argument that questions about hypothetical future behavior are valid because they measure intentions.

This is not to deny that such questions are valid. Indeed, results of meta-analyses provide ample support for the validity of interview questions about hypothetical future behavior (McDaniel et al., 1994), even if results of some recent studies suggest they might not be quite as valid as questions about actual past behavior (Bosshardt, 1992; Campion et al., 1994; Motowidlo & Burnett, 1995; Pulakos & Schmitt, 1995). However, if their validity cannot be compellingly explained through intentional mechanisms, we must consider some other explanation.

Another possible explanation is that they measure a form of job knowledge. This explanation does not require that applicants be truthful when they say how they would handle a hypothetical job situation. Neither does it require that any intentional components to their answers be stable across time. In fact, their intentions are simply not relevant for this explanation. But it does rest on other assumptions. First is the assumption that applicants describe what they believe to be the best way to deal with the hypothetical situation described in the interview question, a reasonable assumption given that applicants are trying to promote a favorable impression in order to get the job. Second is the assumption that incumbents who know what the best action is in a particular job situation are likely to try to perform it, again a reasonable assumption given that incumbents want to perform effectively on the job. Third is the assumption that incumbents who know what action should be taken in a particular situation also have the skills necessary to perform the action effectively. This is a more tenuous assumption. However, if similar kinds of traits and learning opportunities contribute to individual differences in both knowledge and skill (Motowidlo, Borman, & Schmit, 1997), it is at least reasonable to expect a substantial correlation between them.

Conclusions and Implications

A reasonable explanation for the predictive validity of interview questions about actual past behavior is that they measure habitual patterns of intentional behavior in situations that resemble situations that occur on the job. The more consistent the behaviors are across situations in the past, and the more similar the situations are to situations that occur frequently on the job, the more valid those questions should be.

If questions about hypothetical future behavior are answered truthfully and people describe their real intentions about behavior in the situations posed, they might be predictively valid for the same reason, provided that their intentions are stable over time and their intended actions are under their volitional control. However, another and probably more likely explanation for the validity of questions about hypothetical future behavior is that they measure a form of job knowledge. This explanation makes no assumptions about applicants' intentions during the interview, but does assume that applicants report what they think is the best way to deal with situations described in interview questions, will try to perform these actions when the situations occur on the job, and have the skills necessary to perform them effectively. These conclusions have several implications for research and practice:

1. It might be possible to improve the validity of questions about actual past behavior by ensuring that they elicit behavioral reports that are as consistent as possible from one example of a situation to another. This requires studies of the reliability with which applicants give similar responses to questions that ask about different past occurrences of the same type of situation.

2. Another way to improve the validity of past-oriented questions might be to ensure that situations described in the questions resemble as closely as possible situations that occur frequently on the job and that have important consequences for job effectiveness. This requires studies of the kinds of problem situations that occur on the job, their frequencies, their signifi-

cance for overall effectiveness, and variability among incumbents in how effectively they deal with them.

3. The first two points also apply to future-oriented questions. Steps should be taken to ensure that they too elicit consistent responses across different versions of the same hypothetical situation. Also, the hypothetical situations should be psychologically similar to important situations that occur frequently on the job and that show wide variability in the effectiveness with which different incumbents handle them.

4. If future-oriented questions are designed to measure habitual patterns of intentional behavior, we need studies of the stability of intentions formed for different kinds of hypothetical situations. We need to know more about the kinds of intentions that are less likely to change over time, and we should use that information to ensure that future-oriented questions concern intentions that are as stable as possible.

5. If future-oriented questions are designed to measure habitual patterns of intentional behavior, we also need studies of the volitional control associated with different kinds of intentions. We need to know more about the kinds of intentions that are under maximum volitional control, and we should ensure that future-oriented questions target them in particular. An alternative strategy might be to supplement these questions with follow-up questions designed to assess perceived behavioral control (Ajzen, 1991), questions about applicants' beliefs that they can actually succeed in carrying out the intentions they describe, because they might add incremental validity to questions about behavioral intentions.

6. If future-oriented questions are designed to measure job knowledge, perhaps they would measure it more validly if they were reworded to ask applicants what they think is the best thing to do in a hypothetical situation, rather than what they would do.

References

Ajzen, I. (1985). From intentions to actions: A theory of planned behavior. In J. Kuhl & J. Beckman (Eds.), *Action-control: From cognition to behavior* (pp. 11-39). Heidelberg: Springer.

Ajzen, I. (1991). The theory of planned behavior. *Organizational Behavior and Human Decision Processes, 50,* 179-211.

Baron, R. A. (1989). Impression management by applicants during employment interviews: The "too much of a good thing" effect. In R. W. Eder & G. R. Ferris (Eds.), *The employment interview: Theory, research, and practice* (pp. 204-215). Newbury Park, CA: Sage.

Bosshardt, M. J. (1992). *Situational interviews versus behavior description interviews: A comparative validity study.* Unpublished doctoral dissertation, University of Minnesota.

Campion, M. A., Campion, J. E., & Hudson, J. P. (1994). Structured interviewing: A note on incremental validity and alternative question types. *Journal of Applied Psychology, 79,* 998-1002.

Campion, M. A., Pursell, E. D., & Brown, B. K. (1988). Structured interviewing: Raising the psychometric standards of the employment interview. *Personnel Psychology, 41,* 25-42.

Hakel, M. D. (1989). The state of employment interview theory and research. In R. W. Eder & G. R. Ferris (Eds.), *The employment interview: Theory, research, and practice* (pp. 285-293). Newbury Park, CA: Sage.

Huffcutt, A. I., Roth, P. L., & McDaniel, M. A. (1996). A meta-analytic investigation of cognitive ability in employment interview evaluations: Moderating characteristics and implications for incremental validity. *Journal of Applied Psychology, 81,* 459-473.

Janz, J. T. (1982). Initial comparisons of patterned behavior description interviews versus unstructured interviews. *Journal of Applied Psychology, 67,* 577-580.

Janz, J. T. (1989). The patterned behavior description interview: The best prophet of the future is the past. In R. W. Eder & G. R. Ferris (Eds.), *The employment interview: Theory, research, and practice* (pp. 158-168). Newbury Park, CA: Sage.

Latham, G. P. (1989). The reliability, validity, and practicality of the situational interview. In R. W. Eder & G. R. Ferris (Eds.), *The employment interview: Theory, research, and practice* (pp. 169-182). Newbury Park, CA: Sage.

Latham, G. P., Saari, L. M., Pursell, E. D., & Campion, M. A. (1980). The situational interview. *Journal of Applied Psychology, 65,* 422-427.

Locke, E. A. (1968). Towards a theory of task motivation and incentives. *Organizational Behavior and Human Performance, 3,* 157-189.

Locke, E. A., & Latham, G. P. (1990). *A theory of goal setting and task performance.* Englewood Cliffs, NJ: Prentice Hall.

McDaniel, M. A., Whetzel, D. L., Schmidt, F. L., & Maurer, S. D. (1994). The validity of employment interviews: A comprehensive review and meta-analysis. *Journal of Applied Psychology, 79,* 599-616.

Motowidlo, S. J., Borman, W. C., & Schmit, M. J. (1997). A theory of individual differences in task and contextual performance. *Human Performance, 10,* 71-83.

Motowidlo, S. J., & Burnett, J. R. (1995). Aural and visual sources of validity in structured employment interviews. *Organizational Behavior and Human Decision Processes, 61,* 239-249.

Motowidlo, S. J., Carter, G. W., Dunnette, M. D., Tippins, N., Werner, S., Burnett, J. R., & Vaughan, M. J. (1992). Studies of the structured behavioral interview. *Journal of Applied Psychology, 77,* 571-587.

Motowidlo, S. J., Dunnette, M. D., & Carter, G. W. (1990). An alternative selection procedure: The low-fidelity simulation. *Journal of Applied Psychology, 75,* 640-647.

Motowidlo, S. J., Hanson, M. A., & Crafts, J. L. (in press). Low fidelity simulations. In D. L. Whetzel & G. R. Wheaton (Eds.), *Applied measurement methods in industrial psychology.* Palo Alto, CA: Consulting Psychologists Press.

Motowidlo, S. J., & Schmit, M. J. (in press). Performance assessment in unique jobs. In D. R. Ilgen & E. D. Pulakos (Eds.), *The changing nature of work performance: Implications for staffing, personnel actions, and development.* San Francisco: Jossey-Bass.

Motowidlo, S. J., & Tippins, N. (1993). Further studies of the low-fidelity simulation in the form of a situational inventory. *Journal of Occupational and Organizational Psychology, 66,* 337-344.

Pulakos, E. D., & Schmitt, N. (1995). Experience-based and situational interview questions: Studies of validity. *Personnel Psychology, 48,* 289-308.

Schuler, H., & Funke, U. (1989). The interview as a multimodal procedure. In R. W. Eder & G. R. Ferris (Eds.), *The employment interview: Theory, research, and practice* (pp. 183-192). Newbury Park, CA: Sage.

Tubbs, M. E., & Ekeberg, S. E. (1991). The role of intentions in work motivation: Implications for goal-setting theory and research. *Academy of Management Review, 16,* 180-199.

Wiesner, W. H., & Cronshaw, S. F. (1988). A meta-analytic investigation of the impact of interview format and degree of structure on the validity of the employment interview. *Journal of Occupational Psychology, 61,* 275-290.

Part III

The Interviewer's
Decision-Making Process

The contributions to Part III examine interviewer decision-making processes. In Chapter 11, Eder addresses the context of the interview. Perhaps because of its use as a selection test, there has been limited research regarding the role of context on interview processes and outcomes. Eder attempts to correct this state of affairs by proposing four distinct dimensions of perceived interview context from an interactionist perspective: task clarity, interview purpose, consequentiality, and accountability. Because of the very limited research on several of these variables as they apply to the employment interview, Eder draws upon research from other areas, such as performance appraisal, to offer insight into how these contextual factors may influence interviewer decision making.

Of particular focus in Eder's chapter is the section on accountability, which Dipboye and Jackson also address in Chapter 15 as a potential explanation for why more experienced interviewers do not necessarily make more accurate selection decisions. The suggestion that interviewers be held accountable for their judgments may be effective, although this raises the question, Accountable to whom?—a question that we address at greater length in Chapter 21.

To what extent is the interviewer motivated to ask the right questions, spend time gathering relevant information, and process carefully the gathered information to make the best decision? A model of the determinants and outcomes of interviewer motivation is overdue.

There are potentially other contextual factors beyond the four that Eder discusses in Chapter 11. One potentially interesting aspect of context that researchers might want to consider is the nature of the relationship between the interviewer and the applicant. That is, the applicant may be a current employee (e.g., seeking a promotion), a past employee (e.g., returning to the organization), or someone the interviewer knows personally. Although there has been some research in the performance appraisal area on degree of personal acquaintance, we know of no such research in the employment interview area. Perceived legal consequences (e.g., likelihood that a lawsuit might be filed) may also constitute a contextual factor of some interest (see Roehling, Campion, & Arvey, Chapter 3, this volume). It seems reasonable to expect that interviewer fear of legal repercussions will affect decision making, yet there has been very little research on this contextual variable. Aside from some rather obvious factors that are likely to be affected by this variable (e.g., what questions are asked), concern over legal consequences may affect the importance accorded various factors (e.g., perhaps more objective factors, such as grade point average, would be weighted more heavily than more subjective factors, such as enthusiasm), use of note taking, and amount of time spent in making a decision. Given the attention paid to legal considerations in staffing decisions, this variable may be an important contextual factor.

The second and third chapters in this section address information processing during the interview. In Chapter 12, Dougherty and Turban discuss research regarding the tendency of interviewers to confirm their initial perceptions of applicants. As these authors conclude, the results of these studies are somewhat mixed, and there has been only limited field research, where the effect may be stronger. It is important to note that this research has been conducted in interview settings with little or no structure. The effects of confirmatory behavior using more structured interview approaches has not been examined. One important task for future research, then, is the examination of the effect of confirmatory behavior on more structured interview approaches. For example, for moderately structured interviews where there is some choice of questions, one might examine whether confirmatory behavior leads to one question being picked over a different question. As Dougherty and Turban discuss near the end of their chapter, confirmatory behavior may also affect the use of nonverbal behavior, through which even a highly structured interview may be affected.

A major question that Dougherty and Turban pose concerns whether confirmatory behavior reduces validity. Although the presumption of this literature is that such behavior reduces interview validity, these authors argue that confirmatory behavior may actually increase validity. Their argument is based on the premise that in attempting to confirm various assumptions about the candidate, the interviewer will become more engaged in seeking out information. This is an interesting thesis in need of empirical examination.

We suggest two additional questions that future researchers should explore. First, what is the effect of confirmatory behavior on applicant perceptions? It seems likely that an interviewer who is trying to confirm his or her first impressions may be perceived more positively by a highly qualified candidate than would an interviewer who is not using this strategy, whereas an interviewer who is trying to confirm his or her first impressions may be perceived more negatively by a poorly qualified candidate. Thus, we would predict an interaction between degree of confirmatory behavior and candidate qualifications.

Second, we recommend that the construct of confirmatory behavior be more fully developed. Most of the research that Dougherty and Turban describe addresses the type (i.e., confirmatory or disconfirmatory) of questions asked. Only one study they review included a larger range of predictor variables, such as number of questions asked and use of follow-up questions. We suggest that a more complete understanding of confirmatory behavior will be gained when researchers consider a wider variety of measures.

In Chapter 13, Kacmar and Young extend the concept of unfavorable information by distinguishing between direct and indirect types of information. After first reviewing the extant literature on unfavorable information, they proceed to define what is meant by "indirect" unfavorable information and, based on a content analysis of some interviews, offer three categories of such information: missing the information, missing the mark, and missing the opportunity. They then describe how these categories may mesh with impression management and identify components of the interview process that may be most affected by indirect unfavorable information.

The distinction that Kacmar and Young introduce between direct and indirect unfavorable information may be a potentially important one, for a variety of reasons. First, we suspect that interviewers will interpret indirect information quite differently, even using structured interviews, depending on other factors. For example, an answer that involves "missing the mark," in which the applicant gives an inappropriate answer, might be interpreted quite differently by different interviewers, depending on the circumstances. Consider Dougherty and Turban's argument that initial impressions will affect interviewer behavior and judgments. It seems quite likely that depending on whether the interviewer's initial impression is positive or negative, the effects of missing the mark might differ greatly. If the interviewer's initial impression is positive, he or she may choose to discount or perhaps completely ignore an answer that has missed the mark. If the interviewer's initial impression is negative, however, he or she may interpret the same response in a negative light. More work is needed to determine the factors that affect interviewers' interpretations of and responses to indirect unfavorable information.

Second, we may find that different categories of indirect unfavorable information may be interpreted differently. For example, "missing the mark" may have consequences that are different from those for "missing the opportunity." One type of indirect unfavorable information may affect whether further probes are used, and another type of indirect unfavorable information may determine whether the interviewer attempts to hurry through the remainder of the interview. Given the dynamic nature of the interview, variables such as the temporal placement of the information may have important effects on the interpretation and weight placed on indirect unfavorable information.

Finally, we believe that under certain circumstances, indirect unfavorable information may be viewed as even more negative than direct unfavorable information. For example, an interviewer might regard an applicant's misunderstanding of a question as a direct indicator of how the applicant will behave on the job. Such behavior, then, might be considered even more probative than a self-report of similar behavior.

The authors of the fourth and fifth chapters in this section examine the possibility of between-interviewer differences in decision-making processes. In Chapter 14, Graves and Karren review research addressing the basic question of whether differences between interviewers exist. They note that most of the research has supported the thesis of differences between interviewers. However, this research tends to be based on very small numbers. The one study that has been conducted with a reasonably large sample found no differences in interviewer validity, but this may have been due to the use of a highly structured format. Graves and Karren point out that between-interviewer differences have been examined in regard to just two stages in the employment interview and that the range of variables should be expanded.

Researchers need to go beyond the question of whether or not different interviewers use different decision-making processes and begin testing individual difference variables that are related to these different processes. Aside from some factors discussed by Dipboye and Jackson in Chapter 15, there has been a dearth of theorizing here. In their chapter in this section, Dougherty and Turban suggest two individual difference variables that may be important: conscientiousness and need for cognition. In addition, although both a situational and a personal variable, interviewer mood may be a factor affecting interview decision processes.

In Chapter 15, Dipboye and Jackson address experience as a potential factor that affects interviewer decision-making processes. They assert that experience may actually be a multidimensional construct, because interviewing experience may have taken place in different organizations, different roles (e.g., college recruiting, in-house interviewing), and different types of interview used (e.g., how structured). Managers who have extensive experience interviewing college students for one organization may not have the acquired experience to conduct interviews for midlevel managers in a different organization. Dipboye and Jackson offer three possible reasons that experience should lead to improved interviewer decision-making processes: Experience leads to superior knowledge structures; experience allows for greater automaticity, allowing for improved use of cognitive resources; and experience leads to increased motivation. They then proceed to review the limited research in the interviewing area on the question of experience, incorporating findings from other domains. Their general conclusion is that there is little evidence that experienced interviewers make superior judgments compared with less experienced interviewers. They offer some possible explanations as to why this is so, including lack of feedback and overconfidence on the part of experienced interviewers. It would appear that interviewer experience fails to generalize to the degree that new knowledge structures must be acquired by the interviewer. If the jobs being interviewed for are the same, the only difference would seem to be in knowledge structures of organizational aspects such as culture. More research should investigate the role of interviewing experience across organizations, jobs, roles, and interview formats. Furthermore, as we have pointed out in Chapter 1, the interview may measure four basic constructs: KSAs, reliability, values, and motivation. We think it is important that future research examine these constructs separately to determine whether interviewer experience can be helpful in the measurement of any of these.

Finally, we agree with Dipboye and Jackson that it will be difficult for interviewers to learn from their previous decisions. In support of this, the authors cite research from the decision-making literature indicating that the most effective way for interviewers to improve would be for them to be provided with information about the intercorrelation and validity of various cues. We suspect, however, that for many interviewers such information would rarely be made available, and if available, it would be difficult for most hiring managers to understand without instruction in statistics and decision making.

In the final chapter in this section, Tullar and Kaiser address the application of the group support system (GSS) to multiple-interviewer situations. This chapter links two under-researched aspects of interviewing research: the use of information technology and group dynamics. As we have noted in Chapter 1, organizations are making increasing use of interview-related information technology (e.g., decision support software and electronic hardware). Yet there is a paucity of research on how these alternative communication mechanisms affect interviewing processes and outcomes. Likewise, despite the widespread use of panel interviews, there are almost no studies of group processes in this setting.

The premise of Tullar and Kaiser's chapter is that the use of GSS will improve group functioning by reducing the cognitive costs of communication, deliberation, and acquisition of information. Another possible advantage of the GSS approach is that it allows comments to be made anonymously, which appears to encourage participants to be less inhibited. Tullar and Kaiser point out a number of possible disadvantages of the GSS process as well, including high costs and the need for skilled facilitators. They acknowledge that the use of group support systems does not eliminate the fact that some people (e.g., extroverts) will talk more than others (e.g., introverts).

A major advantage of the GSS approach is that it facilitates discussion. Identification of the precise advantages of this method for interviewer discourse is sorely needed. Although GSS procedures have been found to be helpful in other decision contexts, they must be empirically tested in the interview setting, because the nature of the interviewing task differs from other tasks in a variety of ways.

Although a virtue in some settings, the lack of identifiability offered by the GSS approach may have some potential negative consequences in the interview context. For example, research on social loafing indicates that lack of identifiability may decrease perceived accountability, which in turn may decrease the quality of interview decisions. Further, although maintaining a permanent record of the decision panel's discussion may have benefits, it may also discourage some interviewers from making comments that could cause them harm, such as speaking out against a candidate who might later become their supervisor. (It should be noted that any comments that are recorded through group support systems are likely to be discoverable in a lawsuit, and therefore could come back to hurt the organization.)

11

Contextual Effects

Robert W. Eder

In comparison with biographical inquiries, aptitude tests, and performance simulations, the employment interview is usually conducted under conditions that can best be called variable. Even experienced, well-trained interviewers operate under a variety of situational constraints, some of which are a function of organizational requirements (e.g., level of assigned decision-making responsibility) and some of which are directly perceived by the interviewer (e.g., risk in making false positive decisions). Yet little is known about how the interview context affects interviewer judgment.

Prior to 1985, reviews of the employment interview literature concluded that the likely cause of faulty interview judgment rests largely within the individual interviewer (see Arvey & Campion, 1982; Hakel, 1982; Hunter & Hunter, 1984; Reilly & Chao, 1982; Schmitt, 1976). Each of these reviews concluded that low selection interview validities, relative to biographical data, aptitude testing, and work samples, are likely the result of interviewer information-processing errors. Originally driven by person

AUTHOR'S NOTE: This chapter updates and extends the discussion on contextual effects in interview decisions, particularly in the area of interviewer accountability, provided in Eder (1989).

perception theory, and later by cognitive information-processing theory, employment interview research focused on the perceptual processes that interact to create assessments of applicant qualifications, reflective of the "cognitive miser" metaphor used to depict human judgment biasing (see Dipboye, 1982, 1994).

Six recent meta-analytic reviews (Conway, Jako, & Goodman, 1995; Huffcutt & Arthur, 1994; Marchese & Muchinsky, 1993; McDaniel, Whetzel, Schmidt, & Maurer, 1994; Wiesner & Cronshaw, 1988; Wright, Lichtenfels, & Pursell, 1989) and one qualitative review (Harris, 1989) on the reliability and validity of the interview are more encouraging about the efficacy of the employment interview, especially the structured interview. Recent research has supported the enhanced validity of structured interviewing (Campion, Pursell, & Brown, 1988) and the incremental validity of the structured interview beyond cognitive ability tests (Campion, Campion, & Hudson, 1994; Huffcutt, Roth, & McDaniel, 1996; Motowidlo et al., 1992; Pulakos & Schmitt, 1995). In these studies, as is generally implied by both researchers and practitioners alike, the primary attribute of these structured interviews was the development and use of situational interviewing (SI) questions (e.g., Latham, Saari, Pursell, & Campion, 1980) or behavioral description interviewing (BDI) questions (e.g., Janz, Hellervik, & Gilmore, 1986).

However, as Huffcutt and Arthur (1994) and Campion, Palmer, and Campion (1996) have pointed out, there are likely other ways to increase the structure of the interview, beyond the use of SI or BDI questions. Dimensions of structure may include the degree of question standardization across applicants, the extent to which the applicant is allowed to ask questions, and the degree to which explicit scoring is employed. Even prior to the advent of structured interviews, published research reported that the practice of having the interviewer use a guide or framework to organize the interview improves judgment reliability and predictive validity (see Carlson, Schwab, & Heneman, 1970; Heneman, Schwab, Huett, & Ford, 1975; Schwab & Heneman, 1969). In essence, engineering the interview context, or structuring the interview, includes more than the standardization of interview content. Engineering the interview context also includes interviewer and organizational efforts, conscious or unconscious, that systematically alter situational parameters of the interview context (e.g., allotted interview length, relative importance of candidate attraction and/or selection to the interviewer, decision accountability) and, subsequently, how interviewers form their judgments.

This chapter examines four facets of the interview context that may systematically interact with the interviewer's information processing: task clarity, interview purpose, consequentiality, and accountability. The theoretical foundations for proposing these facets of the interview context are grounded in interactionist psychology. In 1988, Eder and Buckley proposed the adoption of an interactionist perspective to provide a conceptual and theoretical framework for extending existing research on interview judgment to address the effects of contextual or exogenous factors more adequately. Eder and Ferris (1989) employed this interactionist perspective as a framework for reviewing the existing literature and for suggesting new research directions. An interactionist perspective is particularly appropriate given the relative extemporaneous nature of employment interviewing as a selection technique.

Theoretical Foundations: Interactionist Perspective

Both implicit personality theory and cognitive information-processing theory posit that the individual, alone, is the determinant of behavior, and that introspection and self-reports are the primary data collection methods for capturing, respectively, personal trait configurations and specific information-processing strategies.[1] Neither theory offers a research framework for examining either the main or interactive effects of situational factors.

Reliance on intrapsychic explanations for observed variance across interview judgments has not only served to de-emphasize the importance of contextual factors, but has resulted in restricted and/or misplaced organizational efforts to improve interviewer effectiveness. Training interviewers to reduce information-processing errors assumes that it is possible to pinpoint the sources of interviewer bias, distinguish what is "true" perception, and make a permanent change in subsequent interviewer judgment processes. An alternative and more reasonable strategy may be to engineer the interviewing context to elicit a more accurate assessment of job suitability (see Maurer & Fay, 1988). However, such a strategy requires an understanding of how the interview context influences interviewer judgment.

An interactionist perspective conceptualizes behavior as a function of the multidirectional interaction (feedback) between the individual and the situation he or she encounters. In interactionist research, both discrete levels of situation and person factors are used, constrained by researcher control over the heterogeneity of both factors within the research design. The person is assumed not only to react to the situation but also to create or enact the situation, which, in turn, influences the person's future behavior. Schneider (1983) has advocated a definition of interaction as "reciprocal action-transaction." This definition suggests "that the natural ebb and flow of people and settings are continually affected by each other, and that one-way causal inferences fail to adequately represent the reality of most work settings" (p. 10).

On the situation side of the reciprocal interaction, the psychological meaning of the situation for the individual is the determining factor. Rather than a list of objective features of the interview context, such as the physical setting of the interview or the selection ratio (see Arvey &

Campion, 1982), or the extent to which scoring guidelines are provided (see Huffcutt & Arthur, 1994), an interactionist perspective directs the researcher to look for distinctly different ways the interview context is experienced by the interviewer. Atheoretical approaches to identifying situational factors that are relatively stable and yet also naturally variant are unlikely to yield viable taxonomies. For example, Peters, O'Connor, and Rudolf's (1980) free response questionnaire methodology for determining situational constraints on individual performance produced a taxonomy that yielded few substantive effects in field experiments. Commenting on the weak empirical support for their taxonomy, Peters, O'Connor, and Eulberg (1985) noted that individuals viewed these constraints as salient. However, in practice, they perceived their actual work environments to be fairly devoid of these same constraints. Furthermore, the cumulative presence of these objective constraints did not appear to combine in a linear fashion. Following the logic of the interactionist perspective, if cognition and situation interact in a multifaceted fashion, then it is the assigned psychological meaning given to the situation, and not the physical, objective dimensions of the situation, that influences interview judgment.

On the person side of reciprocal interaction, cognitive factors are the essential determinants of behavior. The psychological meaning of a situation can be dominated by the perceiver's cognitive characteristics when exposure and observations are limited. In other words, not all employment interviews would be equally susceptible to the effects of interview context. It is very likely that judgments made by corporate recruiters during brief, informal, and unstructured college campus interviews are predominantly a function of the recruiters' unique cognitive characteristics. However, reliance on interviewer cognitive characteristics to predict final job interview decisions by a supervisor for a specific target position within a work unit is more problematic.

Dipboye (1982) has reported that certain interviewer cognitive characteristics (e.g., schemata and subjective stimulus values from the review of candidate application materials) may be so powerful that they dictate both the conduct of and the decision reached in an interview. He contends that preinterview evaluations of applicants tend to be self-fulfilling; information is attended to, recalled, and interpreted consistent with preinterview evaluations (see Macan & Dipboye, 1990). However, Dipboye (1982) cautions that preinterview evaluations are likely to affect interviewer judgment "only to the extent that . . . the organizational policies, standards, and procedures for conducting the interview are unstructured" (p. 585). The role of interview context and, in particular, the perceived psychological meaning of the interview situation may both interact with and diminish the main effect of interviewer cognitive characteristics on interviewer judgment.

The point is, of course, that individual cognitive differences exist at the very beginning, before "objective" differences in the situation can have any part in modifying them. Thus, from the beginning, the situation must be specified in terms of the particular individual experiencing it. This inseparability of the interviewer's cognitive makeup and what the interviewer perceives, creating a "personal reality," is precisely the interactionist perspective. From the interactionist perspective the individual is seen as an active agent, capable of directing behavior and enacting environments in a goal-oriented fashion. However, choices of actions are partially limited by the variability of the situations that are enacted and by each person's unique cognitive processes.

Typically, interviewers have considerable discretion in how interviews are conducted. Dipboye (1994) contends that, despite the efficacy of structured interviewing, most interviewers will likely continue to interview in an unstructured and highly variant manner. Clearly, substantial systematic differences exist across interviewers in their decision strategies (Graves & Karren, 1992) and schemata (Dougherty, Ebert, & Callender, 1986), which likely adds consistent error variance and suppresses the interview's validity coefficient when the ratings across multiple interviewers are aggregated (Dreher, Ash, & Hancock, 1988).

Likewise, employment interviews are conducted under a variety of situational constraints, some self-imposed and some mandated by the organization's staffing process. Consistency in interviewer judgments across applicants can be explained either in terms of consistency in the individual's choice of enacted interview context and the predictable effects the context has on interview judgment or in terms of the consistency of an individual's information-processing pattern across interview situations. In essence, the quest, from an interview context perspective, is to identify dimensions of assigned psychological meaning that are salient, vary across interview settings, alter the interviewer's information processing, and substantially change interviewer judgment.

Contextual Factors

The first two contextual factors, *task clarity* and *purpose*, provide direction and focus to the interviewer's task. The sparseness of recent research does not diminish their importance in interviewer judgment. In fact, the dynamics surrounding perceived task clarity and purpose may be more complex than initially thought. For example, Dipboye (1994) argues that a variety of personal, projective, and political forces work against the alleged benefits of structured interviews, particularly if interviewers extend their notions of "fit" beyond job specifications to organizational culture or values compatibility (e.g., Bowen, Ledford, & Nathan, 1991; Rynes & Gerhart, 1990). In contrast, there has been substantial advancement of research on *accountability* and to a lesser extent on *consequentiality* as motivational influences on interviewer judgment formation.

Task Clarity

Task clarity for the interviewer is a function of two broad issues: (a) the array and clarity of task demands placed on the interviewer and (b) the extent of interviewer preparation and training. Clarity of task demands in the interview and training in how to prepare for and conduct an employment interview combine to enhance the interviewer's confidence in knowing what to look for in the interview and how to treat the information provided by the applicant.

Osburn, Timmrick, and Bigby (1981) found that specificity of evaluation criteria facilitates discriminability across job applicants. Behaviorally specific criteria that capture job-relevant information not previously tapped by other sources (e.g., review of application, résumé, or other biographical data) and that are recorded on a scored interview report form increase incremental validity. Likewise, familiarity with target job content, skill requirements, and historical performance difficulties may also improve interview validity by focusing the interviewer's attention on more salient job information.

Interviewers who are given more complete job information make decisions with higher interrater reliability (Langdale & Weitz, 1973), a necessary precondition of interview validity. Frequently, only broad job categories or occupational groups form the basis against which interview judgment is rendered (e.g., recruitment interviews), where only a general suitability rating is requested rather than detailed assessment across several rating factors. Naturally, the more complex the job, the greater difficulty the interviewer will likely have in adequately assessing a candidate's diverse qualifications, and hence the more reliance will be placed on the interviewer's cognitive skills to form a valid judgment. By historical standards, organizational work is becoming more complex, creating an even greater set of task demands on the interviewer to assess critical competencies. Increasingly, work has a larger cognitive and affective component as the postindustrial economy becomes more dependent on information and services. Correspondingly, organizations will need to provide interviewers with more guidance on the competencies to be assessed (i.e., task clarity) during the interview that are believed to be predictive of specific performance standards.

Further complicating the interviewer's task demands may be the time allotted to the interviewer to conduct the interview. Tullar, Mullins, and Caldwell (1979) have demonstrated that as allotted interview time increases, decision time increases and "primacy" effects wane. These researchers found that interviewers made decisions more quickly when they were informed that the interview was to last only 15 minutes; when they were told that the interview was to last 30 minutes, their decision times were significantly longer. Tullar et al. also found a potential interaction between allotted interview time and job complexity. With complex jobs, longer allotted interview time may increase interview validity. With less complex jobs, longer allotted interview time may cause the interviewer to drift into issues that are less likely to be job relevant, reducing interview validity. Provided that the interviewer is afforded adequate time to conduct the interview, efforts to improve task clarity and focus attention on job-relevant criteria should delay the onset of a "snap decision" by the interviewer (see Buckley & Eder, 1988), which might otherwise be grounded on candidate appearance, stereotyping, and personal liking.

One approach to improving task clarity that is frequently employed by organizations is the implementation of interviewer training (see Palmer, Campion, & Green, Chapter 19, this volume). Interviewers can be taught to ask job-relevant questions, use rating scales, and improve their interviewing practice (Dougherty et al., 1986; Howard, Dailey, & Gulanick, 1979; Pulakos, Nee, & Kolmstetter, 1995), with corresponding improvements in interviewer judgment. Interviewer training clarifies preinterview expectations and modifies the interviewer's behavior during the interview so that he or she can elicit, observe, and evaluate more information relevant to the determination of applicant qualifications. What is less clear from the literature is what aspects of interviewer training, alone or in combination with other training techniques, yield the greatest improvement in interviewer performance.

Interviewer training has not always produced significant improvements in interviewer judgment. According to Zedeck, Tziner, and Middlestadt (1983), interviewers may use only a few rating dimensions in determining their decisions, even when given a more extensive list of evaluation criteria, especially for assessing qualifications for relatively complex jobs, such as manager or teacher. Whether interviewers can be trained to use a more complete range of information categories, and whether such interventions will result in better decisions, is a question in need of further empirical testing. Maurer and Fay (1988) found no significant increase in interrater reliability after 8 hours of training, raising concerns about whether interviewer training makes an incremental contribution when given to experienced interviewers who use more structured interviews (i.e., situational interviewing). Experienced interviewers appear to learn new interviewing tools and how to use them, but may readily revert to their idiosyncratic judgment processes.

Investigating the upper limits of interviewer training on cognitive processes may also require more systematic research on judgment patterns across divergent sets of interview situations. Interview situations in which the interviewer has not been trained and the interviewing task is unclear will likely yield quicker, more extreme interviewer judgments (see Tullar et al., 1979), a reluctance to quantify candidate performance, higher short-term memory loss, and decisions made more frequently on the basis of nonspecific, non-job-relevant criteria.

Interview Purpose

As Dipboye (1994) points out, a wide variety of personal, political, and organizational purposes may potentially affect the interviewer's conduct and judgment. For the sake of argument, let's examine two of the dominant purposes that drive the employment interview: applicant recruitment and selection. In this more limited framework, each interviewer interprets the extent to which a greater or lesser importance is to be placed on each purpose against which information is gathered. Recruitment interviews may prompt interviewers to search for and organize information around the candidate's own career goals, whereas selection interviews may prompt interviewers to search for and organize information about the candidate's possession of traits assumed to be associated with job success (see Hoffman, Mischel, & Mazze, 1981). Furthermore, there are instances in which applicant attraction, rather than selection, becomes a prime consideration. Early interviews in the selection process may be recruitment efforts to generate a large qualified applicant pool, and final interviews may be conducted as "closers" to be sure the applicant has been sold on the advantages of joining the organization. Ignoring applicant attraction may reduce offer acceptances by applicants who may perceive the organization, through the interview experience, as being indifferent toward the applicant.

Few empirical studies have directly examined the effects of interview purpose. The majority of published interview studies have been conducted using what can best be described as initial screening interviews, where, with limited exposure, the interviewer is asked to make an overall assessment of candidate suitability. Even when the stated interview purpose is to make an accept/reject decision, frequently the decision is made in the fictitious context of a "for-research-only purpose." Carlson, Thayer, Mayfield, and Peterson's (1971) study was one of the first to approximate the effects of interview purpose on interview judgment. These researchers found that in a situation where quotas were stressed, the inexperienced interviewer was more likely to accept a less qualified candidate than was an experienced interviewer. Though Carlson et al. did not examine interviewer cognitive processes directly, their findings suggest that experienced interviewers are more able to enact the psychological meaning of judging candidates under heightened selection utility purposes.

Barber, Hollenbeck, Tower, and Phillips (1994) conducted the only direct test to date of the effects of interview purpose on interview outcomes, although their focus was on applicant, not interviewer, information processing and judgment. Interestingly, they found that applicants were able to gather and retain more information when the interview was conducted for the single purpose of recruitment or selection than when the explicit purpose was a combination of recruitment and selection. Apparently, one possible effect of increased perceived duality of interview purpose is obfuscation of the applicant's information processing. Perhaps this is also the case for the interviewer, whose judgment may be improved by clarification of the purpose or purposes for which he or she is conducting the interview.

Perceived complexity of purpose may also be a source of reduced predictive validity. For example, validation studies on the employment interview that are conducted for purely research-only purposes would likely not have the same complexity of perceived purpose as validation studies that use actual job interviews of real applicants who are subsequently evaluated against the organization's existing performance appraisal system. In fact, McDaniel et al. (1994) found in their meta-analysis that the mean validities for the interviews obtained on job performance criteria collected for research purposes only were larger than those obtained on job performance criteria collected for administrative purposes. They contend that this decrement in judgment accuracy is likely due to the greater prevalence of biases and contaminants in performance ratings conducted for administrative purposes. However, another possibility, based on Barber et al.'s (1994) findings, is that interviewer judgment processes themselves may be directly degraded when the complexity of perceived interview purposes increases; such is more often the case with actual job applicant interviews than with interviews staged solely for research purposes.

Performance appraisal research on the role of purpose in information processing may offer additional insight. For example, two consistent findings are that performance ratings are higher (i.e., more lenient) when the rating purpose is conducted for administrative rather than for counseling or feedback-only purposes (see McCall & DeVries, 1976; Meyer, Kay, & French, 1965) and that different purposes may also trigger rater preferences for distinctiveness versus consensus information (Williams, DeNisi, Blenco, & Cafferty, 1985). With parallel logic, it may well be that recruiters in their interviews search for consensus information that this candidate is or is not in the feasible set, whereas interviewers who are making a choice from among a handful of finalists are looking for distinctiveness information.

The evidence to date, though scant, suggests that an interviewer's information processing may be substantially modified by interview purpose and complicated by the perceived complexity of interview purposes. Whether influenced by the selection situation or as a function of preferred style, interviewers differentially perceive the extent to which candidate attraction and selection are to be emphasized, among other interview purposes. Clarity of purpose provides the interviewer with focus and direction, but complexity of perceived purpose likely makes a difficult judgment task only more strenuous for the interviewer. As more employment interview research is conducted with actual job interviews to enhance external validity, additional opportunities will emerge for researchers to assess the full impact of purpose on interviewer judgment.

Consequentiality

In the related field of performance appraisal ratings, researchers have differentiated between automatic and controlled information processing (see Feldman, 1986) and have noted the significant contribution of rater motivation to the controlled aspects of judgment formation that may subsequently enhance rating accuracy (see Bernardin & Buckley, 1981; DeCotiis & Petit, 1978). Logically, one way to increase interviewer motivation may be to create a situation in which the interviewer "feels responsible" for the decision outcome. For example, McAllister, Mitchell, and Beach (1979) found that participants in a business simulation experiment employed more analytic and complex judgment strategies the more personally responsible they felt for their decisions. This was particularly true when the decision was perceived to be important and irreversible. The perception of feeling responsible, or consequentiality, is likely a function of a number of factors, including personal decision risk to the interviewer and the utility of the interviewer's judgment within the entire selection process, including the false positive cost to the organization.

At one extreme, the interviewer may have sole responsibility for the hiring decision based on just one interview with the applicant. That hiring decision may be crucial to the very success of the interviewer's firm or work unit. At the other extreme, the interviewer may be only one of many people whose opinions are sought on an applicant who will likely have only tertiary impact. When consequentiality is low, the interviewer is likely to save his or her cognitive energies, rely on intuitive impressions, and discount the importance of the interview itself as just one event on the day's busy schedule.

Consequentiality is decision risk couched in both organizational and personal terms. In organizational terms, the selection process presents varying degrees of risk and responsibility for the decision maker. One facet of risk is the probability of making a false positive decision (i.e., hiring someone who subsequently fails on the job). A false positive probability is a function of the historical record of incumbent success and the validity coefficient of the interview (i.e., strength of association between test score and subsequent job success). Jobs in which few incumbents fail reflect lower false positive risk compared with jobs that more frequently experience poor performers. In turn, incremental selection utility is directly affected by the selection ratio (i.e., hires/applicants). The selection ratio is a function of the changes in the relative demand for employees in the job category (i.e., hiring quotas) and the recruitment effort put forth to generate a large pool of qualified applicants. As perceived selection utility increases, consequentiality or felt responsibility increases for the decision maker.

Interestingly, feelings of greater responsibility do not necessarily increase decision risk. For example, a supervisor could conduct a 10-minute interview to hire a clerical worker and hire the person "on the spot," immediately after a cursory interview. Clearly, there is sole responsibility for the decision, but a hiring mistake may not be seen as a major cost. Although base rate, selection ratio, and interview validity determine the probability of a false positive, the cost of making a hiring mistake is a direct function of the economic importance of the job to the organization (e.g., clerical worker versus middle manager) and to the interviewer (e.g., likely colleague versus a hire for another department). In personal terms, decision risk is affected to the extent to which the interviewer is likely to be the job candidate's eventual supervisor or coworker. Hence, decision risk can be increased by exogenous factors (e.g., expansion of labor supply, inherent difficulties of succeeding in the job), deliberate human resource practices (e.g., decreased recruitment effort), and the interviewer's potential work role in relation to the selected candidate.

Webster (1982) was among the first to posit that changing labor market dynamics, both internal and external, that affect the size of the applicant pool may also alter the interviewer's judgment. Candidates with equivalent qualifications may be evaluated differentially as a function of perceived labor market conditions (see Carlson, 1967). If recruitment efforts have been only moderately successful and market conditions appear tight, applicants may receive inflated ratings as interviewers' efforts shift from selecting to attracting qualified candidates. On the other hand, if the available pool of qualified candidates appears to be large by historical standards, applicants may receive more stringent ratings.

This suggests that the effects of decision risk (e.g., "I should take my time and be careful in deciding") may interact with perceived candidate qualifications. For example, Tullar et al. (1979) found in a scheduled 15-minute interview that interviewers who took less time to decide tended to give low-quality candidates lower ratings and high-quality candidates higher ratings. Overall, this suggests that if greater decision risk increases interviewer motivation to be careful in judgment formation, then decision time will be extended, reducing the extreme ratings of high- and low-quality candidates. This suggests that decision risk may both modify the "snap decision" tendency by interviewers (see Buckley & Eder, 1988) and reduce the rating differential between low- and high-quality candidates.

To date, no published research has systematically examined interviewer judgment across interviews that vary in selection utility for the organization and/or personal risk for the interviewer, or the extent to which either may modify interviewer motivation toward the interview judgment task.

Accountability

Being held accountable presents the interviewer with the social pressure to justify his or her judgment to others (i.e., an external validity threat), especially if the account must be made "in person" (Klimoski & Inks, 1990). The strategies individuals develop for coping with the contextual demand for accountability depend, in part, on whether the perception of accountability is pre- or postjudgment and the degree of ambiguity that exists in the interview context with regard to the person or persons to whom the individuals are held accountable. In the early research on accountability, Tetlock (1983b) demonstrated that the simple expectation that one may have to justify a forthcoming decision appears to reduce information primacy effects, increase recall of significant information, and activate a more multidimensional information-processing framework. Perceived accountability, as a dimension of interview context, recognizes that interviewers also act, in part, as "political persons" who desire to adopt positions likely to gain favor and who inherently seek approval and respect from others in the organization.

Rozelle and Baxter (1981) manipulated accountability and responsibility for judges prior to their assignment to watch interview videotapes. Those in the high-accountability condition were told their ratings would be discussed at a staff meeting and that applicants had access to their reports. Other judges were assured that all ratings were confidential and would not be revealed to anyone (the low-accountability condition). Similarly, members of the high-responsibility team were assured their ratings would be used to reach a decision, whereas those with low responsibility knew that a decision had already been reached. Judges who worked under the constraint of high accountability and, to a lesser extent, high responsibility provided descriptions that more accurately reflected applicant characteristics. Thus, preexposure accountability may induce interviewers to become more thorough and vigilant information processors and may make them more willing to revise initial impressions in response to changing evidence (Tetlock, 1983b; Tetlock & Boettger, 1989). When they do not know the views of the person to whom they will be held accountable, interviewers likely engage in preemptive self-criticism (Tetlock, 1985, p. 316). In such situations, interviewers may formulate counterarguments that potential critics could raise in order to avert the appearance of flawed reasoning and subsequent loss of esteem.

Early work on accountability suggests that it is critical to create the accountability context for the decision maker prior to the gathering of information. In contrast, felt postjudgment accountability produces more variance in interviewer decision levels, though not necessarily more accuracy, when compared with a nonaccountability context. In other words, it is not enough to inform interviewers after the fact that they will be expected to justify their judgments. Expressed rationale will be equally as elaborate as under the preaccountability intervention, but it will be no more accurate a judgment. One cannot easily undo the information gathering and integration process once it has already occurred.

However, more recent research suggests that the effects of accountability are not only complex, but sometimes even perverse. Tetlock (1992) has identified three distinct coping strategies used by individuals when confronted with accountability expectations. The acceptability heuristic (i.e., the direct adjustment of one's espoused judgment to meet the expectations of others) is perhaps the best-known effect of accountability. This coping strategy is more likely to be used when consequentiality is low and aversion to risk taking is high (Weigold & Schlenker, 1991). Furthermore, the espoused judgment, though different from what the individual actually believes, appears to have no lasting effect on prior judgment or attitude. In other words, interviewers are likely to adjust their judgments to conform with those to whom they are accountable to the extent that they see their role as minor in the selection process, they see the decision itself to be inconsequential, and they wish to avoid rendering a conflicting opinion. By itself, this coping strategy reduces cognitive effort, emotional strain, and potential interpersonal controversy for the interviewer. The perverse result of higher accountability in this case can be a "snap decision" tendency (Hattrup & Ford, 1995) and a tendency to lock in initial biases (Gordon, Rozelle, & Baxter, 1988).

The second coping strategy, preemptive self-criticism, has the potential to reduce overconfidence and encourage greater effort to gather information and reconcile inconsistent information. The individual conducts a more objective and rational analysis of the available information to avoid anticipated potential criticism by others (see Simonson & Nye, 1992). Preemptive self-criticism is more likely to occur if the audience's viewpoints are not previously known to the individual and the individual is not strongly committed to a particular point of view. This might help explain why it might be wise to have diverse groups involved in selection decision making and why it is important to ask everyone to resist quick judgment before the group deliberates. In some extreme cases, individuals may experience vacillation and may be viewed as "fence-sitters," unable to make up their minds. In contrast, members of an experienced interviewing team may know each other's biases and preferences too well, and may expect others to provide the expected accounting of their decisions. The result is defensive bolstering, Tetlock's third coping strategy, which can lead to considerable information distortion.

Further compounding the effects of accountability is the extent to which the interviewer knows the views of the audience to whom he or she is accountable. When the interviewer knows the views of those to whom he or she will be held accountable, he or she is more likely to shift opinions toward those of others in the interview context (see Tetlock, 1983a), provided the interviewer has not made a prior commitment concerning candidates in opposition to the target audience (Tetlock, Skitka, & Boettger, 1989). In that case, rather than a strategic evaluative shift toward the views of the target audience, the interviewer is more likely to engage in defensive bolstering in anticipation of a hostile reception to his or her judgment (Tetlock et al., 1989). If the interviewer has made no precommitment, his or her subsequent judgment will strategically shift toward the target audience to the extent that the interviewer engages in political behaviors such as impression management or self-serving attributions.

The label of *self-serving attributions* refers to the tendency of a highly accountable interviewer to take credit for hiring successes and to deflect blame for hiring failures. Staw, McKechnie, and Puffer (1983) found that corporate administrators made more self-serving attributions in letters to stockholders as a function of their concern about the volatility in the company's stock price. Of interest is the finding that enhancement statements when the stock price rose were as prevalent as defensive statements when the stock price dropped. Again, rationale is more enmeshed, not necessarily more valid.

Tetlock's work on accountability in decision making may help to reconcile the conflicting evidence of whether board interviews (i.e., panel interviews) improve judgment accuracy over individual interviews. For example, in their meta-analysis of employment interview research, McDaniel et al. (1994) found the mean predictive validity for individual interviews to be larger than that for board or panel interviews, despite the apparent advantage board interviews have for enhancing interrater reliability. Albanese and Van Fleet (1985) argue that the presence of other interviewers may dilute responsibility rather than enhance individual effort. Hence, one might expect that individual, rather than board, interviews increase individual interviewer felt responsibility or consequentiality in making the final determination. For example, Weldon and Gargano (1985) found support for the concept of "social loafing" in decision-making groups; shared responsibility leads to less effortful judgment. However, they note that when the individual's contribution to the group decision was known, not anonymous, social loafing disappeared.

The issue may be how a board operates, rather than whether the decision is an individual or group product. The individual's perceived psychological meaning of accountability in a group interview context would largely depend on the decision-making guidelines of the group. If the history of the group is to share individual assessments and decision rationales before group consensus is formed, then a preaccountability context is created with optimal effects on judgment accuracy. Board members who expect to be actively involved in the group deliberations are more likely to be motivated to show flexibility in their judgments, to rethink values and beliefs, and to take control of the cognitive processes that are activated in the judgment task (Tetlock & Kim, 1987). However, if individuals simply summate their individual ratings without expected discussion, or if there is a dominant view with which everyone is expected to comply (see Peterson, 1997), then judgment accuracy will not likely be enhanced over individual judgment.

In many ways, accountability and consequentiality can have similar effects on the vigilance of the interviewer in attending to and integrating relevant information. Both dimensions of the psychological meaning of the situation directly enhance decision maker motivation. Tetlock et al. (1989) found at least one distinction between the effects each contextual dimension has on decision makers. Increased consequentiality increases judgment overconfidence, whereas increased accountability reduces judgment overconfidence. In an accountability context, the interviewer is more likely to engage in preemptive self-criticism, resulting in more equivocation in the confidence with which the interviewer reports his or her judgment to others. In the consequentiality context, the more felt responsibility for the decision, the more likely the person is to take an explicit position.

Methodological Implications

First, research on situational dimensions of perceived consequentiality and accountability requires more realistic decision-making settings that naturally vary across these salient contextual factors. The relative sterility of a lab setting minimizes the transferability of judgment research such as that concerning the employment interview, whose results are highly modified across different interview contexts. When researchers use subject or stimulus extremes while sampling minor situational variation, we should not be surprised that personalistic theories of interview judgment are once again confirmed. Tetlock (1985) has argued that the findings on accountability "support contingency models of judgment and decision-making which challenge the universality of the cognitive miser portrait of how people think" (p. 320). This literature suggests that interviewers have a capacity to adopt different strategies and styles of information processing in response to changing interview circumstances. At the very least, future researchers should confirm how interviewers perceive the clarity of their judgment task, the purpose(s) of their interviewing, their felt responsibility for reaching accurate decisions, and the extent to which interviewers expect to have to explain their judgment (i.e., accountability).

Second, employment interview research that is conducted outside the reality of organizational life may offer little insight into how interviews are actually performed. Most experiments on the employment interview are conducted "for research only," and subjects are not held accountable for their evaluations. Even when researchers attempt to manipulate accountability in simulated employment interview studies (see Gordon et al., 1988), it is unclear whether the participants simply feel a greater need to meet researcher expectations or whether they actually feel more accountable for their judgments.

Furthermore, in simulated interview research the interview is almost always treated as the sole component of a hypothetical selection process. In actual selection models, interview information is combined with other predictor information and with the judgments of other interviewers before a final summative decision is rendered. However, in most published research studies interviewers have been asked to make a single rating of suitability or to accept or reject applicants based solely on the interviewers' own brief interviews. The innate multidimensionality of the selection task has been ignored. In reality, selection processes often include a variety of steps in a sequential decision process, each contributing to the determination of applicants' overall qualifications. The incremental validity of the employment interview in different contextual settings will remain an unanswered question until interview research is conducted within organizations' actual selection processes.

Finally, the contextual dimensions of consequentiality and accountability continue to evolve; these require construct validation and clearer delineation of how each affects decision making and how each is distinct from other contextual dimensions, such as purpose and task clarity.

Note

1. For a more complete review of the literature on the interactionist perspective, see Eder and Buckley (1988).

References

Albanese, R., & Van Fleet, D. D. (1985). Rational behavior in groups: The free riding tendency. *Academy of Management Review, 10,* 244-255.

Arvey, R. D., & Campion, J. E. (1982). The employment interview: A summary and review of recent research. *Personnel Psychology, 35,* 281-322.

Barber, A. E., Hollenbeck, J. R., Tower, S. L., & Phillips, J. M. (1994). The effects of interview focus on recruitment effectiveness: A field experiment. *Journal of Applied Psychology, 79,* 886-896.

Bernardin, H. J., & Buckley, M. R. (1981). Strategies in rater training. *Academy of Management Review, 6,* 205-212.

Bowen, D. E., Ledford, G. E., & Nathan, B. R. (1991). Hiring for the organization, not the job. *Academy of Management Executive, 5,* 35-51.

Buckley, M. R., & Eder, R. W. (1988). B. M. Springbett and the notion of the "snap decision" in the interview. *Journal of Management, 14,* 59-67.

Campion, M. A., Campion, J. E., & Hudson, J. P. (1994). Structured interviewing: A note on incremental validity and alternative question types. *Journal of Applied Psychology, 79,* 998-1002.

Campion, M. A., Palmer, D. K., & Campion, J. E. (1996, April). *A review of structure in the selection interview.* Paper presented at the annual meeting of the Society for Industrial and Organizational Psychology, San Diego, CA.

Campion, M. A., Pursell, E. D., & Brown, B. K. (1988). Structured interviewing: Raising the psychometric properties of the employment interview. *Personnel Psychology, 41,* 25-42.

Carlson, R. E. (1967). Selection interview decisions: The effect of interview experience, relative quota situation, and applicant sample on interview decisions. *Personnel Psychology, 20,* 259-280.

Carlson, R. E., Schwab, D. P., & Heneman, H. G. (1970). Agreement among selection interview styles. *Journal of Applied Psychology, 5,* 8-17.

Carlson, R. E., Thayer, P. W., Mayfield. E. C., & Peterson, D. A. (1971). Research on the selection interview. *Personnel Journal, 50,* 268-275.

Conway, J. M., Jako, R. A., & Goodman, D. F. (1995). A meta-analysis of interrater and internal consistency reliability of selection interviews. *Journal of Applied Psychology, 80,* 565-579.

DeCotiis, T. A., & Petit, A. (1978). The performance appraisal process: A model and some testable propositions. *Academy of Management Review, 3,* 635-645.

Dipboye, R. L. (1982). Self-fulfilling prophecies in the selection interview. *Academy of Management Review, 7,* 579-586.

Dipboye, R. L. (1994). Structured and unstructured selection interviews: Beyond the job-fit model. In G. R. Ferris (Ed.), *Research in personnel and human resources management* (Vol. 12, pp. 79-123). Greenwich, CT: JAI.

Dougherty, T. W., Ebert, R. J., & Callender, J. C. (1986). Policy capturing in the employment interview. *Journal of Applied Psychology, 71,* 9-15.

Dreher, G. W., Ash, R. A., & Hancock, P. (1988). The role of the traditional research design in underestimating the validity of the employment interview. *Personnel Psychology, 41,* 315-327.

Eder, R. W. (1989). Contextual effects on interview decisions. In R. W. Eder & G. R. Ferris (Eds.), *The employment interview: Theory, research, and practice* (pp. 113-126). Newbury Park, CA: Sage.

Eder, R. W., & Buckley, M. R. (1988). The employment interview: An interactionist perspective. In G. R. Ferris & K. M. Rowland (Eds.), *Research in personnel and human resources management* (Vol. 6, pp. 75-107). Greenwich, CT: JAI.

Eder, R. W., & Ferris, G. R. (Eds.). (1989). *The employment interview: Theory, research, and practice.* Newbury Park, CA: Sage.

Feldman, J. M. (1986). Instrumentation and training for performance appraisal: A perceptual-cognitive viewpoint. In K. M. Rowland & G. R. Ferris (Eds.), *Research in personnel and human resources management* (Vol. 4, pp. 45-100). Greenwich, CT: JAI.

Gordon, R. A., Rozelle, R. M., & Baxter, J. C. (1988). The effect of applicant age, job level, and accountability on the evaluation of job applicants. *Organizational Behavior and Human Decision Processes, 41,* 20-33.

Graves, L. M., & Karren, R. J. (1992). Interviewer decision processes and effectiveness: An experimental policy-capturing investigation. *Personnel Psychology, 45,* 313-340.

Hakel, M. D. (1982). Employment interviewing. In K. M. Rowland & G. R. Ferris (Eds.), *Personnel management* (pp. 102-124). Boston: Allyn & Bacon.

Harris, M. M. (1989). Reconsidering the employment interview: A review of recent literature and suggestions for future research. *Personnel Psychology, 42,* 691-726.

Hattrup, K., & Ford, J. K. (1995). The roles of information characteristics and accountability in moderating stereotype-driven processes during social decision making. *Organizational Behavior and Human Decision Processes, 63,* 73-86.

Heneman, H. G., Schwab, D. P., Huett, D. L., & Ford, J. J. (1975). Interviewer validity as a function of interview structure, biographical data, and interviewee order. *Journal of Applied Psychology, 60,* 748-753.

Hoffman, C., Mischel, W., & Mazze, K. (1981). The role of purpose in the organization of information about behavior: Trait-based versus goal-based categories in person cognition. *Journal of Personality and Social Psychology, 40,* 211-225.

Howard, G. S., Dailey, P. R., & Gulanick, N. A. (1979). The feasibility of informed pretests in attenuating response-shift bias. *Applied Psychological Measurement, 3,* 481-494.

Huffcutt, A. I., & Arthur, W., Jr. (1994). Hunter and Hunter (1984) revisited: Interview validity for entry-level jobs. *Journal of Applied Psychology, 79,* 184-190.

Huffcutt, A. I., Roth, P. L., & McDaniel, M. A.(1996). A meta-analytic investigation of cognitive ability in employment interview evaluations: Moderating characteristics and implications for incremental validity. *Journal of Applied Psychology, 81,* 459-473.

Hunter, J. E., & Hunter, R. F. (1984). Validity and utility of alternative prediction of job performance. *Journal of Applied Psychology, 96,* 72-98.

Janz, J. T., Hellervik, L., & Gilmore, D. C. (1986). *Behavior description interviewing: New, accurate, cost effective.* Newton, MA: Allyn & Bacon.

Klimoski, R., & Inks, L. (1990). Accountability forces in performance appraisal. *Organizational Behavior and Human Decision Processes, 45,* 194-208.

Langdale, J. A., & Weitz, J. (1973). Estimating the influence of job information on interviewer agreement. *Journal of Applied Psychology, 57,* 23-27.

Latham, G. P., Saari, L. M., Pursell, E. D., & Campion, M. A. (1980). The situational interview. *Journal of Applied Psychology, 65,* 422-427.

Macan, T. H., & Dipboye, R. L. (1990). The relationship of interviewers' preinterview Impressions to selection and recruitment outcomes. *Personnel Psychology, 43,* 745-768.

Marchese, M. C., & Muchinsky, P. M. (1993). The validity of the employment interview: A meta-analysis. *International Journal of Selection and Assessment, 1,* 18-26.

Maurer, S. D., & Fay, C. (1988). Effects of situational interviews, conventional structured interviews, and training on interview rating agreement: An experimental analysis. *Personnel Psychology, 41,* 329-344.

McAllister, P. W., Mitchell, T. R., & Beach, L. R. (1979). The contingency model for the selection of decision strategies: An empirical test of the effects of significance, accountability, and reversibility. *Organizational Behavior and Human Performance, 24,* 228-244.

McCall, N. W., & DeVries, D. L. (1976). *Appraisal in context: Clashing with organizational realities.* Paper presented at the annual meeting of the American Psychological Association, Washington, DC.

McDaniel, M. A., Whetzel, D. L., Schmidt, F. L., & Maurer, S. D. (1994). The validity of employment interviews: A comprehensive review and meta-analysis. *Journal of Applied Psychology, 79,* 599-616.

Meyer, H. H., Kay, E., & French, J. R. P. (1965). Split roles in performance appraisal. *Harvard Business Review, 43,* 123-219.

Motowidlo, S. J., Carter, G. W., Dunnette, M. D., Tippins, N., Werner, S., Burnett, J. R., & Vaughan, M. J. (1992). Studies of the structured behavioral interview. *Journal of Applied Psychology, 77,* 571-587.

Osburn, H. G., Timmrick, C., & Bigby, D. (1981). Effect of dimensional relevance and accuracy of stimulated hiring decisions by employment interviews. *Journal of Applied Psychology, 66,* 159-165.

Peters, L., O'Connor, E. J., & Eulberg, J. (1985). Situational constraints: Sources, consequences, and future considerations. In K. M. Rowland & G. R. Ferris (Eds.), *Research in personnel and human resources management* (Vol. 3, pp. 79-114). Greenwich, CT: JAI.

Peters, L., O'Connor, E. J., & Rudolf, C. J. (1980). The behavioral and affective consequences of performance-relevant situational variables. *Organizational Behavior and Human Performance, 25,* 79-96.

Peterson, R. S. (1997). A directive leadership style in group decision making can be both virtue and vice: Evidence from elite and experimental groups. *Journal of Personality and Social Psychology, 72,* 1107-1121.

Pulakos, E. D., Nee, M. T., & Kolmstetter, E. B. (1995, May). Effects of training and individual differences on interviewer rating accuracy. In E. B. Kolmstetter (Chair), *Interviewer and contextual factors that make a difference in interviewer validity.* Symposium conducted at the annual meeting of the Society for Industrial and Organizational Psychology, Orlando, FL.

Pulakos, E. D., & Schmitt, N. (1995). Experience-based and situational interview questions: Studies of validity. *Personnel Psychology, 48,* 289-308.

Reilly, R. R., & Chao, G. T. (1982). Validity and fairness of some alternative employee selection procedures. *Personnel Psychology, 35,* 1-62.

Rozelle, R. M., & Baxter, J. C. (1981). Influence of role pressures on the perceiver: Judgments of videotaped interviews varying judge accountability and responsibility. *Journal of Applied Psychology, 66,* 437-441.

Rynes, S. L., & Gerhart, B. (1990). Interviewer assessments of applicant "fit": An exploratory investigation. *Personnel Psychology, 43,* 13-35.

Schmitt, N. (1976). Social and situational determinants of interview decisions: Implications for the employment interview. *Personnel Psychology, 29,* 79-101.

Schneider, B. (1983). Interactionist psychology and organizational behavior. In L. L. Cummings & B. M. Staw (Eds.), *Research in organizational behavior* (Vol. 5, pp. 1-31). Greenwich, CT: JAI.

Schwab, D. P., & Heneman, H. G. (1969). Relationship between structure and interviewer reliability in an employment situation. *Journal of Applied Psychology, 53,* 214-217.

Simonson, I., & Nye, P. (1992). The effect of accountability on susceptibility to decision errors. *Organizational Behavior and Human Decision Processes, 51,* 416-446.

Staw, B. M., McKechnie, P. I., & Puffer, S. M. (1983). The justification of organizational performance. *Administrative Science Quarterly, 28,* 582-600.

Tetlock, P. E. (1983a). Accountability and the complexity of thought. *Journal of Personality and Social Psychology, 45,* 74-83.

Tetlock, P. E. (1983b). Accountability and the perseverance of first impressions. *Social Psychology Quarterly, 46,* 285-292.

Tetlock, P. E. (1985). Accountability: The neglected social context of judgment and choice. In L. L. Cummings & B. M. Staw (Eds.), *Research in organizational behavior* (Vol. 7, pp. 297-332). Greenwich, CT: JAI.

Tetlock, P. E. (1992). The impact of accountability on judgment and choice: Toward a social contingency model. *Advances in Experimental Social Psychology, 25,* 331-376.

Tetlock, P. E., & Boettger, R. (1989). Accountability: A social magnifier of the dilution effect. *Journal of Personality and Social Psychology, 57,* 388-398.

Tetlock, P. E., & Kim, J. (1987). Accountability and judgment processes in personality prediction task. *Journal of Personality and Social Psychology, 52,* 700-709.

Tetlock, P. E, Skitka, L., & Boettger, R. (1989). Social and cognitive strategies for coping with accountability: Conformity, complexity, and bolstering. *Journal of Personality and Social Psychology, 57,* 632-640.

Tullar, W. L., Mullins, T. W., & Caldwell, S. A. (1979). Effects of interview length and applicant quality on interview decision time. *Journal of Applied Psychology, 64,* 669-674.

Webster, E. C. (1982). *The employment interview: A social judgment process.* Schomberg, ON: SIP.

Weigold, M. F., & Schlenker, B. R. (1991). Accountability and risk taking. *Personality and Social Psychology Bulletin, 17,* 25-29.

Weldon, E., & Gargano, G. M. (1985). Cognitive effort in additive task groups: The effects of shared responsibility on the quality of multiattribute judgments. *Organizational Behavior and Human Decision Processes, 36,* 348-361.

Wiesner, W. H., & Cronshaw, S. F. (1988). A meta-analytic investigation of the impact of interview format and degree of structure on the validity of the employment interview. *Journal of Occupational Psychology, 61,* 275-290.

Williams, K. J., DeNisi, A. S., Blenco, A. G., & Cafferty, T. P. (1985). The role of appraisal purpose: Effects of purpose on information acquisition and utilization. *Organizational Behavior and Human Decision Processes, 35,* 314-339.

Wright, P. M., Lichtenfels, P. A., & Pursell, E. D. (1989). The structured interview: Additional studies and a meta-analysis. *Journal of Occupational Psychology, 62,* 191-199.

Zedeck, S., Tziner, A., & Middlestadt, S. E. (1983). Interviewer validity and reliability: An individual analysis approach. *Personnel Psychology, 36,* 355-370.

12

Behavioral Confirmation of Interviewer Expectations

Thomas W. Dougherty
Daniel B. Turban

Kim felt good about her interviewing skills as she headed off to lunch after her first morning of conducting campus interviews at Midwestern State. Although she had not received any training and had not interviewed applicants before today, she felt that she was doing an excellent job. Kim had always thought she was a good judge of other people, and her interviewing experience confirmed that belief. She could look at an applicant's résumé and predict, with almost infallible accuracy, whether the person would perform well in the interview or not. Applicants who Kim thought would be outstanding employees, based on her review of their résumés, performed well in their interviews. Kim rated them highly and decided she would have them invited for follow-up visits to company headquarters. Applicants who Kim thought would be poor employees, based on their résumés, turned out to be poor communicators. Kim immediately rejected them from additional consideration as potential employees. As she sat down to her lunch, Kim thought to herself that interviewing applicants is relatively easy. In fact, she wondered whether the interview is even necessary; although the interview serves a public relations role, perusing the résumé seems to provide sufficient information about the applicant.

Kim may be an excellent judge of other people, or she may be behaving toward applicants in such a manner that she influences their behavior toward her so as to confirm her initial expectations. This chapter examines theory and research dealing with the second possibility—more specifically, that interviewers form initial expectations toward applicants and then behave toward them in such a manner as to elicit applicant behaviors that confirm the interviewers' preinterview impressions. The notion that interviewers may influence applicants' behaviors to conform with their initial perceptions of the applicants is an aspect of the process known as "self-fulfilling prophecy" in the interview (Dipboye, 1982).

In general, the self-fulfilling prophecy consists of three stages: (a) A person has a belief or expectation concerning another person's (target's) behavior, (b) the expectation leads the individual to behave in a specific manner toward the target, and (c) the target behaves in the expected manner, confirming the expectation (Eden, 1990; Merton, 1948). Merton (1948) describes the self-fulfilling prophecy as a false belief of the situation that evokes a new behavior (of the target) that makes the original false belief come true. However, we will not highlight the veracity of the original expectation in our discussion of the self-fulfilling prophecy in the employment interview. For example, in the case of the interviewer in our opening scenario, Kim's initial perceptions of applicants may have shaped her behavior toward those applicants, which in turn led the applicants to behave in a manner confirming Kim's initial perceptions. Kim's original perceptions of the applicants may have been inaccurate or they may have been accurate. In both cases, the preinterview impressions were "confirmed" by the interview, regardless of whether the impressions were accurate or inaccurate.

Confirmatory behavior could possibly be an enhancement to or a detraction from interview validity, in part as a function of the accuracy or inaccuracy of the first impression. For example, an interviewer who has an accurate negative first impression of an applicant may engage in more probing questions and more follow-up questioning, which then contributes to an accurate negative final evaluation (and to interview validity). However, if a negative first impression is not accurate, such confirmatory probing and follow-up will tend to lead the interviewer to an invalid final judgment. The presence of confirmatory behavior in the interview may also have an effect on other important interview outcomes. For example, an interviewer with a positive first impression of the applicant might display confirmatory behavior such as a positive interview style and a positive vocal style, and may signal a likelihood of extending an offer, all of which could increase an applicant's *attraction* to the organization. As another example, interviewers' confirmatory behavior could be part of the process by which interviewers give higher evaluations to applicants of the same race, as found in some recent research (see Lin, Dobbins, & Farh, 1992; Prewett-Livingston, Feild, Veres, & Lewis, 1996). In this chapter we do not focus on the issue of whether the preinterview impression is accurate or inaccurate. Rather, we examine the processes through which preinterview impressions influence interviewers' behavior in the interview.

As a number of scholars have noted, the self-fulfilling prophecy has been used to describe many types of social and psychological phenomena, from bank closures to students' classroom learning to employment interviews (Dipboye, 1982; Eden, 1984, 1990). Dipboye (1982) discusses a model of the self-fulfilling prophecy process in the context of employment interviews. His model suggests that both behavioral and cognitive biases mediate the effects of interviewers' expectations on evaluations of applicants. Cognitive biases occur when interviewers distort information to support their expectations concerning applicants, for example, with selective attention and recall of information. Behavioral biases, which are the focus of this chapter, occur when interviewers behave in a manner based on their initial perceptions of the applicants. For example, interviewers may display personal interest and positive regard or a lack of interest and negative regard toward candidates based on their initial evaluations of those candidates. In this chapter we examine what has been called *behavioral confirmation* in the interview (Dipboye, 1982): how preinterview impressions influence interviewers' behavior toward applicants. We begin by providing an overview of key studies on interviewers' confirmatory behavior.

The Interviewer as Hypothesis Tester: Experimental Studies

Studies investigating interviewers' use of confirmatory questioning strategies are based upon social psychological studies demonstrating the tendency for people to behave in ways that confirm already held beliefs (Snyder, 1984; Snyder, Campbell, & Preston, 1982; Snyder & Swann, 1978). For example, in an initial study of confirmatory strategies, Snyder and Swann (1978) examined the questioning strategies used by undergraduates in social interactions with others. Subjects were given information about a target person to be interviewed that suggested the person was either an introvert or an extrovert; they then selected interview questions from a list. Subjects were found to use confirmatory questioning strategies, such as selecting more "introverted" question to ask of introverts. Further, in a second study in which actual interviews were conducted, subjects also engaged in confirmatory questioning strategies, with the result that applicants behaved in the expected direction.

Sackett (1982) conducted four studies that extended Snyder and Swann's (1978) research to employment contexts and found little evidence for confirmatory questioning strategies. Overall, Sackett did not find consistent confirmatory strategies when experienced interviewers were used, when an employment interview context was created, or when characteristics other than introvert/extrovert were used. McDonald and Hakel (1985) also investigated expectancy confirmation behaviors, using 170 undergraduate subjects in simulated interviews. Subjects formed first impressions by reviewing résumés of hypothetical applicants; they were then asked to select 10 questions from a list of 30 questions to ask the applicants. Each subject selected a question from the list, read a written response to the question, and then selected another question until 10 questions were selected. The results indicated no clear confirmatory questioning bias.

Macan and Dipboye (1988) extended this line of research, using 26 persons with varied interviewing experience. The subjects formed first impressions by reviewing the credentials of a "paper" applicant and then generated questions to ask the applicant in a subsequent interview. In general, results indicated that interviewers who assessed poorly qualified applicants asked more difficult questions and asked fewer "positive" questions than did interviewers who examined more qualified applicants. However, interviewers did *not* structure questions in a manner forcing applicants' responses to confirm preinterview impressions. Thus, Macan and Dipboye conclude that they found little evidence supporting the view that preinterview impressions lead to strong confirmatory biases.

Binning, Goldstein, Garcia, Harding, and Scattaregia (1988) also used a free question-generation approach to assess the effects of preinterview impressions on student interviewers' questioning strategies. They found that both men and women did adopt confirmatory strategies and that interviewers adopted "disconfirmatory" questioning strategies when interviewing applicants of the opposite sex. However, in addition to generating questions to ask in the interview, subjects also *chose* questions from Sackett's (1982) list of questions. The results indicated that preinterview impressions did not influence the selection of questions. Thus, Binning et al. found support for confirmatory questioning strategies when subjects freely generated their own questions. Their results also suggest that previous studies' requirements that subjects select questions from lists posed a limiting factor for the observation of confirmatory questioning biases.

In a recent replication, Binning, Kaiser, LeBreton, and Williams (1996) examined confirmatory questioning behavior for 135 supervisors in a social service agency. Preinterview impressions significantly affected the supervisors' generation of questions for hypothetical applicants for staff positions. One interesting finding was that interviewers in opposite-gender dyads planned to ask a greater number of questions of low-quality candidates compared with high-quality candidates. In same-gender dyads, however, the total number of questions generated was relatively unaffected by preinterview impressions.

In summary, although the (predominantly) laboratory experiments reviewed above had mixed findings, the results suggest that preinterview impressions do influence interviewers' questioning strategies when interviewers are allowed to generate their own questions. However, these studies all included procedures that may have limited their generalizability to natural interview settings. First, either interviewers were presented with hypotheses about applicants or applicant favorability was manipulated as opposed to naturally generated. Second, in some studies interviewers selected questions from lists, rather than freely generating their own questions. Third, these studies examined the effects of preinterview impressions only on the verbal content of questions, not on other aspects of interviewer behavior. Finally, none of these studies examined expectancy confirmation in actual interview settings.

Research in Actual Interview Settings

Dougherty, Turban, and Callender (1994) examined the influences of interviewers' preinterview impressions on their behaviors in the context of actual interviews in the headquarters employment center of a large energy corporation. This study also differed from the previous laboratory research in that interviewers, in the context of semistructured interviews, were free to ask any questions they wished and to conduct interviews using any format, for any length of time. Dougherty et al. also analyzed both interviewer and applicant behavior, and the study included individual analysis of interviewer behavior as well.

Three interviewers formed first impressions based on application blank and test information and then conducted the interviews, which were audiotaped across 8 months. Coders independently coded 79 interviews for the study. The results demonstrated that first impressions, especially as formed from application blank information, were related to confirmatory behavior. First, interviewers' first impressions from examining application blanks and test scores tended to be positively linked to use of a positive interview style, positive vocal style, and a favorable orientation toward extending a job offer. In addition, interviewers' first impressions from application blanks (but not test scores) tended to be positively related to "selling" the company and job and providing job information to applicants. Although interviewers' first impressions were not related to time spent in interviews, favorable first impressions from application blanks tended to be followed by fewer total questions asked, fewer closed-ended questions, fewer initial questions, and fewer follow-up/probing questions. The study also found that first impressions were related to applicants' use of positive communication styles and rapport with interviewers. An analysis of individual interviewers revealed several differences in their use of expectancy-confirming behaviors and styles, and a number of interviewer behaviors, especially the showing of positive regard, were related to applicant communication style and rapport with interviewers.

In summary, laboratory and field studies have produced some evidence that interviewers behave in ways that confirm their initial expectations of applicants. If interviewers engage in confirmatory behavior, an obvious initial question is, What are the potential costs and benefits of interviewers' confirmatory behavior in terms of the incremental validity of interviews?

Value of Interviewers' Confirmatory Behavior for the Selection Process

Are interviewers who engage in confirmatory behavior guilty of a bias with serious implications for the interview and its validity? Confirmatory behavior may be a bias because the interviewer could be distorting the process of collecting job-relevant information from applicants in an accurate and objective fashion. It is interesting to note that this particular source of bias is unique because it can be measured only through the assessment of the *relationships* of first impressions with interviewer behavior. It may be important to assess which of an organization's interviewers are "more susceptible" to the expectancy confirmation bias, especially if this bias is related to the incremental validity of the employment interview.

The notion of the incremental validity of the interview focuses on whether the interview explains additional variance in the criterion (e.g., job success) beyond whatever information is available about applicants before the interview. Dipboye (1992) notes that the small number of studies that have attempted to establish this incremental contribution of interview information are not encouraging. He also points out that even the studies that appear to provide evidence of incremental validity are extremely limited in their support. In addition, inexpensive methods such as paper-and-pencil measures have often been found to achieve the same level of prediction of applicant success as the (more expensive) interview.

It may be that confirmatory behavior on the part of interviewers plays some role in the interview's incremental validity. Consider the potential effects of an extremely high level of interviewer confirmatory behavior. In this scenario, the interviewer assesses the applicant's credentials, perhaps based on test scores or the résumé, and then behaves during the interview in a manner consistent with the preinterview impression. This behavior toward an applicant could have the effect of eliciting behavior from the applicant that is also consistent with the preinterview impression. Because this interview provides essentially no new information about the applicant, there would likely be little incremental validity beyond the preinterview information.

In contrast, consider an interviewer who engages in little or no confirmatory behavior. We might also question the value of this strategy. For example, an interviewer with no motivation to confirm first impressions may not be doing enough probing, following up, and eliciting of job-relevant information from the applicant—some of the behaviors that would appear to constitute a confirmatory style (see Dougherty et al., 1994). This interviewer may not be contributing enough job-relevant information for the interview to offer any incremental validity beyond preinterview information. Thus, for different reasons, extremely high and extremely low levels of confirmatory behavior may result in little incremental validity for the interview.

Given the reasoning presented above, is it possible that some "moderate" or intermediate level of confirmatory behavior is optimal for interview validity? The research conducted by Dougherty and his colleagues with three corporate interviewers identified one interviewer who made decisions that were valid predictors of applicant job success (Dougherty, Ebert, & Callender, 1986; Dougherty et al., 1994). Interestingly, this same interviewer was also found to be in the *middle* of the three interviewers on "susceptibility" to confirmatory behavior. Of course, although this interviewer was "in the middle," we cannot be sure that this was a "moderate" level of confirmatory behavior. The naturally occurring variance in confirmatory behavior is not yet known. Important issues for future research include exactly what observable behaviors constitute confirmatory behavior, how variant they are in a typical interviewer population, and what portion of the variance can be systematically explained.

We also need a better understanding of the connection between confirmatory and *disconfirmatory* interview behavior. Rowe (1989) points out that research on confirmatory behavior provides evidence that interviewers prefer to ask "positive" questions and that the interview is not a search for negative information. Given that positive questions could be either confirmatory or disconfirmatory, the linkages among confirmatory, disconfirmatory, positive, and negative questioning could be fruitful avenues to explore in future research.

We should also note that interviewers' confirmatory behavior is likely to be influenced by the extent to which the organization *formalizes* interviewers' first impressions of applicants. In the Dougherty et al. (1994) study, for example, interviewers were asked to *rate* applicant qualifications based on test scores and the application blank on an interview rating form at the beginning of each interview. Such a requirement for formal ratings of applicant qualifications may encourage the forming of, or make more salient, first impressions of the applicant, which are then followed by confirmatory behavior in the interview. As a research issue this procedure can be seen as a boundary condition of the study, in that confirmatory behavior may be more likely to be observed when first impressions have been solidified. Formalizing first impressions also has practical implications for encouraging or discouraging confirmatory behavior by interviewers. As we have pointed out, however, it is not clear how desirable or undesirable some level of confirmatory behavior might be for the validity of the interview.

The preceding discussion suggests that we have much to learn about the sources of interviewers' first impressions and the relative impacts of various factors on first impressions and on confirmatory behavior. In the next section we suggest several contextual and individual difference factors that may be sources of, or may constitute limitations on, confirmatory behavior.

Limits on Confirmatory Behavior: Contextual and Individual Difference Factors

Contextual Factors

It seems likely that both contextual factors and individual difference factors influence the extent to which individuals engage in confirmatory behaviors in the interview. Any contextual factor that constrains interviewer behavior is expected to influence the extent to which individuals engage in confirmatory behaviors. For example, interviews that are highly *structured* in terms of the questions asked, the order of questions, how questions are evaluated, and so on should be less amenable to interviewer confirmatory behaviors than more unstructured interviews. The increased structure of the interview limits variability in interviewer behavior and therefore limits the possible effects of preinterview expectations.

Interviews of different "planned interview lengths" may also produce different amounts of confirmatory behavior (see Buckley & Eder, 1988). Tullar, Mullins, and Caldwell (1979) found that the planned length of an interview had an effect on the *time* needed for interviewers to make decisions. Confirmatory behavior could be related to, and in fact may be part of, this process.

The training of interviewers may result in fewer confirmatory behaviors if interviewers are trained to ask questions in a set manner. In this vein, however, Dougherty et al. (1994) found essentially no changes in interviewers' confirmatory behavior over a 4-month period following a week of interviewer training oriented toward questioning techniques and the conduct of semistructured interviews. Additionally, training could focus on the importance of recruiting applicants and "selling" the organization in addition to the traditional focus on evaluating applicants (Rynes, 1989). We expect that interviewers who are trained to focus on recruiting (versus evaluating) applicants will engage in fewer confirmatory behaviors because they will instead engage in positive selling behaviors toward all applicants. Similarly, a high selection ratio (few applicants per open position) may also constrain confirmatory behaviors if interviewers sell the job and the organization to all applicants.

In summary, it seems likely that contextual factors may influence the extent of interviewer confirmatory behaviors, although we are not aware of research investigating such effects.

Individual Differences in Susceptibility to Confirmatory Behavior

As discussed earlier, some evidence suggests that individuals vary in their susceptibility to exhibiting confirmatory behavior in interviews (Dougherty et al., 1994), although no research has investigated factors influencing such differences in susceptibility. We suggest that researchers consider investigating individual differences that may affect confirmatory behavior. To assist that process, we speculate below on some potential variables that may influence variability in confirmatory behaviors in interviews.

Considerable evidence indicates that individuals vary in the extent to which they engage in and enjoy cognitive endeavors, which has been called *need for cognition* (Cacioppo, Petty, Feinstein, & Jarvis, 1996). Individuals high in need for cognition are more likely to seek, acquire, and think about stimuli and events in their world, whereas individuals low in need for cognition are more likely to rely on cognitive heuristics in understanding events in their world. We would speculate that interviewers high in need for cognition, who have a desire to seek detailed information about their world (and therefore the applicant), would exhibit fewer confirmatory behaviors in interviews than would interviewers low in need for cognition. In contrast, we expect that interviewers low in need for cognition would be more likely to make decisions about applicants on the basis of preinterview information. These interviewers would engage in more confirmatory behaviors than would individuals high in need for cognition, who are more likely to continue seeking information about applicants. Note that, consistent with the topic of this chapter, we focus here on the effects of need for cognition on interviewer confirmatory *behavior*. However, need for cognition may also influence the cognitive processing of interviewers. More specifically, interviewers who are low in need for cognition would be expected to engage in less cognitive processing than would interviewers who are high in need for cognition, and thus would be more susceptible to preinterview effects.

Much of the current work in personality deals with what has been called the Big Five factor structure (Barrick & Mount, 1991; Hogan, 1991). Of the Big Five personality dimensions, we expect that *conscientiousness* is the dimension most likely to influence interviewers' engaging in confirmatory behavior in interviews. Individuals high in conscientiousness are more dependable, careful, and thorough than are individuals low in conscientiousness. If interviewers who are more careful and thorough are more likely to conduct detailed, thorough interviews, regardless of the applicants' credentials, then these interviewers are less susceptible to exhibiting confirmatory behavior than are individuals who are lower in conscientiousness.

Finally, we expect that *self-monitoring* (Snyder, 1984) may be related to the extent to which individuals engage in confirmatory behaviors. Individuals low in self-monitoring tend to behave consistently across situations, in part because they lack the ability or motivation to change their behavior in response to various situations. In contrast, individuals high in self-monitoring have the ability and the motivation to change their behaviors across situations and exhibit considerable variability across situations. Therefore, we expect that interviewers high in self-monitoring will engage in more confirmatory behaviors than will interviewers low in self-monitoring because of the expected greater variability in their behaviors across situations; we expect low self-monitors, in contrast, to behave consistently across interviews.

In summary, in an attempt to spur additional research, we have proposed several contextual factors and individual difference factors that may account for the extent to which interviewers are influenced by preinterview information and behave in a confirmatory manner. No doubt there are other contextual and individual factors that also influence interviewers' confirmatory behaviors.

Nonverbal and Applicant Behavior

Research on expectancy confirmation in interviews can be extended to the investigation of interviewer *nonverbal* behaviors that may be influenced by preinterview expectations. Dougherty et al. (1994), using audiotaped interviews, measured interviewers' vocal styles and use of a positive interview style. Future researchers might videotape interviews so that they can measure additional interviewer nonverbal behaviors, such as facial expressions, extent of eye contact, and posture. Researchers might find that these physical nonverbal behaviors are more influenced by preinterview expectations than are the vocal nonverbal measures.

One study has investigated the effects of *applicant* preinterview beliefs on applicant behavior in the interview. Stevens (1997) found that applicants' preinterview beliefs about the job affected their behavior in interviews such that applicants with greater expectancies of receiving a job offer from the company engaged in more impression management behavior and asked more confirmatory questions than did applicants with lower expectancies. Such results suggest that both applicants and interviewers engage in confirmatory behaviors in interviews.

Research investigating confirmatory behavior in interviews can also be extended to attempts to measure the self-fulfilling aspect of preinterview expectations. An interviewer's self-fulfilling prophecy results when the interviewer's behavior toward an applicant causes the applicant to behave in the manner expected by the interviewer. Much of the research has examined whether interviewers' behavior is influenced by their expectations about applicants, and some evidence supports the idea that preinterview expectations influence interviewers' behavior toward applicants.

Research is needed, however, to investigate whether *applicants* behave differently in interviews based on the *interviewers'* preinterview expectations.

Conclusion

Confirmatory behavior by interviewers is but one component of an overall interview process in which preinterview evaluations of applicants become self-fulfilling. The overall process takes place across several interview phases: an implicit or explicit evaluation of applicant credentials, a face-to-face interview, and a final, explicit evaluation of the applicant (Dipboye, 1982). Several of the studies reviewed here provide evidence that interviewers do engage in behavior that confirms initial impressions of applicants. In this chapter we have attempted to provide some insights about this research and its implications for research and practice. For example, we have pointed out that we still know little about the determinants of, or constraints on, confirmatory behavior. There also is little understanding of the consequences of confirmatory behavior for interview validity. We must acknowledge that many additional issues and questions remain. Nevertheless, we hope that our discussion will serve as a stimulus for future investigations of interviewers' confirmatory behavior, which is still relatively uncharted territory in the study of the employment interview.

References

Barrick, M., & Mount, M. (1991). The Big Five personality dimensions and job performance: A meta-analysis. *Personnel Psychology, 44,* 1-26.

Binning, J. F., Goldstein, M. A., Garcia, M. F., Harding, J. L., & Scattaregia, J. H. (1988). Effects of preinterview impressions on questioning strategies in same- and opposite-sex employment interviews. *Journal of Applied Psychology, 73,* 30-37.

Binning, J. F., Kaiser, R. B., LeBreton, J. M., & Williams, K. B. (1996). *A field study of preinterview effects on interviewers' questioning strategies in same- and opposite-gender employment interviews.* Unpublished manuscript.

Buckley, M. R., & Eder, R. W. (1988). B. M. Springbett and the notion of the "snap decision" in the interview. *Journal of Management, 14,* 59-67.

Cacioppo, J. T., Petty, R. E., Feinstein, J. A., & Jarvis, W. B. G. (1996). Dispositional differences in cognitive motivation: The life and times of individuals varying in need for cognition. *Psychological Bulletin, 119,* 197-253.

Dipboye, R. L. (1982). Self-fulfilling prophecies in the selection interview. *Academy of Management Review, 7,* 579-586.

Dipboye, R. L. (1992). *Selection interviews: Process perspectives.* Cincinnati, OH: South-Western.

Dougherty, T. W., Ebert, R. J., & Callender, J. C. (1986). Policy capturing in the employment interview. *Journal of Applied Psychology, 71,* 9-15.

Dougherty, T. W., Turban, D. B., & Callender, J. C. (1994). Confirming first impressions in the employment interview: A field study of interviewer behavior. *Journal of Applied Psychology, 79,* 659-665.

Eden, D. (1984). Self-fulfilling prophecy as a management tool: Harnessing Pygmalion. *Academy of Management Review, 9,* 64-73.

Eden, D. (1990). *Pygmalion in management.* Lexington, MA: Lexington.

Hogan, R. T. (1991). Personality and personality measurement. In M. D. Dunnette & L. M. Hough (Eds.), *Handbook of industrial and organizational psychology* (2nd ed., Vol. 2, pp. 873-919). Palo Alto, CA: Consulting Psychologists Press.

Lin, T.-R., Dobbins, G. H., & Farh, J.-L. (1992). A field study of race and age similarity effects on interview ratings in conventional and situational interviews. *Journal of Applied Psychology, 77,* 363-371.

Macan, T. H., & Dipboye, R. L. (1988). The effects of interviewers' initial impressions on information gathering. *Organizational Behavior and Human Decision Processes, 42,* 364-387.

McDonald, T., & Hakel, M. D. (1985). Effects of applicant race, sex, suitability, and answers on interviewers' questioning strategy and ratings. *Personnel Psychology, 38,* 321-334.

Merton, R. K. (1948). The self-fulfilling prophecy. *Antioch Review, 8*(1), 193-210.

Prewett-Livingston, A. J., Feild, H. S., Veres, J. G., III, & Lewis, P. M. (1996). Effects of race on interview ratings in a situational panel interview. *Journal of Applied Psychology, 81,* 178-186.

Rowe, P. M. (1989). Unfavorable information and interview decisions. In R. W. Eder & G. R. Ferris (Eds.), *The employment interview: Theory, research, and practice* (pp. 77-89). Newbury Park, CA: Sage.

Rynes, S. L. (1989). The employment interview as a recruitment device. In R. W. Eder & G. R. Ferris (Eds.), *The employment interview: Theory, research, and practice* (pp. 127-141). Newbury Park, CA: Sage.

Sackett, P. R. (1982). The interviewer as hypothesis tester: The effects of impressions of an applicant on interviewer questioning strategy. *Personnel Psychology, 35,* 789-804.

Snyder, M. (1984). When belief creates reality. In L. Berkowitz (Ed.), *Advances in experimental social psychology* (Vol. 18, pp. 247-305). New York: Academic Press.

Snyder, M., Campbell, B., & Preston, E. (1982). Testing hypotheses about human nature: Assessing the accuracy of social stereotypes. *Social Cognition, 1,* 256-272.

Snyder, M., & Swann, W. B. (1978). Hypothesis-testing processes in social interaction. *Journal of Personality and Social Psychology, 36,* 1202-1212.

Stevens, C. K. (1997). The effects of preinterview beliefs on applicants' reactions to campus interviews. *Academy of Management Journal, 40,* 947-966.

Tullar, W. L., Mullins, T. W., & Caldwell, S. A. (1979). Effects of interview length and applicant quality on interview decision time. *Journal of Applied Psychology, 64,* 669-674.

13

How Indirect Unfavorable Information Is Evaluated

K. Michele Kacmar
Angela M. Young

Accurately selecting job applicants remains a central issue in human resource management. Hiring an applicant who is ineffective can cost the organization time, money, and even goodwill. Given the high stakes of interview decisions, one of the main goals of an interviewer is to find ways during the interview to eliminate unacceptable candidates. Unacceptable candidates in an interviewer's eyes are those who do not perform adequately in the interview. This lack of performance can result from a variety of causes, but is often uncovered when unfavorable information about an applicant is presented. Therefore, the interview has been characterized as a search for negative applicant information (Dipboye, 1992; Webster, 1982).

Past research in negativity effects in the interview has focused mainly on direct types of unfavorable information. Direct unfavorable information consists of negative aspects about the applicant, such as a low grade point average (Dipboye, Stamler, & Fontenelle, 1984), poor letters of reference (Belec & Rowe, 1983; Tucker & Rowe, 1979), and negative statements taken from personnel reports (Bolster & Springbett, 1961). Direct unfavorable information clearly has been found to have a negative impact on interviewers' decisions. What has not been explored is the identification of indirect unfavorable forms of information presented by applicants; that is the focus of this chapter.

Prior to exploring the new concept of indirect unfavorable information, we present a theoretical foundation for the current study. We build this foundation by reviewing the research on negativity effects in the interview. The stream of negativity effects research provides evidence of the relevance and impact of negative information on interviewer decision making. Direct forms of negative information have been examined in previous studies, but we seek to expand the concept of negative information to include direct and indirect forms of unfavorable information in the employment interview.

Negativity Effects Research

The fact that interviewers seek negative information in an interview has been confirmed in a variety of studies (Blakeney & MacNaughton, 1971; Bolster & Springbett, 1961; Carlson, 1971; Dipboye et al., 1984; Hollman, 1972; Peters & Terborg, 1975; Springbett, 1958). This line of research was begun by Springbett (1958), who found that early impressions formed by an interviewer played a major role in the final decision, and that the final decision was made early in the interview, after only a few minutes. Given that his findings revealed that uncovering even one unfavorable item about a candidate resulted in rejection in 90% of the cases, Springbett dubbed the interview a "search for negative information."

In an effort to confirm Springbett's (1958) findings, Bolster and Springbett (1961) undertook a study in which 16 U.S. Army officers were provided with favorable and unfavorable statements taken from officer selection reports. Their responses to these items indicated that decision shifts from acceptance to rejection were more easily made than the opposite. That is, negative information carried more weight than did positive information.

Hollman (1972) criticized the scales used by Springbett (1958) and Bolster and Springbett (1961) and set out to conduct a more sound study of negativity effects. Hollman asked experienced interviewers to evaluate applicants after each new piece of information was presented so that decision shifts based on the new information could be determined. He found that interviewers did not weigh positive information heavily enough, but that they did apply the appropriate weight to negative information.

In another study, Miller and Rowe (1967) found that a heavier weight was applied for unfavorable information. These researchers tested five different favorable/unfavorable information conditions: three favorable/one unfavorable; three favorable/two unfavorable; three favorable/three unfavorable; two favorable/three unfavorable; and one favorable/three unfavorable. In all but the first condition, the unfavorable information was more influential in the decision process than was the favorable.

Temporal Placement of Unfavorable Information

One specific aspect of negativity effects that has been explored is at what point in the interview the negative information is presented. For example, Peters and Terborg (1975) placed three unfavorable or favorable pieces of information at the beginning of the interview and then alternated the presentation of the remaining neutral, favorable, and unfavorable information pieces (i.e., U U U F N F N F versus F F F U N U N U). Their results indicated that subjects were less likely to hire an applicant in the early unfavorable information condition. This suggests that early presentation of negative information can negatively bias an interviewer.

Confirmation of the importance of ordering unfavorable information can be found in Farr's (1973) work. Specifically, Farr manipulated the order in which favorable and unfavorable information was presented. The most variance was accounted for by the order in which the favorable information was presented, with recency effects being the most prominent. Hakel, Dobmeyer, and Dunnette (1970) found that unfavorable information could be overcome if the area of the interview in which it occurred was less important than other areas in which favorable information was presented. For example, Hakel et al. found that raters gave applicants with average grades, excellent work experience, and appropriate interests *lower* ratings than they gave applicants with poor work experience and appropriate interests who had higher scholastic standings. In this case, because scholastic standing was extremely important to the raters, individuals with two pieces of unfavorable information were preferred to those with only one unfavorable piece of information about scholastic standing.

All of the research discussed above indicates that interviewers often weight unfavorable information more heavily than favorable information. Further, it has been shown that as little as one piece of negative information can result in a rejection. Although the impact of negative information on the interview process is clear, *why* negative information is so important in the decision-making process has not been investigated as thoroughly. However, explanations for using negative information are relevant to a complete understanding of negativity effects. Thus, we review next the theories posited to explain why this phenomenon occurs.

Explanations of Negativity Effects

A variety of explanations or theories have been presented to explain why the interview is a search for negative information. Webster (1964) suggests that because interviewers receive only negative feedback about past hires (i.e., reports on those who failed), this is the only information they have to use in subsequent interviews. Hence, to avoid making the same mistakes, they attempt to solicit information that would indicate that other candidates may fail in the same ways. Tullar (1989) gives a somewhat related explanation, suggesting that interviewer and applicant behavior is often determined by the cognitive scripts both hold for the interview event. According to Tullar, the impact of the unfavorable information in the interview is likely to be influenced by the temporal placement of the negative information during the interview given the cognitive script held by the interviewer. If negative information occurs at a point where the interviewer's cognitive script calls for an extremely important response, the negative information could have a greater impact.

Another explanation for negativity effects has been provided by Skowronski and Carlston (1989), who suggest that negativity effects are found when negative cues are more useful (i.e., more diagnostic) in the decision-making process. For example, they assert that negative information is more useful in morality judgments because even bad people act good sometimes, but good people rarely act bad. So, if negative morality information is found, the decision maker will assume that the applicant is a bad person. Positive information, on the other hand, is more useful in ability judgments because high-ability people may fail, but low-ability persons rarely succeed. Hence, if the interviewer encounters positive ability information during the interview, he or she will be correct more often, assuming that the information describes a common occurrence for a high-ability applicant rather than a freak occurrence for a low-ability one.

Rowe (1984, 1989) also provides an explanation for why negative information is more important than positive information to interviewers in the decision-making process. She suggests that the interviewer develops a picture of the best applicant for the position. This picture of the ideal candidate may be based on the interviewer's beliefs, stereotypes, and biases as well as on the requirements for the job. During the interview, the interviewer seeks information that will indicate how closely the applicant matches the ideal candidate. So the interviewer must make a hire decision based upon the amount of deviance the applicant has from the ideal candidate. In this case, the interviewer seeks information that will affirm his or her stereotypical ideal candidate, but instead finds mismatches (i.e., negative information) between the candidate and the ideal.

In all of the studies reviewed above, unfavorable information took the form of disparaging remarks made by the applicant or about the applicant by someone else. These were all direct comments spoken or written by or about the applicant. The impact of such direct unfavorable pieces of information is evident in past studies. What is missing from these examinations is the influence of *indirect* unfavorable information. Expanding the breadth of negativity effects by investigating and defining indirect unfavorable information contributes to our existing knowledge of the interview process in several ways. First, defining indirect types of negative information refines the existing idea of negativity effects. Second, it is likely that indirect unfavorable information is distinct from direct forms of negative information, and thus the impact of indirect unfavorable information could differ from that of direct forms of negative information. Distinguishing between these two broad categories of negative information is a start toward pinpointing precise behaviors, verbal and nonverbal, displayed by successful and unsuccessful candidates. Finally, no emergent categories or definitions of unfavorable information have been introduced, and no suggestions have been made to guide future research.

Our purpose in this chapter is to investigate the occurrence of unfavorable indirect responses in a sample of interviews. From this investigation, the concept of indirect unfavorable information can be developed. The study reported here was based on a content analysis of actual interviews. Responses made by applicants in 34 different interviews were coded; an indirect unfavorable response was coded if a candidate was unable to respond to a question or responded inappropriately.

Indirect Unfavorable Information Defined

Given that indirect unfavorable information in the employment interview has not been examined previously, we need to begin our investigation with a definition. We define indirect unfavorable information as verbal or nonverbal behaviors that weaken the applicant's position in the eyes of the interviewer. Interview responses that convey indirect unfavorable information can take one of three forms. First, an unfavorable response can occur when an applicant is simply unable to respond to a question. Second, an unfavorable response may take the form of an inappropriate response to a question, such as when the interviewer asks specifically about an experience in a work setting and the applicant relates a story about school. Finally, an unfavorable response occurs when an applicant answers an interviewer's question, but fails to cast the response in the most positive light possible— for example, when an interviewer comments on the level of difficulty of

the courses the applicant has taken and the applicant assures the interviewer that the course titles make them sound much more difficult than
they really were.

Interview Transcripts

In order to isolate the types of statements that are indicative of indirect
unfavorable information, we conducted a content analysis of 34 interview
transcripts from actual interviews that were conducted as part of two
different training classes for a *Fortune* 500 company. Each training class
lasted 3 days and included a total of 10 interviewers. The first day of the
class was taken up entirely with classroom work, during which the structured interviewing technique used by the firm was taught. The second day
focused on the on-site interview format, which is used when an applicant
is brought to the company for a full day of interviewing. During the
afternoon of the second day, students from a university near the training
facility were brought to the training location so that the interviewers could
perform practice interviews with actual applicants. The third day of training focused on the on-campus interview format, with the afternoon being
reserved for a second set of practice interviews with a different group of
actual applicants.

Just prior to each interview, both a video camera and an audiocassette
recorder were turned on to record the interview. At the completion of the
interview, the equipment was stopped and the interviewer was asked to rate
the applicant. A total of 34 of these taped interviews were later transcribed
and used in this study. Because the applicants were rotated from room to
room until each interviewer had performed an interview, each applicant
may have participated in more than one interview. However, the 34 interview transcripts analyzed for this study were based on unique interviewer-
applicant combinations. Although the main purpose of these interviews
was to provide training for the recruiters, applicants who performed well
in the interviews were scheduled for on-site interviews and were eventually
hired.

Content Analysis

In applicant responses to interviewer questions, a number of different
messages can be sent based on words, gestures, and intonation. In the
content analysis, the statements uttered by the applicant in response to an
interviewer's questions were the focus of analysis. Three categories of
indirect unfavorable information emerged based on the content analysis:
missing the information, missing the mark, and missing the opportunity.

We describe these categories in turn below and present sample responses for each type.

Missing the Information

In some cases, an applicant simply does not understand the question or what type of information the interviewer is seeking. Although the applicant may not give a direct negative response, a request for clarification or an admission of misunderstanding occurs. An example of missing the information can be seen in the following excerpt from an interview session. The applicant was discussing a test-taking experience in a college course. The test, according to the applicant, was very difficult, and studying for the test was a formidable task. This exchange is from the subsequent discussion, in which the interviewer attempted to glean more detail from the applicant:

Applicant: It was just the stress and it was a very difficult test.
Interviewer: Did you do anything in particular to help yourself?
Applicant: To help myself?
Interviewer: With the test.
Applicant: With the test?

The applicant may have needed to ask the series of clarification questions in order eventually to answer the initial question; however, such continual misunderstanding and subsequent inability to answer a question may have a negative effect on an interviewer's overall rating of an applicant.

Another example of missing the information is present in an exchange that took place later in the same interview. The interviewer was closing the interview with an invitation to the applicant to ask some questions:

Interviewer: . . . I'd like to ask if you have any questions of me or uhm anything maybe that we haven't covered in this discussion of the two situations that maybe I can answer for you?
Applicant: Not that I can think of.
Interviewer: Uh huh.
Applicant: I'm not quite sure what to ask. Actually I'm not quite sure what you're looking for, what's going on, so I don't know.

In this exchange, the applicant is making an admission of misunderstanding and is unable to answer the question. Such a lack of understanding at this point in the interview is likely to be viewed negatively by the interviewer.

Missing the Mark

Another form of misunderstanding comes from an applicant's providing an inappropriate answer to an interviewer's question. The difference between missing the mark and missing the information has to do with the applicant's response itself. An applicant who is missing the information simply does not attempt to answer the question, and requests clarification or admits a lack of comprehension. An applicant who is missing the mark answers the question, but provides an inappropriate response, and is thus off the mark. An example of an applicant missing the mark can be seen in the following exchange, in which the interviewer requested that the applicant provide more information on an interview experience the applicant discussed earlier:

Interviewer: Let me backtrack to the interview. After the interview was over with uh, what happened next.
Applicant: I went to Dairy Queen and got an ice tea because my mouth was so dry I thought I was going, my lips were stuck to my teeth and so—you mean what happened next as far as the . . .
Interviewer: Yes, after that, as far as the process.

In this exchange the applicant provided an answer to the interviewer's question, but the answer was not in direct response to the question.

Missing the Opportunity

Missing the opportunity occurs when an applicant understands the question and provides an answer, but the answer does not convey information about the applicant's knowledge, skills, or abilities in the most positive light possible. Following is an example of missing the opportunity; in this exchange, the interviewer was asking the applicant a series of questions to pinpoint the applicant's particular role in a group project:

Interviewer: So, how did you become the group's leader?
Applicant: Well, I was chosen by the people in the group.

At this point in the interview, the applicant could have represented him- or herself more positively, by identifying particular skills or reasons for leadership. In other words, the applicant missed the opportunity to expound on some of his or her positive attributes and skills, such as desire or ability to lead the group. Later in the same interview, the applicant failed to take advantage of an opportunity to elaborate on effort and achievement during a group project:

Interviewer: The ah describe a little bit maybe what you did in the group to make it work?

Applicant: Well, pretty much what we did we ah we did do a lot of research. Uh, a lot of it was uh out of class time and uh in which we got together. And uhm, we talked about it, it was it was really more than anything it really was a group's effort. So, I can't take credit for it uh completely, but uh . . .

In this example, the applicant could easily have complimented the group effort while delineating his or her personal achievements. Instead, the applicant's statement drops off, with neither a closing point nor an account of effort or achievement.

Missing the opportunity differs from missing the information and missing the mark in that missing the opportunity is a case of an applicant indicating the possession of some knowledge, skill, or ability without framing the KSA in the most positive light possible. In the case of the last applicant discussed, for example, if he or she had missed the mark, a likely response might have included information unrelated to the group activity. If he or she had missed the information, the response would have indicated a lack of understanding of the question.

Future Research

Each of our proposed categories of indirect unfavorable information represents some obstacle in the exchange of interviewer questions and applicant responses. The extent to which these indirect negative responses will hinder an applicant's ratings of performance and hirability remains to be seen through empirical verification. How we can isolate negative information in the interview and test its effects on interview outcomes requires further investigation. Therefore, we discuss below some ideas for future research.

Identifying Categories of Indirect Unfavorable Information

The study reported in this chapter was exploratory in nature. Based on this study, we have introduced three prospective categories of indirect negative information presented in statements uttered by applicants in response to interviewers' questions. We readily admit that these categories may not constitute a comprehensive taxonomy; further research is needed to confirm and expand our list. Therefore, first and foremost, our initial categories must be tested for discriminant and construct validity.

Distinguishing among the categories of indirect unfavorable information is somewhat subjective, just as other events and behaviors in the interview setting are perhaps reliably detectable but not perfectly objective. Such subjective behaviors include dress, gestures, and intonation. Just as the detection of these behaviors varies among observers, the impacts of these behaviors vary depending on the interviewers, job requirements, applicant KSAs, and so on. Although indirect information is somewhat subjective, there are objective and identifiable elements in most statements uttered by applicants. For instance, in the last exchange offered as an example above, the interviewer requested information on what the applicant did to make the group effort a success. The objective elements in this question are the applicant's work in a group and the group's achievement, which had been previously established.

The extent to which an applicant defines, embellishes, and describes his or her efforts or achievements depends on many elements, such as the exchange quality between the interviewer and applicant and the applicant's verbal ability, nervousness, general knowledge, past experiences, and interview experience. Despite the reason for the applicant's presenting indirect unfavorable information, the occurrence of the unfavorable information remains. In this chapter we have established the occurrence of indirect unfavorable information as a first step in studying this new concept. The reasons applicants present unfavorable information and the impacts of such information are yet to be investigated.

In terms of the construct of indirect unfavorable information, distinctiveness and validity of the construct itself must be verified. We presume that indirect forms of unfavorable information are indeed distinct from direct forms of negative information. Whether or not this presumption is accurate requires further investigation. Moreover, researchers must further examine negative information in general in order to refine the concept of indirect unfavorable information and to determine the role that indirect information plays in negativity effects. We have framed our discussion here in terms of negativity effects, but it may prove beneficial for researchers to explore broader theoretical foundations, such as impression management.

Impression management may encompass a broader range of behaviors, including direct as well as indirect negative information. Although impression management is usually associated with the presentation of oneself in the best possible light, the breadth of accepted applications of impression management is increasing (see Rosenfeld & Giacalone, 1991). Evidence of the growing breadth and application of impression management research is provided by Becker and Martin (1995), who studied forms and motives of purposely developing a negative impression for oneself at work. In keeping with impression management as a tactic to shape impressions that others may form, Becker and Martin found that individuals may seek to present negative information about themselves. These authors reason that individuals control information, both positive and negative, about themselves in order to obtain desired purposes, which may be achieved through poor rather than positive impressions. In light of existing research on impression management as a framework for studying the interview process, more research is needed on where negativity effects, direct and indirect, fit into the existing body of knowledge of impression management.

Indirect Unfavorable Information in the Interview Process

Eder, Kacmar, and Ferris (1989) have presented an integrated framework to illustrate the relationships among various streams of employment interview research. Using that framework, we can pinpoint several relevant areas in which to study indirect unfavorable information in the employment interview process as well as the relevant antecedent factors and outcomes related to the presence of indirect unfavorable information.

Information Processing and Impression Formation

Indirect unfavorable information is a central part of information processing in the employment interview. A direct assessment of the effect of indirect unfavorable information on interviewer perceptions would shed light on the interview exchange itself and how indirect unfavorable information influences impressions made by the applicant. Further exploration of the different decision styles and cognitive structures of interviewers, such as those presented by Schuh (1989), is one potential approach to studying the influence of indirect unfavorable information presented by the applicant.

Further, extending Rowe's (1989) discussion on unfavorable information effects, the basis on which an interviewer forms his or her decisions is likely to influence the interview and its outcomes. Specifically, the interviewer's use of a positive or negative test strategy has been shown to influence decisions made by the interviewer throughout the interview process (Binning, Goldstein, Garcia, Harding, & Scattaregia, 1988; Klayman & Ha, 1987; Rowe, 1989; Sackett, 1982). According to Rowe (1989), an interviewer who uses a negative hypothesis test presumes that an applicant is an ill fit to the position, and thus any negative information the applicant presents will confirm the interviewer's hypothesis. An interviewer who uses a positive hypothesis test examines the applicant for possession of knowledge, skills, and abilities that fit the position. Given the interviewer's predisposition toward positive or negative testing of an applicant, questions dealing with effects of indirect unfavorable information in each scenario would advance knowledge of the effects of information processing during the interview.

From a slightly different perspective, interviewer verbal and nonverbal behavior during the interview is another useful focus for the study of indirect unfavorable information. The employment interview is often used as more than a screening device to select applicants; it is also the foundation for presenting an organization to applicants (Rynes, 1989). Relevant research issues include the indirect unfavorable information presented by an interviewer through verbal and nonverbal behaviors and specific statements or questions that may be perceived negatively by the applicant.

Antecedent Factors

Antecedent factors relevant to the interview exchange itself include applicant and interviewer characteristics and preinterview impression effects (see Eder et al., 1989). Relevant research questions dealing with the preinterview impressions formed by an interviewer may provide additional information on the stability of preinterview impressions and the resilience of those impressions in the face of indirect unfavorable information. Macan and Dipboye (1990) found that interviewers gave higher performance ratings to applicants when the preinterview evaluation was favorable. Moreover, they found that positive perceptions of an applicant in the preinterview phase were less likely to change than were negative perceptions held over from the preinterview phase.

The preinterview assessment itself may influence not only the interviewer's perceptions of the applicant's suitability, but the interview process. It follows, then, that the presentation of indirect unfavorable information could influence interviewer perceptions, and thus interview outcomes, differently depending on the preinterview impressions an interviewer forms about an applicant.

Interview Outcomes

The outcomes of the employment interview, such as perceptions of an applicant and the ultimate hiring decision, are relevant dependent variables that are likely to be influenced by the presence of indirect unfavorable information. Some pertinent research issues relevant to interview outcomes include the influence of indirect unfavorable information and the effectual differences between indirect and direct negative information. We have presented here three categories of indirect unfavorable information. The varied degrees of influence of these categories constitute another important and pending issue. Also, the frequency of indirect unfavorable information in relation to positive information presented during the interview is relevant to perceptual and behavioral outcomes.

In this chapter we have introduced three categories of indirect unfavorable information and presented suggestions for future research on negative information and indirect unfavorable information in particular. A better understanding of the influence of indirect unfavorable information on the interview process would allow for a more complete picture of the employment interview and its usefulness in the selection process.

References

Becker, T. E., & Martin, S. L. (1995). Trying to look bad at work: Methods and motives for managing poor impressions in organizations. *Academy of Management Journal, 38,* 174-199.

Belec, B. E., & Rowe, P. M. (1983). Temporal placement of information, expectancy, causal attributions, and overall final judgments in employment decision making. *Canadian Journal of Behavior Science, 53,* 61-70.

Binning, J. F., Goldstein, M. A., Garcia, M. F., Harding, J. L., & Scattaregia, J. H. (1988). Effects of preinterview impressions on questioning strategies in same- and opposite-sex employment interviews. *Journal of Applied Psychology, 71,* 30-37.

Blakeney, R. N., & MacNaughton, J. F. (1971). Effects of temporal placement of unfavorable information on decision making during the selection interview. *Journal of Applied Psychology, 55,* 138-142.

Bolster, B. I., & Springbett, B. M. (1961). The reaction of interviewers to favorable and unfavorable information. *Journal of Applied Psychology, 45,* 97-103.

Carlson, R. E. (1971). Effect of interview information in altering valid impressions. *Journal of Applied Psychology, 55,* 66-72.

Dipboye, R. L. (1992). *Selection interviews: Process perspectives.* Cincinnati, OH: South-Western.

Dipboye, R. L., Stamler, C., & Fontenelle, G. A. (1984). The effects of the application on recall of information from the interview. *Academy of Management Journal, 27,* 561-575.

Eder, R. W., Kacmar, K. M., & Ferris, G. R. (1989). Employment interview research: History and synthesis. In R. W. Eder & G. R. Ferris (Eds.), *The employment interview: Theory, research, and practice* (pp. 17-31). Newbury Park, CA: Sage.

Farr, J. L. (1973). Response requirements and primary-recency effects in a simulated selection interview. *Journal of Applied Psychology, 58,* 228-233.

Hakel, M. D., Dobmeyer, T. W., & Dunnette, M. D. (1970). Relative importance of three content dimensions in overall suitability ratings of job applicants' resumes. *Journal of Applied Psychology, 54,* 65-71.

Hollman, T. D. (1972). Employment interviewers' errors in processing positive and negative information. *Journal of Applied Psychology, 56,* 130-134.

Klayman, J., & Ha, M. (1987). Confirmation, disconfirmation, and information in hypothesis testing. *Psychological Review, 94,* 211-228.

Macan, T. H., & Dipboye, R. L. (1990). The relationship of interviewers' preinterview impressions to selection and recruitment outcomes. *Personnel Psychology, 43,* 745-768.

Miller, J. W., & Rowe, P. M. (1967). Influence of favorable and unfavorable information upon assessment decisions. *Journal of Applied Psychology, 31,* 432-435.

Peters, L. H., & Terborg, J. R. (1975). The effects of temporal placement of unfavorable information and of attitude similarity on personnel selection decisions. *Organizational Behavior and Human Performance, 13,* 279-293.

Rosenfeld, P., & Giacalone, R. A. (1991). From extreme to mainstream: Applied impression management in organizations. In R. A. Giacalone & P. Rosenfeld (Eds.), *Applied impression management* (pp. 3-12). Hillsdale, NJ: Lawrence Erlbaum.

Rowe, P. M. (1984). Decision processes in personnel decisions. *Canadian Journal of Behavioral Science, 16,* 326-337.

Rowe, P. M. (1989). Unfavorable information and interview decisions. In R. W. Eder & G. R. Ferris (Eds.), *The employment interview: Theory, research, and practice* (pp. 77-89). Newbury Park, CA: Sage.

Rynes, S. L. (1989). The employment interview as a recruitment device. In R. W. Eder & G. R. Ferris (Eds.), *The employment interview: Theory, research, and practice* (pp. 127-141). Newbury Park, CA: Sage.

Sackett, P. R. (1982). The interviewer as hypothesis tester: The effects of impressions of an applicant on interviewer questioning strategy. *Personnel Psychology, 35,* 789-804.

Schuh, A. J. (1989). Interviewer decision styles. In R. W. Eder & G. R. Ferris (Eds.), *The employment interview: Theory, research, and practice* (pp. 90-96). Newbury Park, CA: Sage.

Skowronski, J. J., & Carlston, D. E. (1989). Negativity and extremity biases in impression formation: A review and explanation. *Psychological Bulletin, 105,* 131-142.

Springbett, B. M. (1958). Factors affecting the final decision in the employment interview. *Canadian Journal of Psychology, 12,* 13-22.

Tucker, D. H., & Rowe, P. M. (1979). Relationships between expectancy and causal attributions, and final hiring decisions in the employment interview. *Journal of Applied Psychology, 64,* 27-34.

Tullar, W. L. (1989). The employment interview as a cognitive performing script. In R. W. Eder & G. R. Ferris (Eds.), *The employment interview: Theory, research, and practice* (pp. 233-246). Newbury Park, CA: Sage.

Webster, E. C. (1964). *Decision making in the employment interview.* Montreal: Eagle.

Webster, E. C. (1982). *The employment interview: A social judgment process.* Schomberg, ON: SIP.

14

Are Some Interviewers Better Than Others?

Laura M. Graves
Ronald J. Karren

A growing body of evidence indicates that there are individual differences in employment interviewers' decision processes. For instance, several recent studies have revealed differences in information utilization and validity across interviewers (e.g., Dipboye, Gaugler, & Hayes, 1990; Dougherty, Ebert, & Callender, 1986; Kinicki, Lockwood, Hom, & Griffeth, 1990). Further, individual differences appear to account for a substantial portion of the variance in interviewers' hiring decisions and ratings of applicants (Conard, 1988; Graves & Powell, 1996). In one recent study, individual differences explained 28% of the variance in interviewers' hiring decisions and 20% to 34% of the variance across eight rating dimensions (Conard, 1988).

Individual differences in interviewers' decision processes have potentially serious consequences for organizations. They may erode the quality of selection decisions and negatively affect outcomes such as employee performance, satisfaction, and turnover (Graves & Karren, 1996). In addi-

243

tion, the courts have used variation in interviewers' decision processes as a basis for legal rulings against organizations. Moreover, individual differences in interviewers' decision processes are likely to lead to erroneous research findings. Individual differences may suppress the size of validity coefficients and may result in biased estimates of the size of other relationships of interest to researchers (Dreher, Ash, & Hancock, 1988; Gehrlein, Dipboye, & Shahani, 1993; Graves & Powell, 1996).

Despite the potentially serious effects of individual differences in interviewers' decision processes, existing research provides only perfunctory information about the nature and consequences of these differences. The lack of attention to individual differences stems, at least in part, from evidence indicating that highly structured interviews are a promising means for ensuring that interviews are effective (e.g., Conway, Jako, & Goodman, 1995; Janz, 1989; Latham, 1989; McDaniel, Whetzel, Schmidt, & Maurer, 1994). Highly structured interviews, which include standardization of questions and the use of formal scoring keys to evaluate applicants' responses, closely resemble tests and are likely to generate high reliability and validity. One would expect the psychometric properties of highly structured interviews to reduce the occurrence of individual differences in interviewers' decision processes (Pulakos, Schmitt, Whitney, & Smith, 1996). Indeed, standardization across interviewers is the intent of such interviews.

However, it is premature to conclude that the availability of highly structured interviews will eliminate individual differences across interviewers. First, unstructured interviews continue to be the most popular selection technique in today's organizations, perhaps because they allow interviewers to exercise their own idiosyncratic preferences (Dipboye, 1992, 1994). Second, structured interviews may not necessarily eliminate individual differences. Individual differences in the use of structured interviews are likely to emerge over time as interviewers modify these interviews to suit their own needs (Dipboye, 1994). Also, the extent to which a structured interview eliminates individual differences may depend on the exact nature of the interview. For instance, structured interviews with features such as standardized scoring keys and objective techniques for combining multiple ratings should reduce individual differences to a greater extent than structured interviews that do not possess these characteristics (Conway et al., 1995).

Given the persistence of unstructured interviews, as well as the possibility that individual differences may occur in some structured interviews, a better understanding of individual differences is needed to safeguard the quality of interview decisions. To that end, in this chapter we review existing evidence on individual differences in employment interviewers' decision processes. We then outline an agenda for a new generation of research on individual differences in interviewers' decision processes.

Existing Research on Individual Differences

Research on individual differences in employment interviewers' decision processes has focused primarily on individual differences in validity and information utilization.

Individual Differences in Validity

Existing evidence on individual differences in interviewer validity is somewhat limited. Only six studies to date have examined individual differences in the validity of interviewers' judgments (Dipboye et al., 1990; Dougherty et al., 1986; Gehrlein et al., 1993; Kinicki et al., 1990; Pulakos et al., 1996; Zedeck, Tziner, & Middlestadt, 1983). In most of these studies, participating interviewers conducted interviews with multiple applicants, and performance data were gathered for applicants who were selected. Validity coefficients were then calculated for each interviewer.

Five of the six studies provide evidence of individual differences in interviewer validity. Dougherty et al. (1986) found that the validity of three corporate interviewers' judgments for predicting the job performance of 60 applicants ranged from .02 to .26, with only one of the three interviewers making valid predictions. Similarly, Kinicki et al. (1990) found differences in the validity with which three interviewers predicted organizational commitment and satisfaction, but not performance and retention. In addition, Zedeck et al. (1983) found that candidates selected by three interviewers had higher training performance ratings than did candidates selected by seven other interviewers. However, validity coefficients were not calculated for each interviewer because there were only a few applicants actually selected per interviewer. Further, Dipboye et al. (1990) found that the validity of five interviewers' ratings for predicting employee performance ranged from .02 to .25, with only two of five interviewers making valid judgments. Finally, a related study of college admissions interviewers found that only two of six interviewers made judgments that were valid predictors of students' academic records (Gehrlein et al., 1993).

The methodology used in these five studies makes it difficult to assess formally the extent of variation in validity across interviewers. In each investigation, there was a small sample of interviewers (i.e., 3 to 10 interviewers), which yielded insufficient statistical power to test for individual differences in validity using meta-analysis (Graves, 1993; Harris, 1989). Moreover, in two of the studies, interviewers evaluated at least some of the same applicants (Dipboye et al., 1990; Dougherty et al., 1986). Consequently, interviewers' validity coefficients were not completely independent of one another, which made it inappropriate to test statistically for differences in validity coefficients across interviewers (Dipboye et al.,

1990). However, Kinicki et al. (1990) used moderated regression analysis to confirm that there were differences in the accuracy with which hiring managers' assessments of applicants predicted outcomes.

The sixth study, conducted by Pulakos et al. (1996), was the only study that found no evidence of individual differences in interviewer validity. In this study, 62 interviewers in a government agency received extensive training in the use of a highly structured behavior-based panel interview. The members of the interview panels then conducted interviews, recorded individual ratings of applicants on behaviorally anchored rating scales, and developed consensual ratings of applicants. Each interviewer evaluated from 11 to 48 applicants. A meta-analysis was conducted on the validity coefficients of the individual interviewers. The purposes of the meta-analysis were (a) to summarize the results for all of the interviewers by estimating the average validity for the entire sample and (b) to determine whether the variation in validity across interviewers was due to sampling error or other factors, such as moderators (e.g., individual difference variables). The results of the meta-analysis indicated that the observed differences in validity across individual interviewers were due to sampling error.

The absence of individual differences in interviewer validity in the Pulakos et al. (1996) study may have been due to the use of highly structured interviews. Whereas all of the studies that reported individual differences in validity were based on interviews that had some degree of structure (e.g., rating forms for evaluating applicants, lists of selection criteria, sample questions), Pulakos et al.'s findings were based on highly structured behavior-based interviews. One would expect the psychometric properties of such interviews to reduce the occurrence of individual differences. In addition, as Pulakos et al. note, standardization was especially likely in their study because participants received intensive training in the structured interview format and reached consensus within a panel interview setting.

Further, it is also possible that the meta-analysis performed in the Pulakos et al. (1996) study was not a comprehensive test of the significance of individual differences in validity. In particular, there may have been insufficient statistical power to detect individual differences in validity. With a sample size of 62 interviewers, Pulakos et al. had a sufficient number of interviewers to perform meta-analysis. However, 42 of the 62 interviewers evaluated fewer than 30 applicants. The small number of applicants for these interviewers may have led to large amounts of sampling error that obscured true differences in validity (Motowidlo, Mero, & DeGroot, 1995; Sackett, Harris, & Orr, 1986).

Thus, existing research evidence supports the notion that there are differences in validity across interviewers, but suggests that these differences are less likely to occur in highly structured interviews. However, given the relatively small amount of research, as well as the methodological issues raised above, it would be inappropriate to draw firm conclusions about the extent of individual differences in validity. Moreover, existing evidence focuses almost exclusively on individual differences in the accuracy with which interviewers can predict employee performance. With the exception of the results obtained by Kinicki et al. (1990), there is almost no information about individual differences in the accuracy with which interviewers predict outcomes such as commitment, satisfaction, and turnover.

Individual Differences in Information Utilization

Much of the research on individual differences in the interview has focused on differences in information utilization. In fact, some of the studies described above looked not only at individual differences in validity, but also at the individual differences in information utilization (i.e., Dipboye et al., 1990; Kinicki et al., 1990; Zedeck et al., 1983). Generally, information utilization studies have used policy-capturing methodology (Slovic & Lichtenstein, 1971) to build weighted-additive models of interviewers' decision rules. Some of the studies were experimental studies in which profiles of hypothetical applicants were created through the manipulation of selection criteria in a balanced factorial design. Other studies were nonexperimental studies (i.e., selection criteria were not manipulated) in which interviewers evaluated real applicants on several criteria and made overall judgments. In both types of studies, each interviewer's evaluations of applicants were analyzed to determine the weights he or she assigned to particular selection criteria.

Both experimental (e.g., Graves & Karren, 1992; Stumpf & London, 1981; Valenzi & Andrews, 1973) and nonexperimental (Dipboye et al., 1990; Dougherty et al., 1986; Zedeck et al., 1983) studies consistently revealed differences in information utilization across interviewers. For instance, one study found that 29 recruiters had 13 different ways of combining five different criteria to judge applicants (Graves & Karren, 1992). Similarly, Kinicki et al. (1990) found differences in the importance that interviewers attached to interview impressions versus qualifications in evaluating applicants. Moreover, several of the studies found that differences in cue utilization were linked to differences in validity. Interviewers who were effective utilized different cues than did interviewers who were ineffective (e.g., Dipboye et al., 1990; Graves & Karren, 1992; Kinicki et al., 1990; Zedeck et al., 1983).

Although this research indicates that there are differences in information utilization across interviewers and suggests that these differences lead to differences in validity, it provides an inadequate description of the true nature of individual differences in interviewers' decision-making processes. In particular, the policy-capturing methodology used in this research produces simple linear models that mimic individuals' decisions but do not provide detailed information about the processes that underlie decisions (Carroll & Johnson, 1990). This focus on linear models has created an overly narrow view of the nature of individual differences in interviewers' decision processes. Moreover, it is in direct conflict with the literature on employment interview decisions (e.g., Dipboye, 1992) and other organizational decisions (e.g., image theory; Beach 1990; Mitchell & Beach, 1990), which recognizes the importance of underlying decision processes and stresses their intuitive, affective nature.

In conclusion, existing evidence suggests that there are differences in both validity and information utilization across interviewers. However, these findings provide only a glimpse of the true nature of individual differences in interviewers' decision processes. As noted earlier, research on individual differences in interviewer validity is limited and somewhat inconclusive. Similarly, research on individual differences in information utilization has not provided information about differences in the processes that underlie interviewers' judgments.

Moreover, the fact that researchers have focused primarily on differences in validity and information utilization leaves many potentially important aspects of individual differences unexplored. The employment interview is a multistage process (Dipboye, 1992), yet we have almost no information about the differences that occur in stages other than the information integration stage. Further, despite the fact that contextual factors (e.g., interview purpose, accountability for the decision) may influence the likelihood of individual differences by altering or interacting with interviewers' cognitive processes (Eder, 1989; Eder & Buckley, 1988), we have little understanding of the contextual factors that are most likely to evoke individual differences.

Agenda for Future Research

In order to develop a better understanding of individual differences in interviewers' decision processes, a new generation of research is needed. In this section, we outline an agenda for this new wave of research. The conceptual issues that researchers must address, as well as the methodological challenges associated with them, are described below and summarized in Table 14.1. Because some of the limitations of prior research stem from the difficulties of obtaining adequate samples of interviewers and applicants per interviewer, where possible, we identify methodologies that will allow researchers to explore individual differences without large samples.

First, researchers should determine whether there are consequential individual differences in interviewer validity across a broad range of criteria (e.g., performance, organizational commitment, turnover, person-organization fit, ability to work as a team member). Moreover, it would be

Table 14.1   Agenda for Future Research on Individual Differences

Research Issue to Be Addressed	*Methodology for Exploring Issue*
Test individual differences in interviewer validity across a broad set of criteria.	Conduct meta-analysis of validity data from adequate numbers of interviewers and applicants per interviewer for multiple criteria.
Examine the causes of individual differences in interviewers' preinterview evaluations.	Use policy capturing, verbal protocol analysis, and information search techniques to examine differences in the ways in which interviewers form preinterview impressions.
Identify individual differences in interviewer conduct during the interview.	Code and analyze videotapes or audiotapes of real or mock interviews. Employ adequate samples of interviewers and applicants per interviewer.
Identify individual differences in the general steps that interviewers use to make selection decisions.	Use verbal protocol analysis and information search techniques to explore individual interviewers' decision processes in realistic selection simulations.
Determine which individual differences in interviewers' decision processes have the greatest impacts on interviewer validity.	Collect validity data from adequate samples of interviewers and applicants per interviewer. Assess individual differences across interviewers on several variables (e.g., decision steps, interview behaviors). Determine how much of the variance in validity is determined by a given individual difference variable.
Identify how the nature of the interview and the interview context affect the incidence of individual differences across interviewers.	Perform meta-analysis of validity data collected from interviewers who use different interview techniques to test whether the nature of the interview moderates the incidence of individual differences. Use experimental designs to test the effects of contextual factors on the occurrence of individual differences.

useful to examine whether differences in validity are more likely to occur for some criteria than for others. This would allow researchers to target future efforts toward understanding and addressing those differences in validity that are most important.

In conducting this research, researchers must address the methodological problems that have interfered with the interpretation of earlier research on individual differences in validity. In particular, researchers must design studies that permit formal tests of individual differences in validity across interviewers using meta-analysis. These investigations must include large enough numbers of interviewers and applicants hired per interviewer to provide sufficient statistical power to ensure the adequacy of the tests. For example, a sample of 64 interviewers and 50 applicants per interviewer would be needed to produce sufficient power (i.e., .80) to detect a single moderator or individual difference variable with a moderate effect size (Sackett et al., 1986). Further, if the effect of the moderator variable is small, a very large sample of applicants per interviewer (e.g., 200) would be required to obtain a power of .80.

Moreover, when performing meta-analysis, researchers should utilize the random-effects statistical model rather than the fixed-effects statistical model, which is typically used in meta-analysis (see Erez, Bloom, & Wells, 1996). The random-effects statistical model provides a more comprehensive means of assessing between-studies or, in this case, between-interviewer variance than the fixed-effects statistical model. Thus, it is particularly well suited to the measurement of individual differences in interviewer validity.

Second, research should focus on individual differences at the various stages of the interview process, including the preinterview, interview, and decision-making stages. Space limitations prohibit detailed discussion of all of the issues that deserve attention at each stage, but we describe below some of the research questions that should be addressed.

With respect to individual differences at the preinterview stage of the process, researchers should focus on differences in interviewers' evaluations of applicants' paper credentials. Substantial research evidence indicates that interviewers' evaluations of applicants' paper credentials are likely to differ (e.g., Graves & Karren, 1992; Stumpf & London, 1981; Valenzi & Andrews, 1973). Research is needed to explore the underlying causes of these differences. One likely source of variation in interviewers' preinterview impressions is differences in their views of the ideal applicant, particularly differences in the dimensions that they believe are important for successful job performance (Graves, 1993). Disparities in interviewers' preinterview evaluations of applicants may also come from differences in the basic steps that they use to form their impressions of applicants (e.g., how they break up the task, the order in which they notice various attributes).

To examine thoroughly individual differences in interviewers' preinterview evaluations of applicants, researchers should use a variety of research methodologies. For instance, policy-capturing methodology might be used to explore differences in how interviewers weight specific dimensions in forming preinterview impressions. In addition, qualitative methodologies such as verbal protocol analysis and information search techniques, which we describe later in the chapter, may be used to examine individual differences in the steps interviewers use to form preinterview impressions.

With respect to individual differences in the conduct of the interview, there are a number of issues that should be explored. For example, examination of individual differences in interviewers' interpersonal behaviors toward applicants could be useful. Existing theory and research on applicant attraction suggests that the extent to which interviewers exhibit empathy and positive nonverbal behaviors toward applicants may influence applicants' reactions to the interview (see Rynes, 1991). Moreover, these behaviors determine whether applicants are willing to share information with the interviewer, and consequently influence interviewer validity (Graves, 1993).

Further, researchers might examine individual differences in the questioning process across interviewers (Dipboye, 1992). For instance, researchers might examine individual differences in the job relatedness of interviewers' questions (Graves, 1993). In addition, researchers might investigate differences in the types of the questions (e.g., open-ended, closed-ended, probing questions) interviewers ask or the ways in which they sequence these questions (e.g., closed-ended followed by open-ended versus open-ended followed by closed-ended). Obviously, the job relatedness, type, and sequencing of interviewers' questions may affect the nature of the information shared by applicants, and ultimately will influence interviewer effectiveness (Dipboye, 1992; Wiesner & Cronshaw, 1988).

In addition, researchers might examine whether there are individual differences in the extent to which interviewers' behaviors reflect various cognitive biases. Existing work on the employment interview has uncovered several biases that may affect the conduct of the interview. For example, the work of Dipboye and his colleagues suggests that interviewers behave in a manner that is consistent with their preinterview impressions of applicants (e.g., Dipboye, 1982, 1992; Dipboye & Macan, 1988). Similarly, research based on the similarity-attraction paradigm suggests that interviewers are likely to exhibit positive behaviors toward applicants whom they view as similar to themselves (Graves & Powell, 1988). Yet some evidence also indicates that the behaviors of all interviewers may not be affected by these biases (Dougherty, Turban, & Callender, 1994; Frank & Hackman, 1975). An examination of individual differences in the extent to which interviewers' behaviors mirror cognitive biases would be desirable because the behaviors evoked by these biases are likely to reduce interviewer effectiveness.

Studying individual differences in the conduct of the interview poses serious methodological challenges for researchers. Researchers may obtain some information about individual differences in interview conduct by surveying or interviewing applicants and interviewers immediately following the employment interview. However, these techniques are likely to produce incorrect or incomplete data about interviewers' behaviors. In order to collect more accurate data, researchers should videotape actual employment interviews. These videotaped interviews might then be coded and analyzed to test for differences across interviewers on a host of dimensions. Unfortunately, obtaining videotapes of real interviews will be difficult. Neither organizations nor applicants are likely to consent to videotaping of actual employment interviews. Audiotaping of such interviews may be more feasible (e.g., Dougherty et al., 1994), but will be somewhat less informative.

A more practical strategy might be to use videotaping as part of an interview training program for M.B.A. students. Corporate recruiters might be invited to conduct mock interviews with students, and these interviews could be videotaped to provide feedback to the students. Assuming that sufficient numbers of recruiters and students per recruiter participated in the program (i.e., adequate statistical power), analysis of the videotapes might provide useful information about individual differences in interviewer behavior. Of course, caution must be used in generalizing from data collected in mock interviews. The contextual demands created by mock interviews are likely to differ from those of real interviews. For instance, interviewers conducting mock interviews may experience low levels of decision risk and little sense of accountability for their decisions (Eder, 1989). Consequently, they may be especially likely to engage in idiosyncratic behaviors.

With respect to individual differences at the decision-making stage of the interview process, in-depth examination of the underlying processes by which interviewers make decisions is needed. Rather than simply focusing on differences in how interviewers weight criteria, researchers should study differences in the broader processes that interviewers use to reach their decisions.

Image theory (Beach, 1990; Mitchell & Beach, 1990), which describes the processes used in individual and organizational decision making, provides some clues about the basic processes that some interviewers might use to form their judgments. It suggests that interviewers may use a two-step process to make selection decisions. Initially, interviewers should determine whether candidates are compatible with their prototypes or images of candidates for the position. An interviewer's judgment of the compatibility between a candidate and the position would be based on the number of negative violations that occur when the candidate is compared with a limited set of relevant standards. Compatibility judgments are typically passive and simple, based primarily on intuition and affect.

Next, interviewers should compare the relative merits of the candidates who survived the compatibility test and choose the best one. Interviewers might perform a second type of test, the profitability test, to choose the best candidate. The strategies that interviewers use to perform this test may range from complex, analytic approaches based on formal decision models to simple, nonanalytic approaches that require little time or thought (Beach, 1990).

Of course, the two-step process suggested by image theory is only one of many possible processes that interviewers might use to make their decisions. Extensive research is needed to uncover the basic steps that interviewers actually use and to determine how these steps differ across interviewers. In addition, researchers should explore whether interviewers use different strategies for executing specific steps in the decision process. We would expect such differences to occur. For instance, the intuitive, affective nature of compatibility judgments, as well as the fact that interviewers may not hold identical prototypes of candidates for the position, may create individual differences in the nature of interviewers' compatibility judgments. Similarly, individual differences in the strategies interviewers use to perform profitability tests are likely because each individual has a limited number of decision strategies at his or her disposal, and some of these strategies are wholly unique to the individual (Beach, 1990).

Qualitative research methodologies such as verbal protocol analysis (Carroll & Johnson, 1990; Ericsson & Simon, 1993) and information search techniques (Carroll & Johnson, 1990; Ford, Schmitt, Schechtman, Hults, & Doherty, 1989) should be especially useful for exploring differences in decision processes across interviewers. These methodologies provide broad, descriptive information about the decision-making process.

In verbal protocol analysis, subjects are presented with written materials about a decision situation (e.g., choosing an apartment to rent) and asked to think aloud as they reach a decision. Subjects' comments are recorded, transcribed, and analyzed. Analysis can be informal (e.g., reading of transcripts) or formal (e.g., development of a flowchart of each subject's thinking process) (Carroll & Johnson, 1990). Analysis provides information about how decision makers break up the task, the order in which attributes are noticed, which attributes seem important, how attributes are combined, and whether there are differences across decision makers (Carroll & Johnson, 1990).

In information search studies, subjects are given access to information about the attributes of several decision alternatives (e.g., an information display might give information about six models of automobiles on 10 different dimensions) (Carroll & Johnson, 1990; Ford et al., 1989). Subjects access only the information that they believe they need to make their decisions and then make choices among the decision alternatives. Each individual's information search pattern is examined to identify the strategies underlying his or her decision. The decision strategies of individuals can then be compared.

Both verbal protocol analysis and information search techniques might provide useful information about individual differences in interviewers' decision-making processes. The primary drawback of these techniques is that real interviews cannot be studied. However, both techniques might be used in the context of a realistic selection simulation. For instance, the Center for Creative Leadership has developed a computer simulation of an executive selection decision that contains a host of information (e.g., video interviews, résumés, others' opinions, search firm reports) about applicants for an executive position (Campbell, Sessa, & Taylor, 1995). Verbal protocol analysis or information search techniques could be used to study subjects' decisions in such a simulation.

Third, researchers need to determine which individual differences have the greatest impact on validity. To date, we have little information about the links between differences in interviewers' cognitions and behaviors and their effectiveness. Obtaining such information will be a daunting task. Sample sizes similar to those required for meta-analysis are needed. Researchers must assess the validity of interviewers' judgments for predicting one or more criteria (e.g., performance, commitment). Individual differences across interviewers on variety of dimensions (e.g., interviewer behaviors, cognitive strategies) also must be measured. Researchers can then determine how much unique variance in validity is explained by a given individual difference variable. Moreover, for individual differences in cognitions and behaviors that have consequences for validity, researchers should be able to identify the most effective cognitive and behavioral strategies.

Fourth, a better understanding of the circumstances under which individual differences occur is needed. In particular, researchers should examine how the nature of the interview affects the occurrence of individual differences. It would be especially useful to identify the components of structured interviews that are most important in reducing individual differences. Further, researchers should examine whether panel interviews affect the incidence of individual differences. Although panel interviews should reduce the extent of individual differences (Graves, 1993), they may not eliminate all individual differences. For instance, recent evidence suggests that individual differences associated with demographic similarity may occur in some panel interview settings (Prewett-Livingston, Feild, Veres, & Lewis, 1996).

In addition, researchers might examine whether aspects of the interview context affect the prevalence of individual differences. Contextual factors such as accountability and task clarity (knowledge of target job and evaluation criteria, complexity of target job) should reduce the likelihood of individual differences. Interviewers who are accountable to others should be more motivated to form accurate evaluations of job candidates (Dipboye, 1992; Eder, 1989; Eder & Buckley, 1988; Graves, 1993; Pulakos et al., 1996). As a result, they may ask questions that are indicative of success on the job, thereby reducing the occurrence of individual differences. Similarly, when task clarity is high, interviewers are likely to possess a common understanding of the personal attributes underlying performance of the job (Dipboye, 1994; Eder, 1989). Thus, individual differences in interviewers' decision processes should be reduced.

There are several different approaches that researchers might use to identify the circumstances under which individual differences are most likely to occur. Field research might be useful in determining how the nature of the interview affects the incidence of individual differences. For example, to examine the effects of interview structure on the occurrence of individual differences in validity, researchers might locate an organization with a large enough sample of interviewers and applicants hired per interviewer to permit the use of meta-analysis. Half of the sample of interviewers could be trained in the use of a highly structured interview (e.g., Pulakos et al., 1996), and the other half could be trained in the use of a semistructured interview. Validity coefficients could be calculated for each interviewer, and meta-analysis might be used to test the moderating effect of structure on the occurrence of individual differences in interviewer validity.

Further, experimental research designs can be used to test the effects of contextual variables such as accountability and task clarity on the occurrence of individual differences. Researchers can present subjects with written materials that manipulate the interview context and then ask them to view a videotape of a simulated employment interview (e.g., Rozelle & Baxter, 1981). The effect of the manipulation on the amount of variation on interviewers' responses can then be assessed. Clearly, the advantage of such experimental designs is that they do not require the participation of large numbers of interviewers.

Once researchers have determined which individual differences are important and when they occur, strategies for reducing the negative effects of individual differences on the interview process can be developed. Although structuring the interview may be one way to reduce individual differences, researchers should consider other strategies as well. For instance, individual differences might be reduced through improved selection of interviewers. If interviewer characteristics (e.g., personality, cognitive complexity), behaviors, or decision strategies account for differences in validity, these factors might be used as the basis for interviewer selection. Another possible strategy for ameliorating individual differences across interviewers is training. Organizations might train interviewers to engage in those cognitive and behavioral strategies that seem to be most effective. Finally, individual differences might be reduced through alteration of the interview context. If research indicates that individual differences across interviewers are less prevalent when certain contextual factors are present, these factors might be manipulated to decrease the extent of individual differences.

Conclusion

Although existing research suggests that there are individual differences in interviewer validity and information utilization, it provides only perfunctory information about the true nature of individual differences across interviewers. A new wave of research on individual differences in interviewers' decision processes is needed. In this chapter we have outlined an agenda for this research. We have suggested that researchers must determine whether there are consequential individual differences in validity across interviewers. To assess the true extent of individual differences in validity, researchers must address the methodological problems that have clouded the interpretation of past research.

Further, in-depth examination of the individual differences that occur at each stage of the interview process is needed. To understand these differences fully, researchers will need to use qualitative methodologies that provide detailed descriptions of how interviewers conduct interviews and make judgments, as well as conventional quantitative methodologies. Moreover, once individual differences in interviewers' decision processes have been identified, researchers must determine which ones are important and when they occur. Such research is essential to safeguard the quality of interview judgments.

References

Beach, L. R. (1990). *Image theory: Decision making in personal and organizational contexts.* Chichester: John Wiley.

Campbell, R. J., Sessa, V. I., & Taylor, J. (1995). Choosing top leaders: Learning to do better. *Issues and Observations, 15*(4), 1-5.

Carroll, J. S., & Johnson, E. J. (1990). *Decision research: A field guide.* Newbury Park, CA: Sage.

Conard, M. A. (1988). *The contribution of the interview to the prediction of job performance* (Report No. MRRR1-1988). Farmington, CT: LIMRA International.

Conway, J. M., Jako, R. A., & Goodman, D. F. (1995). A meta-analysis of interrater and internal consistency reliability of selection interviews. *Journal of Applied Psychology, 80,* 565-579.

Dipboye, R. L. (1982). Self-fulfilling prophecies in the selection interview. *Academy of Management Review, 7,* 579-586.

Dipboye, R. L. (1992). *Selection interviews: Process perspectives.* Cincinnati, OH: South-Western.

Dipboye, R. L. (1994). Structured and unstructured selection interviews: Beyond the job-fit model. In G. R. Ferris (Ed.), *Research in personnel and human resources management* (Vol. 12, pp. 79-123). Greenwich, CT: JAI.

Dipboye, R. L., Gaugler, B. B., & Hayes, T. L. (1990). *Differences among interviewers in the incremental validity of their judgments.* Paper presented at the annual meeting of the Society for Industrial and Organizational Psychology, Miami, FL.

Dipboye, R. L., & Macan, T. H. (1988). A process view of the selection/recruitment interview. In R. S. Schuler, S. A. Youngblood, & V. L. Huber (Eds.), *Readings in personnel and human resource management* (pp. 217-232). St. Paul, MN: West.

Dougherty, T. W., Ebert, R. J., & Callender, J. C. (1986). Policy capturing in the employment interview. *Journal of Applied Psychology, 71,* 9-15.

Dougherty, T. W., Turban, D. B., & Callender, J. C. (1994). Confirming first impressions in the employment interview: A field study of interviewer behavior. *Journal of Applied Psychology, 79*, 659-665.

Dreher, G. W., Ash, R. A., & Hancock, P. (1988). The role of the traditional research design in underestimating the validity of the employment interview. *Personnel Psychology, 41*, 315-327.

Eder, R. W. (1989). Contextual effects on interview decisions. In R. W. Eder & G. R. Ferris (Eds.), *The employment interview: Theory, research, and practice* (pp. 113-126). Newbury Park, CA: Sage.

Eder, R. W., & Buckley, M. R. (1988). The employment interview: An interactionist perspective. In G. R. Ferris & K. M. Rowland (Eds.), *Research in personnel and human resources management* (Vol. 6, pp. 75-107). Greenwich, CT: JAI.

Erez, A., Bloom, M. C., & Wells, M. T. (1996). Using random rather than fixed effects models in meta-analysis: Implications for situational specificity and validity generalization. *Personnel Psychology, 49*, 275-306.

Ericsson, K. A., & Simon, H. A. (1993). *Protocol analysis: Verbal reports as data* (Rev. ed.). Cambridge: MIT Press.

Ford, J. K., Schmitt, N., Schechtman, S. L., Hults, B. M., & Doherty, M. L. (1989). Process tracing methods: Contributions, problems, and neglected research questions. *Organizational Behavior and Human Decision Processes, 43*, 75-117.

Frank, L. L., & Hackman, J. R. (1975). Effects of interviewer-applicant similarity on interviewer objectivity in college admissions interviews. *Journal of Applied Psychology, 60*, 356-360.

Gehrlein, T. M., Dipboye, R. L., & Shahani, C. (1993). Nontraditional validity calculations and differential interviewer experience: Implications for selection interviews. *Educational and Psychological Measurement, 52*, 457-469.

Graves, L. M. (1993). Sources of individual differences in interviewer effectiveness: A model and implications for future research. *Journal of Organizational Behavior, 14*, 349-370.

Graves, L. M., & Karren, R. J. (1992). Interviewer decision processes and effectiveness: An experimental policy-capturing investigation. *Personnel Psychology, 45*, 313-340.

Graves, L. M., & Karren, R. J. (1996). The employee selection interview: A fresh look at an old problem. *Human Resource Management, 35*, 163-180.

Graves, L. M., & Powell, G. N. (1988). An investigation of sex discrimination in recruiters' evaluations of actual applicants. *Journal of Applied Psychology, 73*, 20-29.

Graves, L. M., & Powell, G. N. (1996). Sex similarity, quality of the employment interview and recruiters' evaluations of actual applicants. *Journal of Occupational and Organizational Psychology, 69*, 243-261.

Harris, M. M. (1989). Reconsidering the employment interview: A review of recent literature and suggestions for future research. *Personnel Psychology, 42*, 691-726.

Janz, J. T. (1989). The patterned behavior description interview: The best prophet of the future is the past. In R. W. Eder & G. R. Ferris (Eds.), *The employment interview: Theory, research, and practice* (pp. 158-168). Newbury Park, CA: Sage.

Kinicki, A. J., Lockwood, C. A., Hom, P. A., & Griffeth, R. W. (1990). Interviewer predictions of applicant qualifications and interviewer validity: Aggregate and individual analyses. *Journal of Applied Psychology, 75*, 477-486.

Latham, G. P. (1989). The reliability, validity, and practicality of the situational interview. In R. W. Eder & G. R. Ferris (Eds.), *The employment interview: Theory, research, and practice* (pp. 169-182). Newbury Park, CA: Sage.

McDaniel, M. A., Whetzel, D. L., Schmidt, F. L., & Maurer, S. D. (1994). The validity of employment interviews: A comprehensive review and meta-analysis. *Journal of Applied Psychology, 79,* 599-616.

Mitchell, T. R., & Beach, L. R. (1990). "... Do I love thee? Let me count ...": Toward an understanding of intuitive and automatic decision making. *Organizational Behavior and Human Decision Processes, 47,* 1-20.

Motowidlo, S. J., Mero, N. P., & DeGroot, T. (1995, May). Predicting and controlling individual variability in interviewers' judgments. In E. B. Kolmstetter (Chair), *Interviewer and contextual factors that make a difference in interview validity.* Symposium conducted at the annual meeting of the Society for Industrial and Organizational Psychology, Orlando, FL.

Prewett-Livingston, A. J., Feild, H. S., Veres, J. G., III, & Lewis, P. M. (1996). Effects of race on interview ratings in a situational panel interview. *Journal of Applied Psychology, 81,* 178-186.

Pulakos, E. D., Schmitt, N., Whitney, D., & Smith, M. (1996). Individual differences in interviewer ratings: The impact of standardization, consensus discussion, and sampling error on the validity of a structured interview. *Personnel Psychology, 49,* 85-102.

Rozelle, R. M., & Baxter, J. C. (1981). Influence of role pressures on the perceiver: Judgments of videotaped interviews varying judge accountability and responsibility. *Journal of Applied Psychology, 66,* 437-441.

Rynes, S. L. (1991). Recruitment, job choice, and post-hire consequences: A call for new research directions. In M. D. Dunnette & L. M. Hough (Eds.), *Handbook of industrial and organizational psychology* (2nd ed., Vol. 2, pp. 399-444). Palo Alto, CA: Consulting Psychologists Press.

Sackett, P. R., Harris, M. M., & Orr, J. M. (1986). On seeking moderator variables in the meta-analysis of correlational data: A Monte Carlo investigation of statistical power and resistance to Type I error. *Journal of Applied Psychology, 71,* 302-310.

Slovic, P., & Lichtenstein, S. (1971). Comparison of Bayesian and regression approaches to the study of information processing in judgment. *Organizational Behavior and Human Performance, 6,* 649-744.

Stumpf, S. A., & London, M. (1981). Capturing rater policies in evaluating candidates for promotion. *Academy of Management Journal, 24,* 752-766.

Valenzi, E., & Andrews, I. R. (1973). Individual differences in the decision processes of employment interviewers. *Journal of Applied Psychology, 58,* 49-53.

Wiesner, W. H., & Cronshaw, S. F. (1988). A meta-analytic investigation of the impact of interview format and degree of structure on the validity of the employment interview. *Journal of Occupational Psychology, 61,* 275-290.

Zedeck, S., Tziner, A., & Middlestadt, S. E. (1983). Interviewer validity and reliability: An individual analysis approach. *Personnel Psychology, 36,* 355-370.

15

Interviewer Experience and Expertise Effects

Robert L. Dipboye
Stacy L. Jackson

The selection interview is the most frequently used means of screening and selecting applicants for positions and is at the heart of the selection process in most organizations. Given the central role that interviews play, it is reassuring that meta-analyses have shown that interviewers can achieve respectable levels of validity (McDaniel, Whetzel, Schmidt, & Maurer, 1994). To a greater extent than most other selection techniques, however, the effectiveness of selection interviews depends on the individuals implementing them. Over time, an interview procedure may degrade in validity in the process of being implemented by some interviewers or may improve in validity in the hands of other interviewers. In this chapter we examine the most obvious of the individual difference factors that possibly can account for variations among interviewers: their experience in conducting interview sessions and assessing applicants.

Experience is a major determinant of how much competence is attributed to people for a wide variety of tasks, including the interview.

Interviewer experience is typically treated as a unidimensional continuum, anchored at the lowest level by a complete lack of experience and at the high end by a large number of interviews and time spent interviewing. A common assumption is that experience leads to expertise, as manifested in more knowledge of the selection task, superior processing of information on applicants, and, most important, higher-quality judgments. Thus, naive interviewers who have no experience and novice interviewers who have relatively little experience differ dramatically from highly experienced (i.e., expert) interviewers in how they perform in assessing applicants. But is this assumption correct? As we will show, the research on the interview does not make a convincing case for the notion that experience in interviewing translates into expertise. Experience can incur costs as well as benefits, and the costs can detract from, and in some cases completely negate, the benefits. We propose that experience should be examined as a multidimensional construct rather than as unidimensional. We also set forth several research questions for future research on interviewer experience and the possible conditions under which one might expect experience to translate into expertise.

The Cognitive, Behavioral, and Affective Benefits of Experience

Research on a variety of tasks suggests that experience can benefit performance. Recent meta-analyses have shown that experience is positively related to job performance, although the strength of the relationship is modest in magnitude and moderated by study characteristics (Quinones, Ford, & Teachout, 1995). Also, the research on practice has shown that achievement of master status in the performance of complex tasks does not come naturally to high-ability persons but appears to require years of deliberate practice coupled with feedback (Ericsson, Krampe, & Tesch-Romer, 1993). Comparisons of experts with novices on structured tasks such as chess suggest that there are three primary benefits of experience. First, the experienced performer develops richer and more differentiated knowledge structures with which he or she can represent the task and process information. A second potential benefit is automaticity in the performance of the task, which allows the individual more flexibility and freedom in investing cognitive resources. A third benefit is motivational, taking the form of higher self-efficacy and task involvement (Fiske & Kinder, 1981). All three of these benefits are purported to allow the experienced individual to process information more effectively. Experts appear to achieve high levels of performance as a consequence of their ability to perceive and recall large patterns of events, the quickness with which they can size up a task and execute solutions, superior short-term and long-term memory, the use of general principles to organize knowledge, and self-monitoring skills that allow continuous improvement (Glaser & Chi, 1988).

Research on the Effects of Interviewer Experience

Previous research has shown that experience can benefit task performance. But can we say that experience leads to the development of expertise in selection interviewing in the same ways that it appears to enhance performance on the job and on the structured tasks (e.g., chess) used in research on expertise? As described by Dipboye and Gaugler (1993), interviewers possess knowledge structures that influence their initial impressions of applicants in the preinterview phase and their information gathering and evaluation of applicants in subsequent phases of the interview. Consistent with this model, we will address three questions in examining the effects of interviewer experience. First, how do experienced interviewers differ from inexperienced interviewers in the knowledge structures and attitudes that they bring to the interviewing task? Second, how do they differ in the effects of initial impressions on information gathering? Third, what is the relationship of experience to the quality with which interviewers can judge applicant qualifications and make decisions?

Differences in Knowledge Structures

The superior performance of experts is usually attributed to the knowledge structures that they have developed as a result of their task experiences (Glaser & Chi, 1988). In a recent attempt to extrapolate from this research to the interview, Graves (1993) found that interviewers' experience in evaluating and selecting applicants for a particular job led to higher effectiveness as a consequence of more complex and organized knowledge structures. Thus, one can propose that as interviewers gain experience in specific selection situations, they extract from their experiences mental representations in the form of schemata, cognitive categories, and scripts that allow them to gather and process information more efficiently and accurately. Knowledge structures, as we will refer to these mental representations, can exist in the form of interviewers' beliefs about the requirements of jobs, the characteristics of applicants, and the manner in which interviews should be conducted. Knowledge structures contain *what* is believed or known about applicants, positions, and interview procedures as well as the *relationships* among these beliefs and ideas.

Based on research comparing experts and novices on structured tasks, one could expect experienced interviewers to have knowledge structures that are more detailed, complex, and organized (Graves, 1993). As a result, the experienced interviewer should be able to retrieve from memory more information in a more efficient manner than can the inexperienced interviewer. Several studies outside of the interviewing context provide support for this contention. For instance, Lurigio and Carroll (1985) found that experienced probation officers described probationers in terms of schemata that were fewer in number but more detailed. According to these authors, "Rather than simply adding schemata as new experiences were accumulated, experienced POs seem to have weeded out many useless stereotypes and enriched a smaller number of useful schemata" (p. 1124). Moreover, highly experienced individuals have been shown to process information in a more efficient and effective manner as a consequence of their knowledge structures.

The research conducted so far with employment interviews has focused mostly on differences in conceptions of occupational requirements between experienced interviewers and students with little or no experience. Contrary to what one might expect from previous research on expertise, the findings of the interview research suggest that there are minimal differences between experienced and experienced interviewers in the content and the quality of their descriptions of the typical incumbent of an occupation. Paunonen and Jackson (1987) found that inexperienced students were similar to personnel managers in their perceptions of the personality attributes of the typical computer programmer. Marks and Webb (1969) found that engineers and students had similar conceptions of the characteristics of engineers. Both Hakel, Hollman, and Dunnette (1970) and Imada, Fletcher, and Dalessio (1980) found that interviewers, accountants, and students attributed different personality characteristics and vocational interests to accountants but did not differ in the accuracy of their perceptions. In one of the few studies that have compared interviewers (nonstudents) with varying degrees of experience, Keenan (1976) found that experience was unrelated to ratings of the importance of 12 applicant characteristics (e.g., intelligence).

In addition to developing different conceptions of the typical applicant and the requirements of the job, one might also expect that experience would lead interviewers to form beliefs about how interviews should be conducted that differ from those of inexperienced interviewers. These beliefs include interviewers' evaluation of the interview as a selection technique and their ideas about how sessions should be conducted. One could predict that increased experience will be associated with greater involvement in the interviewing task as indicated by higher self-confidence and motivation (Fiske & Kinder, 1981). In a preliminary investigation of the relation of interviewer experience to beliefs and attitudes about the interview, we surveyed a sample of 274 managers, personnel specialists, and recruiters from an aerospace, a petrochemical, and a manufacturing organization. The primary measure of experience consisted of one item in the survey in which respondents were asked to estimate how much experience they had in conducting an interview, using a 5-point scale that ranged from very little (1) to quite a lot (5).

Consistent with the idea that experience brings more involvement in the task, the more experienced interviewers evaluated their own performance more positively ($r = .47, p < .01$) and were more likely to express enjoyment in the interviewing task ($r = .32, p < .01$). Indicative of their faith in interviews, experienced interviewers were more likely to express faith in the interview's ability to measure accurately 12 personal attributes, such as intelligence, social skills, and honesty ($r = .16, p < .05$). Experienced interviewers were also more likely to disagree with statements that were negative toward the interview as a selection technique, such as "No two interviewers are likely to agree very much on the qualifications of the same candidate" ($r = -.19, p < .05$); "An interviewer seldom acquires information that could not be obtained from the application and resume" ($r = -.21, p < .05$); and "An interviewer's judgment of an applicant is likely to depend on chance factors such as how the interviewer feels that day" ($r = -.25, p < .05$). Experienced interviewers were more likely to agree with statements that support the interview, such as "A skilled interviewer can read between the lines and detect what an applicant really feels" ($r = .13, p < .05$).

Although interviewers' experience was associated with increased confidence in the validity of the interview and their own ability to evaluate applicants, experience was unrelated to interviewers' beliefs about how interviews should be conducted. Perhaps the most interesting aspect of these findings is that both experienced and inexperienced interviewers tended to reject what could be considered structured interviewing procedures. More respondents agreed than disagreed that the interviewer's evaluation should be an essay rather than ratings (41% versus 27%), that the interviewer should ask any question he or she wishes (45.7% versus 31.3%), and that nonverbal behavior is an important indicator of future behavior (59.4% versus 28.4%). More also disagreed than agreed that interviewers should ask exactly the same questions across applicants (48.4% versus 32.6%) and should stick to specific job qualifications (57.7% versus 29%).

In summary, the research reviewed here shows that experience engenders positive attitudes toward the interview but provides little support for the hypothesis that experienced interviewers differ from inexperienced interviewers in their beliefs about requirements of positions or how interviews should be conducted. It should be noted that the research so far on differences in the knowledge structures of experienced and inexperienced interviewers is quite limited. The focus has been on perceptions of occupations, where one might expect to find stereotypes that are widely shared by experienced and inexperienced interviewers. Also, in our survey we focused on beliefs regarding isolated interviewing practices (e.g., Should you preview the application?) rather than examine differences in the con-

264 THE INTERVIEWER'S DECISION-MAKING PROCESS

tent and organization of prototypes of the ideal applicant, schemata relating applicant behavior to dispositions, and cognitive scripts for conducting the interview.

Effects of Experience on Information Gathering

The essence of the interview is the questioning of applicants by interviewers to gather information (Dougherty, Turban, & Callender, 1994; Macan & Dipboye, 1988). The research on expertise would suggest that, as a consequence of their more complex and organized knowledge structures, experienced interviewers are more diagnostic in their information searches (Glaser & Chi, 1988). However, the questioning of both students (Binning, Goldstein, Garcia, Harding, & Scattaregia, 1988) and experienced interviewers (Dougherty et al., 1994; Kohn, Dipboye, & Gaugler, 1995) appears to be biased by the interviewers' initial impressions. In the only direct comparison of experienced and inexperienced interviewers that we could find, initial impressions were found to influence questioning regardless of the experience of the interviewer (Macan & Dipboye, 1988).

A potentially important factor to consider, which has been missing in previous research, is whether interviewers are held accountable for their judgments (Eder, 1989). Initial information on an applicant seems most likely to bias information gathering when the interviewer is inexperienced and accountability for the accuracy of the judgments is low. On the other hand, the combination of interviewer experience and accountability should attenuate the biasing effects of initial information. To explore whether accountability moderates the effects of interviewer experience and initial impressions on the diagnosticity of questioning, we conducted an experiment in which 83 M.B.A. students were assigned randomly to one of six conditions in a 2 × 3 factorial experiment. The first factor in this experiment was accountability (high versus low); the second factor was initial information on the applicant's grade point average (high, low, no information). In addition to these two manipulated factors, a third measured factor was included in the form of the subjects' previous interviewing experience (experience, no experience). Each subject was presented with a fictitious application and letter of reference for an individual who was described as having applied for a sales position. A set of specifications was provided for the position that defined a high GPA along with seven other factors (e.g., sales-relevant knowledge and skills) as requirements. Subjects examined the paper credentials and then wrote questions they would ask of the applicant.

The grade point average of the applicant was manipulated so that one-third of the subjects received a high-GPA candidate (3.85), another third received a low-GPA candidate (2.25), and the remaining subjects received no GPA information. Subjects assigned to the high-accountability condition were told that their answers would be scored on how well they assessed the applicant's requirements and that they would later have to justify their questions, whereas those in the low-accountability condition were told that their questions would be anonymous and would not have to be justified. The third independent variable was interviewer experience, with 56% of the subjects classified as experienced and the remainder as inexperienced on the basis of their answers to an item asking if they had ever conducted interviews. The paper credentials were constructed so that some information was missing and some was inconsistent. The primary measure of diagnosticity was the number of questions generated that addressed these gaps and inconsistencies in the paper credentials. The average age of the subjects was 30, with 66% employed full-time and 17% employed part-time at the time of the study. A set of specifications was provided for the position that defined the key job requirements to be a high grade point average; sales-consistent personality characteristics; evidence of hard work and dependability; leadership in school, work, and other activities; sales-relevant knowledge and skills; and involvement in extracurricular activities consistent with sales. Subjects were instructed to examine the application and write as many questions as they wished and to phrase them exactly as they would in a face-to-face interview. The major dependent measure was the number of diagnostic questions, operationalized as the number of questions generated that dealt with gaps and inconsistencies in the paper credentials. Similar effects were found for the proportion of the total questions asked that were diagnostic. Consequently, we report here only the effects found for number of diagnostic questions.

Analyses of several manipulation checks showed that the initial impression and accountability manipulations were successful. A main effect for the applicant's GPA was found in which subjects given a high-GPA applicant asked fewer diagnostic questions ($M = 3.66$) than did subjects given an applicant with no GPA ($M = 5.77$) or a low GPA ($M = 6.54$), $F(2, 62) = 3.85$, $p < .05$. Consistent with previous research showing that initial impressions can bias information gathering, the participants were least likely to pursue gaps and inconsistencies in the credentials when the applicants had high GPAs and most likely to ask diagnostic questions when the applicants had low GPAs. An interaction between GPA and interviewer experience revealed that this effect of GPA on questioning was moderated by interviewer experience, $F(2, 62) = 3.22$, $p < .05$. The means for this interaction are plotted in Figure 15.1.

The biasing effect of initial information on questioning was more pronounced for experienced than for inexperienced interviewers. Specifically, experienced interviewers asked more diagnostic questions of the low-GPA applicant ($M = 7.67$) than they did of the applicant with high GPA ($M = 4.46$) or no GPA ($M = 4.43$). The inexperienced interviewers were less influenced by GPA ($Ms = 5.00$ and 3.09 for the low- and high-GPA applicants, respectively) and asked the most diagnostic questions in the no GPA condition ($M = 6.73$). In interpreting these findings,

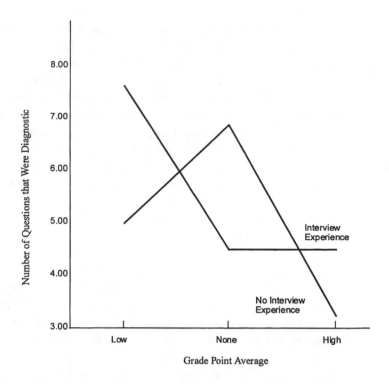

Figure 15.1. Number of Diagnostic Questions Asked as a Function of Experience and Applicant GPA

it is important to recognize that a high GPA was only one of several requirements set forth in the specifications, and the respondents were instructed to consider all requirements to be equally important. Consequently, there was little reason to expect the experienced interviewers to ask as many diagnostic questions as they did of the low-GPA candidate. On the basis of previous research showing that experienced judges are prone to overreact to highly salient and novel information (Johnson, 1988), we would speculate that the experienced interviewers in this experiment overreacted to the GPA information. The low-GPA applicant was especially salient for the experienced interviewers, who were perhaps accustomed to seeing more inflated GPAs.

Contrary to our initial hypotheses, initial information influenced question diagnosticity to the same extent in the two accountability conditions. However, accountability and experience were found to interact in their influence on the diagnosticity of questioning, $F(1, 62) = 4.39, p < .05$. Larger effects of accountability were found for high-experience subjects than for low-experience subjects. Whereas the fewest diagnostic questions were asked by the experienced interviewers under low accountability ($M = 2.92$), the largest number of diagnostic questions were asked by the experienced interviewers under high accountability ($M = 6.42$). By contrast, the low-experience subjects asked about the same number of diagnostic questions under low accountability ($M = 5.82$) as under high accountability ($M = 5.37$). One possible explanation for these findings is that experienced interviewers approached the selection situation "on automatic," with questions that they tended to ask of most applicants. As a consequence, they may have given less thought to what they were doing in their evaluation of the applicants. The freeing of cognitive resources as a consequence of experience is beneficial in some respects, but the automaticity with which experienced interviewers perform the selection task can make them more vulnerable to biases (see Gilbert, Pelham, & Krull, 1988). As the result of being held accountable for their questions, the experienced interviewers may have reverted to "manual control" and subsequently approached the task in a more deliberate and attentive fashion. In contrast, we would speculate that the inexperienced participants were more self-conscious and tended to devote the same degree of attention to the gaps and inconsistencies across both accountability conditions.

Our explanations of these findings are consistent with previous research and theory relating to expertise (see Johnson, 1988; Sternberg & Frensch, 1992), but are obviously speculative. For instance, a possible alternative explanation for the low number of diagnostic questions generated under low accountability is that the experienced interviewers found the entire process to be trivial and perhaps dismissed the task. However, the total number of questions generated did not differ as a function of either accountability or experience. Moreover, in an analysis of additional items, the experienced interviewers were as motivated to perform the task as were the inexperienced interviewers. We consider possible differences in automaticity to provide a plausible interpretation, but additional research is required to determine the relative merits of this and alternative interpretations.

Effects of Experience on Ratings

The outcome of the interviewer's information gathering and processing is that a judgment is rendered regarding the qualifications of the applicant. One would expect from research showing the beneficial effects of experience that the ratings of experienced interviewers would be less biased, more reliable, less influenced by irrelevant factors, more complex in the utilization of information, and more valid and accurate than those of inexperienced interviewers. Once again, previous research suggests that the effects of interviewer experience are more complex than suggested by research on structured tasks.

Previous research has demonstrated a variety of rating biases, including halo effects, order effects, leniency, contrast, and negativity. The only consistent difference between experienced and inexperienced raters in this research is that the former are less lenient in their evaluations (Carlson, 1967; Dipboye, Fromkin, & Wiback, 1975; Gehrlein, Dipboye, & Shahani, 1993; Gilmore, Beehr, & Love, 1986; Hakel, Dobmeyer, & Dunnette, 1970; Rowe, 1963; Singer & Bruhns, 1991; Wiener & Schneiderman, 1974). One possible explanation is that experience changes the schema of the qualified applicant, so that the interviewer sees a narrower range of applicant attributes as acceptable (Rowe, 1963). In an actual employment interview, one might also expect the experienced interviewer to be more sensitive to hiring quotas and more apt to weed out applicants. In discussing the effects of experience on leniency, Webster (1982) has observed that implications of leniency for judgment quality are not entirely clear and are dependent on other factors, such as whether the interviewer is held accountable for mistakes.

Another question pertaining to the quality of ratings is whether irrelevant factors influence inexperienced interviewers to a greater extent than they do experienced interviewers. Although academic performance and work experience of the applicant have the largest influence on the ratings of applicant qualifications (Olian, 1985), there are other factors that influence ratings that are largely irrelevant to job qualifications. Among the most consistent findings is that physically unattractive applicants receive less favorable ratings than do attractive applicants (Stone, Stone, & Dipboye, 1992). Two experiments have examined the relative reactions of experienced and inexperienced interviewers to the physical appearance of applicants. Carlson (1967) had life insurance managers evaluate the qualifications of eight hypothetical candidates who were either described in written information or shown to them in photographs. Experience of the managers was measured in terms of either the numbers of interviews they had conducted or their number of years of experience. The interviewers who were most prone to attractiveness bias were the high-tenure/low-activity managers, who had been on the job for a long time but had conducted relatively few interviews, whereas the least prone to these biases were the low-tenure/high-activity managers, who had conducted high numbers of interviews but had been on the job for shorter periods of time.

In the most recent experiments examining the influence of experience on the attractiveness bias, Marlowe, Schneider, and Nelson (1996) provided 112 managers with four equivalent résumé data sheets to which photographs were attached, with the photographs varying in terms of the gender and attractiveness of the applicant. The participants, 46 male and 66 female financial institution supervisors and managers, evaluated all of the applicants on their qualifications for a position that could eventually lead to an executive vice presidential position. According to Marlowe et al., the task was seen as realistic by the participants. Consistent with previous findings in both the lab and the field (Stone et al., 1992), the managers evaluated the highly attractive candidates as more qualified than the "marginally attractive" candidates. Also, they judged the male candidates to be more qualified than the female candidates. These biases were found for both experienced and inexperienced managers, although there was evidence that the experienced managers were more biased against unattractive candidates.

Related to attractiveness bias, interviewers may tend to evaluate applicants they personally like as more qualified. One might expect that professional experience would reduce the influence of personal liking for the applicant on evaluations of qualifications. However, Keenan (1978) found the opposite to be true. He had college recruiters evaluate applicants on suitability for the position and whether they would personally like the applicants as individuals. The correlation between likability and overall suitability was $r = .66$ ($n = 139, p < .01$) for the experienced interviewers and $r = .35$ ($n = 253, p < .01$) for the inexperienced interviewers.

One might also expect experienced interviewers to show more complexity in their use of information on applicants in their evaluations of qualifications. Again, there is some indication that the opposite may occur. Barr and Hitt (1986) found that experienced managers and students were both influenced by irrelevant factors such as age, sex, and race, but the students actually appeared more complex in their processing of cues to the extent that there were more higher-order interactions in the effects of the cues. Singer and Bruhns (1991) found that students tended to use both academic qualifications and work experience in the evaluation of applicant qualifications, whereas managers tended to use mostly work experience in their evaluations. Similarly, Johnson (1988) found that experienced judges tended to use much less information from the application files of medical school applicants than did undergraduates.

The most important issue is how experience influences the validity, reliability, and accuracy of the interviewer's final judgments of the applicant. Unfortunately, only a few studies have addressed this issue. Ryan and Sackett (1989) found that industrial/organizational psychologists who were experienced in individual assessment did not differ in their ratings and recommendations of candidates from those who were inexperienced. Johnson (1988) found little evidence that physicians having experience in the selection of medical school residents achieved higher validities in the selection of residents than inexperienced students. Dougherty, Ebert, and Callender (1986) found that an interviewer with 10 years of experience had higher validities in the prediction of relative job success than either an interviewer with 26 years' experience or an interviewer with 6 years' experience. However, the latter two interviewers did not differ substantially in the validities of their judgments. Moreover, all three interviewers were influenced by their initial impressions of the applicants' test scores.

Gehrlein et al. (1993) were able to examine this issue with a large sample of interviewers involved in undergraduate admissions at a university. Each interview session lasted approximately 30 minutes, and at the conclusion the interviewer completed a rating form designed to measure the applicant's motivation and oral communication on 12 dimensions.

Interviews were conducted by six full-time admissions officers, who constituted the experienced interviewers. A large group of volunteers constituted the inexperienced group and included alumni, faculty, and a few students. The experienced interviewers had interviewed a total of 843 applicants over the previous 2 years, for a mean number of 140 per interviewer. Over the same period, 487 inexperienced interviewers evaluated a total of 1,679 applicants, for a mean of 3 per interviewer. The inexperienced interviewers were found to have a corrected validity of .26 ($p < .001$) in the prediction of the quantitative GPA and .13 ($p < .05$) in the prediction of the nonquantitative GPA. In comparison, the experienced interviewers had a validity of .05 (*ns*) in the prediction of the quantitative GPA and .10 (*ns*) in the prediction of the nonquantitative GPA. One possible reason for the lower validities of the experienced interviewers is that they were more likely to stray from prescribed procedures. The experienced interviewers were observed to complain openly about what they considered overly formal procedures and were much more likely to omit several rating dimensions in evaluating the applicants than were the inexperienced interviewers.

There has been scant research on the relation of experience of interviewer accuracy and validity, and the few studies that have been conducted have produced results that are far from conclusive. Fortunately, there has been research on this issue in other judgment domains that appears generalizable to employment interviews. Experience has been found to have little relation to judgmental accuracy in research on clinical diagnoses of psychologists (Garb, 1989; Goldberg, 1970), graduate admissions (Dawes, 1971), economic forecasting (Armstrong, 1978), and task analyses (Richman & Quinones, 1996). Although experienced judges can be a valuable source of information, one of the most consistent findings in the psychological literature is that linear models can outperform even the most experienced judges in predicting outcomes (Dawes, 1988). The predictive success of linear models reflects the difficulty that human judges encounter in consistently using predictive cues. Judges frequently have little insight into their own judgment policies and tend to believe they are using more cues, and in a more complex manner, than they really are (Dawes, 1988). In contrast, a statistical equation does not stray and is consistent over time.

To summarize, the results of research on the effects of experience on the ratings of interviewers seem to run counter to what one might expect based on research that has shown the beneficial influence of experience. Although experienced interviewers are less lenient than inexperienced interviewers, there is some evidence that experienced interviewers are not immune to the biasing effects of attractiveness and personal liking and may even be more prone to these effects. Moreover, there is little evidence from either interview research or research on other types of clinical judgment tasks that experience enhances the validity of judgments.

Under What Conditions Does Interviewer Experience Become Expertise?

The research reviewed here has shown little support for the hypothesis that experienced enhances the quality of interviewer judgments. We believe that these results are important to the extent that they cast doubt on experience as a source of interviewer wisdom. These findings also reveal problems in the conceptualization and operationalization of experience in past research. As we stated earlier in this chapter, experience can incur costs at the same time that it bestows benefits. For instance, experience may lead to overly complex knowledge structures, an overemphasis on highly salient or vivid information, and rigidity at the same time that it allows interviewers to perform their tasks with less effort and frees their cognitive resources. Sternberg and Frensch (1992) note this paradox when they observe that "although the expert may have more processing resources available to deal with novelty than does the novice, it may be the novice who is better able to deal with this novelty" (p. 197). More systematic and theory-driven investigations are needed to examine the conditions under which the benefits of interviewing experience outweigh the costs and bring improvements to the quality of interviewer judgments. As a guide to this research, we now consider situations in which interviewer experience becomes expertise.

> *Proposition 1:* The importance that interviewers place on the fit of applicant knowledge, skills, and abilities (KSAs) to the job relative to the fit of applicant characteristics to the job context (i.e., the work group, the organization) depends on the role the interviewers have played in the selection process. The more experience interviewers have in screening applicants for organizational membership, the more likely they are to judge applicants on their fit to the organization. On the other hand, the more experience interviewers have in evaluating applicants for a specific job, the more likely they are to base their evaluations on the fit of the applicant's KSAs to the job.

As shown by Carlson (1967), the amount of interviewing experience and the time spent in a managerial role can have very different consequences, and the failure to separate these two dimensions may account for some of the effects that have been found in previous research. For instance, the confounding of these two dimensions may explain why several previous studies have shown somewhat more vulnerability of experienced interviewers to rating biases (Gehrlein et al., 1993; Keenan, 1978; Marlowe et al., 1996). For example, the recruiters in Keenan's (1978) study may been more influenced by their personal liking as the result of demands on them to serve as an initial filter rather than as judges of specific KSAs. Likewise, the experienced admission staff in Gehrlein et al.'s (1993) experiment seemed more concerned than their inexperienced counterparts with the extent to which applicants would contribute to the quality of campus life. Consequently, they seemed more resistant than inexperienced interviewers to focusing on academic abilities in evaluating applicants. We would expect that these two tendencies could work in opposition, such that increasing attention to person-organization fit undermines the beneficial effects that derive from experience in evaluating applicants for positions. Although evaluating the fit of applicants to the work context seems warranted in many cases, we believe that there continues to be merit in selecting applicants who have the KSAs to do the job. The remaining propositions focus on conditions in which experience in evaluating applicants will improve the performance of interviewers in evaluating person-job fit.

> *Proposition 2:* The interviewer's evaluations of applicant fit to job requirements will increase in quality the more applicants that are evaluated only to the extent that (a) the experience is limited to a specific domain of jobs, (b) feedback is provided that allows the interviewer to learn from experience, and (c) the interviewer is held accountable for the quality of decisions.

Quality, in the context of this proposition, refers to the reliability and criterion-related validity with which interviewers assess applicants on their fit to the KSAs and other requirements of jobs. Previous research has not provided convincing evidence that experience enhances the quality of interviewer evaluations. However, we would argue that experience is likely to translate into higher quality when interviewers have the opportunity to evaluate a large number of applicants for a specific job. Thus, we would suggest that interviewer expertise in evaluating applicants is not a broad ability that generalizes across varied positions, but a capability that is limited to a narrow domain of positions. Our proposition is consistent with previous research showing that expertise is limited to specific task domains (Glaser & Chi, 1988). An example of an interviewer who apparently developed expertise within a narrow domain is Edwin Ghiselli (1966), who interviewed stockbroker applicants over a 17-year period and was able to achieve a corrected criterion-related validity of .51. We would suggest that the high validities that Ghiselli achieved resulted from his intimate knowledge of the position and candidate pool.

An additional contingency in Proposition 2 pertains to feedback. As interviewers assess more candidates for positions, they are likely to show improvements in the quality of their judgments only to the extent that their experience allows them to learn from their mistakes and their successes. Outcome feedback may not be the ideal form of feedback, however. Balzer, Doherty, and O'Connor (1989) have reviewed evidence that simple knowledge of results does not improve the accuracy of prediction and may harm judgmental accuracy. This research suggests that a superior approach is to provide interviewers with their judgmental policies and task information in the form of the validity of predictive cues (e.g., the correlation of background characteristics of applicants to job success), the predictability of the criterion, and the interrelations among predictive cues. Hogarth (1987) further recommends that judges be required to take notes on their decisions in which they state the reasons for their actions and then use these notes to evaluate their decisions against subsequent outcomes.

Experience must not only allow the interviewer to learn, it must motivate the interviewer to improve. Increased experience with the screening and selection of applicants appears to enhance interviewer self-efficacy as the interviewer becomes more efficient and less self-conscious in the actual conduct of interview procedures. However, experience can also be associated with a hubris that can lead to overconfidence and an unwillingness to learn. Holding interviewers accountable for the quality of their judgments should help to avoid these problems.

> *Proposition 3:* Experience in interviewing and evaluating applicants is associated with higher-quality judgments to the extent that interviewers acquire knowledge structures that facilitate their gathering and processing of information.

We would further propose that the beneficial effects of experience on the quality of interviewer evaluations of applicants stated in Proposition 2 are mediated by the knowledge structures that the interviewer acquires. As we noted earlier, previous research has not shown convincing differences in knowledge structures, and this failure to show strong differences may reflect the fact that interviewers learn what they know about jobs and interviewing under less-than-ideal circumstances. When people can learn from their experiences, the research on expertise would suggest that those who achieve master status in the performance of a task domain develop abstract representations and principles that allow them to process information more efficiently (Glaser & Chi, 1988). The acquisition of knowledge structures should also free cognitive resources. In other words, experienced interviewers can ask questions, evaluate, recruit, answer questions, and perform other tasks without having to devote as much thought to the process as would novice interviewers. As a consequence, experienced interviewers may be more likely to give full consideration to more of the specific data on individual applicants and may be less prone to make snap judgments.

> *Proposition 4:* The influence of interviewer experience on the quality of judgments is moderated by the interview structure. Specifically, more pronounced effects of experience will be shown with unstructured interviews than with highly structured interviews.

The beneficial effects of experience stated in Proposition 2 are unlikely to occur to the same extent on all types of interviews. Although this hypothesis has not been tested directly, a high degree of interview structure seems to reduce individual differences among interviewers (Pulakos, Schmitt, Whitney, & Smith, 1996) and seems likely to attenuate the effects of experience. The effect of highly structured interviews is to reduce the cognitive demands on the interviewer (Dipboye & Gaugler, 1993). As a consequence, relatively little experience should be needed to achieve quality judgments with a structured procedure.

There are several areas in which research on interviewer experience could be improved. For one, a multidimensional conceptualization of experience is needed to replace the simplistic views that have dominated past research. It is especially important to distinguish among the amount of interviewing, the diversity of experience (i.e., the different types of interviewing), and time spent in organizational roles (Quinones et al., 1995). In future research it will be important also to distinguish among the various types of experience, including experience with (a) the rating task; (b) the position, job, and organization for which applicants are being considered; (c) the applicant population; (d) the interviewing role (e.g., college recruiting, in-house interviews); and (e) the interviewing procedures (e.g., semistructured, unstructured). A second improvement for this research would be to sample a wider range of experience, so that master interviewers, as defined by high levels of validity and accuracy, can be compared to novice and naive interviewers. Given the difficulty of access and the limited availability of master interviewers, this research will probably require laboratory simulations in which experts are "manufactured" under controlled conditions. Another way to improve future research would be to use more realistic, face-to-face interview situations. In suggesting this we do not mean to imply that past research using paper credentials has not provided insights into the effects of experience. Most employment decisions (especially decisions to not interview) are based on no more than paper, and more, not less, research is needed on how interviewers judge applicants and gather information in the preinterview phase of the interview process. However, it is risky to generalize from these studies to the face-to-face interview. There have been too few studies of how experience influences interview outcomes when the interviewer not only observes and evaluates but also asks questions and recruits.

Conclusion

We began this chapter by stating a common assumption—that interviewers who are more experienced in interviewing and evaluating applicants are superior to inexperienced interviewers in their knowledge structures, their gathering of information, and their judgments. Research on this issue has cast doubt on this assumption. Experienced interviewers appear less lenient, more confident of their own abilities as interviewers, more satisfied by the interviewing task, and more positive toward interviews as selection procedures than do inexperienced interviewers. However, there is evidence that experience can harm as well as help the quality of interviewer judgments. The propositions stated above for the conditions under which experience leads to interviewer expertise are speculative and must be tested in future research. Nevertheless, interviewer experience seems fundamental to understanding and improving selection interviews and deserves more attention from researchers and theorists.

We have focused solely on the quality of the interviewer's judgments in selecting applicants. It is important to recognize, however, that the interviewer role involves more than just selection and that the interview process may serve other important functions besides finding the right person for the job. A broader conception of expertise may be needed to take into account the organizational context. Similarly, Sternberg and Frensch (1992) recently observed that "in the real world—as opposed to many psychological laboratories—expertise is, in large part, an attribution. A person is an expert because she is regarded as such by others" (p. 194). In ambiguous situations, interviewer "success" may depend more on impression management than on the interviewer's actual accuracy in picking the right people for the job. Moreover, one could argue that the confidence that others have in the "expert" may serve important system functions even though the expert falls short of psychometric standards for evaluating judgments. Exploration of these possibilities goes beyond the scope of this chapter, but it is crucial to the achievement of a comprehensive understanding of expertise in the organizational context.

References

Armstrong, J. S. (1978). *Long range forecasting: From crystal ball to computer.* New York: John Wiley.

Balzer, W. K., Doherty, M. E., & O'Connor, R., Jr. (1989). Effects of cognitive feedback on performance. *Psychological Bulletin, 106,* 410-433.

Barr, S. H., & Hitt, M. A. (1986). A comparison of selection decision models in manager versus student samples. *Personnel Psychology, 39,* 599-617.

Binning, J. F., Goldstein, M. A., Garcia, M. F., Harding, J. L., & Scattaregia, J. H. (1988). Effects of preinterview impressions on questioning strategies in same- and opposite-sex employment interviews. *Journal of Applied Psychology, 73,* 30-37.

Carlson, R. E. (1967). Selection interview decisions: The effect of interviewer experience, relative quota situation, and applicant sample on interviewer decisions. *Personnel Psychology, 20,* 259-280.

Dawes, R. M. (1971). A case study of graduate admissions: Application of three principles of human decision making. *American Psychologist, 26,* 180-188.

Dawes, R. M. (1988). *Rational choice in an uncertain world.* San Diego, CA: Harcourt Brace Jovanovich.

Dipboye, R. L., Fromkin, H. L., & Wiback, K. (1975). Relative importance of applicant sex, attractiveness, and scholastic standing in evaluation of job applicant resumes. *Journal of Applied Psychology, 60,* 39-43.

Dipboye, R. L., & Gaugler, B. (1993). Cognitive and behavioral processes in the selection interviews. In N. Schmitt, W. C. Borman, & Associates (Eds.), *Personnel selection in organizations* (pp. 135-171). San Francisco: Jossey-Bass.

Dougherty, T. W., Ebert, R. J., & Callender, J. C. (1986). Policy capturing in the employment interview. *Journal of Applied Psychology, 71,* 9-15.

Dougherty, T. W., Turban, D. B., & Callender, J. C. (1994). Confirming first impressions in the employment interview: A field study of interviewer behavior. *Journal of Applied Psychology, 79,* 659-665.

Eder, R. W. (1989). Contextual effects on interview decisions. In R. W. Eder & G. R. Ferris (Eds.), *The employment interview: Theory, research, and practice* (pp. 113-126). Newbury Park, CA: Sage.

Ericsson, K. A., Krampe, R. T., & Tesch-Romer, C. (1993). The role of deliberate practice in the acquisition of expert performance. *Psychological Review, 100,* 363-406.

Fiske, S. T., & Kinder, D. R. (1981). Involvement, expertise, and schema use. In N. Cantor & J. F. Kihlstrom (Eds.), *Personality, cognition, and social interaction* (pp. 171-187). Hillsdale, NJ: Lawrence Erlbaum.

Garb, H. N. (1989). Clinical judgment, clinical training, and professional experience. *Psychological Bulletin, 105,* 387-396.

Gehrlein, T. M., Dipboye, R. L., & Shahani, C. (1993). Nontraditional validity calculations and differential interviewer experience: Implications for selection interviews. *Educational and Psychological Measurement, 52,* 457-469.

Ghiselli, E. E. (1966). The validity of a personnel interview. *Personnel Psychology, 19,* 389-394.

Gilbert, D. T., Pelham, B. W., & Krull, D. S. (1988). On cognitive busyness: When person perceivers meet persons perceived. *Journal of Personality and Social Psychology, 54,* 733-740.

Gilmore, D. C., Beehr, T. A., & Love, K. G. (1986). Effects of applicant sex, applicant physical attractiveness, type of rater, and type of job on interview decisions. *Journal of Occupational Psychology, 59,* 103-109.

Glaser, R., & Chi, M. T. H. (1988). Overview. In M. T. H. Chi, R. Glaser, & M. J. Farr (Eds.), *The nature of expertise* (pp. xvii-xx). Hillsdale, NJ: Lawrence Erlbaum.

Goldberg, L. R. (1970). Man versus model of man: A rationale, plus some evidence, for a method of improving on clinical inferences. *Psychological Bulletin, 73,* 422-432.

Graves, L. M. (1993). Sources of individual differences in interviewer effectiveness: A model and implications for future research. *Journal of Organizational Behavior, 14,* 349-370.

Hakel, M. D., Dobmeyer, T. W., & Dunnette, M. D. (1970). Relative importance of three content dimensions in overall suitability ratings of job applicants' resumes. *Journal of Applied Psychology, 54,* 65-71.

Hakel, M. D., Hollman, T. D., & Dunnette, M. D. (1970). Accuracy of interviewers, certified public accountants, and students in identifying the interests of accountants. *Journal of Applied Psychology, 54,* 115-119.

Hogarth, R. M. (1987). *Judgement and choice.* Chichester: John Wiley.

Imada, A. S., Fletcher, C., & Dalessio, A. (1980). Individual correlates of an occupational stereotype: A reexamination of the stereotype of accountants. *Journal of Applied Psychology, 65,* 436-439.

Johnson, E. J. (1988). Expertise and decision under uncertainty: Performance and process. In M. T. H. Chi, R. Glaser, & M. J. Farr (Eds.), *The nature of expertise* (pp. 209-228). Hillsdale, NJ: Lawrence Erlbaum.

Keenan, A. (1976). Interviewers' evaluation of applicant characteristics: Differences between personnel and non-personnel managers. *Journal of Occupational Psychology, 49,* 223-230.

Keenan, A. (1978). Selection interview outcomes in relation to interviewer training and experience. *Journal of Social Psychology, 106,* 249-260.

Kohn, L. S., Dipboye, R. L., & Gaugler, B. B. (1995, May). *Predicting postinterview impressions from preinterview information: A correlational test of behavioral mediators.* Poster presented at the annual meeting of the Society for Industrial and Organizational Psychology, Orlando, FL.

Lurigio, A. J., & Carroll, J. S. (1985). Probation officers' schemata of offenders: Content, development and impact on treatment decisions. *Journal of Personality and Social Psychology, 48,* 1112-1127.

Macan, T. H., & Dipboye, R. L. (1988). The effects of interviewers' initial impressions on information gathering. *Organizational Behavior and Human Decision Processes, 42,* 364-387.

Marks, E., & Webb, S. C. (1969). Vocational choice and professional experience as factors in occupational image. *Journal of Applied Psychology, 53,* 292-300.

Marlowe, C. M., Schneider, S. L., & Nelson, C. E. (1996). Gender and attractiveness biases in hiring decisions: Are more experienced managers less biased? *Journal of Applied Psychology, 81,* 11-21.

McDaniel, M. A., Whetzel, D. L., Schmidt, F. L., & Maurer, S. D. (1994). The validity of employment interviews: A comprehensive review and meta-analysis. *Journal of Applied Psychology, 79,* 599-616.

Olian, J. D. (1985). Staffing. In E. A. Locke (Ed.), *Generalizing from laboratory studies to field settings* (pp. 13-42). Lexington, MA: Lexington Books.

Paunonen, S. V., & Jackson, D. N. (1987). Accuracy of interviewers and students in identifying the personality characteristics of personnel managers and computer programmers. *Journal of Vocational Behavior, 31,* 26-36.

Pulakos, E. D., Schmitt, N., Whitney, D., & Smith, M. (1996). Individual differences in interviewer ratings: The impact of standardization, consensus discussion, and sampling error on the validity of a structured interview. *Personnel Psychology, 49,* 85-102.

Quinones, M. A., Ford, J. K., & Teachout, M. S. (1995). The relationship between work experience and job performance: A meta-analytic review. *Personnel Psychology, 48,* 887-910.

Richman, W. L., & Quinones, M. A. (1996). Task frequency rating accuracy: The effect of task engagement and experience. *Journal of Applied Psychology, 81,* 512-524.

Rowe, P. M. (1963). Individual differences in selection decisions. *Journal of Applied Psychology, 47,* 304-307.

Ryan, A. M., & Sackett, P. R. (1989). Exploratory study of individual assessment practices: Interrater reliability and judgments of assessor effectiveness. *Journal of Applied Psychology, 74,* 568-579.

Singer, M. S., & Bruhns, C. (1991). Relative effect of applicant work experience and academic qualification on selection interview decisions: A study of between-sample generalizability. *Journal of Applied Psychology, 76,* 550-559.

Sternberg, R. J., & Frensch, P. A. (1992). On being an expert: A cost-benefit analysis. In R. R. Hoffman (Ed.), *The psychology of expertise* (pp. 191-203). New York: Springer-Verlag.

Stone, E. F., Stone, D. L., & Dipboye, R. L. (1992). Stigmas in organizations: Race, handicaps, and physical unattractiveness. In K. Kelley (Ed.), *Issues, theory, and research in industrial and organizational psychology.* Amsterdam: Elsevier Science.

Webster, E. C. (1982). *The employment interview: A social judgment process.* Schomberg, ON: SIP.

Wiener, Y., & Schneiderman, M. L. (1974). Use of job information as a criterion in employment decisions of interviewers. *Journal of Applied Psychology, 59,* 699-704.

16

Using New Technology

The Group Support System

William L. Tullar
Paula R. Kaiser

For more than 30 years, interviewing research has indicated that the use of multiple interviewers is a promising approach for improving interview reliability and validity (see Mayfield, 1964). The use of multiple interviewers (panel or serial) may benefit the interview through several means. First, sharing their different perceptions may help interviewers to reduce or eliminate irrelevant inferences they make that are not job related (Arvey & Campion, 1982). Second, the sharing of different perceptions may help to eliminate idiosyncratic biases among interviewers (Hakel, 1982). Third, there is a range of information and judgment that different interviewers may contribute that may lead to more accurate predictions (Dipboye, 1992). Fourth, using more than one interviewer is akin to having a longer test. Longer tests are more reliable than shorter tests; thus, the combined scores of more interviewers should be more reliable than the score of a single interviewer (Hakel, 1982).

This chapter examines the potential contribution of the group support system (GSS) to the theory and practice of using multiple interviewers. A group support system is a combination of computer hardware and software that makes it possible for group members sitting together in a room to have a discussion through their computer keyboards and a central projection screen that all participants can view. As the discussion proceeds, each participant can respond to the topic at hand by reading what others have written on the central screen and typing responses. In most setups, all the written comments are anonymous, so face-to-face social conventions do not dominate the content or the process. Moreover, because all the comments are written using computers, it is possible for investigators to trace lines of thought carefully long after the interaction has been concluded.

Using focus theory (Briggs, 1994), we argue that the GSS produces interviews that are generally higher in content validity than face-to-face interacting panel or serial interviews. Focus theory posits that three common group activities—communication, deliberation, and accessing information—compete for scarce cognitive resources. The GSS allows better group process and group decisions because it reduces the cognitive costs of all three activities. We then take up the issues of how best to apply group support systems for interview practice and how best to apply them for testing interviewing theory.

Recent GSS Literature and Group Decision Making

The application of GSS technology to panel or serial interviewing is at once both obvious and subtle. A group support system typically consists of a local area network of microcomputers in a room with software designed to support a meeting. There are several commercially available GSSs that include programs for both exchanging information and expressing preferences. The unique capability of simultaneous communication in written form lets many more people participate effectively and brings more information to bear on a problem than would otherwise be possible. GSSs have been used for electronic brainstorming, organizing ideas, ranking and rating decision alternatives, maintaining participant anonymity, and automated record keeping (Aiken, Hasan, & Vanjani, 1996).

IBM was an early pioneer in group support systems, holding the first trials of electronic meeting systems at its Owego, New York, plant in 1986. In the 2 years that followed, IBM documented that teams using the technology saved up to 55% in labor costs over conventional methods and reduced start-to-finish project time up to 91%. IBM also documented improvements in the quality of results and the satisfaction levels of participants (Nunamaker & Briggs, 1994).

Aiken et al. (1996) found that groups using GSSs have reduced meeting time up to 91% and labor costs up to 71%. They also note that because meetings take less time and are more effective, group members are more satisfied with automated meetings than with traditional, verbal meetings. Bulkeley (1992) and Deutsch (1990) have both reported that organizations using GSSs have achieved superior decisions with meeting times reduced in the range of 70%-90%. In laboratory studies, groups using GSSs have been found to generate many more unique ideas of higher quality than have groups using standard meeting techniques (Dennis, Valacich, & Nunamaker, 1990; Gallupe, Bastianutti, & Cooper, 1991).

Well-known group phenomena are often modified when a GSS is applied. It has long been known that individual risk preferences and group risk preferences are often quite different. In the 1960s, an experiment conducted by Stoner (1968) gave rise to what was later dubbed the *risky shift* phenomenon. Stoner showed that people who made individual choices in a decision simulation and later made the same choices as a group showed a definite shift toward risk. This phenomenon has been studied extensively; later researchers have called it the *choice shift* because, depending on the decision-making situation, some groups have shifted toward caution. Karan, Kerr, Murthy, and Vinze (1996) studied this phenomenon using GSS. Their results suggest that GSS-mediated communication, whether anonymous or nonanonymous, resulted in no significant choice shift, whereas the face-to-face groups produced the expected cautious shift.

Group support systems alter group interaction. GSS groups tend to be more focused, produce more comments, have greater levels of participation, consider more issues, and make better overall judgments. In some cases the advantage is slight and in others it is more pronounced, but in most of the experiments that have compared GSS with face-to-face groups, GSS groups have been shown to be different and usually superior.

The Downside of Using Group Support Systems

Although the use of group support systems offers a multitude of benefits to group decision making and to the interview process, it does carry a potential downside, which must be considered. We describe below some characteristics of GSSs that may create problem areas for some users.

Group process is influenced by personality type. In both traditional meetings and GSS environments, participation in and satisfaction with the group process is influenced by personality type. Yellen, Winniford, and Sanford (1995) used the Myers-Briggs type indicator to create mixed groups of introverts and extroverts that met in traditional face-to-face meetings and in GSS meetings. The extroverts made more comments in both environments. Further, personal satisfaction with the process may be influenced by the individual's desire to use a computer.

Logically, we can assume that people who like working on computers enjoy the GSS environment more than do those who dislike computers.

A GSS does not replace leadership. For a group support system to be used effectively, the leader must sincerely desire group participation and be open to the ideas of the group. Painful issues that would not be discussed in traditional meetings may arise in a GSS environment. A sensitive leader must be receptive to both positive and negative feedback.

GSS facilitators must be skilled. Skilled facilitators are important for success with GSS sessions. GSSs have been developed to be easily and quickly learned by participants, with groups sometimes beginning productive work after less than 30 seconds of instruction (Nunamaker, Briggs, Mittleman, Vogel, & Balthazard, 1997). This short participant learning curve has been accomplished through the off-loading of the system's complexity to the facilitator. A highly skilled technical person is therefore needed to manage the complex software and to keep the appropriate computer files accessible to participants during their deliberations.

Additionally, a leader who understands the content issues is necessary to help the group define the issues and to lead the group to consensus. Generally, these two different skill sets are not available in one person; most groups will require a technical facilitator and a group leader. Future GSS development work should focus on simplifying the facilitator's learning curve so that a larger number of facilitators can be available in many organizations and so that many group leaders can facilitate their own meetings.

GSSs are expensive. The most significant disadvantage to the use of group support systems is its cost. Meeting-room facilities, GSS software, and facilitator training are all costly. Therefore, the use of GSS for interviewing at the present time is limited to those positions for which a false positive decision entails a significant financial risk. As future use of the GSS increases and facilities become more available, the cost will decrease, just as other computing costs have. GSS software is currently being developed for the Internet. Development work is proceeding to make the use of GSSs easier for facilitators to learn. The future points to wider use of GSSs and the feasibility of using this technology in a larger number of interviewing and selection decisions.

Geographically dispersed meetings lack body language. Body language and paralanguage are still present in many GSS meetings, so that an alert leader or facilitator can note the shifting gazes, body positions, and gestures that indicate it is time to move on or that signal discomfort with the current topic. The geographically dispersed meeting loses the advantage of body language, and facilitators must use electronic means of staying in touch with participants' feelings.

Panel and Serial Interviews

Two different designs have generally been employed with multiple interviewers. The most common design used for selecting firefighters, police, and government employees is the panel. The members of the panel sit down in one place at one time, and the applicants sit before the panel. Usually the same questions are asked in the same order, to ensure fairness. Thus, each member of the panel hears the same applicant statements in the same order. In the serial design, interviewers handle each applicant sequentially. Often in this design interviewers coordinate so as *not* to ask the same questions. This approach makes for better coverage of the job content domain but probably produces lower interrater reliability, because each interviewer witnesses a different set of applicant answers.

Many years of interviewing research have sustained the view that the use of multiple interviewers is a promising way to improve reliability and validity of interviews (e.g., Arvey & Campion, 1982; Mayfield, 1964). There may be several reasons for this improvement. It may be that sharing different perceptions helps interviewers become aware of irrelevant inferences they make about variables that are not job related (Arvey & Campion, 1982). Further, most interviewing researchers consider panel or serial interviews to be more structured and therefore more reliable than other kinds of interviews. The use of multiple interviewers may also reduce the impact of idiosyncratic biases among individual interviewers (Campion, Pursell, & Brown, 1988). The aggregation of multiple judgments into a single judgment may balance out the random errors (Dipboye, 1992; Hakel, 1982). The use of multiple interviewers also permits better recall of information (Stasser & Titus, 1987). The range of information and judgments that different interviewers contribute may lead to more accurate predictions (Dipboye, 1992). In addition, using more interviewers is approximately the same thing as including more items in a test. A longer test is more reliable than a shorter test; thus multiple interviewers should be more reliable than a single interviewer (Hakel, 1982).

The most recent meta-analysis of interviewing studies found that panel (versus separate) interviewers correlated .56 with interview reliability (Conway, Jako, & Goodman, 1995). However, if one takes the whole body of evidence currently available through meta-analysis, the evidence for the superiority of panel interviews is mixed. Wiesner and Cronshaw (1988) found that for unstructured interviews, panels were superior, but for structured interviews, there did not appear to be much difference. Marchese and Muchinsky (1993) found no correlation between the number of interviewers and interview validity. We find the results of these latter two studies to be counterintuitive and perhaps suspect.

We argue that the panel interview is superior to most unstructured interviews performed today, and that imposing the structure of a group support system on the panel makes the (structured) panel superior to a structured individual interview. This should be true for both reliability and validity. With Hakel (1982), we hold that using more interviewers is the same as using a longer test and thus more reliable. With Feild and Gatewood (1989), we argue that the multiple experience of several panel members translates into more content points of the applicant's performance and more content points of the position in question. The panel interview combines the advantages of a more thorough examination of the job content domain as well as a good check on the matching of individual knowledge, skills, and abilities to job requirements. The most significant disadvantage of the panel interview is, of course, its cost. However, in those cases where a false positive decision entails a substantial financial risk, the cost of a panel may seem small by comparison.

How a GSS Changes Interview Panel Dynamics

Most of the advantage of the GSS is explained by the focus theory of group productivity, which holds that all group members divide their cognitive resources among three cognitive processes that compete for their attention: communication, deliberation, and accessing of information. Focus theory holds that these processes interfere with one another, limiting group productivity. Considering each of these processes in turn, we can see how each claims scarce cognitive resources of group members. Communication requires that people devote attention to choosing their words, behaviors, images, and artifacts, presenting them through various media to other team members. Deliberation requires that people devote cognitive effort to forming intentions toward accomplishing the group's goal. This includes the classic problem-solving activities: making sense of the problem, developing and evaluating alternatives, selecting and planning a course of action, and so on. The accessing of information requires finding, storing, processing, and retrieving the information needed to support the deliberations.

The interviewing panel has three major tasks: arriving at the best interview criteria (job specifications) possible, examining carefully the match between each candidate and those job specifications, and then arriving at a final decision. Table 16.1 shows how the support aspects of the GSS facilitate the performance of each of these tasks. As the table shows, a group support system improves productivity and accuracy of group deliberations by lessening the attention costs of communication, deliberation, and information access. Information has value only insofar as it is available when a choice must be made, and then it must be complete and accurate. The GSS makes information available at less cognitive cost. This explains why most people find GSS sessions more pleasant than other

Table 16.1   Technology Aspects Versus Interview Phase

	Communication Support	Deliberation Support	Information Access Support
Building criteria (job specifications)	Having a medium in which one can quickly express ideas stimulated by others	Ensuring that group members are able to produce as complete a job specification as possible	Ensuring that all written materials on the position are instantly available
Information absorption process	Being able to articulate criteria with less effort and fewer interruptions	Building categories that will span the job specification space	Making the job specifications and reasoning for them instantly available
Final decision process	Having the ability to see others' reasoning on candidate job specification matches	Driving the group to consensus for each candidate on each dimension	Ensuring that all of the job specification/ candidate matches are examined

decision-making forums, and they usually express a higher level of satisfaction with the decisions they make. Table 16.1 shows, for instance, the lessening of cognitive cost to examine the job specifications another time or to reread what someone else contributed about a point made earlier. Many of the normal cognitive demands of short-term memory, information processing, and decision making are made less taxing by the GSS.

Applying Group Support Systems

The most obvious application of GSSs to interview decision making would be in situations where false positive decisions would be extremely costly. GSS labs are generally expensive to rent, and thus there must be a substantial stake in the applicant. GSSs can be adapted in a number of ways to meet particular groups' needs. We suggest two possible models to support the panel interview.

Model 1

The group charged with the decision would meet in a GSS session to formulate the knowledge, skills, and abilities necessary for the position and to plan for interview questions. Then the interview(s) would be conducted. One model would have the best interviewer conduct all interviews and videotape them. The group would then meet to watch the tapes, examine the job specifications the group members had previously put together,

Table 16.2   GSS Multiple-Interviewer Designs

	Same Location	*Different Locations*
Panel	Classic panel design: Panel meets in one room and interviews applicants sequentially. Panel adjourns to GSS lab and decides.	By means of tele- or videoconferencing, panel members assemble at one time and interview applicants sequentially. GSS session is conducted at distributed locations.
Serial	Classic serial design: Each interviewer sees each applicant one on one. After interviewers finish with all applicants, they adjourn to GSS lab and decide.	Applicants are seen wherever convenient. Teleconferencing, telephone, and e-mail are used. GSS session is conducted at distributed locations and times.

examine the candidates' paper and interview performance credentials, and decide, category by category, how each applicant performed. At the end of the session the GSS facilitator would drive the group toward a final decision.

If, as shown in Table 16.2, it is not possible for the members of the panel to meet at one physical location, they could go to separate locations to view the videos of the interviews through videoconference or Internet. Then the GSS session would be conducted via Internet or e-mail. This method may have extensive application for multinational organizations that have managers in several locations who need to agree on the best candidates for certain jobs. Group facilitation in the distributed circumstance is somewhat more difficult, however.

Interviewers using this model must consider applicants' possible reactions to the videotaping of their interviews. We have videotaped a large number of student screening interviews on campus, and have found that in general students seem to have little reaction to the prospect of being videotaped and appear to behave quite normally soon after the taping begins. How applicants in high-pressure interview situations might be affected by videotaping is, however, a different question. Our own experience with a few such interviews suggests that more senior people have even less problem with videotaping than do students, but we know of no comprehensive research study that has examined this effect.

Model 2

In an equally valid model, the panel members would arrive at job specifications the same way as in Model 1, but then all panel members would interview the applicants separately and sequentially. Panel members would then meet in a GSS session to review the specification/candidate fit, and the facilitator would drive them toward a final decision. This model, however, has the disadvantage that all members of the panel witness different applicant behavior. Because of this, the facilitator needs to encourage an exchange among the panel members that takes account of the various impressions of the applicants.

As in the panel model, it is possible to use the sequential interview model with panel members participating from different locations. Here it is important that videotapes of all the different interviews be available. Given that in this case not all interviewers will have interviewed all the applicants, it is very important that some of each interview be available to interviewers who have not had the opportunity to interview given applicants.

The benefits of conducting the panel or serial interview by the means described above are as follows:

1. The panel produces a better and more thorough job analysis.
2. The panel does a more thorough job of examining the applicant than any single person could do.
3. The panel can integrate all the relevant information about the candidates and match each with the job analysis information.

The evidence shows that GSS groups do these tasks faster than face-to-face groups, and that group members are more satisfied with the interaction. For those interviewing decisions that justify the expenditure of time and resources for a panel, the GSS format will provide better decisions and more satisfying group interaction.

Group Support Systems in Academic Interviewing

The search process used for most important academic positions offers an excellent example of a selection procedure that can benefit from the use of GSS technology. In most universities the selection of a senior administrator involves a large number of diverse constituents in a process that often lasts a year or longer. The search committee assigned the responsibility for screening and interviewing candidates meets frequently throughout the period of the search.

The collegial and self-governing traditions of the university make the search process a slow and arduous task, as various priorities are pushed forward and distinctly different personal agendas become apparent. Members of the search committee, already burdened with other service responsibilities, become weary reviewing applicant files and attempting to reach consensus. Even after the last round of interviews, the process ends with less than optimal decision making and low satisfaction on the part of the participants.

On most campuses, computer laboratories are already in place for student use. With the addition of GSS software, such a computer lab could be used for a GSS facility. The search committee would of course need to find a facilitator to handle technical problems and to facilitate the interaction; the chair of the committee could then convene the committee in the GSS lab.

Although a number of models are possible in the academic setting, we propose the following:

1. The search committee would meet in the GSS facility to establish selection criteria and procedures for the search. Initial GSS sessions might involve people other than committee members to provide guidance on desired characteristics of the incumbent.
2. Reaching consensus in additional meetings, the search committee members would agree on a job description and an appropriate announcement of the position opening.
3. As applications are received, individual search committee members would review applicant files against previously established criteria and individually enter comments and/or ratings.
4. The GSS would compile the various comments/ratings and make them available to search committee members at succeeding group meetings. The facilitator could then bring the group to consensus on which applicants to bring to campus for interviews.
5. Interviews would follow the traditional format, including group or individual meetings with large numbers of people and, depending on the type of position, perhaps an open presentation by the candidate.
6. Following each interview or following the last interview, the search committee would meet in the GSS facility to make comments regarding the applicants' performance on established selection criteria. The chair would then bring the group to a consensus on the committee's recommendation for filling the position.

The use of group support systems in academic decision making should result in better decisions, less time spent in meetings, and higher levels of satisfaction on the part of participants.

Group Support Systems, Multiple Interviewers, and Diversity

One of the real advantages of the GSS is found in the area of diversity among multiple interviewers. There is empirical evidence that diverse groups reach better, more satisfying decisions when they reach them using group support systems rather than in face-to-face groups. This is a prediction derivable from focus theory. Diversity makes demands on scarce cognitive resources. In the area of communication, for example, there may be language barriers. The differences may be as small as the variations in, say, American and Indian English or as great as the differences between two completely distinct languages. In both cases there is good evidence that the GSS facilitates communication. Group support systems enable each participant to contribute in his or her language of choice. A centrally based translator program can then render languages back and forth, so that every person is able to read his or her own native language during the session. Although the translations of such programs are not perfect, they are usually quite understandable, providing that participants learn to avoid using metaphors, idioms, and slang. Preliminary development work at the University of Arizona suggests some potential for the building of automatic translation features into future GSS software (Nunamaker et al., 1997).

The GSS is also especially useful for surfacing hidden agendas and value differences. In groups that have a great deal of diversity, one of the problems is the different value systems that underlie the discussion. A group support system can help to surface these differences and force the group to deal with them. Further, the GSS facilitator can push the group toward a decision even when there is not full consensus.

The GSS has great potential for reducing unfair discrimination biases on the part of interviewers. Because GSS discussions are captured in written form, it is possible to conduct a "sensitivity review" of each person's comments to detect inappropriate or illegal patterns of decision making that might have negative impacts on protected groups.

The accessing of information is also a great problem in diverse groups. Using GSS technology, it is possible for participants to refer continually back to the job analysis and job specifications. These documents can appear in any of the languages being used, so that differential recall is not a factor in the discussion.

It is not surprising, however, that the use of the GSS with diverse groups has been shown to yield varying results in satisfaction with the process. Griffith (1996) related Hofstede's (1980) concept of power distance to differences in satisfaction with GSS interactions and found that high power distance cultures are more resistant to the anonymous and egalitarian status created by GSS technology.

Most research concerning GSS use and most field applications of the technology have centered on the use of group support systems by participants in the same conference room at the same time. As we have noted, it is possible with GSS technology to have participants not bound to the same place and time. This property makes GSS interviews particularly attractive for multinational hiring situations. Nunamaker et al. (1997) point to the future use of the GSS integrated with videoconferencing in global contexts. There has, however, been no research to date that we know of that demonstrates empirical experience with this application of GSS technology.

The group support system is not a panacea for dealing with diversity in interviewing situations. However, it does have proven characteristics that help groups manage their differences, process information, and reach decisions simultaneously. This is an area that calls out for research, because international human resource management is becoming a critical area.

Research Possibilities

In addition, GSS panel groups allow us to examine a number of possible hypotheses about interview structure. We can easily track the contributions of each participant in the process and see how false leads were put right and how right leads were followed. We can check on the hypothesis of multiple recall of information by tracing through various participants' contributions. We can also compare the range of information gathered by GSS groups against that gathered by face-to-face groups or individuals acting alone.

Group support systems might also be used to monitor individual cue processing. For instance, with GSS software it is possible to relate the time each comment is typed in to the exact spot on the videotape of an interview that prompted the comment. Thus, it is possible to see exactly which cues were seized upon by which participants. Moreover, one could subsequently examine the inferences that people drew from those cues and connect them. This would allow for cue processing models to explain how different interviewers can see the same behavior but reach different conclusions about it.

GSS technology makes it possible for researchers to examine the way job analysis material is gathered and how the inference process from job analysis to job specifications proceeds. They can track each member of the group and follow his or her suggestions to trace the cognitive paths of various ideas about the job that eventually end up in the job specifications. GSSs can also be useful for researchers interested in examining the group inference process. The technology allows investigators to see how each participant construes a certain behavior he or she witnessed during the interview and how these impressions are changed by the suggestions that other group members make.

Conclusion

Group support systems constitute an interesting tool that could have profound impacts on several areas of interviewing. In panel and serial interviewing, the GSS process adds reliability and content validity to what are already arguably the most reliable interview methods in widespread use. The GSS has beneficial effects on interview decision making in diverse, even multinational, groups. The method offers considerable promise as a research tool, producing computer-encoded data on the entire interview inference process. It is important that interviewing researchers and practitioners familiarize themselves with group support systems and what they can do.

References

Aiken, M., Hasan, B., & Vanjani, M. (1996). Total quality management: A GSS approach. *Information Systems Management, 13,* 73-73.

Arvey, R. D., & Campion, J. E. (1982). The employment interview: A summary and review of recent research. *Personnel Psychology, 35,* 281-322.

Briggs, R. O. (1994). *The focus theory of group productivity and its application to the development and testing of electronic group support technology.* Unpublished doctoral dissertation, University of Arizona, Tucson.

Bulkeley, W. H. (1992, January 28). Computerizing dull meetings is touted as an antidote to the mouth that bored. *Wall Street Journal,* p. 1.

Campion, M. A., Pursell, E. D., & Brown, B. K. (1988). Structured interviewing: Raising the psychometric properties of the employment interview. *Personnel Psychology, 41,* 25-42.

Conway, J. M., Jako, R. A., & Goodman, D. F. (1995). A meta-analysis of interrater and internal consistency reliability of selection interviews. *Journal of Applied Psychology, 80,* 565-579.

Dennis, A. R., Valacich, J. S., & Nunamaker, J. F., Jr. (1990). An experimental investigation of small, medium, and large groups in an electronic meeting system environment. *IEEE System, Man and Cybernetics, 25,* 1049-1057.

Deutsch, C. (1990, October 21). Business meetings by keyboard. *New York Times.*

Dipboye, R. L. (1992). *Selection interviews: Process perspectives.* Cincinnati, OH: South-Western.

Feild, H. S., & Gatewood, R. D. (1989). Development of a selection interview: A job content strategy. In R. W. Eder & G. R. Ferris (Eds.), *The employment interview: Theory, research, and practice* (pp. 145-157). Newbury Park, CA: Sage.

Gallupe, R. B., Bastianutti, L., & Cooper, W. H. (1991). Unblocking brainstorms. *Journal of Applied Psychology, 76,* 173-182.

Griffith, T. L. (1996). *Cross-cultural and cognitive issues in the implementation of new technology: Focus on group support systems and Bulgaria* (Working paper). St. Louis, MO: Washington University.

Hakel, M. D. (1982). Employment interviewing. In K. M. Rowland & G. R. Ferris (Eds.), *Personnel management* (pp. 102-124). Boston: Allyn & Bacon.

Hofstede, G. (1980). *Culture's consequences: International differences related to values.* Beverly Hills, CA: Sage.

Karan, V., Kerr, D. S., Murthy, U. S., & Vinze, A. S. (1996). Research information technology support for collaborative decision-making in auditing: An experimental investigation. *Decision Support Systems, 16*(3), 181-194.

Marchese, M. C., & Muchinsky, P. M. (1993). The validity of the employment interview: A meta-analysis. *International Journal of Selection and Assessment, 1,* 18-26.

Mayfield, E. C. (1964). The selection interview: A reevaluation of published research. *Personnel Psychology, 17,* 239-260.

Nunamaker, J. F., Jr., Briggs, R. O., Mittleman, D. O., Vogel, D. R., & Balthazard, P. A. (1997). Lessons from a dozen years of group support systems research: A discussion of lab and field findings. *Journal of Management Information Systems, 13*(3).

Nunamaker, J. F., Jr., & Briggs, R. O. (1994, March 14-16). *Groupware user experience: Ten years of lessons with GroupSystems.* Paper presented at the Fifth Annual GroupSystems Users Conference, Tucson, AZ.

Stasser, G., & Titus, W. (1987). Effects of information load and percentage of shared information on the dissemination of unshared information during group discussion. *Journal of Personality and Social Psychology, 53,* 81-93.

Stoner, J. A. F. (1968). Risky and cautious shifts in group decisions: The influence of widely held values. *Journal of Experimental Social Psychology, 4,* 442-459.

Wiesner, W. H., & Cronshaw, S. F. (1988). A meta-analytic investigation of the impact of interview format and degree of structure on the validity of the employment interview. *Journal of Occupational Psychology, 61,* 275-290.

Yellen, R. E., Winniford, M., & Sanford, C. C. (1995). Extroversion and introversion in electronically-supported meetings. *Information and Management, 28,* 63-64.

Part IV

Interviewer-Applicant Dynamics

This section of the handbook examines the nature of the interaction between the interviewer and the job applicant. In Chapter 17, Jablin, Miller, and Sias review the literature on interview process, which they define as the communication and interaction between interviewer and applicant. The chapter is organized around three approaches to studying interview processes, ranging from a descriptive approach that focuses on duration, frequency, and patterns of change of communicative acts to a more recently developed approach that views process as the manifestation of a dynamic social system. These approaches all bring to bear somewhat varying perspectives. Together, however, they provide an understanding of the employment interview that is different from what has been implicit in most of the research to date. For example, Jablin et al. suggest that in addition to eliciting information about job applicants, interviewers' questions may communicate information about the status differences between interviewer and applicant.

As Jablin et al. observe, there has been relatively little recent research on the interview process. In fact, many of the key citations in their chapter are to works published prior to 1990, suggesting that a decline in interview process research has occurred. As we have noted elsewhere in this volume, one likely explanation for this is that structured interviews, which seek to eliminate differences in process, are currently enjoying center stage. Interest in the interview as a communication tool has therefore declined. Nevertheless, we believe that process cannot be completely eliminated from an interview, and that researchers should investigate interaction issues in the context of the structured interview. In particular, Jablin et al. suggest an examination of both interviewer and applicant beliefs regarding the structured interview and how these beliefs influence interviewer-applicant reactions.

Another important research issue is how the interviewer handles the opening and closing of the interview. As Jablin et al. indicate, there is a general paucity of empirical literature on this issue, despite the emphasis practitioners place on how the interview is initiated and ended. Furthermore, it seems quite reasonable to expect that the beginning of the interview would be a potentially important determinant of subsequent interaction. This may be even more true in the case of a highly structured interview, which is likely to be a novel situation for many applicants. The way in which a highly structured interview is introduced may be a critical determinant of subsequent interviewer-applicant dynamics and reactions.

Finally, it seems critical that more researchers address the underlying causal mechanisms between process and interview outcomes. Why, for example, are successful interviews associated with applicant dominance and complementary exchanges, whereas unsuccessful interviews are associated with symmetrical exchanges? One explanation might be that dominant behavior on the part of the applicant is deemed to be an indication of social savvy; to the degree to which this is true and social savvy is job related, this may even be a valid cue. Another explanation is that complementary exchanges are more effective for building interpersonal relationships, and therefore applicants who use that method are more likable, which in turn leads to more favorable interview outcomes (but not necessarily better performance on the job).

In Chapter 18, Gilmore, Stevens, Harrell-Cook, and Ferris address impression management behavior in the interview. By way of summary, these authors invoke a model developed by Ferris and Judge to organize a review of the literature and to develop new hypotheses. Impression management is a topic that has received a great deal of attention in social psychology and appears to be an appropriate issue to study in the interview context.

One area in which Gilmore et al. note a need concerns the precise determination of what is and is not impression management behavior. For example, one of the behaviors often included as self-promoting is "entitlement," which is defined as claiming credit for positive events. In the interview context, however, the interviewer may not be able to distinguish between accurate portrayals of a positive event and inaccurate portrayals of the same incident. In other words, it seems that what might be an entitlement for one applicant may be non-impression management for another. To date, this distinction seems to have been ignored.

Second, as Gilmore et al. state, we need models and theories to explain more completely why impression management behaviors appear to affect interviewer ratings. One thing we do know is that the effects are not simple, because occasionally too much impression management behavior can backfire against the applicant. At least two explanations come to mind for this latter finding. First, perhaps the interviewer assesses the appropriateness of the applicant's behavior such that too much, or too little, impression management behavior is a signal as to how he or she will behave on the job. Note that this explanation is somewhat supported by the literature indicating that the effect of impression management may be moderated by the nature of the job. Or, alternatively, perhaps the interviewer regards too much impression management behavior as a signal that the candidate is disingenuous and therefore the interviewer discounts the sincerity of the candidate's statements.

Third, a largely overlooked factor is individual differences in interviewers' reactions to impression management behaviors. That is, it seems possible that some interviewers are more influenced by applicants' impression management behaviors than are other interviewers. Perhaps novice interviewers, for example, are more susceptible to such influences than are experienced interviewers. This relates to some degree to the previous suggestion that we need a greater understanding of *why* and *how* impression management behaviors affect interview ratings. We suspect that the same behavior or statement displayed by a candidate might be interpreted in different ways by different interviewers; a study examining the factors that determine how an interviewer perceives a particular behavior would be of great value.

Last, we offer two methodological suggestions for future researchers. First, almost all of the research examining impression management behavior has been in the context of unstructured interviews. We need to know much more about the role of this construct in structured interviewing. Second, with a few noteworthy exceptions, the vast majority of this research has been conducted in laboratory contexts; there is a strong need for more investigation in field settings.

In Chapter 19, Palmer, Campion, and Green address the effects of training, particularly as it relates to the roles of interviewers and applicants. As these authors observe, despite the frequency of interview training, there is a paucity of research on this topic. A major point that Palmer et al. make is that there is an inherent conflict between the interviewer's agenda and the applicant's agenda. Based on this, they address a number of issues, including whether interviewer and applicant training cancel each other out or whether such training enhances the accuracy of each party's decision.

Palmer et al. raise a number of interesting points that we would like to highlight. One is that each party may have a unique set of purposes. As described earlier in this volume, the interviewer's purpose (e.g., selection, recruitment) has been largely neglected; Palmer et al. take this issue one step further and argue that we must also consider the goals of the applicant in understanding interview dynamics.

A second important point raised by these authors is that we need to apply general training principles to understand the effects of interviewer training. As an example, to what degree is transfer of training a concern? We speculate that transfer of training may be a large problem here, just as it is for other skills. Many practical issues should be addressed as well. For example, what are the most effective means of conveying information in an interviewer training program (e.g., role-playing, case studies)? Are there individual differences in trainee learning? For example, as some of the contributions to Part III of this volume indicate, there is reason to believe that experienced and inexperienced interviewers may require different strategies for training.

Third, researchers should use a wide array of criteria in assessing the success of an interviewer training program. For example, considering the three basic outcomes examined in Part I of this handbook, a highly successful training program should improve the hiring process in many ways, including validity, protection from legal exposure, and positive applicant reactions. Within these three basic categories are a larger number of possible criteria, such as higher job acceptance rate, lower turnover rate, and higher rate of applicants' recommending the organization to a friend. Using Kirkpatrick's four levels of criteria, concrete results might be measured in a variety of different, yet important, ways.

Finally, with regard to applicant training programs, because most of the training content has been geared toward unstructured interviews, an interesting issue is to what degree information about the purpose and underlying assumptions of structured interview would increase applicant scores. In the assessment center context, for example, research indicates that assessees who know what dimensions are being assessed will attain higher ratings than those who do not know what dimensions are being measured. Similar studies that either manipulate knowledge of the dimensions underlying structured interviewing (i.e., by providing some applicants with training) or simply measure knowledge of the dimensions assessed would be interesting for both practical and theoretical reasons.

17

Communication and Interaction Processes

Fredric M. Jablin
Vernon D. Miller
Patricia M. Sias

Almost any description of the employment interview includes the term *process*. Exactly what is a process? At its most fundamental level, a process is a "pattern that is seen in reference to time" (Monge, Farace, Eisenberg, Miller, & White, 1984, p. 22). Thus, for example, scholars often refer to the interview as a process in their descriptions of interviewers' and applicants' question-asking and -answering patterns (e.g., Jablin & Miller, 1990), as well as in terms of the impressions and judgments of each interview party with respect to suitability of employment (e.g., Jablin & McComb, 1984; Kinicki & Lockwood, 1985; Sackett, 1982). Others use the term *process* when they describe the progression of steps involved in gaining employment—that is, the activities that begin with job search and culminate with the acceptance of a job offer (Adams, 1994; Paunonen, 1987). In brief, the notion of process is considered in a variety of ways in research related to the employment interview. Our purpose here, however, is not to review all the ways in which the notion of process has been studied in the employment interview; rather, we focus on what most researchers and practitioners think of when the notion of process is raised with respect to the interview: the nature of communication/interaction processes between interviewer and applicant.

Curiously, relatively few investigations have been conducted into communication/interaction processes in the employment interview, despite numerous calls for more research in this area (Jablin & McComb, 1984; Liden & Parsons, 1989; Tengler & Jablin, 1983) and past criticisms about the neglect of the study of processes related to organizational phenomena in general (Monge, 1990; Monge et al., 1984; Porter & Roberts, 1976). As Liden and Parsons (1989) suggest, "Acquiring a better understanding of the process dynamics of what actually transpires between an interviewer and applicant during an interview" may resolve the interview's predictive validity problems and aid in the design of more effective interview training programs (p. 231). Along these lines, and in an effort to clarify, organize, and promote research exploring communication/interaction processes in the employment interview, we provide in this chapter a brief review of the literature in this area organized in terms of three approaches that have been used to investigate interview "process" dynamics. We also present examples of the application of each approach and suggest corresponding directions for future research within and across these approaches.

Brief Review of the Process Literature

Just as there are numerous approaches to examining process in organizational settings (Monge, 1990), there are several approaches to investigating communication processes in the employment interview. Although a number of different approaches might be taken to organizing the literature on process in the interview (e.g., kinds of processes studied, behavioral foci), we structure our analysis in terms of a fundamental issue associated with the study of process: the grouping of sequences of communicative behavior. More specifically, three approaches to sequential behavior are reflected in the extant employment interviewing research.

The first approach tends to be descriptive in nature and focuses on profiling the display of particular kinds of discrete communicative acts (for example, questions, statements, hesitancies, response latencies), their duration, frequency, patterns of change, and the like over the course of the interview. The second approach focuses on sequences of pairs of communicative acts and the extent to which they are predictive of subsequent patterns of interview interaction as well as interview outcomes (e.g., offer of "on-site" interview, interview satisfaction). As a series of interconnected events, the fundamental unit of study in this approach is a verbal or nonverbal interact or double interact (Hollander & Willis, 1967). An *interact* may be defined as a pair of acts (or utterances) in which the second act is dependent upon the first act. For instance, an applicant's answer depends upon the interviewer's question. A double interact is a sequence in which a third act is dependent upon the interact. In this case, a statement made by the interviewer depends upon how the applicant responded to the interviewer's initial question. In brief, the second approach to process does not focus on patterns of single acts or behaviors, but draws attention to patterns of verbal behavior as "concatenous and progressive pairs of antecedent and consequent acts" (Hawes, 1973, p. 14). The third and final approach, although a relatively new area of study, also focuses on understanding patterns of interacts and double interacts over the course of the interview, but clusters these patterns of interaction in more "macro" terms. More specifically, the focus of this approach is on understanding the manner in which patterns of interaction define the interview as a social system and create structures (for example, conversational rules and expectations) that enable and constrain interaction processes over time.

In sum, although all of these research approaches emphasize the study of interview process, their purposes vary greatly, and as a consequence each provides distinctive information with respect to the roles and functions of communication/interaction in the interview. In addition, it is important to recognize that selective studies explore multiple issues, and thus in our overview of the literature we discuss some studies in more than one subsection. Finally, the reader should realize that because of space limitations the review that follows is not intended to be comprehensive; rather, it is representative in nature.

Patterns of "Acts"

The first approach to the study of communication/interaction examines changes in the mean score (or a range of scores) in a continuous variable or changes in the frequency of certain acts over some period of time. When applied to interviewer or applicant communication patterns, investigations from this perspective tend to address the following fundamental question: How is behavior structured over time (e.g., Warner, 1991)?

One method that has been used to identify patterns of behavior over time examines changes in mean score or frequency of acts to discover trends. These investigations examine the overall patterns of recruiters' or applicants' interviewing behavior across the interview. By examining the types of questions asked, length of talk time in question asking, question answering, and making statements, or number and types of interruptions, investigators are able to understand how interviewers seek information and how applicants enact their role in the interview. Along these lines, for instance, in an examination of participants' overall talk time, Anderson (1960) found that military interviewers talked more in interviews with applicants who were ultimately accepted and that the amount of time that accepted and rejected applicants talked varied little. In addition, he found that the duration of candidates' talk time varied inversely with the length of the interviewer's talk time.

In a more detailed examination of screening interview participants' talk time, Tengler and Jablin (1983) discovered differences in the talk time of candidates in screening interviews who were offered or not offered a second (on-site) interview. Analyses showed that successful candidates, compared with unsuccessful candidates, spent less time responding to interviewer questions (about half of their total talk time) but spent more time talking in their interviews outside of question-answer sequences. These patterns suggest that recruiters' decisions may be based more on nonquestion interactions than on responses to specific questions.

In examining the overall interview structure of question asking, Tengler and Jablin (1983) also found that interviewers tended to use inverted-funnel questioning sequences. That is, in the first segments of the interview, recruiters asked closed-ended, mostly primary questions and then progressed to more open-ended and secondary questions in the second (middle) interview segment. This sequence indicates that recruiters' use of closed-ended questions may have been restricting candidates' responses in the early portion of the interview and allowing for more expansive responses in the middle portion of the interview.

Research in this area has also examined patterns in the frequency and proportion of interviewers' interruptive statements and questions, probing questions, verbal encouragers, restatements, clarification questions, and question-and-answer response latencies (e.g., the amount of time between an applicant's utterance and an interviewer's question, or the lapse of time between an interviewer's utterance and an applicant's response; see McComb & Jablin, 1984). In addition, at least one study has described the format and timing of applicants' questions. Babbitt and Jablin (1985) found that applicants' questions were characterized as closed-ended, singular in form, and typically not phrased in the first person. Also, applicants asked the great bulk of their questions only after their interviewers solicited questions from them (formally signaled a switch in roles).

A second method that has been used to identify patterns of interview behavior over time involves focusing on behaviors displayed during specific segments of the interview. In particular, research has focused on patterns displayed during the opening minutes of the interview and inter-action patterns associated with particular topics of inquiry. With respect to this latter issue, for example, Matarazzo, Wiens, Jackson, and Manaugh (1970) found that applicants for a clinically oriented position spoke longer and had less hesitancy when discussing their occupational histories than when interview segments focused on their family or educational backgrounds. Results also showed that occupational history was a more important consideration in recruiters' decisions about applicants than was information about family and educational background.

Interest in interaction during the opening minutes of the interview stems from studies that have shown that this period may be critical in recruiters' formation of judgments about the suitability of recruits. In possibly the most controversial investigation of the opening segment of employment interviews, Springbett (1958) found that interviewers tend to make decisions about applicants' employability during the first 4 to 7 minutes of the interview. Subsequent investigations of the "snap decision" suggest that the quickness of interviewers' decisions ranges from the first few minutes to the latter half of the interview and may depend on the purpose and length of the interview as well as the quality of the applicant (Huegli & Tshirgi, 1975; Tucker & Rowe, 1977; Tullar, Mullins, & Caldwell, 1979). Although the quickness with which interviewers judge applicants can be disputed (see Buckley & Eder, 1988), these investigations do provide important information on the threshold of information (i.e., quantity and quality) necessary for recruiters to make decisions about applicants.

In some respects, investigations into interviewers' use of confirmatory and disconfirmatory questioning strategies (e.g., Binning, Goldstein, Garcia, Harding, & Scattaregia, 1988; Sackett, 1982) continue the tradition of examining the initial segments of the employment interview. Along these lines, for example, Dougherty, Turban, and Callender (1994) allowed interviewers to form impressions about applicants by first exposing them to their applications and test scores. Audiotapes of the interviews were subsequently coded for interviewers' verbal behaviors associated with "positive regard," focus (e.g., selling the company), talk time, and information-gathering strategies, among other things. Results revealed that interviewers' first impressions were associated with the use of "confirmatory behavior and styles." Moreover, the more positive interviewers' first impressions, the fewer total questions, closed-ended questions, initial questions, and follow-up/probing questions they asked.

Investigations of the quickness of interviewer decisions coupled with studies of participants' talk time generate several concerns about the quality of interviewers' decisions. Given that interviewers' question sequences often take the form of inverted funnels, with a heavy emphasis on closed-ended questions early in interviews, and that many recruiters spend more time talking in their interviews than do the applicants (Anderson, 1960; Tengler & Jablin, 1983), interviewers may be limiting themselves in the amount of information they obtain at the same point in time they are most impressionable. Job applicants may also be contributing to this situation by being reticent during the early segments of their interviews. In other words, interviewers may be adopting inverted-funnel sequences in reaction to applicants who are cautious about talking early on in their interviews. In some circumstances, the use of inverted-funnel question sequences can help stimulate a respondent and help him or her feel more comfortable in talking, although this is not always the case (Stewart & Cash, 1991) and has not been examined in the employment interview.

In sum, investigations in this research tradition help us to understand how the interview is conducted or enacted by participants. In general, a unique contribution of this approach is its focus on analyzing actual interview dialogue occurring in interviews on college campuses and in organizations. As a consequence, this approach provides valuable information regarding how interviews are structured and the extent to which and how recruiters and candidates participate in interview interactions.

Patterns of Interacts and Double Interacts

As noted earlier, the second approach in the investigation of employment interview processes examines initial interaction "states" and transition patterns. In particular, this type of research examines such states and patterns as predictive of end states or outcomes associated with the process (Monge et al., 1984) and/or studies how participants influence each other's behaviors during interaction (Warner, 1991). One approach within this perspective examines the predictive nature of patterns of discrete variables such as various utterance types, whereas a second analyzes why asymmetrical influence between participants occurs during interviews and how the parties may play dominant or passive roles in the communication process. Central to both sets of investigations is a focus on interacts and double interacts.

In line with the first approach noted above, Axtmann and Jablin (1986), in a study of double interacts in the employment interview, analyzed question-answer-response sequences of interview participants taken from videotapes of screening interviews on a university campus. Participants' utterances were coded according to the source (ER = interviewer; EE = interviewee) and the nature of the utterance (question, answer, statement). Possible sequences thus were ER question-EE answer-ER question, ER question-EE answer-EE statement, ER question-EE question-ER answer, and so on. One particularly notable finding from this study was that applicants who received second interview offers had fewer interrogative interaction patterns characterized by ER question-EE answer-ER question sequences. Instead, successful applicants engaged the interviewer more frequently in conversation sequences such as ER question-EE answer-ER statement and ER question-EE question-EE statement.

In turn, Engler-Parish and Millar (1989) examined how patterns of message types and relational control in employment interview interactions predicted interview success. In this case, message types included assertions, talkovers, extensions, topic changes, and questions. Relational control was measured as one-up (attempts to raise one's status), one-down (attempts to lower one's status), and one-across (communicating similar status) moves. "Success" in the interview was operationalized as participants' communication satisfaction and the extent to which the participants felt they had obtained information sufficient to make a "reasoned" employment decision.

From their examination of interacts from 35 campus screening interviews, Engler-Parish and Millar (1989) found that interviewers most frequently used extension statements and changed topics six times as often as applicants. As interviewers increased their use of extension statements, applicants offered fewer answers and topic changes. When applicants supported statements made by the interviewers, interviewers were unlikely to express support in return or change topics, but more likely to extend the topic of discussion (this is somewhat similar to findings reported by Axtmann & Jablin, 1986). Regarding relational control, Engler-Parish and Millar reported a "cybernetic tension" between interviewers and applicants, where the "recruiter is 'pushing' the student to provide the information deemed necessary for deciding whether to recommend employment. Concurrently, the applicant is 'pulling' the interviewer out of a questioning mode and into an information-giving, storytelling, advising mode" (p. 48). Successful interviews were characterized by a balance in these pushing and pulling behaviors, and unsuccessful interviews resulted from either an interviewer "pushing" too much or an applicant "pulling" too much.

In another study of relational control, Tullar (1989) examined symmetrical and complementary interaction pairs in employment interviews. In symmetrical paired exchanges, an utterance was followed by a similar utterance (e.g., dominance followed by dominance). Complementary exchanges were those in which an act was followed by a dissimilar utterance (e.g., dominance followed by submission). Successful interviews (indicated by the offer of a second interview and higher interviewer ratings of applicant's intelligence, self-assurance, motivation, and sociability) were characterized by applicant dominance and complementary, rather than symmetrical, paired exchanges. In particular, successful applicants followed a dominant interviewer act (an utterance that attempts to restrict the behavioral options of the other party, such as demanding an answer to a question or changing the topic) with a submissive act (an utterance that relinquishes behavioral options to the other party) and a submissive interviewer utterance with a dominant utterance. Unsuccessful interviews, on the other hand, tended to be characterized by symmetrical exchanges. In particular, unsuccessful applicants tended to follow an interviewer's structuring act (an utterance that attempts to restrict the behavioral options of the other party while opening options for oneself, such as expanding on a previous statement) with another structuring act.

More recently, Kacmar and Hochwarter (1995) examined the relationships among interviewer gender, interviewer race, and relational control patterns in structured (training) employment interviews. Their statistical results revealed that neither race nor gender differentiated the communication patterns of applicants and interviewers, although qualitative analyses did suggest that minority interviewers and male interviewers were challenged more (dominant-dominant paired interactions) than were nonminority and female interviewers, respectively.

In an investigation that did not focus on specific pairs of communicative acts but on general forms of communicative behavior, Liden, Martin, and Parsons (1993) conducted a laboratory study in which they assessed applicants' (students in role-play interviews) overall verbal and nonverbal performance (as rated by independent judges viewing audio- or audio/videotapes of the interviews) when interacting with interviewers who displayed either "cold" (no eye contact, backward body lean, no smiling, seated sideways in chair) or "warm" (forward body lean, occasional smiles, facing the applicant, maintaining eye contact 90% of the time) nonverbal behaviors. They found that "an interviewer's manipulated nonverbal behavior greatly influenced independent judges' ratings of applicants' verbal and nonverbal behaviors" (p. 378), and in particular demonstrated the negative effects that "cold" interviewer behavior has on applicants' verbal and nonverbal behaviors (especially among applicants with low self-esteem).

Findings from the research reviewed above suggest that particular patterns of interaction are predictive of subsequent outcomes, such as the receipt of a second interview offer, higher interviewer ratings of applicant characteristics, and perceptions of the usefulness of information obtained in the interview. Research focused on patterns of interacts, however, has also examined interaction to determine why one party in an interview has an asymmetric influence over the other and how interviewers and applicants play active or passive roles in the interview process. For instance, Engler-Parish and Millar's (1989) results suggest that once an applicant communicated to the employer that he or she was unable to begin work at the preferred time or lacked an interest in the job, the recruiter "took over" the interview and tended to dominate the remainder of the interaction. Relatedly, Ragan and Hopper (1981) found that an applicant's use of unsolicited accounts or explanations for problematic issues (e.g., a low grade point average) that introduced negative information regarding the applicant that otherwise may never have come up reinforced the status differential between interviewer and applicant and promoted the powerlessness of the applicant. In sum, examination of patterns of interacts and double interacts can help us understand why interview participants assume passive or active roles during various phases of the interview, and how interviewers and applicants reinforce perceived status differentials through interaction processes.

Enactment of Interview Systems/Structures

The third approach to the study of communication/interaction, which has not received much attention in the empirical research, focuses on how the interviewer and applicant produce and reproduce the interview system through the enactment of structures (e.g., conversation rules, utilization of planned interview questions) that enable as well as constrain their interaction. Thus, from this approach, the employment interview is conceived of as a dynamic social system composed of interdependent beliefs and observable relations between recruiter and applicant that are produced and reproduced through the process of interaction. Emergent interaction structures thus represent the outcome as well as the medium of interaction (e.g., Poole & DeSanctis, 1990).

One type of research falling into this category is research that examines how the nature of the relationship between the interviewer and the applicant emerges during the course of the interview process. In particular, such research can show how both parties contribute to the social construction of meaning and the characteristics and dimensions of their relationship.

Along these lines, Cahn (1976) offers a "self-validation" model of the employment interview that asserts that during the interview process, the applicant and the interviewer both construct perceptions of their respective self-concepts (information regarding the individual's relationship to objects, places, and other individuals) and metaself-concepts (the individual's conception of self as viewed through the other). The model suggests that these perceptions are constructed through the "mutual transfer of symbolic information, verbal and nonverbal," exchanged during the interview process (Cahn, 1976, p. 151). In particular, the self-validation model is a phase model of the interview process in which the interviewer and applicant express their self-concepts to one another during the first phase of the interview, form metaself-concepts during the second phase of the interview, and form an interpersonal relationship during the third phase of the interview based on each person's comparison of his or her self-concept and metaself-concept (pp. 152-153).

In a study also focused on relationship issues, Cheepen (1988) examined (through analysis of language and grammatical patterns) the ways in which interviewers reinforce their greater status over applicants during the interview process. For example, Cheepen found that in the opening phase of the interview, recruiters often provided references to their official status or questioned the applicant's mode of transportation to the interview, behaviors that Cheepen asserts reinforced the interviewer's status over the applicant. Such reinforcement of status also occurred during the closing phase of the interview as well. In particular, interview closing segments were characterized primarily by transactional utterances (which reinforce differential status) rather than interactional utterances (which downplay differential status). In addition, Cheepen noted that the interviewer's use of metastatements (e.g., "Now we'll discuss your previous experience") reinforced the interviewer's status by controlling topics.

Other studies falling into this category of process research have examined how the structure of the interview itself emerges through interaction. Shaw (1983), for instance, found that applicants' "taken-for-granted" assumptions regarding employment interviews influenced the structure of the interview process. Specifically, he identified three primary taken-for-granted assumptions applicants have regarding interviews: (a) Interviewers' primary responsibility was to listen to applicants and acknowledge their qualifications, (b) any questions asked by interviewers were assumed to be appropriate and required a response from the applicant, and (c) the primary responsibility of applicants was to express their qualifications and feelings. These assumptions influenced the structure of employment interviews. For example, when an applicant perceived that the interviewer had violated the first assumption by failing to show an interest in the applicant's qualifications, the applicant became quiet and failed to elaborate or offer information regarding his or her qualifications. With respect to the second assumption (question appropriateness), applicants reported that even when an interviewer asked a question that appeared to be irrelevant to the interview context, they felt obliged to answer the question, and, consequently, the structure of the interview tended to focus on topics other than those the applicant assumed to be relevant (e.g., the applicant's qualifications for the job). Finally, the assumption that applicants must be expressive in the interview led many applicants to avoid silence and pauses. As Shaw (1983) explains, "In an effort to be expressive, applicants filled silence with talk. They strove for free-flowing interaction. But a consequence of that spontaneity was often that they were unable to give much thought to their answers. . . . Paradoxically, to be 'expressive' often meant in practice not talking about oneself much at all" (pp. 152-153). Thus, Shaw's study provides insight into how an applicant's implicit assumptions regarding the employment interview can influence the interview's emergent structure.

Interview system/structure research can also examine the interplay of the various goals of the interviewer and applicant. Both the interviewer and the applicant participate in the employment interview to accomplish particular goals. The interviewer, for example, hopes to obtain information upon which to base a hiring decision. The applicant may hope not only to provide information about him- or herself to make a positive impression on the interviewer, but also to obtain information about the job and the organization in order to make a reasoned employment decision. Consideration of how both persons' implicit beliefs about the interview process affect their ability to accomplish their respective goals is a focal concern of research that takes a system/structure approach. For instance, as part of his investigation of taken-for-granted assumptions, Shaw (1983) found that applicants assumed they would be given an opportunity to express their qualifications for the job during the interview (an instrumental goal). Examination of process, however, revealed that applicants spent a great deal of time discussing topics irrelevant to their qualifications in an attempt to answer the questions of their interviewers (which were assumed to be appropriate). In other words, the interaction process affected applicants' ability to accomplish their goals.

The Approaches in Perspective

For many years, interaction-oriented employment interview research tended to apply linear models of communication that emphasized the creation and reception of messages (e.g., Schramm, 1954; Shannon & Weaver, 1949), with a particular emphasis on the messages of interviewers compared with those of applicants (Jablin & McComb, 1984). In particular, research focused on attributes of message senders (e.g., trustworthiness, competence, empathy) and characteristics of their messages (e.g., message clarity, informativeness). These emphases helped to identify content and stylistic attributes of the messages recruiters and applicants communicate to one another that enhance their respective attractiveness or appeal (see Harris, 1989; Jablin, 1987; Rynes, 1991). However, these traditional conceptualizations of communication "processes" did not provide appropriate models for exploring patterns of interview interaction, dynamic factors shaping discourse in the interview, or how interaction contributes to interview outcomes, among other issues. More recent approaches, as reflected by those discussed in the preceding sections, are more consistent in their efforts to help us understand the development of patterns of communication/interaction processes over time.

Examination of the literature reviewed above suggests several conclusions about research exploring communication/interaction processes in the interview. First, the focal areas of interest in process-oriented research are actual patterns of verbal and nonverbal behavior (Hawes & Foley, 1973). By examining verbal behavior, researchers examine what is actually said and patterns of talk unique to employment interview interaction rather than rely on participants' overall perceptions or self-reports of interview behavior. Further, although unfortunately infrequently incorporated into actual studies, process-oriented interaction research "assumes" that all verbal interview message exchanges are accompanied by nonverbal exchanges that support, emphasize, or contradict concomitant verbal messages (Burgoon, 1994; Knapp, Cody, & Reardon, 1987). In addition, as with verbal behavior, the reciprocal nature of nonverbal behavior (i.e., the manner in which one person's nonverbal acts are accommodated and/or emulated by the other person) is recognized as vital to understanding the interview process. For example, research along these lines might examine how an applicant will respond to a recruiter whose nonverbal messages contradict his or her verbal messages (e.g., recruiter professing interest in the candidate while yawning). Does the applicant respond with a complementary behavior (e.g., backward body lean) or asymmetrical behaviors (e.g., leans forward and initiates and maintains eye contact with the recruiter)? Similarly, an investigation in this area might examine how a recruiter's ability to concentrate on what a job candidate is saying (and ability to consider what to ask next) may be impaired by his or her focus on the applicant's persistent fidgeting. The extent to which the setting of employment interviews (especially campus interviews) may constrain the range of nonverbal behaviors that are displayed and visible in the interview (and therefore possibly affect verbal behavior as well) is also of concern in process-oriented research. For example, the range of nonverbal behaviors that are demonstrated may be restricted in relatively brief, 30-minute exchanges in the context of a small interviewing room, in contrast to less constrained conditions in which a greater range of behaviors are acceptable. In particular, this is likely the case when a physical artifact such as a table or desk separates the interview participants, thus drawing each participant's attention to the other person's upper body, especially the head (Jablin, Hudson, & Sias, 1997).

Second, process-oriented research assumes that all verbal and nonverbal behaviors in the interview can be interpreted as messages, and as messages that contain interdependent content and relational dimensions (Hawes, 1973; Watzlawick, Beavin, & Jackson, 1967). In other words, embedded in an interviewer's question is a focus or substantive content area (e.g., the question, "Why do you want to work for our organization?" solicits a cluster of information on the applicant's perceived job qualifications, motivation, and the like), as well as personal signals about the relationship that may be inferred from the interviewer's verbal and nonverbal message delivery (e.g., friendly, hostile). Consequently, in the interview participants exchange information, draw inferences about the meaning of information, and create social realities regarding power, trust, and affinity in their relationship. By examining the interchange of content and relational messages, investigations of interview process can uncover the means by which rapport is established among the interactants, how participants come to believe they are on the "same wavelength," how "face" is maintained under stress, and strategies that allow the interview parties to support and reinforce their identities (Cheepen, 1988).

Third, communication/interaction process research draws attention to "meaning-making" processes in the interview—that is, how the interview parties construct meaning and "social reality" through their interaction. For example, patterns of interacts or double interacts provide valuable information regarding how conversation develops and how meanings evolve from series of question-answer-statement exchanges. As investigations of conversation and interaction attest (see Poole, Foley, & Hewes, 1987; Tracy, 1991; Watt & VanLear, 1996), what is asked or what information is given tells only part of the story; the relation of an answer to a preceding question creates the context for the next question or answer. In this way, interviewer and applicant patterns of message sending and receiving define social reality and regulate social action. The pattern of interview interacts and double interacts can indicate who is in control of the interview (Tullar, 1989) or who is capable of "holding their own," among other things.

Relatedly, interaction process research appreciates that interactions are constrained by conversational rules regarding the meanings associated with messages and appropriate forms of response (Cronen, Pearce, & Harris, 1982; Pearce & Cronen, 1980; Searle, 1967, 1969). In everyday conversation, participants use constitutive rules to interpret and understand the meaning of any event. Participants also use regulative rules to determine what behaviors or responses are considered to be socially acceptable forms of communication. For instance, if a job candidate "takes it for granted" that she or he is supposed to wait until a recruiter says it is okay to ask questions, clarify remarks made by the interviewer, or seek clarification about information contained in the organization's promotional recruitment literature, then the candidate is imposing self-limits on the timing and frequency of opportunities to participate in conversation (Babbitt & Jablin, 1985; Jablin & Miller, 1990). Further, interview participants may also respond to self- and other-generated cues to create and sustain their own sets of rules to guide their interaction. These parameters (including beliefs about ethical communication; e.g., Kirkwood & Ralston, 1996; Ralston & Kirkwood, 1995) both shape and constrain participants' perceptions of acceptable interview behavior.

Clearly, none of the approaches we have identified in investigating communication/interaction processes in the employment interview reflects all of the generalizations described above. Each approach focuses on fairly unique aspects of communication processes, and as a consequence has something distinct to offer in enhancing our understanding of the employment interview. Along these lines, in Table 17.1 we offer a summary of some of the research questions that each approach seems most suited to answer. In an attempt to unpack further the benefits of research exploring communication processes in the interview from each approach, we offer in the following section some directions for future research with respect to each approach.

Directions for Future Research

Patterns of "Acts"

There are a number of ways that research examining patterns of communicative acts in the interview can enhance our understanding of the interview process. Future researchers might examine the progression of

Table 17.1   Approaches to the Study of Process: Examples of Research Foci

Pattern of Acts	Patterns of Acts and Double Interacts	Enactment of Systems/Structures
How does the content of information asked for and given vary across the interview?	What is the pattern of interacts (e.g., question-answer) and double interacts (e.g., question-answer-statement) in the interview?	How do clusters of acts, interacts, and double interacts encourage the emergence of communication rules and interaction structures in the interview?
How do the types of questions asked vary across the interview?	In what way do interacts and double interacts reflect symmetric and asymmetric relationships?	How does the relationship of interviewer and applicant evolve through their discourses and exchanges?
How does the proportion of time each party speaks (total talk time, time asking or answering questions) vary across the interview?	How do the foci of the interview content shape the pattern of interacts and double interacts?	How do participants' exchanges shape their self-identities and, in turn, the content and interaction patterns of the interview?
What question sequence (e.g., funnel, inverted funnel) characterizes the interview?	What is the relationship between functional and substantive forms of interacts in the interview?	How does the violation of participants' interaction assumptions affect their subsequent interview behavior?
What factors influence patterns of acts in the interview?	How do participants respond to ambiguous or unclear information?	How do participants apply their general knowledge of information seeking and information giving to guide their interview interaction?
How do patterns of nonverbal behavior vary across the interview?	To what extent do participants evidence consistency in their confirmatory questioning behaviors?	How do structures of norms, power, and meaning evolve for participants through their interactions in the interview?
What is the relationship between verbal and nonverbal acts in the interview?	To what extent do conversational versus interrogative patterns of interacts characterize "successful" interviews?	In what ways do applicants and recruiters adapt interview systems/structures to achieve their respective goals?
How do individuals' perceptions of communication acts vary across the employment interview?	What is the relationship of interacts and double interacts and participants' perceptions of the other party?	How do the "meanings" that applicants and interviewers associate with structured forms of interviewing affect, and in turn how are they affected by, their respective behaviors?

recruiters' questions in employment interviews in order to discover what topics they attempt to cover initially and whether they actually proceed in a confirmatory or disconfirmatory manner to explore these topics. Investigations aimed at identifying patterns of interviewer behavior might also examine when and to what extent they present information on organization and job attributes to applicants. Analyses of the content of their presentations (as well as applicant responses) can help us understand how and when organizational representatives attempt to recruit versus just select applicants (e.g., Rynes & Barber, 1991) as well as the extent to which they provide realistic job previews to applicants (Jablin, 1987; Wanous, 1980). In other words, analyses of interview transcripts may reveal the extent to which realistic job previews are given by organizational representatives, whether applicants ask follow-up questions concerning this information, and the extent to which the shared information is clear, accurate, and interesting. Further, the degree to which representatives may provide "inside" information to especially attractive candidates might be examined.

Another important direction for future study involves the examination of interview openings and closings. Openings and closings are considered to be critical segments for establishing rapport, setting candidates at ease, and setting the agenda for the rest of the interview (Komter, 1986; Stewart & Cash, 1991). However, the extent to which interviewers attempt to establish rapport with candidates is unknown, although such attempts may contribute to applicants' evaluations of recruiters and their organizations. Similarly, the extent to which recruiters use the closing of the interview to reestablish rapport and inform the applicant about the organization's next contact with the candidate is also unknown. Openings and closings of interactions serve multiple purposes, and how each interview party manages these sequences may affect the other person's perceptions of the individual's credibility (Knapp, Hart, Friedrich, & Shulman, 1973; Krivonos & Knapp, 1975; Stewart & Cash, 1991).

Patterns of Interacts and Double Interacts

As noted earlier, studies of the interview process that focus on patterns of interacts and double interacts examine how particular sequences of question-answer-statement responses, submissive versus structuring utterances, and symmetrical versus complementary paired exchanges are predictive of various outcomes. A number of important directions are possible for future research utilizing this approach. First, researchers might examine interaction patterns by applying coding schemes other than those that are "functional" in nature (that is, schemes in which utterances are examined and coded according to their function, e.g., dominance, submissiveness, question, answer, statement). Little is known about the predictive nature of patterns of utterance content (e.g., references to applicant qualifications, references to job requirements, references to the interviewer's experience with the organization) in employment interviews. Such research could provide important information about patterns of interaction that distinguish "successful" from "unsuccessful" interviews or lead participants to form particular impressions of one another. Clearly, it would also be highly desirable for studies to examine functional interaction patterns and substantive ones in conjunction with (rather than in isolation from) one another.

Future research might also apply insights associated with the study of interaction processes to other research traditions associated with the employment interview. For example, evidence from studies examining the "confirmatory question hypothesis" is conflicting and inconsistent (Harris, 1989). Several researchers have failed to find support for the prediction that an interviewer will ask questions designed to confirm his or her initial impression of the applicant formed from preinterview materials (McDonald & Hakel, 1985; Sackett, 1982; Snyder, Campbell, & Preston, 1980; Snyder & Swann, 1978). In an exception, Binning et al. (1988) did find support for the hypothesis. Importantly, however, although researchers who have found no support for the hypothesis included applicant feedback in their studies, Binning et al. did not. An examination of process may lead to important insights in this area. To date, research in this area has not examined the extent to which interviewers maintain or modify the consistency of their inquiries in response to candidates' actual answers, statements, or questions. Data on interviewers' reactions to candidates' actual responses to questions might show different styles of confirmatory or disconfirmatory questioning behavior that are not apparent from research that focuses primarily on determining what questions an interviewer might ask, or the order in which these questions might be asked, in response to variations in preinterview information. Consequently, research into confirmatory question asking might benefit from a consideration of interview communication behavior in terms of how interviewers' questions influence applicants' responses as well as interviewers' subsequent questions and/or statements, and so on.

Reflection on some of our current assumptions about the "confirmatory questioning hypothesis" in light of process notions might also lead to alternative conceptualizations of the phenomenon. For example, it seems apparent that current research models make the assumption that it is the interviewer who does the confirming or disconfirming in an interview. It is likely, however, that the applicant may provide confirming or disconfirming statements during the interview, so that the interviewer is not required to do so. The applicant may, for instance, provide an account in order to disconfirm an image that he or she assumes the interviewer may perceive (e.g., Ragan & Hopper, 1981). Once the applicant provides an account intended to disconfirm the interviewer's assumed initial impression, there is no reason for the interviewer to ask a planned confirmatory question regarding that particular issue. In other words, studies that examine the interview process may discover that the communicative behavior of the applicant often explains the lack of support for the confirmatory question hypothesis obtained in earlier studies.

Further research is also needed that examines the ways certain communicative behaviors are predictive of subsequent communicative behaviors and communicative states. Research similar to Hawes and Foley's (1973) examination of the interaction process of medical interviews using Markov analysis, for example, could shed some light on the stochastic or patterned nature of a variety of communication behaviors.

As a follow-up to Tengler and Jablin's (1983) research, investigators might compare the content and sequence of messages within versus outside of question-answer interacts. Given that Tengler and Jablin found that applicants who received second interview offers spoke more outside of the question-answer sequence than did those not receiving offers, it is possible that topics critical to interviewers' decisions may be covered outside of the traditional focus of research attention: the question-answer sequence.

Finally, greater research attention needs to be focused on nonverbal interaction processes (and their relation to verbal interaction processes) in employment interviews. In particular, researchers should work to identify patterns of nonverbal interaction rather than simply observe the nonverbal behavior of one or both participants in isolation from the other. That is, research examining how particular nonverbal behaviors predict subsequent nonverbal behaviors could lead to important insights into how interview participants may accommodate their nonverbal communication to that of their conversation partners. Such studies may identify nonverbal interaction patterns that distinguish "successful" from "unsuccessful" interviews on a variety of "success" criteria.

Interview Systems/Structures

Numerous opportunities exist for research guided by the systems/structures approach. One profitable area for future study might be to identify the taken-for-granted assumptions of interviewers and examine how those assumptions (and their interaction with applicants' assumptions/cognitive scripts) affect interviewers' communicative behavior during the interview process. One could imagine, for example, that some of the assumptions of the interviewer may clash with those of the applicant, causing disruptions in the interview process and hindering the ability for either or both parties to accomplish their goals.

One particular theoretical model of social systems that has received considerable attention in the study of communication processes generally in recent years, and is amenable to the study of the interview, is structuration theory (Dipboye, 1994; Giddens, 1976, 1984). As adapted by communication researchers, structuration "refers to the process by which systems are produced and reproduced through members' use of rules and resources" (Poole & DeSanctis, 1990, p. 179). The rules (e.g., in the interview context, that the organizational representative is responsible for initiating interaction) and resources (e.g., a recruiter's structured interview protocol) used in the production and reproduction of the interview system are considered to be structures that represent both the outcome and the medium of interaction. Thus, structures "form the basis for action, but only through entering into action are they themselves produced and reproduced. System and structure form a duality, codetermining each other in a continuous process of structuration" (Poole, 1985, p. 101). Hence, it is through processes that occur in interaction that participants in interviews produce and reproduce their own structures-in-use (Poole & DeSanctis, 1990, p. 180).

In addition to trying to understand how rules and resources affect and are affected by interaction in the interview, structuration theory implies that interaction in the interview is best understood as a process involving norms (structures of legitimation), power (structures of authority/domination), and meaning (structures of signification). For example, if a recruiter uses a highly structured approach to interviewing, the effect of this approach on interview interaction is mediated by the meanings (or lack thereof) of this practice to the applicant (structures of signification; that is, the use of a structured versus unstructured approach may be perceived of as metacommunication about the interview communication process generally), alternative ways the applicant might respond to or resist the implementation of this practice of information seeking (power resources, e.g., responding to questions with questions, engaging the interviewer in conversation versus answering questions), and the applicant's beliefs about the appropriateness of such interviewing practices (norms or structures of legitimation). Interview interaction will also be mediated by what a highly structured approach to interviewing "means" to the recruiter (what is "appropriated" of the practice, e.g., one interviewer might always follow the interview protocol, whereas another interviewer interprets it as a tool to be adapted), what he or she perceives as the regulating function of structured interviewing (e.g., to control interviewer behavior and/or applicant behavior), and the recruiter's attitude about the practice (e.g., is it just a burden or is it useful?). Moreover, it is important to recognize that (a) practices such as structured interviewing may be enacted in varying ways by recruiters, depending on the extent to which the organization enforces following the practice (power resources); and (b) structures are not only created by interviewer and applicant through interaction, but also "appropriated" through larger social institutions (for example, from general social knowledge of effective information-seeking and decision-making procedures).

The mediating forces or structures central to structuration theory also provide a "dialectic of control" (Giddens, 1991) wherein agents (interview participants) are able to exert some control over the interview process. In particular, the notion of dialectic of control acknowledges and emphasizes the role of the individual (regardless of the interaction context and institutional constraints) in exerting some degree of control over the interaction. As Banks and Riley (1993) explain, "Agents always have the capacity to make a difference, even in the face of institutional settings predicated on others' power and control . . . agents never are completely compelled by others' power, but always have options for doing otherwise" (p. 172). For example, as alluded to above, control in highly structured interviews takes on distinctive meanings when considered from this perspective. Structured interview protocols (as in behavior description interviews) might be seen to exert control at two levels. First, and perhaps most explicit, the structured interview is intended to control the applicant's behavior, limiting his or her response and question choices to those elicited by the planned structure. Second, and perhaps more implicit but equally important, the structured interview is intended to control the behavior of the interviewer by limiting his or her behavioral options during the interview. (This raises an interesting issue: If most interviewers were well trained, actually did follow the interviewing methods and procedures they were taught, and were knowledgeable about the positions for which they were seeking to hire applicants, would highly structured interview formats with standardized questions be necessary?) Thus, the institution (i.e., the organization) seeks to control the agents in the interview process through the use of a particular resource, the structured interview. The dialectic of control, however, suggests that both agents can "make a difference" despite these structural constraints (i.e., they will adapt the structured interview so that it "works" for them, something that has been implicitly recognized in research exploring applicant impression management tactics; e.g., Stevens & Kristof, 1995). Hence, the interview structure that is produced by or emerges from the interview communication process is the result of the mediation of the behavior of both the interviewer and the applicant and can be understood in terms of structures of legitimation, authority, and signification.

Research aimed at examining structuration in employment interviews is not easy to conduct and requires some creativity. For example, Charoenngam (1996) used a method in a study of communication in employment interviews in Thailand that might be adapted to explore structuration in the interview. She videotaped actual employment interviews in eight Thai organizations; two copies of each interview were simultaneously recorded. Subsequent to each interview, both the applicant and the recruiter watched the videotaped interview in separate rooms and provided phenomenological reports about their interactions (respondents stopped the videotape at "meaningful" junctures and explained why they asked certain questions, answered as they did, and so on; see Charoenngam & Jablin, 1999). Although Charoenngam did not incorporate structuration theory into her study, her data are amenable to such analysis in that they can be considered in terms of participants' identification of structures of legitimation, authority, and signification. Further, it is possible to analyze (code in terms of function and content) the videotape records of the specific interactions that are representative of such structures in terms of the actual sequencing of acts, interacts, double interacts, and so on. Such method triangulation could shed light on the ways that structures of legitimation and authority influence, and are influenced by, emergent interaction processes in the interview. If successful, research along these lines would also reveal the potential for structuration theory to serve as a conceptual mechanism for integrating the various approaches to the study of process identified in this chapter, a possibility deserving of consideration in future research.

Concluding Comment

As several contributors to this handbook note, there are considerable advantages for interviewers in the use of structured interviews (behavior description and situational interviews). To date, however, communication/interaction process research has not considered how interaction patterns vary between highly structured interviews and more traditional moderately structured interviews. Such investigations are necessary and may provide valuable information about the quantity and quality of information obtained from applicants, the nature of interview interaction sequences, and the assumptions guiding interviewers' and applicants' decision making in these varying interview contexts.

Some researchers and practitioners may question the importance of examining communication process, given evidence that the structured interview has (relatively speaking) predictive validity. We believe that variability likely exists among interviewers using structured interview formats, as we have indicated in the previous section. Regardless of planned structure, interviewers may differ with respect to their overall communication competence, follow-up questioning abilities, relationship development skills, and ability to adhere to an interview structure. Thus, examination of communication/interaction processes can help identify the degree to which interviewers can adhere to the planned structure necessary for the interview to retain its predictive validity, identify elements of structure that may require modification so as to increase the interview's usefulness as a predictor, and/or suggest interviewer communication skills that require development for structured interviews to be most effective.

References

Adams, G. A. (1994). The employment interview as a sociometric selection technique. *Journal of Group Psychotherapy, Psychodrama and Sociometry, 47*, 99-113.

Anderson, C. W. (1960). The relation between speaking times and decisions in the employment interview. *Journal of Applied Psychology, 44*, 267-268.

Axtmann, L., & Jablin, F. M. (1986, May). *Distributional and sequential interaction structure in the employment screening interview.* Paper presented at the annual meeting of the International Communication Association, Chicago.

Babbitt, L. V., & Jablin, F. M. (1985). Characteristics of applicants' questions and employment screening interview outcomes. *Human Communication Research, 11*, 507-535.

Banks, S. P., & Riley, P. (1993). Structuration theory as an ontology for communication research. In S. A. Deetz (Ed.), *Communication yearbook 16* (pp. 167-196). Newbury Park, CA: Sage.

Binning, J. F., Goldstein, M. A., Garcia, M. F., Harding, J. L., & Scattaregia, J. H. (1988). Effects of preinterview impressions on questioning strategies in same- and opposite-sex employment interviews. *Journal of Applied Psychology, 73*, 30-37.

Buckley, M. R., & Eder, R. W. (1988). B. M. Springbett and the notion of the "snap decision" in the interview. *Journal of Management, 14*, 59-67.

Burgoon, J. K. (1994). Nonverbal signals. In M. L. Knapp & G. R. Miller (Eds.), *Handbook of interpersonal communication* (2nd ed., pp. 229-285). Thousand Oaks, CA: Sage.

Cahn, D. D. (1976). The employment interview: A self-validation model. *Journal of Employment Counseling, 13*, 150-155.

Charoenngam, N. S. (1996). *Communication in employment interviews: An exploratory study in Thailand.* Unpublished doctoral dissertation, University of Texas, Austin.

Charoenngam, N. S., & Jablin, F. M. (1999). *Communication interaction and behavior in employment interviews in Thai organizations.* Paper presented at the annual meeting of the International Communication Association, San Francisco.

Cheepen, C. (1988). *The predictability of informal conversation.* New York: Pinter.

Cronen, V. E., Pearce, W. B., & Harris, L. (1982). The coordinated management of meaning. In F. E. X. Dance (Ed.), *Human communication theory* (pp. 61-89). New York: Holt, Rinehart & Winston.

Dipboye, R. L. (1994). Structured and unstructured selection interviews: Beyond the job-fit model. In G. R. Ferris (Ed.), *Research in personnel and human resources management* (Vol. 12, pp. 79-123). Greenwich, CT: JAI.

Dougherty, T. W., Turban, D. B., & Callender, J. C. (1994). Confirming first impressions in the employment interview: A field study of interviewer behavior. *Journal of Applied Psychology, 79*, 659-665.

Engler-Parish, P. G., & Millar, F. E. (1989). An exploratory relational control analysis of the employment screening interview. *Western Journal of Speech Communication, 53*, 30-51.

Giddens, A. (1976). *New rules of sociological method: A positive critique of interpretative sociologies.* New York: Basic Books.

Giddens, A. (1984). *The constitution of society: Outline of the theory of structuration.* Berkeley: University of California Press.

Giddens, A. (1991). *Modernity and self-identity: Self and society in the late modern age.* Stanford, CA: Stanford University Press.

Harris, M. M. (1989). Reconsidering the employment interview: A review of recent literature and suggestions for future research. *Personnel Psychology, 42,* 691-726.

Hawes, L. C. (1973). Elements of a model for communication processes. *Quarterly Journal of Speech, 40,* 11-21.

Hawes, L. C., & Foley, J. M. (1973). A Markov analysis of interview communication. *Speech Monographs, 40,* 208-219.

Hollander, E. P., & Willis, R. H. (1967). Some current issues in the psychology of conformity and nonconformity. *Psychological Bulletin, 68,* 62-76.

Huegli, J. M., & Tshirgi, H. (1975). An investigation of the relationship of time to recruitment interview decision making. *Proceedings of the National Academy of Management,* pp. 234-236.

Jablin, F. M. (1987). Organizational entry, assimilation, and exit. In F. M. Jablin, L. L. Putnam, K. H. Roberts, & L. Porter (Eds.), *Handbook of organizational communication: An interdisciplinary perspective* (pp. 679-740). Newbury Park, CA: Sage.

Jablin, F. M., Hudson, D., & Sias, P. (1997). *Verbal and nonverbal correlates of communication satisfaction in employment screening interviews.* Unpublished manuscript, University of Richmond, Virginia.

Jablin, F. M., & McComb, K. B. (1984). The employment screening interview: An organizational assimilation and communication perspective. In R. N. Bostrom (Ed.), *Communication yearbook 8* (pp. 137-163). Beverly Hills, CA: Sage.

Jablin, F. M., & Miller, V. D. (1990). Interviewer and applicant questioning behavior in employment interviews. *Management Communication Quarterly, 4,* 51-86.

Kacmar, K. M., & Hochwarter, W. A. (1995). The interview as a communication event: A field examination of demographic effects on interview outcomes. *Journal of Business Communication, 32,* 207-232.

Kinicki, A., & Lockwood, C. A. (1985). The interview process: An examination of factors recruiters use in evaluating job applicants. *Journal of Vocational Behavior, 26,* 117-125.

Kirkwood, W. G., & Ralston, S. M. (1996). Ethics and teaching employment interviewing. *Communication Education, 45,* 167-179.

Knapp, M. L., Cody, M. J., & Reardon, K. K. (1987). Nonverbal signals. In C. R. Berger & S. H. Chaffee (Eds.), *Handbook of communication science* (pp. 385-418). Newbury Park, CA: Sage.

Knapp, M. L., Hart, R. P., Friedrich, G. W., & Shulman, G. M. (1973). The rhetoric of goodbye: Verbal and nonverbal correlates of human leave-taking. *Speech Monographs, 40,* 182-198.

Komter, M. (1986). Token up-dates: The reiteration of mutual knowledge in the opening stages of job interviews. *Human Studies, 9,* 247-259.

Krivonos, P. D., & Knapp, M. L. (1975). Initiating communication: What do you say when you say hello? *Central States Speech Journal, 26,* 115-125.

Liden, R. C., Martin, C. L., & Parsons, C. K. (1993). Interviewer and applicant behaviors in employment interviews. *Academy of Management Journal, 36,* 372-386.

Liden, R. C., & Parsons, C. K. (1989). Understanding interpersonal behavior in the employment interview: A reciprocal interaction analysis. In R. W. Eder & G. R.

Ferris (Eds.), *The employment interview: Theory, research, and practice* (pp. 219-232). Newbury Park, CA: Sage.

Matarazzo, J. D., Wiens, A. N., Jackson, R. H., & Manaugh, T. S. (1970). Interviewee speech behavior under different content conditions. *Journal of Applied Psychology, 54,* 15-26.

McComb, K. B., & Jablin, F. M. (1984). Verbal correlates of interviewer empathic listening and employment interview outcomes. *Communication Monographs, 51,* 353-371.

McDonald, T., & Hakel, M. D. (1985). Effects of applicant race, sex, suitability, and answers on interviewers' questioning strategy and ratings. *Personnel Psychology, 38,* 321-334.

Monge, P. R. (1990). Theoretical and analytical issues in studying organizational processes. *Organizational Science, 1,* 406-430.

Monge, P. R., Farace, R. V., Eisenberg, E. M., Miller, K. I., & White, L. (1984). The process of studying process in organizational communication. *Journal of Communication, 34,* 22-43.

Paunonen, S. V. (1987). Accuracy of interviewers and students in identifying the personality characteristics of personnel managers and computer programmers. *Journal of Vocational Behavior, 31,* 26-36.

Pearce, W. B., & Cronen, V. (1980). *Communication, action, and meaning.* New York: Praeger.

Poole, M. S. (1985). Communication and organizational climates: Review, critique, and a new perspective. In R. D. McPhee & P. K. Tompkins (Eds.), *Organizational communication: Traditional themes and new directions* (pp. 79-108). Beverly Hills, CA: Sage.

Poole, M. S., & DeSanctis, G. (1990). Understanding the use of group decision support systems: The theory of adaptive structuration. In J. Fulk & C. W. Steinfield (Eds.), *Organizations and communication technologies* (pp. 173-193). Newbury Park, CA: Sage.

Poole, M. S., Foley, J. P., & Hewes, D. E. (1987). Analyzing interpersonal interaction. In M. E. Roloff & G. R. Miller (Eds.), *Interpersonal processes: New directions in communication research* (pp. 220-256). Newbury Park, CA: Sage.

Porter, L., & Roberts, K. (1976). Communication in organizations. In M. D. Dunnette (Ed.), *Handbook of industrial and organizational psychology* (pp. 1553-1589). Chicago: Rand McNally.

Ragan, S. L., & Hopper, R. (1981). Alignment talk in the job interview. *Journal of Applied Communication Research, 9,* 85-103.

Ralston, S. M., & Kirkwood, W. G. (1995). Overcoming managerial bias in employment interviewing. *Journal of Applied Communication Research, 23,* 75-92.

Rynes, S. L. (1991). Recruitment, job choice, and post-hire consequences: A call for new research directions. In M. D. Dunnette & L. M. Hough (Eds.), *Handbook of industrial and organizational psychology* (2nd ed., Vol. 2, pp. 399-444). Palo Alto, CA: Consulting Psychologists Press.

Rynes, S. L., & Barber, A. E. (1991). Applicant attraction strategies: An organizational perspective. *Academy of Management Review, 15,* 286-310.

Sackett, P. R. (1982). The interviewer as hypothesis tester: The effects of impression of an applicant on interviewer questioning strategy. *Personnel Psychology, 35,* 789-804.

Schramm, W. (1954). *The process and effects of mass communication.* Urbana: University of Illinois Press.

Searle, J. (1967). Human communication theory and the philosophy of language: Some remarks. In F. E. X. Dance (Ed.), *Human communication theory* (pp. 116-129). New York: Holt, Rinehart & Winston.

Searle, J. (1969). *Speech acts: An essay in the philosophy of language.* Cambridge: Cambridge University Press.

Shannon, C., & Weaver, W. (1949). *The mathematical theory of communication.* Urbana: University of Illinois Press.

Shaw, M. R. (1983). Taken-for-granted assumptions of applicants in simulated selection interviews. *Western Journal of Speech Communication, 47,* 138-156.

Snyder, M., Campbell, B., & Preston, E. (1982). Testing hypotheses about human nature: Assessing the accuracy of social stereotypes. *Social Cognition, 1,* 256-272.

Snyder, M., & Swann, W. (1978). Hypothesis-testing processes in social interactions. *Journal of Personality and Social Psychology, 36,* 1202-1212.

Springbett, B. M. (1958). Factors affecting the final decision in the employment interview. *Canadian Journal of Psychology, 12,* 13-22.

Stevens, C. K., & Kristof, A. L. (1995). Making the right impression: A field study of applicant impression management during job interviews. *Journal of Applied Psychology, 80,* 587-606.

Stewart, C. J., & Cash, W. B. (1991). *Interviewing: Principles and practices* (5th ed.). Dubuque, IA: W. C. Brown.

Tengler, C. D., & Jablin, F. M. (1983). Effects of question type, orientation, and sequencing in the employment screening interview. *Communication Monographs, 50,* 245-263.

Tracy, K. (1991). Discourse. In B. M. Montgomery & S. Duck (Eds.), *Studying interpersonal interaction* (pp. 179-196). New York: Guilford.

Tucker, D. H., & Rowe, P. M. (1977). Relationship between expectancy, causal attribution and final hiring decisions in the employment interview. *Journal of Applied Psychology, 64,* 27-34.

Tullar, W. L. (1989). Relational control in the employment interview. *Journal of Applied Psychology, 74,* 971-977.

Tullar, W. L., Mullins, T. W., & Caldwell, S. A. (1979). Effects of interview length and applicant quality on interview decision time. *Journal of Applied Psychology, 64,* 669-674.

Wanous, J. P. (1980). *Organizational entry: Recruitment, selection, and socialization of newcomers.* Reading, MA: Addison-Wesley.

Warner, R. (1991). Incorporating time. In B. M. Montgomery & S. Duck (Eds.), *Studying interpersonal interaction* (pp. 82-102). New York: Guilford.

Watt, J. H., & VanLear, C. A. (1996). *Dynamic patterns in communication processes.* Thousand Oaks, CA: Sage.

Watzlawick, P., Beavin, J., & Jackson, D. (1967). *Pragmatics of human communication: A study of interaction patterns, pathologies, and paradoxes.* New York: W. W. Norton.

18

Impression Management Tactics

David C. Gilmore
Cynthia Kay Stevens
Gloria Harrell-Cook
Gerald R. Ferris

Interpersonal influence and impression management are fundamental processes of social behavior in organizations. In recent years, organizational scientists have gained considerable insight into the role played by social influence and impression management in key human resource decisions such as selection, performance evaluation, promotion, and compensation (Ferris & Judge, 1991). Our focus in this chapter is on the impact of impression management on one component of human resource selection decisions: the employment interview.

The employment interview is one of the most thoroughly researched topics in human resource management. However, systematic research has focused on social influence and impression management within the interview context only in recent years. The purposes of this chapter are to provide a critical analysis of existing research on impression management in the employment interview process and to enhance the theoretical understanding of influence dynamics by strengthening explanations of how and why impression management processes during the interview affect applicants' and interviewers' employment decisions.

Theoretical Foundations

Symbolic Interactionist Roots
of Impression Management

Prevailing notions about organizations and the people within them assume that both are rational entities that can be understood using objective methods of the natural sciences (Burrell & Morgan, 1979). This contrasts sharply with interpretive paradigms, which hold that objective reality does not exist outside the beliefs and social constructions of individuals (Burrell & Morgan, 1979). The symbolic interactionist perspective, from which impression management research derives, comprises a range of positions between these extremes. Its core idea is that people negotiate the interpretations attached to behavior and events in social settings (Schlenker, 1980).

Although impression management researchers accept this core idea, they often disagree in their underlying assumptions about the nature of social science. In practice, this has led to confusion regarding construct definitions and acceptable methodologies (Tetlock & Manstead, 1985). For example, some researchers lean toward objective methods and definitions; they have defined impression management as conscious attempts to manipulate others, and they focus on discrete behaviors that occur in the presence of an audience (e.g., Gaes, Kalle, & Tedeschi, 1978). In contrast, other researchers adopt interpretive approaches. For these researchers, impression management need not be conscious or deliberate—all behavior may have impression management value—and the "audience" may include imagined others or oneself (e.g., Goffman, 1959). To avoid confusion, it is essential that impression management researchers state their assumptions and construct definitions explicitly. In this chapter, we define *impression management* as conscious or unconscious attempts to influence images during interaction and *self-presentation* as attempts to influence self-relevant images. Furthermore, we assume that impression management concerns are heightened in the presence of an evaluative external audience and lowered by circumstances that induce a strong task focus, spontaneous emotional expression, and normatively ritualized behavior (Jones & Pittman, 1982). Accordingly, the interview context is one that should raise impression management concerns for both interviewers and applicants.

Taxonomies of Impression
Management Behavior

Researchers have identified several classes of behavior that may be used to manage others' impressions. One early classification was provided by

Schneider (1981), who suggested that impression management includes verbal behaviors, nonverbal behaviors, artifactual displays (e.g., one's apparel, "props" used during interaction, the physical setting), and integrated behavior patterns. Given the short duration of most interviews, the appropriate foci for research in the interview context would be verbal and nonverbal behavior and some artifactual displays.

Other researchers have classified impression management behavior according to the types of attributions sought from the audience (Jones & Pittman, 1982) and according to the time orientation and general purpose of the impression management attempt (Tedeschi & Melburg, 1984). Because impression managers (also called actors) seek to control the images that arise during social interaction, insight into their behavior can be gained through examination of their desired outcomes—that is, the attributions they want others to draw. Jones and Pittman (1982) propose that several common attributions are sought by actors, including likability, competence, fearfulness, moral worthiness, and helplessness. In the employment interview context, it seems likely that the first three would be most relevant. Jones and Pittman suggest that actors may elicit attributions of likability through ingratiation, which includes opinion conformity (agreeing with others' opinions), other-enhancement (flattery or compliments), and offers to do favors. Competence attributions may be achieved through the use of such self-promotion behaviors as positive self-descriptions, entitlements (claiming credit for positive events), and enhancements (claiming increased value of positive events for which one is responsible). These attributions may be sought by both applicants and interviewers during employment interviews. Finally, Jones and Pittman suggest that actors can foster attributions of fearfulness through intimidating behaviors, such as threats or displays of anger. These behaviors might be used by interviewers to underscore their power during interviews.

Tedeschi and Melburg (1984) extended this work by constructing a 2 × 2 typology of impression management behavior on the basis of time orientation (tactical or short-term versus strategic or long-term) and the general purpose of the behavior (assertive or image construction versus defensive or image repair). Assertive-tactical behaviors are considered an appropriate focus for investigation, as applicants generally attempt to construct attractive images of themselves within a limited period of time. However, assertive-strategic behaviors may also play a role, as these behaviors influence how applicants establish their credentials. For example, applicants may undertake volunteer work or extracurricular activities to enhance their résumés.

Having summarized current knowledge regarding the scope and definition of impression management, we now review existing research concerning the role of impression management in employment interviews.

Research on Impression Management in the Employment Interview

Influence Processes in Human Resource Decisions

Organizational researchers have shown that individual differences influence the propensity to engage in impression management. Furthermore, impression management behavior may be interpreted differently by perceivers depending on perceiver (or target) characteristics and the context in which impression management occurs. To summarize these factors, Ferris and Judge (1991) have proposed an analytic framework for understanding how social influence processes, including impression management, affect human resource decisions such as employment interview decisions (see Figure 18.1). According to this framework, impression management tactics are a function of actor and target characteristics and characteristics of the situation or context in which impression management behavior occurs. Impression management tactics affect human resource decisions through three mediating variables: affect or liking, perceived fit, and assessments of competence. Finally, human resource management decisions result in attitudinal and behavioral outcomes. Below, we briefly summarize the major variables in this framework as a springboard to our summary of relevant research findings.

Actor and Target Characteristics

The Ferris and Judge (1991) framework indicates that several characteristics of both applicants and interviewers may affect the use and impact of influence tactics, including demographic and personality variables. Because gender is linked with socialization and with power differences in organizations, it has been studied as an antecedent of influence tactics. For example, Fletcher and Spencer (1984) found that female applicants intended to be more open during upcoming interviews, particularly if the interviewers were also female. Graves and Powell (1995) found that the effects of applicant and interviewer gender similarity were mediated by perceived similarity and interpersonal attraction.

Another demographic variable of interest is applicant and interviewer age and experience. Fletcher (1990) found that applicants who had more interview experience had stronger intentions to maintain eye contact, project a positive image, and ask questions than did applicants who had less interview experience. Similarly, Delery and Kacmar (1995) found that applicants who were older and who had more training in interview skills made fewer requests and were less likely to use entitlements during interviews. Interestingly, when interviewers in their study had stronger communication skills and greater experience and were older, applicants also made

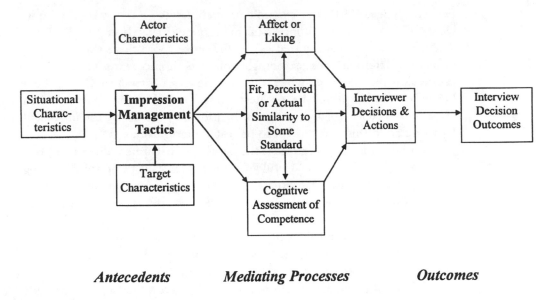

Figure 18.1. Adaptation of the Ferris and Judge (1991) Framework

fewer requests and used fewer entitlements, but used more self-enhancing and self-promoting statements.

The role of personality variables in affecting impression management during the interview is less certain. Fletcher (1990) found evidence that applicants high in Machiavellianism (a trait in which one's self-interests are pursued even at the expense of others) reported that they would be more likely to bluff and less likely to give honest answers during interviews. However, applicants' personality traits generally were not strongly linked with their intended self-presentation tactics. Similarly, Delery and Kacmar (1995) found no relationship between self-monitoring (a trait associated with careful tracking of the situational appropriateness of one's behavior) and applicants' actual use of impression management tactics. It may be that the situational demands associated with employment interviews are such that they create a "floor" effect; that is, applicants may engage in impression management regardless of personality traits that would predispose them to do so or inhibit them from doing so. Additional research is needed to examine this issue.

Situational Characteristics

Because behavior may be more or less appropriate depending on the context in which it occurs, several researchers have proposed that situational characteristics may be important in influencing the prevalence and interpretation of impression management (e.g., Eder & Buckley, 1988;

Ferris & Judge, 1991). For example, the ambiguity or clarity of the interview task should affect impression management (Ferris & Judge, 1991). The greater the ambiguity that exists, the more room there should be for influence. Extending this reasoning, applicants should be most likely to use impression management when the interview is unstructured, and these behaviors should have the greatest impact on decision making when interviewers lack information about the job and purpose of the interview. Unfortunately, this idea has yet to be tested empirically.

Another situational variable is the perceived instrumentality of impression management, or how useful an actor perceives it to be for obtaining desired outcomes in a given situation. For both applicants and interviewers, impression management may be more prevalent if it is seen as useful in obtaining job offers or increasing applicant attraction, respectively. This idea is supported by the work of Stevens (1997), who found that applicants were more likely to use ingratiation tactics during actual interviews if they thought a job offer was likely to be forthcoming.

A third situational variable is accountability, or the need to provide justification for one's decisions given possible counterarguments. Eder and Buckley (1988) suggest that interviewers who are held accountable for their recommendations may provide more accurate descriptions of applicant characteristics. Although research has not examined the effects of interviewer accountability on interviewers' reactions to applicant impression management, Gordon, Rozelle, and Baxter's (1988, 1989) studies of the effects of interviewer accountability on age discrimination shed some light on this issue. In both of Gordon et al.'s studies, interviewer accountability led to stereotyped, polarized reactions to applicants of different ages; younger applicants were evaluated more positively than were older applicants under high but not low accountability. Moreover, Gordon et al. (1989) found that interviewers who expected to explain their recommendations made more dispositional attributions than did interviewers who had no such expectations. Additional research is needed to determine whether a similar pattern would hold for interviewers' evaluations for different patterns in applicant impression management.

Situational variables also may moderate the effects of impression management. For example, Stevens, Mitchell, and Tripp (1990) found that the order of presentation for recruiters who used different impression management tactics moderated the effectiveness of their impression management tactics. Recruiters who used self-enhancement (i.e., boasting) were generally less effective in eliciting positive attributions and encouraging offer acceptance than were recruiters who used other-enhancement or opinion conformity. However, when self-enhancing recruiters were seen first, they were more effective. Similarly, Anderson (1991) found order of presentation effects in ratings of applicants who used different verbal and nonverbal tactic combinations. These findings suggest that the types and degrees of impression management observed across several interviews may provide a context for interpreting given impression management attempts.

Another likely moderator of impression management is the type of job for which applicants are being evaluated. Dipboye and Wiley (1978) found that a moderately aggressive self-presentational style resulted in higher evaluations than did a passive style when the position involved a super- visory job. However, this pattern was reversed when the position was for an editorial assistant: A passive style elicited higher evaluations. Although this finding has not been replicated, other evidence points to a moderating influence of job type. For example, Gilmore and Ferris (1989) speculate that they found strong effects for impression management but no effect of applicant credentials because the opening described a customer service representative job. For that position, effective self-presentation might be regarded as essential for job success.

Impression Management Tactics and Their Effects

Most research on impression management in interviews has concen- trated on how these tactics affect interviewers' judgments. For example, Tullar (1989) and Engler-Parish and Millar (1989) examined the effects of relational control in applicants' interview outcomes. Relational control was operationalized in terms of interviewers' and applicants' dominance and submission patterns in response to each other. These researchers found that successful applicants dominated more frequently than did unsuccess- ful applicants. In addition, successful applicants behaved less competitively than did unsuccessful applicants in response to interviewers' attempts to structure the conversation.

By far, most research in this area has concentrated on applicants' nonverbal behaviors during the interview. Nonverbal behaviors include eye contact, facial expressions, head nodding, gestures, posture, paralinguistic cues (e.g., tone of voice, disfluencies), physical orientation, and spatial distance. Because nonverbal behaviors convey information about emo- tional and cognitive states, and because they are difficult to feign (DePaulo, 1992), they are often seen as a useful source of information about appli- cants. Research has consistently shown that friendly nonverbal behavior is associated with higher interviewer evaluations (e.g., Anderson, 1991; An- derson & Shackleton, 1990; Forbes & Jackson, 1980; Gifford, Ng, & Wilkinson, 1985; Hollandsworth, Kazelskis, Stevens, & Dressel, 1979; Imada & Hakel, 1977; McGovern, Jones, Warwick, & Jackson, 1981; Par- sons & Liden, 1984).

Researchers have also examined the effects of various combinations of verbal and nonverbal tactics. For example, Gilmore and Ferris (1989) found that several tactical-assertive behaviors (eye contact, smiling, ingra- tiation, and self-promotion) were more effective in raising interviewers' evaluations than were applicants' paper credentials. Similarly, Kacmar,

Delery, and Ferris (1992) found that self-focused tactics (such as self-promotion) were more effective in increasing interviewers' evaluations than were other-focused tactics (such as ingratiation). Rasmussen (1984) found that friendly nonverbal behaviors were effective only when corresponding verbal behaviors were present.

Fewer studies have examined the role of artifactual displays such as clothing and grooming aids. In general, clean clothing and a professional appearance are associated with better interviewer evaluations (Parsons & Liden, 1984). However, Baron (1989) has reported interactive effects of different artifacts—dress and artificial scent—and of artifacts in combination with nonverbal behavior. Specifically, he found that the combination of professional dress and artificial scent or of friendly nonverbal behaviors and artificial scent led to lower ratings than did professional dress, scent, or friendly nonverbal behaviors alone. This pattern, which Baron labels the "too much of a good thing" effect, suggests that particular combinations of impression management tactics may vary in effectiveness. Future research needs to examine more closely why and how such effects occur.

Mediating Variables

The processes through which impression management influences interviewers' and applicants' judgments and decisions are not well understood. Essentially, personal and situational variables shape the target's reaction to the actor's impression management, which in turn determines the target's perceptions of the actor. This perception feeds into subsequent judgments and decisions. Ferris and Judge (1991) suggest that three types of perceptions are important in later decisions: likability, assessments of competence, and perceived fit.

Several studies have explored the relationships between impression management and interviewers' perceptions of applicant likability and competence or between these perceptions and subsequent decisions. Graves and Powell (1988) found that interviewer liking for applicants was influenced by how similar interviewers thought applicants were; liking in turn affected interviewers' subjective assessments of applicants' qualifications. Howard and Ferris (1996), using an experimental design, found that interviewers' judgments of applicant competence were positively influenced by nonverbal behaviors but negatively influenced by self-promotion. Furthermore, perceived similarity contributed to both perceived competence and likability, which affected interviewers' final evaluations of applicants.

Identifying the antecedents and role of perceived fit between the applicant and organization has proven to be more difficult. Kristof (1996) defines *fit* as the compatibility between people and organizations that occurs when one entity provides what the other needs or when they share similar characteristics. Most research on fit has focused on similarity in individual and organizational goals and values (Chatman, 1989), although it seems probable that similarity in individuals' knowledge, skills, and abilities and job demands would also affect selection decisions and job choice. Because detailed information about value, goal, and KSA-job compatibility may not be routinely available during the hiring process, impression management is likely to factor heavily into the fit perceptions of both applicants and interviewers.

Decisions and Outcomes

Most studies of the effects of impression management have focused on short-term measures, such as interviewers' evaluations of applicant suitability or their estimates of the likelihood that applicants will be offered a job (e.g., Anderson & Shackleton, 1990; Fletcher, 1990; Hollandsworth et al., 1979; Parsons & Liden, 1984). In laboratory studies, participants are asked to make hypothetical decisions such as whether or not they would offer a job to particular applicants (e.g., Gilmore & Ferris, 1989; Kacmar et al., 1992) or which applicant or opening they would choose (e.g., Anderson, 1991; Stevens et al., 1990). Studies examining the impacts of impression management on actual decisions have been sparse. One field study found evidence of significant relationships between applicant impression management in the initial interview and actual site-visit invitations (Stevens & Kristof, 1995). Nonetheless, the combined results across these lab and field studies point in the same direction: Impression management appears to influence selection decisions.

This pattern raises a second important but often overlooked question: What is the longer-term impact of impression management on recruitment and selection? Some researchers have suggested that impression management constitutes a source of validity-reducing bias in selection (e.g., Anderson, 1991). Similarly, one implication of the realistic job preview research is that too much impression management during recruitment can reduce the quality of applicants' job choices and ultimately increase turnover. These issues, which have not been studied, depend in part on how impression management is defined and whether it is seen as distinct from misrepresentation. We believe that the two constructs are separable and distinct, and that the impact of impression management on longer-term outcomes may be positive or negative, depending on how it is used. However, an important first step would be to examine the longer-term recruitment and selection outcomes affected by impression management.

Critique and Future Research Directions

Ferris and Judge's (1991) framework, as a tool to review existing research, elucidates gaps in understanding and highlights issues that should be considered in the design of future studies. One obvious gap is the focus of research: Most studies have concentrated on applicant impression management, yet interviewers may also manage applicants' impressions. Specifically, interviewers provide early information about the job and organization as well as direct or indirect information about the culture and people who work in the organization. This information affects applicants' evaluations of the job opportunity and shapes their expectations for future interactions with organizational representatives (Harris & Fink, 1987; Rynes, 1989). In the extreme case, a poor initial impression may prompt an applicant to eliminate the job opportunity from further consideration. Much of the recruitment literature has emphasized the importance of providing realistic information; however, we would argue that it is possible to do so while still accentuating positive features of the job (see Wanous, 1989). Future research needs to concentrate on what impression management tactics interviewers use, which ones are effective in stimulating applicant interest, and whether interviewers can be trained to use effective tactics to improve recruitment outcomes.

Another notable gap in the research is the limited range of impression management tactics that have been investigated. Existing studies have measured or manipulated small subsets of nonverbal or verbal tactics. However, actual interviews present simultaneous combinations of verbal and nonverbal tactics and artifactual displays (e.g., dress, grooming). Two problems result from this oversight. One is that, particularly among laboratory studies, the types and ranges of impression management studied may not parallel those found in actual interviews. Not only does this potentially reduce the generalizability of the findings, it may also yield misleading conclusions about the underlying influence processes. For example, Stevens and Kristof (1995) found that applicants made extensive use of self-promotion but limited use of ingratiation during actual interviews. Laboratory studies that do not examine self-promotion or that manipulate self-promotion and ingratiation to be equivalent may therefore clarify influence dynamics that are irrelevant to most interview settings. For these reasons, future researchers should work to clarify the variety and level of impression management tactics that are exhibited in naturally occurring interview situations (e.g., campus interviews, on-site interviews). Systematic analysis of videotaped interviews may help us to understand more fully the range, frequency, and complexity of various impression management behaviors.

The second problem with the current focus on a limited range of impression management tactics is that their effects may be moderated by tactics not investigated. Several laboratory studies have shown that verbal and nonverbal tactics (Rasmussen, 1984), and nonverbal tactics and artifactual displays (Baron, 1989), interact in their effects on interviewers' judgments. Moreover, the forms of these interactions differ: In one case, the tactic combinations led to higher ratings, whereas in the other they led to lower ratings. This pattern suggests that the impact of impression management is highly dependent on the configuration of tactics present. For this reason, it is essential that researchers begin to investigate a broader range of tactic combinations in a more systematic fashion. One strategy would be to manipulate or measure all three classes of impression management (verbal tactics, nonverbal behavior, and artifactual displays) in future studies. If a particular class of impression management is held constant in laboratory research (e.g., dress), it should still be described in the methods section to facilitate cross-study comparisons of results. Another strategy would be to conduct further investigations of tactic combinations that have surfaced in the literature (e.g., moderately aggressive self-presentation style [Dipboye & Wiley, 1977], self-focused tactics [Kacmar et al., 1992]). Studies should determine whether the impacts of these styles change as component tactics are varied systematically. Systematic study of a broader range of impression management tactics can help tremendously in identifying the patterns of impression management that affect applicants' and interviewers' judgments.

A related issue is the need for greater attention to the moderating influences of important contextual variables. Two salient moderators include order of presentation effects and the job type. Order effects are especially problematic because, despite current reliance on study designs involving between-subjects assessments (i.e., ratings for a single applicant or opening), most interviews involve within-subjects assessments (i.e., ratings for a succession of applicants or openings). As a result, most selection decisions and job choices are likely to be made relative to a pool of options that can color the evaluation of any single option. For example, assume that most applicants engage in impression management tactics during their interviews. This might raise the baseline expectations of interviewers and potentially counteract the problems that have been observed with the "too much of a good thing" effect. Similarly, the type of job provides an important context for evaluating the appropriateness and impact of impression management exhibited by both applicants and interviewers. It may be possible to explore these effects more systematically, for example, by comparing reactions to impression management across openings in several different job families. At a minimum, researchers must be more sensitive to contextual features when designing studies and interpreting findings.

Our review has highlighted several personal and situational characteristics that have been examined, yet many interesting variables remain unexplored, including interviewer accountability, interview structure, and task ambiguity. Additionally, attention needs to be devoted to improving knowledge of how these variables affect targets' perceptions and decision processes. For example, studies have shown that interviewers can be grouped according to which cues they use to evaluate applicants (e.g., Graves & Karren, 1992; Zedeck, Tziner, & Middlestadt, 1983). It is possible that the underlying schemata associated with patterns of cue use also lead to differential susceptibility to applicant impression management. Perhaps interviewers differ in how they assess and weight applicant likability, competence, and fit. Investigating the development and use of various judgmental schemata and their relationship to interviewers' perceptions holds promise for clarifying interviewers' decision processes. Furthermore, training of interviewers may affect their susceptibility to applicant impression management efforts. Howard and Ferris (1996) found that interviewers who received formal training rated applicants who used self-promotion tactics lower than did untrained interviewers.

Another area that warrants study is the characteristics and situational perceptions that affect applicants' and interviewers' choices of impression management tactics. Leary and Kowalski (1990) propose that actors choose impression management tactics on the basis of their own self-concepts and desired identities as well as an assessment of role constraints, target values, and perceived social images of themselves. However, an analysis of these components has not been provided for the interview context. By breaking down these components, researchers may be able to identify trends in claimed images according to personality and demographic variables, thereby clarifying how various factors affect the types of images claimed in interview settings.

Implications for Practice

It is increasingly clear that impression management can be used to explain many interview dynamics and that we should acknowledge that applicants and interviewers both use impression management tactics to influence each other. Once that is acknowledged and research clarifies the impression management dynamics, then definitive advice can be offered to both interviewers and applicants on what should work and how to interpret impression management in an interview. We need to acknowledge impression management and calibrate the phenomenon with systematic research before we can begin to suggest exactly how it may be used in practice.

One obvious implication concerns the job relevance of impression management techniques. Once particular impression management tactics have been identified as appropriate for a job, candidates could be evaluated for hire based on more specific behaviors, such as self-promotion, rather than more generalized behaviors, such as marketing techniques. Potential employees could be evaluated using more specific standards, such as those that might be contained in behaviorally anchored rating scales focusing on different impression management tactics.

Applications of impression management research to benefit organizations in an interview context typically focus on the recruiting process. Research is needed to investigate which impression management tactics are effective in portraying an organization's image to an applicant and how that image corresponds to reality. For example, should an organization that has a bad environmental track record use defensive impression management tactics to repair its image, or are assertive tactics more likely to be viewed positively by applicants? And what is the relative impact of an organization's record compared with pronouncements made by a recruiter in what must be an obvious impression management situation? The likely curvilinear relationship between the amount of any impression management tactic and perceived effectiveness is most obvious in the discussion of how much recruiters try to influence applicants. We need some calibration of the optimum amounts of impression management tactics. We suspect that the most successful impression management actors are not only good at initiating tactics but adept at gauging how much impression management is needed to result in the desired outcome. The ability to "read" others may be taught to actors once we have a better description of impression management dynamics. In the future, organizational recruiters could be selected based on their sensitivities and then, through impression management training, could become even more effective organizational representatives.

Conclusion

We need a better understanding of the complex interactions that occur in employment interviews, particularly when multiple impression management tactics are being used simultaneously. We also need more precision in estimates of the impacts of various levels of impression management tactics and how different actors are influenced by them. Viewing the interview from an impression management perspective should allow researchers to help practitioners make dramatic improvements in a much maligned process.

References

Anderson, N. R. (1991). Decision making in the graduate selection interview: An experimental investigation. *Human Relations, 44,* 403-417.

Anderson, N. R., & Shackleton, V. (1990). Decision making in the graduate selection interview: A field study. *Journal of Occupational Psychology, 63,* 63-76.

Baron, R. A. (1989). Impression management by applicants during employment interviews: The "too much of a good thing" effect. In R. W. Eder & G. R. Ferris (Eds.), *The employment interview: Theory, research, and practice* (pp. 204-215). Newbury Park, CA: Sage.

Burrell, G., & Morgan, G. (1979). *Sociological paradigms and organisational analysis.* Portsmouth, England: Heinemann.

Chatman, J. A. (1989). Improving interactional organizational research: A model of person-organization fit. *Academy of Management Review, 14,* 333-349.

Delery, J. E., & Kacmar, K. M. (1995). *The use of impression management tactics in the employment interview: An investigation of the influence of applicant and interviewer characteristics.* Paper presented at the annual meeting of the Society for Industrial and Organizational Psychology, Orlando, FL.

DePaulo, B. M. (1992). Nonverbal behavior and self-presentation. *Psychological Bulletin, 111,* 203-242.

Dipboye, R. L., & Wiley, J. W. (1977). Reactions of college recruiters to interviewee sex and self-presentation style. *Journal of Vocational Behavior, 10,* 1-12.

Dipboye, R. L., & Wiley, J. W. (1978). Reactions of male raters to interviewee self-presentation style and sex: Extensions of previous research. *Journal of Vocational Behavior, 13,* 192-203.

Eder, R. W., & Buckley, M. R. (1988). The employment interview: An interactionist perspective. In G. R. Ferris & K. M. Rowland (Eds.), *Research in personnel and human resources management* (Vol. 6, pp. 75-107). Greenwich, CT: JAI.

Engler-Parish, P. G., & Millar, F. E. (1989). An exploratory relational control analysis of the employment screening interview. *Western Journal of Speech Communication, 53,* 30-51.

Ferris, G. R., & Judge, T. A. (1991). Personnel/human resources management: A political influence perspective. *Journal of Management, 17,* 447-488.

Fletcher, C. (1990). The relationships between candidate personality, self-presentation strategies, and interviewer assessment in selection interviews: An empirical study. *Human Relations, 43,* 739-749.

Fletcher, C., & Spencer, A. (1984). Sex of candidate and sex of interviewer as determinants of self-presentation orientation in interviews: An experimental study. *International Review of Applied Psychology, 33,* 305-313.

Forbes, R. J., & Jackson, P. R. (1980). Non-verbal behavior and the outcome of selection interviews. *Journal of Occupational Psychology, 53,* 65-72.

Gaes, G. G., Kalle, R. J., & Tedeschi, J. T. (1978). Impression management in the forced compliance paradigm: Two studies using the bogus pipeline. *Journal of Experimental Social Psychology, 14,* 493-510.

Gifford, R., Ng, C. F., & Wilkinson, M. (1985). Nonverbal cues in the employment interview: Links between applicant qualities and interviewer judgments. *Journal of Applied Psychology, 70,* 729-736.

Gilmore, D. C., & Ferris, G. R. (1989). The effects of applicant impression management tactics on interviewer judgments. *Journal of Management, 15,* 557-564.

Goffman, E. (1959). *The presentation of self in everyday life.* Garden City, NY: Doubleday.

Gordon, R. A., Rozelle, R. M., & Baxter, J. C. (1988). The effect of applicant age, job level, and accountability on the evaluation of job applicants. *Organizational Behavior and Human Decision Processes, 41,* 20-33.

Gordon, R. A., Rozelle, R. M., & Baxter, J. C. (1989). The effect of applicant age, job level, and accountability on perceptions of female applicants. *Journal of Psychology, 123,* 59-68.

Graves, L. M., & Karren, R. J. (1992). Interviewer decision processes and effectiveness: An experimental policy-capturing investigation. *Personnel Psychology, 45,* 313-340.

Graves, L. M., & Powell, G. N. (1988). An investigation of sex discrimination in recruiters' evaluations of actual applicants. *Journal of Applied Psychology, 73,* 20-29.

Graves, L. M., & Powell, G. N. (1995). The effect of sex similarity on recruiters' evaluations of actual applicants: A test of the similarity-attraction paradigm. *Personnel Psychology, 48,* 85-98.

Harris, M. M., & Fink, L. S. (1987). A field study of applicant reactions to employment opportunities: Does the recruiter make a difference? *Personnel Psychology, 40,* 765-784.

Hollandsworth, J. G., Jr., Kazelskis, R., Stevens, J., & Dressel, M. E. (1979). Relative contributions of verbal, articulative, and nonverbal communication to employment decisions in the job interview setting. *Personnel Psychology, 32,* 359-367.

Howard, J. L., & Ferris, G. R. (1996). The employment interview context: Social and situational influences on interviewer decisions. *Journal of Applied Social Psychology, 81,* 112-136.

Imada, A. S., & Hakel, M. D. (1977). Influence of nonverbal communication and rater proximity on impressions and decisions in simulated employment interviews. *Journal of Applied Psychology, 62,* 295-300.

Jones, E. E., & Pittman, T. S. (1982). Toward a general theory of strategic self-presentation. In J. Suls (Ed.), *Psychological perspectives on the self* (Vol. 1, pp. 231-262). Hillsdale, NJ: Lawrence Erlbaum.

Kacmar, K. M., Delery, J. E., & Ferris, G. R. (1992). Differential effectiveness of applicant impression management tactics on employment interview decisions. *Journal of Applied Social Psychology, 22,* 1250-1272.

Kristof, A. L. (1996). Person-organization fit: An integrative review of its conceptualizations, measurement, and implications. *Personnel Psychology, 49,* 1-49.

Leary, M. R., & Kowalski, R. M. (1990). Impression management: A literature review and two-component model. *Psychological Bulletin, 107,* 34-47.

McGovern, T. V., Jones, B. W., Warwick, C. L., & Jackson, R. W. (1981). A comparison of job interviewee behavior on four channels of communication. *Journal of Counseling Psychology, 28,* 369-372.

Parsons, C. K., & Liden, R. C. (1984). Interviewer perceptions of applicant qualifications: A multivariate field study of demographic characteristics and nonverbal cues. *Journal of Applied Psychology, 69,* 557-568.

Rasmussen, K. G., Jr. (1984). Nonverbal behavior, verbal behavior, resume credentials, and selection interview outcomes. *Journal of Applied Psychology, 69,* 551-556.

Rynes, S. L. (1989). The employment interview as a recruitment device. In R. W. Eder & G. R. Ferris (Eds.), *The employment interview: Theory, research, and practice* (pp. 127-141). Newbury Park, CA: Sage.

Schlenker, B. R. (1980). *Impression management: The self-concept, social identity, and interpersonal relations.* Monterey, CA: Brooks/Cole.

Schneider, D. J. (1981). Tactical self-presentations: Toward a broader conception. In J. T. Tedeschi (Ed.), *Impression management theory and social psychological research* (pp. 23-40). New York: Academic Press.

Stevens, C. K. (1997). The effects of preinterview beliefs on applicants' reactions to campus interviews. *Academy of Management Journal, 40,* 947-966.

Stevens, C. K., & Kristof, A. L. (1995). Making the right impression: A field study of applicant impression management during job interviews. *Journal of Applied Psychology, 80,* 587-606.

Stevens, C. K., Mitchell, T. R., & Tripp, T. M. (1990). Order of presentation and verbal recruitment strategy effectiveness. *Journal of Applied Social Psychology, 20,* 1076-1092.

Tedeschi, J. T., & Melburg, V. (1984). Impression management and influence in the organization. In S. B. Bacharach & E. J. Lawler (Eds.), *Research in the sociology of organizations* (Vol. 3, pp. 31-58). Greenwich, CT: JAI.

Tetlock, P. E., & Manstead, A. S. R. (1985). Impression management versus intrapsychic explanations in social psychology: A useful dichotomy? *Psychological Review, 92,* 59-77.

Tullar, W. L. (1989). Relational control in the employment interview. *Journal of Applied Psychology, 74,* 971-977.

Wanous, J. P. (1989). Installing a realistic job preview: Ten tough choices. *Personnel Psychology, 42,* 117-124.

Zedeck, S., Tziner, A., & Middlestadt, S. E. (1983). Interviewer validity and reliability: An individual analysis approach. *Personnel Psychology, 36,* 355-370.

19

Interviewing Training for Both Applicant and Interviewer

David K. Palmer
Michael A. Campion
Paul C. Green

The purpose of this chapter is to investigate interview training from the perspectives of both interviewers and applicants. Is the focus of one perspective interchangeable with the other, or are there subtle differences that could meaningfully inform research and practice?

It is recognized that the interview can serve many purposes, including both selection and recruitment (Dipboye, 1992). The interview is a dynamic interaction in which both the interviewer and the applicant often fulfill multiple roles simultaneously (e.g., information gatherer, evaluator, presenter). Training can be directed at enhancing the performance of any one or more of these roles and their associated behaviors. Sackett, Burris, and Ryan (1989) have envisioned three possible outcomes of interview training: (a) the reduction of error through the elimination of some sources of deficiency, such as test anxiety; (b) the improvement of the underlying characteristic being tested without affecting the test's construct or predictive validity; and (c) an increase in the test taker's score without improvement on the underlying characteristic or construct. The first two outcomes are positive for both the interviewer and the applicant, whereas the latter is positive only for the applicant. Regarding subsequent good performers, there may be a decision to accept ("hit") or reject ("miss"). Regarding subsequent poor performers, there may be a decision to accept ("false positive") or reject ("correct rejection"). Interviewers are striving to achieve hits and correct rejections, whereas applicants are striving to elicit job offers, both hits and false positives.

The literature on interview training can be categorized according to its focus on either the interviewer (organizational perspective) or the applicant (individual job seeker's perspective). There is some identifiable academic research literature on both interviewer training and applicant training. There is also a practitioner-oriented literature concerned with both. Furthermore, there is a large industry devoted to providing training and consulting on these topics, but it is proprietary and not in the public domain. Thus, we focus in this chapter only on published books and articles.

Interviewer Training

Training is probably the most common technique used by organizations to improve their interviewing (Dipboye, 1992). Indeed, an appreciation of the importance of training for interview success is not new (e.g., Wonderlic, 1942). Training is integral to improving the structuring of interviews, and hence their psychometric properties (Campion, Palmer, & Campion, 1997). Howard, Dailey, and Gulanick (1979) note that aspects of interviewing structure can be easily taught. Additionally, Eder and Buckley (1988) state that training can improve the selection interview through situational factors (e.g., increased interviewer role clarity).

Training is indeed a key component and represents one of the most offered courses in organizations today, with an estimated 65% of organizations providing some sort of interview training ("Who's Learning What?" 1996). These surveys reveal that 32% provide training that is designed and delivered only by in-house staff, 8% use only external sources for interview training, and 25% use a combination of internal and external sources ("Who's Learning What?" 1996). Although some of this training is conducted by consultants, there are a number of popular press books and guides that can supplement training with self-initiated study.

Research

The main emphasis of research on interview training has been on improving the selection function of the employment interview. The focus has been on the interviewer's ability to gather and evaluate information within the context of the employment decision. However, training is generally incidental in many studies; very few researchers have examined interview training as their primary research question. Instead, most have focused on testing the validity of structured interviewing; they have included training only to prepare interviewers to implement the system correctly. Reports of research of this type usually mention the kind of training used only in passing, making no effort to assess its effectiveness and offering no discussion as to why a certain form of training was chosen over others. An interesting aspect of much research has been the dearth of explicit integration of the training literature and theory (e.g., Goldstein, 1991).

However, a few researchers have directly addressed interviewer training. Many of these have attempted to improve interviewer judgments by improving the quality of observation and evaluation (e.g., Dougherty, Ebert, & Callender, 1986; Maurer & Fay, 1988; Vance, Kuhnert, & Farr, 1978). The results of these studies have been ambiguous. The training employed by Vance et al. (1978) in a lab study (e.g., informing subjects of the types of rating errors and admonishing them to use the full scale) had no positive effect on rating accuracy. However, Dougherty et al. (1986) found that more extensive training involving job-related questions, rating scales, and practice interviews with feedback improved the interviewers' predictive validities. Likewise, Pulakos, Nee, and Kolmstetter (1995) found that an extensive interviewer training program improved rating accuracy.

Research concerning the effects of different types of training is rare. The studies reported by Gatewood, Lahiff, Deter, and Hargrove (1989) are an exception. In the first of two studies, Gatewood et al. investigated whether trained interviewers would use different characteristics of applicants when making decisions about acceptability for a position than would untrained interviewers. They found no difference between the trained and untrained interviewers in their sample of 23 recruiters. The trained/untrained status of the interviewers was assessed with self-report measures. In a second study, Gatewood et al. attempted to determine if different types of training would influence subsequent interviewer behaviors. Three different training approaches were used: One focused on the establishment of a warm and positive atmosphere for the interview, another focused on the development of better questions, and the final approach focused on the reduction of rating errors. The only difference among the different training conditions was in the manner in which interviewers trained to avoid rater errors conducted the interview. These interviewers asked more questions, talked more, and conducted longer interviews, all in an attempt to gather more information. Gatewood et al. suggest that this type of behavior, because it is generally unnatural in everyday interactions but specific to and crucial for interviews (i.e., direct and continued questioning of one party by another), is more easily changed than other interview behaviors that are not interview specific but common to other inter-personal interactions (e.g., developing rapport, evaluating others).

Generally, interviewer training research has not attended to the recruit-ment function, in which the interviewer presents information to the appli-cant so as to influence his or her job choice decision. Minor exceptions include some studies that have addressed interviewer behaviors that may be positively received by candidates, such as building rapport and the use of "icebreakers" (e.g., Motowidlo et al., 1992; Robertson, Gratton, & Rout, 1990; Roth & Campion, 1992). Barber, Hollenbeck, Tower, and Phillips (1994) found evidence that candidates are able to gather more information from single-purpose recruitment interviews than from interviews explicitly combining the selection and recruitment functions. However, the conduct of the selection interview itself can serve as an influence/recruitment tactic (Harris & Fink, 1987; Rynes, 1991). Further research is necessary to elaborate this issue fully and to investigate the interplay of the various "recruitment" and "selection" behaviors in the interview.

Some issues noted by Arvey and Campion (1982) and Dipboye (1992) remain unexplored. For example, what are the broader effects of interview training on interviewer behavior, and how does interviewer behavior influ-ence candidate behavior? Gatewood et al. (1989) suggest that it may be necessary to differentiate among those behaviors peculiar to interviews and those common to many other interpersonal activities. What are the best training methods and techniques? What is the long-term effectiveness of interview training? Do gains from training decay over time? Additional-ly, do interviewers maintain the new skills or modify them over time to adapt to changing demands (e.g., changes in the quality of the applicant pool) or to alleviate personal boredom (Dipboye, 1994)?

Practice

Practitioner-focused books do offer some evidence of the conflict in outcome agenda engendered by Sackett et al.'s (1989) discussion, in that interviewers and applicants may not necessarily wish to achieve the same outcomes. A palatable sense of a conflict with applicants, especially trained applicants, comes through in some of these books. A theme running throughout many of these books is the necessity for the interviewer to keep control of the interview. Pinkster (1991) notes that "once the inter-view starts, some candidates will immediately try to take control of the process. . . . you cannot lose control of the interview or else you will not find out the information you are seeking" (p. 91). This sentiment is echoed by Yate (1987), who describes the interview as a conversation and notes that "the person asking the questions in any conversation controls and directs its flow. As the interviewer . . . you should establish that control now" (p. 71). According to Yate, when applicants attempt to take control, it may be because they want to find "ways to hide vital information you [the interviewer] need or to direct the conversation away from your aims" (p. 71). There is an implied sense that the interviewer should not be outmaneuvered, because this may lead to a "false positive" decision desired by some applicants. As Bell (1989) comments, "What adds zest to the process, of course, is that a double game is being played" between interviewer and applicant (p. 12).

Many practitioner-oriented volumes take this sense of conflict a step further and explicitly acknowledge that interviewers may be dealing with trained applicants who are attempting to subvert the interview process and advance their own agendas. Fear (1984) notes that "trained applicants will make a subtle but immediate attempt to take charge of the interview" (p. 37), and the interviewer must recognize and resist such attempts. Smart (1989) has explicitly designed a program to thwart trained applicants by countering "canned" answers—answers that have been prepared in advance and that may allow the applicant to avoid disclosing negative information.

In summary, some general characterizations of the interviewer training literature are possible. For example, relatively few studies have directly addressed interview training, although it has been addressed tangentially in a number of studies. The selection function, as opposed to the recruitment function, is the primary emphasis of most of the extant research. The theories and research issues discussed in the training literature have not been explicitly integrated into the interviewing training literature. Finally, an investigation of the practice literature underscores an inherent conflict between interviewers and applicants as they struggle to gain control of the interview. This conflict has not been addressed by research.

Applicant Training

It is difficult to estimate the number of individuals who seek out training to improve their interview skills. One indication comes from a U.S. Department of Labor study that identified 8.4 million people who were displaced from their jobs between January 1993 and December 1995 (Gardner, 1996). Although it is impossible to be precise about how many people can be regarded as job applicants who might benefit from interview training, it is reasonable to say that there are large numbers of persons on a continuous basis who are potential beneficiaries of training.

Research

Campion and Campion (1987), Dipboye (1992), and Sackett et al. (1989) provide brief reviews of the literature in which the focus of interview training is on the applicant. By and large, applicant training research has dealt with very specialized and narrowly defined populations (e.g., the chronically unemployed/disadvantaged, substance abusers, prison inmates, the mentally or physically impaired, college and high school students). The generalizability of many of the findings of this research is a concern, given its reliance on specialized and narrowly defined populations. These are populations that may be lacking in job interview experience, knowledge, and past success, and that may be burdened by characteristics negatively valued by employers (e.g., record of drug abuse, prison record; Speas, 1979) but that must be overcome to achieve success in the employment interview. The emphasis has been on the acquisition of behaviors considered appropriate for the interview and the workplace. Many of these studies have also focused on appropriate nonverbal behaviors in the interview (Sigelman & Davis, 1978; Trent, 1987). Very few studies have investigated interview training for more mainstream applicants. This leads to uncertainties regarding the generalizability of these research findings to the broader job-seeking population.

Overall, applicant training has been studied in relatively few of the populations that could potentially benefit. Several other populations may benefit from further study; we note some of these below.

New entrants. The research literature addressing the population of new entrants to the workforce—those with very little work experience or interviewing experience (e.g., high school or college students)—has been limited (e.g., Hollandsworth, Dressel, & Stevens, 1977).

Homemakers. This group may consist of individuals returning to the workforce after absences of many years or entering the workforce essentially for the first time. Little of the interview training research has addressed this group specifically. An interesting possible line of research would be to investigate training that facilitates the translation of homemaking skills (e.g., time management, budgeting, conflict resolution) into terms that interviewers would readily recognize as applicable to the needs of their organizations.

Special needs populations. Special needs individuals may include potential applicants who in the past have been excluded from consideration due to various disabilities; the Americans With Disabilities Act of 1990 may facilitate the integration of some of these individuals into the workplace. Hayes, Citera, Brady, and Jenkins (1995) found that persons with disabilities perceived structured interviews to be less fair than did nondisabled individuals. They suggest that because structured interviews are built around job analyses for fully able incumbents and do not take into account applicant answers built around possible reasonable accommodation, structured interviews place disabled applicants at a disadvantage. Training of interviewers to appreciate a fuller range of appropriate responses may be warranted. Additionally, research is needed to guide applicant training so as to best prepare applicants for structured interview situations where their special needs may not have been accounted for in the development of questions and rating scales.

Experienced workers. Generally, experienced workers have not been studied, although the work of Campion and Campion (1987) represents a rare exception. They examined a mainstream work population (i.e., current employees eligible for internal transfer). Although the majority of subjects taking training indicated positive responses to it, and test scores indicated that they learned the training material, they did not receive more offers than those who did not participate in the training. It is possible that the actual work experiences of the candidates were much more important than interview performance as a factor in subsequent job offers.

In line with an emphasis on selection, the focus of much of this research is often upon improving some set of interview behaviors (e.g., head nods and voice quality), with the (presumed) goal of improving the likelihood of a job offer. Generally, this stream of research has assumed that these behaviors lead to interview success, although this has rarely been tested, and interview success has rarely been used as a direct criterion. The link between training and the acquisition of certain interview behaviors is well established (e.g., Dipboye, 1992; Sackett et al., 1989); however, the link between those behaviors and subsequent measures of interview success (e.g., job offers) has not been explored extensively. However, in practitioner-oriented books, the linkage between training and behavior acquisition, and between behavior acquisition and interview success, defined as job offers, is made more explicit. Job offers and employment are the criteria for practitioner-oriented books, as opposed to academic research, where the criterion is the acquisition of interviewing behaviors assumed to be of positive value.

Additionally, from the applicant's perspective, the information-gathering and evaluation function of the interview has not been addressed. Schwab, Rynes, and Aldag (1987) note that the broad job search process includes an evaluation component. However, there is little evidence that the development of analytic skills for evaluating prospective employers and job offers is emphasized in applicant interview training. Little attention has been given to the process whereby the applicant must gather information and evaluate the merits of a job offer and then decide to either accept or reject it. Eliciting job offers is seen as an end in itself and not as a means to an end. Perhaps research should examine the relative merits of training applicants to make better job choice decisions.

Practice

Although research has generally been concerned only with the applicant's ability to acquire certain behaviors presumed to lead to the narrow criterion of job offers, the practice literature does offer some emphasis on a broader range of job search imperatives. Many job seekers use how-to books to train themselves in interview preparation. The primary emphasis of this literature is on the applicant's presenting information, responding, and selling, as it relates to the interview's selection function. However, there is a subset of this literature, employing insights from career planning, personal development, and counseling, that also informs the applicant's ability to make job choices by addressing information-gathering and evaluation skills. Therefore, this literature can be partitioned into two distinct groups: answer-driven books and preparation-driven books.

Answer-driven books. Typically, answer-driven books provide general information on interviewing along with lists of interview questions and suggested answers. They are prescriptive, providing advice on how to answer specific interview questions and what to avoid saying (e.g., Allen, 1988; Camden, 1990; Hirsch, 1994; Kaufman & Corrigan, 1988; Komar, 1979; Medley, 1984; Morin & Cabrera, 1982; Ryan, 1994; Washington, 1995). They usually take a short-term approach (e.g., get a job now). To some extent it is unclear what these books have to say regarding interview score improvement, error reduction, and construct improvement (Sackett et al., 1989). Additionally, they raise very real concerns as to how poor performers are being trained—are they being trained to become good performers (a potentially win-win situation, with both the individual and the organization benefiting) or simply to be selected ("false positive"; a potentially long-term lose-lose situation)? Although none of the books sampled endorses lying, an ethical issue is raised. What is the best way to train and prepare poor performers? Underlying that question is a need to explore the reasons for poor performance and whether or not interview training is the most appropriate vehicle for addressing performance deficiencies.

Preparation-driven books. In contrast to answer-driven books, preparation-driven books encourage candidates to conduct self-assessment and then identify ways to answer interview questions. Some of these books should be described as career guides rather than interview training handbooks. Not only do they offer advice and training on how to get a job (e.g., preparing the best answers for expected questions), they take a more career-oriented approach, giving candidates guidance on self-assessment that can lead to the identification of appropriate career paths and the development of strategies to achieve their career goals, supplemented by training in the interview and other job search skills (e.g., Azrin & Besalel, 1982; Beatty, 1986; Caple, 1991; Green, 1996; Nadler, 1994). Preparation-driven books encourage candidates to provide honest, insightful answers to interview questions. More so than answer-driven books, they attempt to help candidates develop the skills necessary for a lifelong series of career progressions.

Both approaches attempt to help those with the potential for satisfactory job performance achieve "hits" and avoid "misses." The difference between the two may lie in the advice offered to applicants who may ultimately be evaluated as poor performers once they are on the job. The answer-driven books may be attempting to increase "false positives" and decrease "correct rejections," whereas the preparation-driven books may be attempting to change candidates fundamentally from poor performers to good performers, thus transforming a "correct rejection" into a "hit." Additionally, and somewhat paradoxically, the preparation-driven books may also be attempting to increase correct rejections. Although this may appear to be at odds with the criterion of getting the candidate a job offer, it makes sense if one considers the focus to be on getting the "right" job offer. These two approaches may have differential impacts on the validity of subsequent interviews (Sackett et al., 1989). The answer-driven approach may have a negative impact on the interview's validity (e.g., through impression management tactics that mask job deficiencies), whereas the preparation-driven approach may improve validity by training candidates in career-relevant skills and helping them achieve person-job and person-career fit (Holland, 1985; Kristof, 1996).

There is some confusion in the literature as to the purpose of applicant training. Is the intent to reduce error of measurement, or to produce false positive selection decisions? Stevens and Kristof (1995) examined the impression management tactics of candidates and their impact on interview success. In part, their study was motivated by a desire to test the advice of popular press books that suggest various impression management techniques (e.g., Medley, 1984). They found some evidence to support the generalizability of earlier laboratory studies (e.g., Gilmore & Ferris, 1989): Such impression management tactics may be influencing interview validity, possibly producing false positive selection decisions.

Finally, although it is often more muted than depicted in the practitioner-oriented interviewer training books, there is still a sense of a fundamental conflict between interviewers and applicants. Figler (1988) notes that there may even be a danger in the applicant's approaching the interview as a contest as opposed to a problem-solving conversation conducted with a prospective employer and aimed at achieving a mutually satisfying outcome. Medley (1984) emphasizes the need for applicant honesty and candor. However, Faux (1985), in her advice to applicants for executive positions, explicitly acknowledges the role of conflict and the need to control the interview. She notes that "the success of the executive interview depends upon your ability to psych out the person interviewing you" (p. 83).

In summary, some general characterizations of the applicant training literature are possible. For example, most of the extant research has investigated narrowly defined populations of job seekers, which calls into question the generalizability of much of the research. The major focus of research is upon the selection function and the acquisition of behaviors that will enhance the applicant's chances of being selected. The importance of certain interview behaviors is generally assumed, but more needs to be done to establish the relationship between applicant behaviors and interviewer reactions and subsequent decisions. A subset of the practice literature (i.e., preparation-driven books) attempts to integrate interview training into the broader areas of job search and career development. Finally, a sense of inherent conflict between interviewers and applicants is evident in the practice literature, although it is generally downplayed or ignored in the extant research.

Recommendations for Future Research

There does appear to be an inherent conflict in the interview between the agendas of the interviewer and the applicant. This conflict is most explicitly addressed in the practitioner literature. Research is needed to examine how this inherent conflict influences the value of the interview as a selection device and recruiting tool, and whether it is in the best interest of the applicant's job search process.

Much of the research to date has been concerned primarily with the selection function of the employment interview, where the influence and information path moves from the candidate to the interviewer. The emphasis has been upon the applicant's presenting information and the interviewer's gathering and evaluating information. In the strict sense of a structured selection interview, the interviewer is trying to gather the most reliable and valid information. At the same time, the applicant is attempting to influence the interviewer's information-gathering and decision-making process. The key notion is that *when the interviewer is trying to evaluate objectively, the applicant is trying to sell; and when the applicant is trying to evaluate objectively, the interviewer is trying to sell.* This essential conflict is not removed when organizations explicitly separate the interview process into a recruitment phase (e.g., initial campus visit, job fairs) and a selection phase (e.g., plant visits). If anything, the conflict is set in stark relief because all that remains is either one or the other path of potential conflict (i.e., either the interviewer is selling or the applicant is selling).

It is clear that interviewers and applicants have different goals, motivations, and approaches to the selection interview. As such, it is possible that the training of interviewers and applicants to improve performance in the interview may have different emphases. For example, interviewers may be trained to be objective, whereas applicants may be trained in how best to present themselves. This asymmetrical dynamic implicit in the interview process is reflected to some degree in the practitioner literature, but it is ignored in the academic literature.

Is there a fundamental ethical issue that needs to be addressed, or does this simply reflect the give-and-take of a buyer-seller relationship, where both parties need to be prepared to exercise due caution as each attempts to maximize his or her outcomes? Bostwick (1981) notes that "the interviewer/applicant relationship is like a looking glass showing the reverse image of the same subject" (p. 220). We have found no studies that have specifically examined the interaction of applicant and interviewer training. Do they cancel each other out, or do they lead to a more reliable, valid, acceptable, and successful interview for both parties?

Additionally, the purpose of the interview and potentially of interview training need not be limited to a selection or a recruitment function. Not only do interviews serve the potentially conflicting purposes of selection and recruitment, they may also be used by organizations as a form of socialization, as opportunities to advise job candidates, and for internal political reasons (Dipboye, 1992, 1994). Taking a broader perspective may illuminate other areas of potential synergy and conflict in training agendas and objectives.

Further, there should be a recruiting- or persuasion-oriented component to interviewer training. This notion is suggested by the thrust of the applicant training literature and is thus an example of one literature informing another. This has been neglected in the past; the sole emphasis has been on increasing validity. This is especially important given the tightening job market and the demonstrated utility of having the "best" candidate actually accept the job offer (Murphy, 1986). Research is needed to determine if this should be part of the training and whether it would actually increase job acceptance rates.

We also need to know more about the effectiveness of applicant training. Regarding the interviewer, research has shown that training can improve the implementation of interview structure, which in turn improves the reliability and validity of the interview (Campion et al., 1997). However, no corresponding claims can be made for applicant training, for two reasons. First, the findings from past studies on special populations may not generalize to mainstream or experienced candidates. Second, more thought needs to be given to criteria used to measure effectiveness. Research has shown that candidates can readily be trained to acquire certain behaviors (e.g., Sackett et al., 1989); however, measures of these same behaviors are then typically used as surrogates for interview effectiveness. The criteria of interview success need to be reevaluated and their linkages to trainable behaviors investigated. Regarding behaviors, we also need to know more about what behaviors are positively and negatively interpreted by interviewers and applicants within the context of the employment interview. For example, do more appropriate nonverbal behaviors (e.g., eye

Table 19.1 Criteria for the Evaluation of Commercially Available Training Programs

1. Was a needs analysis conducted?
2. Is the content of the training driven by learning objectives?
3. Do course contents reflect the components of a good selection system?
   Job analysis
   Legal guidelines
   Use of structured interviews
   Instruction on rating
   Modeling followed by skill demonstration
   Tests of learning
4. Are course contents based on research?
5. Does the provider furnish evidence of validity?
6. Is there evidence of training effectiveness?
7. Does the program contribute to broad organizational objectives?

contact) translate into more job offers? Also, research is needed to examine what kinds of training are most effective (e.g., answer-driven training versus preparation-driven training).

Finally, more research is needed that integrates the interview training literature and the broader training literature. As we have noted, very little of the interviewer training research has addressed the issue of identifying the effectiveness of a training intervention. However, the application of mainstream training research may, for example, help in identifying important professional criteria for the evaluation of commercially available programs. Such criteria are listed in Table 19.1, which incorporates insights from the training literature (e.g., Kirkpatrick, 1983; Leibler & Parkman, 1992; Mager, 1984; Robinson & Robinson, 1989; Stolovitch & Keeps, 1992). Given the number of potential users of interview training and the vast array of training options available, paying greater attention to the evaluation of training effectiveness appears warranted. The integration of training theories and methodologies should inform future interview training research and designs.

References

Allen, J. G. (1988). *The complete Q&A job interview book.* New York: John Wiley.

Arvey, R. D., & Campion, J. E. (1982). The employment interview: A summary and review of recent research. *Personnel Psychology, 35,* 281-322.

Azrin, N. H., & Besalel, V. (1982). *Finding a job.* Berkeley, CA: Ten Speed.

Barber, A. E., Hollenbeck, J. R., Tower, S. L., & Phillips, J. M. (1994). The effects of interview focus on recruitment effectiveness: A field experiment. *Journal of Applied Psychology, 79,* 886-896.

Beatty, R. H. (1986). *The five-minute interview.* New York: John Wiley.

Bell, A. H. (1989). *The complete manager's guide to interviewing: How to hire the best.* Homewood, IL: Dow Jones/Irwin.

Bostwick, B. E. (1981). *111 proven techniques and strategies for getting the job interview.* New York: John Wiley.

Camden, T. M. (1990). *The job hunter's final exam.* Chicago: Surrey.

Campion, M. A., & Campion, J. E. (1987). Evaluation of an interview skills training program in a natural field experiment. *Personnel Psychology, 40,* 675-691.

Campion, M. A., Palmer, D. K., & Campion, J. E. (1997). A review of structure in the selection interview. *Personnel Psychology, 50,* 655-702.

Caple, J. (1991). *The ultimate interview.* Garden City, NY: Doubleday.

Dipboye, R. L. (1992). *Selection interviews: Process perspectives.* Cincinnati, OH: South-Western.

Dipboye, R. L. (1994). Structured and unstructured selection interviews: Beyond the job-fit model. In G. R. Ferris (Ed.), *Research in personnel and human resources management* (Vol. 12, pp. 79-123). Greenwich, CT: JAI.

Dougherty, T. W., Ebert, R. J., & Callender, J. C. (1986). Policy capturing in the employment interview. *Journal of Applied Psychology, 71,* 9-15.

Eder, R. W., & Buckley, M. R. (1988). The employment interview: An interactionist perspective. In G. R. Ferris & K. M. Rowland (Eds.), *Research in personnel and human resource management* (Vol. 6, pp. 75-107). Greenwich, CT: JAI.

Faux, M. (1985). *The executive interview.* New York: St. Martin's.

Fear, R. A. (1984). *The evaluation interview.* New York: McGraw-Hill.

Figler, H. (1988). *The complete job-search handbook: All the skills you need to get any job and have a good time doing it* (Rev. ed.). New York: Henry Holt.

Gardner, J. (1996, August 22). *Worker displacement during the mid-1990's.* Washington, DC: U.S. Department of Labor, Bureau of Labor Statistics.

Gatewood, R., Lahiff, J., Deter, R., & Hargrove, L. (1989). Effects of training on behaviors of the selection interview. *Journal of Business Communication, 26,* 17-31.

Gilmore, D. C., & Ferris, G. R. (1989). The effects of applicant impression management tactics on interviewer judgments. *Journal of Management, 15,* 557-564.

Goldstein, I. L. (1991). Training in organizations. In M. D. Dunnette & L. M. Hough (Eds.), *Handbook of industrial and organizational psychology* (2nd ed., Vol. 2, pp. 507-619). Palo Alto, CA: Consulting Psychologists Press.

Green, P. C. (1996). *Get hired! Winning strategies to ace the interview.* Austin, TX: Bard.

Harris, M. M., & Fink, L. S. (1987). A field study of applicant reactions to employment opportunities: Does the recruiter make a difference? *Personnel Psychology, 40,* 765-784.

Hayes, T. L., Citera, M., Brady, L. M., & Jenkins, N. M. (1995). Staffing for persons with disabilities: What is "fair" and "job related"? *Public Personnel Management, 24,* 413-427.

Hirsch, A. S. (1994). *Interviewing.* New York: John Wiley.

Holland, J. L. (1985). *Making vocational choices: A theory of careers* (2nd ed.). Englewood Cliffs, NJ: Prentice Hall.

Hollandsworth, J. G., Jr., Dressel, M. E., & Stevens, J. (1977). Use of behavioral versus traditional procedures for increasing job interview skills. *Journal of Counseling Psychology, 24,* 503-510.

Howard, G. S., Dailey, P. R., & Gulanick, N. A. (1979). The feasibility of informed pretests in attenuating response-shift bias. *Applied Psychological Measurement, 3,* 481-494.

Kaufman, P. C., & Corrigan, A. (1988). *No nonsense interviewing: How to get the job you want.* Stamford, CT: Longmeadow.

Kirkpatrick, D. A. (1983). *A practical guide for supervisory training and development* (2nd ed.). Reading, MA: Addison-Wesley.

Komar, J. J. (1979). *The interview game: Winning strategies for the job seeker.* Chicago: Follett.

Kristof, A. L. (1996). Person-organization fit: An integrative review of its conceptualizations, measurement, and implications. *Personnel Psychology, 49,* 1-49.

Leibler, S. N., & Parkman, A. W. (1992). Personnel selection. In H. D. Stolovitch & E. J. Keeps (Eds.), *Handbook of human performance technology: A comprehensive guide for analyzing and solving performance problems in organizations* (pp. 259-276). San Francisco: Jossey-Bass.

Mager, R. F. (1984). *Preparing instructional objectives* (Rev. ed.). Belmont, CA: Lake.

Maurer, S. D., & Fay, C. (1988). Effects of situational interviews, conventional structured interviews, and training on interview rating agreement: An experimental analysis. *Personnel Psychology, 41,* 329-345.

Medley, H. A. (1984). *Sweaty palms: The neglected art of being interviewed.* Berkeley, CA: Ten Speed.

Morin, W. J., & Cabrera, J. C. (1982). *Parting company: How to survive the loss of a job and find another successfully.* San Diego, CA: Harvest.

Motowidlo, S. J., Carter, G. W., Dunnette, M. D., Tippins, N., Werner, S., Burnett, J. R., & Vaughan, M. J. (1992). Studies of the structured behavioral interview. *Journal of Applied Psychology, 77,* 571-587.

Murphy, K. R. (1986). When your top choice turns you down: Effect of rejected offers on the utility of selection tests. *Psychological Bulletin, 99,* 133-138.

Nadler, B. J. (1994). *Naked at the interview: Tips and quizzes to prepare you for your first real job.* New York: John Wiley.

Pinkster, R. J. (1991). *Hiring winners: Profile, interview, evaluate: A 3-step formula for success.* New York: AMACOM.

Pulakos, E. D., Nee, M. T., & Kolmstetter, E. B. (1995, May). Effects of training and individual differences on interviewer rating accuracy. In E. B. Kolmstetter (Chair), *Interviewer and contextual factors that make a difference in interviewer validity.* Symposium conducted at the annual meeting of the Society for Industrial and Organizational Psychology, Orlando, FL.

Robertson, I. T., Gratton, L., & Rout, U. (1990). The validity of situational interviews for administrative jobs. *Journal of Organizational Behavior, 11,* 69-76.

Robinson, D. G., & Robinson, J. C. (1989). *Training for impact: How to link training to business needs and measure the results.* San Francisco: Jossey-Bass.

Roth, P. L., & Campion, J. E. (1992). An analysis of the predictive power of the panel interview and pre-employment tests. *Journal of Occupational and Organizational Psychology, 65,* 51-60.

Ryan, R. (1994). *60 seconds and you're hired!* Manassas Park, VA: Impact.

Rynes, S. L. (1991). Recruitment, job choice, and post-hire consequences: A call for new research directions. In M. D. Dunnette & L. M. Hough (Eds.), *Handbook of industrial and organizational psychology* (2nd ed., Vol. 2, pp. 399-444). Palo Alto, CA: Consulting Psychologists Press.

Sackett, P. R., Burris, L. R., & Ryan, A. M. (1989). Coaching and practice effects in personnel selection. In C. L. Cooper & I. T. Robertson (Eds.), *International review of industrial and organizational psychology* (Vol. 4, pp. 145-183). New York: John Wiley.

Schwab, D. P., Rynes, S. L., & Aldag, R. J. (1987). Theories and research on job search and choice. In K. M. Rowland & G. R. Ferris (Eds.), *Research in personnel and human resources management* (Vol. 5, pp. 129-166). Greenwich, CT: JAI.

Sigelman, C. K., & Davis, P. J. (1978). Making good impressions in job interviews: Verbal and nonverbal predictors. *Education and Training of the Mentally Retarded, 13,* 71-77.

Smart, B. D. (1989). *The smart interviewer.* New York: John Wiley.

Speas, C. M. (1979). Job-seeking interview skills training: A comparison of four instructional techniques. *Journal of Counseling Psychology, 26,* 405-412.

Stevens, C. K., & Kristof, A. L. (1995). Making the right impression: A field study of applicant impression management during job interviews. *Journal of Applied Psychology, 80,* 587-606.

Stolovitch, H. D., & Keeps, E. J. (Eds.). (1992). *Handbook of human performance technology: A comprehensive guide for analyzing and solving performance problems in organizations.* San Francisco: Jossey-Bass.

Trent, S. D. (1987). The importance of social skills in the employment interview. *Education of the Visually Handicapped, 19,* 7-18.

Vance, R. J., Kuhnert, K. W., & Farr, J. L. (1978). Interview judgments: Using external criteria to compare behavioral and graphic scale ratings. *Organizational Behavior and Human Performance, 22,* 279-294.

Washington, T. (1995). *Interview power: Selling yourself face to face.* Bellevue, WA: Mount Vernon.

Who's learning what? (1996, October). *Training, 33,* 53-65.

Wonderlic, E. F. (1942). Improving interview techniques. *Personnel, 18,* 232-238.

Yate, M. J. (1987). *Hiring the best: A manager's guide to effective interviewing.* Boston: Bob Adams.

Part V

Commentary on Theory,
Research, and Practice

20

The Current and Future Status of Research on the Employment Interview

Neal Schmitt

Researchers have recognized for a long time that the employment interview serves two primary purposes from the point of view of the organization. First, the organization uses the interview to assess the knowledge, skills, and abilities and the degree of fit of job applicants to the positions it is seeking to fill. Second, the organization may use the interview to recruit applicants and to contribute to the socialization of newcomers. The applicant, likewise, is seeking to find a job that he or she finds attractive and to convince the organization that he or she can fill that job. These distinctions among the various purposes the interview serves are important, because it does not seem possible to integrate research and theory across purposes very well. Theories and research that seem to explain behavior in the interview from one of these perspectives are not as relevant when one of the other perspectives is considered. In this handbook, the various contributors provide summaries of research and theory directed to all of these perspectives.

This volume on the employment interview also represents several different research streams that have been pursued sequentially, but sometimes concurrently. In the first four sections of this chapter, I address what

355

I believe to be the central questions in these four different historical periods. In the succeeding two sections, I address the possibilities afforded by a consideration of the interview as an organizational intervention and research on the role of the interview in determining what happens in the interview and as a result of the interview.

The bulk of the research on the employment interview has been directed toward assessing the degree to which the interview provides an adequate assessment of human talent. In my view, this literature can be divided into four phases. Early research was directed toward the assessment of the outcomes associated with the employment interview, and most of that research indicated that the interview is a relatively deficient selection tool. Inter-interviewer reliability was inconsistent across studies and often very low, and validities were almost always found to be near zero (Ulrich & Trumbo, 1965; Wagner, 1949). The second phase of the research was launched to investigate why the interview should produce such deficient outcomes. Highly influential in initiating this research was the work of Webster (1964), who first began researching issues that are still being addressed by contributors to this volume (e.g., Dougherty & Turban, Chapter 12; Kacmar & Young, Chapter 13). Social and cognitive psychological theory have been used to explain a variety of behaviors in the employment interview. The third phase of interview research was oriented toward the improvement of the employment interview. Representative of this effort are the contributions to this handbook by Maurer, Sue-Chan, and Latham (Chapter 9) and Motowidlo (Chapter 10). The next phase of this research, which I believe we are just beginning, seems to be concerned with discovering what constructs are and can be measured in the employment interview. Ulrich and Trumbo (1965) suggested more than 30 years ago that the interview could be used most successfully to assess motivation and interpersonal skills. Three chapters in this volume (Binning, LeBreton, & Adorno, Chapter 6; Parsons, Cable, & Liden, Chapter 7; Harris, Chapter 8) are directed toward a concern for the nature of the constructs measured in the interview.

Assessment of Talent

Eder, Kacmar, and Ferris (1989) cite nine qualitative reviews that are mostly devoted to summarizing the literature on the reliability and validity of the interview. In Chapter 2 of this volume, Buckley and Russell provide an integration of seven meta-analytic reviews of the literature. In some ways, the results of this research are clear. Structured interviews provide validities that are useful and that rival the best of alternative selection procedures, and unstructured interviews are of much less practical value. Buckley and Russell argue convincingly, however, that there is a need for additional primary research on the validity of the interview. Most of the questions they raise concern the context of the interview (see Eder, Chapter 11, this volume, for similar arguments) and the fact that the interview is many times only a small part of the selection system and should be studied as such. I also believe that their plea for a reexamination of the primary research that constitutes the meta-analytic database should be heeded. Much of the database on interview validities, as well as the validities of other procedures, is based on articles and technical reports that were written several decades ago. Buckley and Russell note that qualitative reviews often report results of research absent of any criticism of the research. This may often be true as well of meta-analytic research, in which efforts seem to be directed only at getting an estimate of an effect size and perhaps coding several moderators. One often suspects that there has been little in-depth consideration of the way in which the primary studies that are the source of the data were conducted. Nor does the typical meta-analytic report include much effort to describe observations about the quality of the primary research. Fortunately, good, but certainly not flawless, studies of the validity of interviews continue to be conducted (e.g., Campion, Pursell, & Brown, 1988; Latham & Saari, 1984; Latham & Skarlicki, 1995; Pulakos & Schmitt, 1995).

Social and Cognitive Influences on Interview Outcomes

As indicated above, the social and decision-making approaches to the study of interviews appear to have been stimulated by the need to understand why interviews were not valid and reliable. This body of literature is difficult to evaluate. Certainly the interview provides a wonderful real-world context in which to assess social and cognitive theories. However, the payback from these "microanalytic" studies is unclear. After 20 years of research on the role of confirmatory biases in interviews, Dougherty and Turban (Chapter 12, this volume) are still forced to conclude somewhat tentatively that the results suggest that preinterview impressions do influence interviewers' questioning strategies when interviewers are allowed to generate their own questions. They also offer an interesting hypothesis and a reason this research seems so confusing. They suggest that confirmatory bias of moderate nature may actually result in better decisions and incremental validity. Some skepticism and questioning on the part of the interviewer may allow him or her to gain better information about a candidate, whereas a completely closed mind will filter all new information and a completely open mind about the applicant will leave the interviewer open to the "marketing" skills of the applicant. Dougherty and Turban also make the important observation that the interview is one small part of an overall process that often includes several other data-gathering and presentation events, so that the confirmatory questioning that takes place in the interview may realistically account for a very small portion of the variance in the interview outcomes most often studied (i.e., acceptance or rejection of candidates, validity and reliability of judgments).

The situation appears to be the same with respect to the role of negative information in the interview. Bolster and Springbett (1961) first pointed to the importance of negative information in interviews. Although subsequent research has confirmed that negative information is more likely than positive information to influence interviewer decision making, the reason this is true and its impact on interview reliability and validity have not been ascertained. In Chapter 13 of this handbook, Kacmar and Young describe ways in which negative information might work and provide an interesting analysis of how applicants might communicate negative information inadvertently.

Perhaps the most recent effort in this regard is the work on individual differences in interviewer validity and reliability summarized by Graves and Karren in Chapter 14. In this instance, too, the data are not clear, nor do the effects appear to be large. Documentation that there are individual differences in validity demands that each interviewer in the study conduct a large number of interviews. Given that this is rarely the case in most studies and organizations, an alternate explanation for what appear to be large individual differences is sampling error, as was the case in the Pulakos and Schmitt (1996) study. The existence of theory or hypotheses about the nature of individual differences and how they might affect the validity and reliability of the interviews conducted would alleviate some of the demand for very large sample sizes. Dipboye and Jackson's discussion of experience in Chapter 15 is relevant in this regard, in that one certainly should expect that experience would have some influence on the manner in which interviews are conducted and the quality of the outcomes of those interviews. Dipboye and Jackson also differentiate between aspects of interviewers' experience and speculate on the mechanisms by which experience may affect interview outcomes. Graves and Karren provide a large list of potential cognitive processing variables that might represent important individual difference variables; good qualitative information-processing research such as they describe might serve to shorten their list. With a better sense of variability across interviewers in these cognitive processes, a researcher might narrow the focus of interest to cut down the data collection burden inherent in the study of individual differences in interviewer outcomes.

The research on discrimination in interviews seems to have advanced the most in terms of the quality of research, based on the review provided by Roehling, Campion, and Arvey in Chapter 3 of this volume. Researchers are relying less on "paper people" studies and are becoming much more sophisticated in the development of realistic research scenarios and the manipulation of independent variables (e.g., Pingitore, Dugoni, Tindale, & Spring, 1994). Moreover, there seem to be some generalizable results across studies of sex, race, and weight bias. Specifically, main effects do not seem to occur, or, when they do, they do not account for large portions of the variance in interview outcomes. There does seem to be interaction among the type of job, the information presented, the potential bias factors, and maybe the interviewer (or the context) that produces biased interview decisions. What is most generalizable, then, is the subtlety of bias effects.

Improving the Interview

Over the past 15 years, and even since the first collection of work on the employment interview (Eder & Ferris, 1989), there have been dramatic improvements in what seems to be achievable in terms of reliability and validity. If we were to give someone advice about how to develop and conduct interviews, there would be several rules. First, develop a structured interview in which all applicants are asked the same questions. Second, base these questions on a job analysis and direct them toward the gathering of job-relevant information. Third, provide the interviewers with rating scales that are anchored with what are determined to be good and bad answers to the interview questions. Fourth, use multiple interviewers who have to discuss their judgments of candidates and perhaps be accountable to the other interviewers for their ratings of candidates. Fifth, provide interviewer training that includes explanation of the purposes of the interview, information on some common sources of error and how to avoid those errors, and explanation of the questions and ratings required. Most of these elements, if not all, are present in studies when the interview is considered structured. As indicated above, the validity of structured interviews is markedly superior to that of unstructured interviews and rivals that of the most valid selection procedures.

Interestingly, these improvements probably minimize or eliminate the effects of various social, cognitive, and individual difference factors discussed in the preceding section. Whether by design or, as I suspect, inadvertently, these improvements have served to address the idiosyncrasies of the unstructured interview that led to the inconsistencies in judgment derived from unstructured interviews and to low reliability and validity. In effect, these improvements may have addressed the "biases" recognized by the "microanalytic" efforts described in the previous section.

We do not know which of the "improvements" minimizes which of the "biases," but we do know that cumulatively these improvements result in a superior product. We also do not know precisely which of the improvements listed above produces the superior reliability or validity. This is why the efforts of Motowidlo (Chapter 10) and Maurer et al. (Chapter 9) in this volume are important, though difficult. Maurer et al. seek to uncover what accounts for differences across studies in the validity of situational interviews (SI) and, in some cases, differences between SIs and patterned behavior description interviews (PBDIs). The existing body of literature includes studies with a large variety of operationalizations of these two interview types; isolating the specific factor or factors that produced the differences within and across interview types is nearly impossible. Maurer et al. assert that three features are critical to the success of SIs: the use of questions that represent dilemmas for which there are no clearly socially desirable answers, the use of rating guides by the interviewers, and the requirement that ratings be done after each interview question. It is also not clear which of these attributes, or combination of attributes, is responsible for the improved validity of the interview based on the existing research base.

Motowidlo addresses a much narrower question about comparable interview techniques, namely, whether past-oriented or intention-based questions yield superior validity. It appears to be true that past-oriented, experience-based questions are superior, though again the four studies reviewed probably differed on other dimensions as well. Motowidlo also argues logically that intention-based questions should have lower validity. These questions require that intentions be stable and that subsequent behavior be under volitional control. Although the data do not exist to answer definitively the questions posed in Chapters 9 and 10, they are very important questions, both theoretically and practically. Maurer et al. and Motowidlo reach conclusions that are at least in indirect contradiction. Because SIs and PBDIs differ on dimensions other than question format, we do not know the extent of the contradiction in the conclusions reached.

What Constructs Are Measured in the Interview?

It is perhaps amazing that much of the research on selection procedure validity focuses on the validity of particular procedures (e.g., biodata, interviews, personality tests). A far more central issue is the degree to which the interview, or any other procedure, can provide valid assessments of particular constructs. Does the interview provide valid assessments of motivation, social skills, cognitive ability, physical ability, and so forth? If we do not consider the question this way, it is equivalent to saying that it does not matter what questions are asked in the interview. In Chapter 8 of this handbook, Harris refers to the same disturbing conclusion, but then develops the proposition that the interview may represent a measure of a person's ability to engage in one-on-one conversation, with no reference to the topics addressed in that conversation. Recently, there has been more attention to the nature of the constructs assessed in the interview, and it is important that chapters on personality, work values, and constructs in general have been included in this volume.

In Chapter 6, Binning et al. present a number of interesting propositions. First, there is the idea that the interview be used to explore in more depth personality scores that have been produced by a standardized personality test and that have attracted an interviewer's attention for some reason. I think the interview can also be used, and has been used, to assess job-related personality or work styles directly. When the dimensions assessed in interview research are mentioned, they almost always include concepts associated with personality (dependability, cooperation, motivation, and so on). Binning et al. suggest that the interviewer be left some latitude to explore questions that he or she has about the candidate and that the interview be structured around the personality constructs assessed in the entire selection process. The interview would be part of an attempt to "triangulate" and gather information from multiple sources in an effort to resolve discrepancies or uncertainties. This approach is very different from the typical structured interview and may actually serve as a means to confirm or disconfirm the confirmation biases discussed by Dougherty and Turban in Chapter 12 of this volume. It places a great deal of control and burden on the interviewer to understand the relevant constructs and the information provided by various sources. It also demands that the interviewer have a great deal of ability to probe for information that the applicant may not want to reveal. This kind of interview should heighten the importance of individual differences in the skill and training of interviewers. Binning et al. also challenge the research that supports the use of highly structured and standardized interview questions.

In Chapter 7, Parsons et al. propose the use of the interview to assess work values and the degree to which the candidates' values fit organizational demands and culture. They point to the need to establish that interviewers actually assess fit or can be trained to assess fit; the emphasis in most of the chapters in this book is on the degree to which interviewers can assess work-related skills. Both Binning et al. and Parsons et al. suggest the use of outcome measures other than job performance. Worker satisfaction, withdrawal behavior, and organizational citizenship behavior are more relevant outcome variables if the target constructs in an interview are correlates of these variables.

In Chapter 8, Harris discusses the notion that the structured interview approximates, or can be constructed to approximate, an orally administered cognitive ability test. This notion originates with Campion et al.'s (1988) findings that the interview is related to scores on several employment aptitude tests and that the interview does not add incrementally to the prediction of performance ratings beyond these tests. These are not typical findings; the low correlations between tests and interviews reported by Pulakos and Schmitt (1996) are much more common. However, the controversy suggests that we should pay much more attention to the relationship between interview ratings and measures of relatively well-known constructs. These "marker" variables may provide a great deal of information about what is or is not (as Harris concludes is true of cognitive ability) being measured in the interview as well as what biases one might expect.

An important research question is whether interviewers can be trained to assess specific constructs in interviews and whether they can simultaneously assess more than one construct. Campion et al. (1988) emphasize the importance of distinguishing between motivation and ability interviews. In addition, the fact that interview ratings are typically so highly intercorrelated that researchers simply combine them to produce a single interview score suggests that interviewers cannot provide more than global assessments of single abilities. This may also be a function of the fact that researchers have rarely thought in construct terms and have never tried to establish a degree of discriminant validity with respect to interview rating dimensions. Establishing what should be measured and then assessing whether it was in fact measured may contribute to progress in understanding the interview. It may even provide a basis upon which to assess the contributions and meanings of the social and cognitive microanalytic research approaches if researchers also include measures of the hypothesized biases in their studies of interviews (Schmitt, 1994). The overwhelming conclusion with respect to all three chapters on the constructs measured in the interview is that we have not come a great distance since Ulrich and Trumbo (1965) concluded their review of the interview literature with the guess that the interview best measures interpersonal skills and motivation.

The Interview as an Intervention

Several authors in this volume, but especially Eder (Chapter 11) and Maurer et al. (Chapter 9), discuss the role of the context in which the interview is used. Maurer et al. examine in detail the reasons organizational personnel might not use situational interviews in spite of evidence regarding their efficacy and allude to data that indicate some interviewers do not like the structure that is imposed on them in the typical SI or PBDI. Moreover, I have had similar experiences with interviewers who have favorite questions or who simply want to talk with applicants. In one organization, I even established a system of audiotaping and monitoring to ensure that interviewers were following an interview protocol. This research and my own observations suggest that we should give much more attention to the implementation and survival of the structured interview. This means we must begin to treat the interview as an organizational intervention and study its introduction to an organization and then assess the degree to which established procedures are changed to accommodate individual interviewer preferences or organizational demands. Much about structured interviews can easily be changed, and as the user group is extended to individuals who were not instrumental in its development, it is almost certain that this intervention will decay or be modified in important ways. The degree to which we understand the centrality of certain aspects of the interview process (see Maurer et al., Chapter 9; Motowidlo, Chapter 10) becomes extremely important in this circumstance.

Johns (1993) has examined the innovation-diffusion process for personnel practices in general, and his work suggests both research questions and practical solutions to the problems surrounding the use and durability of structured interview technologies. He points to the fact that industrial/organizational psychologists, in particular, are convinced that the technical merits of interventions will win the day. However, interventions are more often adopted because "someone else does it that way" or because of environmental threats, governmental regulation (see Roehling et al., Chapter 3, this volume, for an excellent discussion of EEO considerations in the use of the interview), and political processes internal to the organization. Johns also maintains that personnel practices are viewed as administrative rather than technical innovations by managers and as such are viewed as matters of management "style" as opposed to technical improvements in personnel practices. Viewed in this way, a structured interview will be relatively more difficult to implement in an organization that gives its employees a great deal of latitude with respect to how they do their work. Moreover, the rather rigid structured interview may be incongruent with an open, friendly, nonbureaucratic climate. The negative reaction to the structured interview reported by some researchers is predictable in such an environment. Certainly also, ignoring the social context within the organization jeopardizes the implementation and fidelity of use of innovations. Anyone who has attempted to implement any innovation in an organization knows how important it is to have a strong and knowledgeable internal organizational ally.

These issues have been ignored by researchers in personnel selection in general, but they are particularly important to the interview because it is so vulnerable to changes that can destroy its efficacy. Our validation studies are most often completed prior to implementation. In fact, they are used to convince organizational personnel of the worth of our efforts. What we need are studies of the long-term efficacy of the interview that document how this intervention is actually used or adapted to meet the idiosyncrasies of the organization.

The Role of the Interviewee

To this point, the discussion has centered on the effectiveness of the interview in identifying organizational talent. A second area of research has been directed toward the study of the applicant or interviewee. In Chapter 4 of this volume, Gilliland and Steiner detail a series of propositions concerning the role that justice perceptions might play in applicants' reactions to the interview. Adoption of the justice framework provides a very large number of researchable issues as well as suggestions for ways to improve applicant reactions. Perhaps the most consistent finding in the relatively small body of literature in this area is that applicants do not react well to highly structured interviews. This may be due to the evaluation apprehension inherent in the interview situation, but it also seems to be a function of the applicant's feeling of lessened control and opportunity to present a case for his or her talents, or even a means by which the applicant's challenges to the system are made less credible (Latham & Finnegan, 1993). On a number of dimensions (consistency of adminis-tration, face validity), the justice perspective would predict that applicants should have positive reactions to SIs and PBDIs. The potential for negative reactions to unstructured interviews is also high and has been documented in an interesting manner by Gilliland (1995).

Probably my most significant reaction to the research on applicant reactions to the interview is that the interview may be only a relatively small part of a larger process in which the individual is attracted and recruited by an organization (Rynes, 1993). This process very likely begins with the recruit's overall image of the organization and changes to an increasingly differentiated view of the organizational and job characteristics that may motivate the acceptance of a job and subsequent job behavior. To some extent, the same can be said of the organization's selection of a person, but in that case, one can usually isolate the point of decision, and one has a quantitative appraisal of the applicant's performance in various aspects of the selection process. Applicant decisions and impressions cannot usually be attributed to a single aspect of the recruitment and selection process. This suggests the need for longitudinal research in which data collection is timed to occur in close proximity to particular key events—most relevant to this chapter, the conduct of the employment interview. A longitudinal data collection effort of this type would allow for the assessment of mean change in impressions as well as changes in the reaction construct itself (Golembiewski, Billingsley, & Yeager, 1976; Millsap & Hartog, 1988).

Three chapters in this book (Jablin, Miller, & Sias, Chapter 17; Gilmore, Stevens, Harrell-Cook, & Ferris, Chapter 18; Palmer, Campion, & Green, Chapter 19) offer discussion of the applicant from a somewhat different perspective—that is, as a major influence on the interviewer and the interview process itself. The thesis of the first two of these chapters is that the applicant actually changes the interview process and the constructs that are assessed both because of the way he or she interacts with the inter-viewer and because of deliberate attempts to manage impressions. Jablin et al. describe a method of examining the sequence of interviewer-appli-cant interactions that take place in the interview and relates these to interview outcomes. These authors suggest extending the use of this technique to interactions regarding specific content; in my opinion, this research would also be informative with respect to its implications for the nature of the constructs measured in the interview. If the sequence of interactions shows that the interviewer's questions about specific topics are always followed by avoidance responses, whereas the introduction of other topics is followed by extended applicant response, and these sequences are differentially related to the interviewer's assessments of the candidates, we may have information about the source of the interviewer's attributions. Impression management tactics (Gilmore et al., Chapter 18) almost certainly occur in the interview and should be related to measures of the same tactics employed by respondents to other selection procedures (Ones, Viswesvaran, & Reiss, 1996) and to measures of the constructs one intends to measure. Finally, Palmer et al. point to the fact that some at least view the interview as a conflict between the interviewer and the applicant. This is an interpretation of the interview about which I believe we have no research information. I suspect that the structured interview minimizes the degree to which the applicant can manipulate or change the interview, just as structure controls the interviewer, but we have little information on any of the processes or variables suggested in these chapters.

Summary and Conclusions

The contributions to this handbook describe advances in research on the employment interview on several different fronts. One of the requests the editors of this volume made of me was that I develop for this chapter some overall integrative theoretical framework for the interview research summarized in this volume. I do not believe that is feasible. As I stated at the outset, and as Palmer et al. note in Chapter 19, the interview research sets forth three very different purposes served by the interview. As a selection device, the model of the interview one devises should be dictated by a model of the performance construct(s) one is trying to predict (Campbell, McCloy, Oppler, & Sager, 1993). If the interview is being considered as a recruitment device, then theories of socialization are appropriate (e.g., Feldman, 1976; Wanous, 1980). Likewise, theories of job or career choice (Hall, 1986) are relevant when one is considering the applicant's selection of an organization. Within each of these relatively broad theoretical domains, there is room for many alternate hypotheses or minitheories of the type that have characterized microanalytic approaches to the study of the interview.

There are several areas of research that I think ought to receive additional attention. First, concern over the nature of the constructs that are measured in the interview, or can be measured in the interview, is long overdue. The emphasis on the method of data collection is a natural by-product of the industrial psychologist's concern with the technical aspects of our discipline, but we must attend more to the substantive constructs measured for a variety of practical and scientific reasons.

Second, more attention should be given to the possibility that interview ratings of certain constructs are related to aspects of performance to which we have not paid much attention. Interviews that are focused on the motivations or social skills of the applicant ought to relate to withdrawal, organizational citizenship behavior, job satisfaction, and the capability to work collaboratively.

A third area toward which research ought to be directed is the length of time an interview continues to be effective in an organization and what contributes to the decay of this intervention. In this respect, we have much to learn from those who have concentrated their efforts on the study of innovation (e.g., Drazin & Schoonhoven, 1996).

Finally, it seems that those interested in applicant reactions to the interview must conduct longitudinal research that ties data collection to the timing of specific selection and recruitment practices if we are ever to identify the role that the employment interview plays in applicants' reactions and behavior.

References

Bolster, B. I., & Springbett, B. M. (1961). The reaction of interviewers to favorable and unfavorable information. *Journal of Applied Psychology, 45*, 97-103.

Campbell, J. P., McCloy, R. A., Oppler, S. H., & Sager, C. E. (1993). A theory of performance. In N. Schmitt & W. C. Borman (Eds.), *Personnel selection in organizations*. San Francisco: Jossey-Bass.

Campion, M. A., Pursell, E. D., & Brown, B. K. (1988). Structured interviewing: Raising the psychometric properties of the employment interview. *Personnel Psychology, 41*, 25-42.

Drazin, R., & Schoonhoven, C. B. (1996). Community, population, and organization effects on innovation: A multilevel perspective. *Academy of Management Journal, 39*, 1065-1083.

Eder, R. W., & Ferris, G. R. (Eds.). (1989). *The employment interview: Theory, research, and practice*. Newbury Park, CA: Sage.

Eder, R. W., Kacmar, K. M., & Ferris, G. R. (1989). Employment interview research: History and synthesis. In R. W. Eder & G. R. Ferris (Eds.), *The employment interview: Theory, research, and practice* (pp. 17-31). Newbury Park, CA: Sage.

Feldman, D. C. (1976). A contingency theory of socialization. *Administrative Science Quarterly, 21*, 433-452.

Gilliland, S. W. (1995). Fairness from the applicant's perspective: Reactions to employee selection procedures. *International Journal of Selection and Assessment, 3*, 11-19.

Golembiewski, R. T., Billingsley, K., & Yeager, S. (1976). Measuring change and persistence in human affairs: Types of change generated by OD designs. *Journal of Applied Behavioral Science, 12*, 133-157.

Hall, D. T. (1986). *Career development in organizations*. San Francisco: Jossey-Bass.

Johns, G. (1993). Constraints on the adoption of psychology-based personnel practices: Lessons from organizational innovation. *Personnel Psychology, 46,* 569-592.

Latham, G. P., & Finnegan, B. J. (1993). Perceived practicality of unstructured, patterned, and situational interviews. In H. Schuler, J. L. Farr, & M. Smith (Eds.), *Personnel selection and assessment: Individual and organizational perspectives* (pp. 41-55). Hillsdale, NJ: Lawrence Erlbaum.

Latham, G. P., & Saari, L. M. (1984). Do people do what they say? Further studies on the situational interview. *Journal of Applied Psychology, 69,* 569-573.

Latham, G. P., & Skarlicki, D. (1995). Criterion-related validity of the situational and patterned behavior description interviews with organizational citizenship behavior. *Human Performance, 8,* 67-80.

Millsap, R. E., & Hartog, S. B. (1988). Alpha, beta, and gamma change in evaluation research: A structural equation approach. *Journal of Applied Psychology, 73,* 574-584.

Ones, D. S., Viswesvaran, C., & Reiss, A. D. (1996). Role of social desirability in personality testing for personnel selection: The red herring. *Journal of Applied Psychology, 81,* 660-679.

Pingitore, R., Dugoni, B. L., Tindale, R. S., & Spring, B. (1994). Bias against overweight job applicants in a simulated employment interview. *Journal of Applied Psychology, 79,* 909-917.

Pulakos, E. D., & Schmitt, N. (1995). Experience-based and situational interview questions: Studies of validity. *Personnel Psychology, 48,* 289-308.

Pulakos, E. D., & Schmitt, N. (1996). An evaluation of two strategies for reducing adverse impact and their effects on criterion-related validity. *Human Performance, 9,* 241-258.

Rynes, S. L. (1993). Who's selecting whom? Effects of selection practices on applicant attitudes and behavior. In N. Schmitt & W. C. Borman (Eds.), *Personnel selection in organizations.* San Francisco: Jossey-Bass.

Schmitt, N. (1994). Method bias: The importance of theory and measurement. *Journal of Organizational Behavior, 15,* 393-398.

Ulrich, L., & Trumbo, D. (1965). The selection interview since 1949. *Psychological Bulletin, 63,* 100-116.

Wagner, R. (1949). The employment interview: A critical review. *Personnel Psychology, 2,* 17-46.

Wanous, J. P. (1980). *Organizational entry: Recruitment, selection, and socialization of newcomers.* Reading, MA: Addison-Wesley.

Webster, E. C. (1964). *Decision making in the employment interview.* Montreal: Eagle.

21

The State of Employment Interview Practice

Commentary and Extension

Michael M. Harris
Robert W. Eder

Our purpose in this chapter is to offer recommendations for interviewing practice based on the information presented in this handbook and other scholarly sources, as well as our own experience in the roles of interviewer, trainer, consultant, and expert witness. In addition, we conducted an analysis of e-mail exchanges on HRNET, a public "listserv" sponsored by the Human Resources Division of the Academy of Management and heavily used by practitioners seeking information on how best to perform a variety of human resource activities. Our intent was to gain further insight into the questions that most interest practitioners. In the period

AUTHORS' NOTE: We would like to thank Laura Heft for her helpful comments on this chapter.

1993-1997, we found there were literally hundreds of e-mail exchanges on recommended employment interview practices. In general, these exchanges fell into the following broad categories, which we address in this chapter:

1. Requests for advice on best practices
2. Discussion of the practical merits of structured interviewing
3. Requests for advice on how to come up with the best questions to ask
4. Discussion of how to ask questions that do not violate the provisions of the Americans With Disabilities Act
5. Discussion of the use of related assessment technologies to enhance interviewer performance

This chapter is divided into two sections. In the first, we provide advice to hiring managers on how to interview job applicants. The focus of this section is on preparing for and conducting the interview, as well as using the information that is obtained from the applicants. In the second section we offer suggestions for human resource management staff who are seeking to introduce, implement, and maintain state-of-the-art interviewing practices in their organizations.

Preparing for, Conducting, and Using Information From the Interview: Advice for Hiring Managers

We discuss the interview process here in terms of three major steps: preparing for the interview, conducting the interview, and using information from the interview to make a selection decision.

Preparing for the Interview

In preparing for the interview, the hiring manager should first consider the following issues: (a) What are the goals of the interview? (b) What are the key factors that should be assessed in the interview? (c) How should questions be developed to assess those factors?

Goals of the Interview

Traditionally, the selection process has included at least two distinct types of interviewing events: a screening interview and a final employment interview. Screening interviews occur early in the selection process, are usually quite brief, are conducted by an organizational representative, and are designed to enhance applicant attraction (i.e., recruit) and to determine if the applicant is qualified to continue in the selection process. In contrast, the employment interview is often the last stage in the selection process, where a handful of finalists are interviewed extensively by likely supervisors and colleagues with the intent of determining the applicant who is best qualified for the position (i.e., selection). It is also important for the interviewer to determine whether the primary purpose of the interview is selection or recruitment (see Eder, Chapter 11, this volume). Specifically, is the primary purpose to assess the applicant or to recruit the applicant (e.g., entice the applicant to accept a job offer)? Barber, Hollenbeck, Tower, and Phillips (1994) found that applicants were better able to retain information given in interviews that focused only on the recruitment aspects, supporting the notion that hiring managers should carefully consider the purpose of the interview. Due to space constraints, we will focus here primarily on how to assess applicants effectively. Readers interested in recruitment should see Breaugh (1992) for an extensive review of and practical advice on how to communicate with applicants about the job and organization.

The second issue an interviewer should consider with regard to the goals of the interview is what constitutes a successful interview. As we note in the introductory chapter of this handbook, an interview will be judged successful to the degree to which it has substantial validity, is legally sound, and produces positive applicant reactions to the job and organization. Achieving all three of these objectives may not be as simple as one might think. It is clear that although we know a great deal about what makes an interview valid (see Buckley & Russell, Chapter 2, this volume) and legally acceptable (see Roehling, Campion, & Arvey, Chapter 3, this volume), we know far less regarding applicant reactions (see Gilliland & Steiner, Chapter 4, this volume). Even more troubling, it appears that the characteristics that make interviews more valid and legally defensible may actually provoke *negative* responses from applicants. For example, Gilliland and Steiner argue in Chapter 4 that many features of structured interviews, such as standardized scoring, militate against two-way communication, which in turn reduces applicants' perceptions of interactional justice. Thus, prioritizing among the objectives for a successful interview may be more complicated than first appears to be the case. We recommend that none of the three objectives be ignored; however, we expect that in most cases, the top two priorities will be the validity and legal defensibility of the interview, and that various tactics, to be described later in this chapter, will be used to maintain positive applicant reactions.

We turn now to a discussion of the key factors that should be assessed in the interview, followed by a discussion of how questions should be developed to assess those factors. We conclude with a discussion of question standardization.

Key Factors to Be Assessed

As we note in Chapter 1 of this volume, the interview may be used to assess a number of factors or constructs, including reliability, KSAs, values, and motivation. As defined in Chapter 1, *reliability* refers to the applicant's likelihood of adhering to the basic rules and policies of the job and organization, such as attendance, overtime, and travel requirements. *KSAs* are those knowledges (e.g., tax laws), skills (e.g., running a team meeting), and abilities (e.g., verbal reasoning) that are necessary to perform job tasks. *Values* are applicant preferences for aspects of the work environment (e.g., supervisory style) and organizational culture (e.g., teamwork) or applicant attitudes about work (e.g., possessing a strong customer service orientation) that the employer believes will drive both employee and firm performance. Applicant *motivation* refers to the different types of rewards desired by the applicant (e.g., promotions, opportunity to learn new skills, performance bonuses).

To assess these factors and the degree to which they are present in the job and organization, we recommend a systematic, quantitative procedure (see, e.g., Gatewood & Feild, 1998). If there are time or financial constraints that limit the degree to which systematic, quantitative procedures can be followed, we recommend that managers/owners simply take the time to identify the key KSAs (often described as key competencies and "fit" factors) that most directly translate into successful hires for their firms. A summary set of steps for this purpose is provided in Table 21.1. These steps include specifying the essential functions performed by the job incumbent, the KSAs needed to perform the essential functions, relevant work rules and regulations (e.g., rotating shifts, attendance), motivators that exist for this job, and a list of key values held by the organization or work unit.

Developing Questions Based on Key Factors

Once the hiring manager determines what factors are to be assessed in the interview, he or she needs to develop questions that tap these factors. As described next, there are several different types of questions that may be used. First, however, we would like to advise *against* a search for the ultimate list of 10 or 15 questions that should always be asked. Although there are numerous practitioner-oriented books that offer such lists, we strongly believe that the "best" questions depend on the specific set of KSAs, reliability requirements, motivations, and values that are necessary for the particular job and organization. It is the responsibility of both hiring managers and HR professionals to understand and identify the core human resource competencies and person-organization fit factors that will produce a high-performing workforce capable of enhancing the firm's competitive advantage. This will vary across economic sectors, organiza-

Table 21.1 Determining the Factors to Be Assessed in the Interview

1. List the tasks performed by the job incumbent; cluster the tasks into broad functions.

2. Rate the importance of each function using a scale from 1 (not at all important) to 5 (most important). Consider the relative frequency of performance, impact of an error, and significance to the organization overall in rating each function. Be sure to focus only on the important and essential functions.

3. For each function, list the KSAs and other requirements (e.g., professional license) necessary for successful performance.

4. List all possible work requirements, such as attendance rules, overtime, rotating shifts, and travel expectations, that are important for success in the job and membership in the organization. Be sure to examine the employee handbook and other relevant documents identifying these policies and rules.

5. List the major motivators that are available for rewarding employees, including intrinsic (e.g., job design characteristics) and extrinsic (e.g., reward practices) factors that may match applicant work motivational preferences and that may be somewhat unique to the organization.

6. List the top four or five unique values held by the organizational culture or work environment that are integral to organizational success that can be assessed through applicant preferences.

7. Determine whether these KSAs, work requirements, motivators, and values will be assessed through the interview or by other assessment techniques (e.g., reference checks, ability tests, work samples).

tions within each sector, and divisions within each organization. Furthermore, these factors may change over time due to changing competitive dynamics and customer expectations. For example, a firm may be moving toward greater use of teams and therefore may require applicants to demonstrate team process skills. Another firm may emphasize "service orientation" as the possession of certain customer attitudes that go beyond the applicants' technical proficiencies to perform their work. Or a third firm may want to hire managers who practice a supportive, facilitative style desired to enhance innovation rates of knowledge workers. We now turn to a discussion of four basic types of interview questions: behaviorally oriented, trait, training and experience, and willingness to work.

Behaviorally oriented questions. Borrowing from the performance appraisal literature, we first discuss a class of questions that may best be described as behaviorally oriented. As noted in this volume by Motowidlo (Chapter 10), Harris (Chapter 8), and Maurer, Sue-Chan, and Latham (Chapter 9), the primary question formats used in the research literature have been the situational interview (SI) question "What *would* you do . . . ?" (i.e., seeking information on intentions or future behavior) and the behavior description interview (BDI) question

"What *did* you do . . . ?" (i.e., seeking information on past behavior). There are, however, other ways to frame such questions. Motowidlo suggests that if the purpose is to assess knowledge, perhaps applicants should be asked, "What is the best thing to do?" in a hypothetical situation, rather than "What would you do?"

A slightly different approach is to focus on specific situations that the applicant will encounter on the job. For instance, consider an organization that is hiring an employee to conduct a marketing campaign for a new product. A BDI question might be, "Tell me about a time when you initiated a marketing campaign for a new product." An SI question might begin, "Imagine you had to initiate a marketing campaign . . . ." We think that in this situation, however, the best way to assess the applicant's proposed marketing campaign might be to give him or her a brief overview of the product and the intended market and then ask, "What *will* you do in this situation?" Although not completely different from the SI approach, this type of question is more similar to a work simulation in its detail and complexity than the typical SI question. We refer to this as the *actual-situational* (AS) question.

The AS question approach may be particularly conducive to interview evaluations that closely follow important performance dimensions or responsibilities. However, it should be noted, at least in the case of the original SI evaluation procedures, that interviewers are instructed to score each question and then summate scores to infer overall competency rather than to score the applicant's answers by performance dimension. Maurer et al. address this disparity in their critique of recent studies intended to compare BDI and SI approaches (e.g., Pulakos & Schmitt, 1995), though it is unclear whether summating ratings by performance dimension or across all behaviorally oriented questions produces any significant differences in the efficacy of the questioning technique.

Although research at this point is inconclusive as to whether BDI or SI questions are more valid (see Maurer et al., Chapter 9), we believe that interviewers should consider several factors in deciding which question format to use. Specifically, complexity, job level, and amount of experience required are factors that may affect the question format used.

■ *Complexity:* For KSAs that require simple, straightforward answers, SI questions might be the most appropriate (e.g., asking a candidate for a nursing job, "How would you handle a patient who had stopped breathing?"). For KSAs that involve complex issues with many possible correct answers, BDI and AS questions might be more appropriate (e.g., asking a candidate for director of human resources from the BDI approach, "Tell me about a time when you implemented a new HRM program. How did you garner support for the new program? What obstacles did you encounter? How did you resolve them?" or, from the AS approach, "Describe how you would go about implementing a gain-sharing plan in our organization. What obstacles do you expect to encounter and how will you address them?"). Answers to these types of questions can be used to evaluate the applicant's working knowledge of how to implement human resource programs, an important responsibility of a prospective HRM director.

■ *Job level:* The higher the job level, the more appropriate BDI and AS questions are likely to be, because applicants for higher-level jobs may have a negative reaction to more simplistic-sounding SI questions. In addition, higher-level jobs are likely to involve more complex KSAs than are lower-level jobs, and thus, as indicated above, the more useful the BDI and AS approaches should be.

■ *Amount of experience required:* BDI questions presuppose that an applicant has engaged in a particular set of behaviors and learned from the experience, whereas SI and AS questions make no such assumptions. Thus, if actual experience in a particular KSA is desirable or required, a BDI question may be most appropriate. If experience using a particular KSA is not necessary, an SI or AS question would be more appropriate, because it does not require that the applicant have actual experience using the KSA.

Some other factors that might affect the choice of format include interviewer comfort with alternative approaches and ease in developing a scoring guide. To date, we are not aware of any research on differences between question format with regard to these issues, but we believe they may be important factors.

Finally, we strongly recommend that a scoring guide be developed for each question. Table 21.2 provides a step-by-step procedure for creating an interview scoring guide. The scoring guide would specify the key points contained in a very good answer, an average answer, and a poor answer. This will not only improve the reliability and validity of the interview, but will serve as documentation of the job relevance of the interview process if there is a legal challenge. The latter advantage may be the most convincing argument to be made in persuading hiring managers to take the time to develop a scoring guide.

Trait questions. Campion, Palmer, and Campion (1997) note that many types of questions inquire about applicants' self-descriptions and opinions and address poorly defined "traits." For example, Smart (1983) describes an interview approach containing a litany of questions covering education, military experience, and other topics to assess factors such as enthusiasm and assertiveness. Other examples of trait-oriented questions include "What is your greatest strength?" and "What is your greatest weakness?" Such questions are generally associated with the unstructured interview format. Although we know of no research

Table 21.2 Creating Interview Question Scoring Guides

1. Assemble a group of three or four subject matter experts (SMEs) who are familiar with the job and its requirements.

2. For each interview question, ask the SMEs to think about either how an average employee would answer the question or how an average employee has actually performed in the situation. List the key points.

3. For each interview question, ask the SMEs to think about either how an outstanding employee would answer the question or how an outstanding employee has actually performed in the situation. List the key points.

4. For each interview question, ask the SMEs to think about either how an unacceptable or below-average employee would answer the question or how an unacceptable employee has actually performed in the situation. List the key points.

5. Be sure to obtain consensus on the key points for average, outstanding, and unacceptable answers. If there is disagreement on a key point, eliminate that point from the scoring guide. If there is a lack of consensus on several key points across two or more levels, it may be best to eliminate the question altogether.

evidence that directly assesses the validity of such questions, we are dubious of the value of this approach (e.g., applicants often have prepared answers). We believe that the trait approach is less valid than other interview question formats and, for the most part, should be avoided.

Training and experience questions. Campion et al. (1997) refer to a group of questions designed to assess work experience, education, and other qualifications as "background questions." We somewhat expand this category to include a variety of work history topics, including reasons for leaving jobs and absenteeism rates from previous jobs, as well as educational background. Even though some of this information may be obtained from the application blank, it may be useful to obtain during the interview as well. First, it can be a good starting point for behaviorally oriented (e.g., BDI and SI) questions. Furthermore, when asked in the interview, such questions can be helpful in covering any omissions or clarifying conflicting information. Finally, such questions can be useful for rapport building with applicants and provide an opportunity for candidates to sell their records, which may be important for applicant reactions.

Willingness-to-work questions. Willingness-to-work questions address the applicant's intentions to show up on time for scheduled work (e.g., adhering to strict attendance rules); to work required overtime, weekends, and holidays; and to work under potentially adverse or hazardous conditions. Although such questions may be useful for screening applicants, there has been little research concerning their validity, despite the increasing variability in work schedules requested of employees.

What Questions Should Applicants Not Be Asked?

In general, inquiries regarding race, age, sex, religion, and other personal information that might be construed as discriminatory (e.g., childcare arrangements) should not be asked in the interview. Even questions that may indirectly affect the employment opportunities for protected groups should be avoided (e.g., arrest records). Since the passage of the Americans With Disabilities Act of 1990 (ADA), there has been a great deal of added complexity in terms of what kinds of preemployment interview questions it is illegal for interviewers to ask (see Roehling et al., Chapter 3, this volume). Simply put, the ADA prohibits any "disability-related" question in the pre-job-offer stage. After a job offer has been made, the employer may ask "disability-related" questions. However, even then the employer must be able to defend the use of these questions if discrimination is charged. A disability-related question either directly addresses possible disabilities (e.g., "Do you have any physical limitations?" or "Do you need a reasonable accommodation to perform this job?") or is likely to elicit information about a disability covered under the ADA. Although the former type of question seems relatively understandable, some degree of confusion and uncertainty may arise concerning questions that are likely to elicit information about a disability. Equal Employment Opportunity Commission enforcement guidance information released on October 10, 1995, for example, states that an interviewer may ask an applicant who has a broken leg how the leg was broken. The logic behind this is that most broken legs are only temporarily in that state, and ADA does not cover temporary disabilities. Conversely, using the same example, the interpretive guidelines indicate that questions such as "Do your bones break easily?" and "Do you think the leg will heal normally?" *are* disability related, because they directly address possible disabilities. Another example is asking whether an applicant drinks alcoholic beverages (not disability related, because many people drink alcoholic beverages and are not alcoholics) versus asking how many alcoholic beverages the applicant typically drinks in a week (disability related, because the question addresses alcoholism). Furthermore, an interviewer may ask an applicant how many unscheduled absences he or she had last year (not disability related, because an applicant may have many reasons for absences aside from disability) but may not ask an applicant how many days he or she was ill (disability related, because the question potentially reveals an impairment). As these examples illustrate, the distinction between disability-related and non-disability-related questions may seem rather elusive at times. We strongly encourage hiring managers to plan all questions ahead of time and to consider carefully whether each question is likely to elicit information about a disability. If there is any uncertainty as to the legality of particular questions, managers should seek either legal counsel or advice from their HR departments.

Question Standardization and Sequence

We have observed in various organizations the use of several different approaches to interview question standardization. At one end of the spectrum, we have worked with organizations that required managers (at least for some positions) to use a prepared booklet containing all the interview questions. At the other end of the spectrum, and probably the most common situation, are organizations that allow hiring managers to ask different questions of different candidates, and they do. Somewhere in the middle are organizations in which managers must use a standard list of questions that are asked of all applicants and can also use questions that are unique to each applicant.

For the following reasons, we recommend the middle of the spectrum with regard to question standardization. First, as Dougherty and Turban suggest in Chapter 12 of this handbook, "probing, following up, and eliciting of job-relevant information from the applicant" is appropriate; they recommend asking some questions that are designed specifically for the individual applicant. Second, our experience indicates that interviewers often have relevant, important questions that are unique to each job candidate. Third, we have found that managers may resent having to use only predetermined questions and view this as an unnecessary restriction. Allowing interviewers some freedom to vary the questions asked (as long as they are legal) will help to reduce resistance to structured interviewing. Fourth, Huffcutt and Arthur (1994) found no decrease in validity of Structure Level III interviews, which allow some leeway in questioning by the interviewer, compared with Structure Level IV interviews, which allow no latitude in terms of questions asked. Finally, the use of follow-up probes may be so clearly necessary that hiring managers will ask additional questions no matter what attempts are made to stop them.

At the same time, we believe that a core set of standard questions is essential to effective interviewing. We suggest that one way to convince hiring managers to adopt a core set of common questions is to explain the difficulty of making objective comparisons among candidates if they have been asked different questions. Or, stated somewhat differently, one might explain that having a standard set of questions for all applicants creates a "level playing field," and therefore is the fairest way to make assessments.

Although there are many different possible ways to sequence the interview, we recommend that interviewers use a four-part questioning sequence. First, interviewers should normally begin with training and experience questions (e.g., inquiries about the applicant's previous jobs). The advantage of starting here is that candidates usually expect such questions, so this provides an opportunity for the interviewer to build rapport and to make the candidate comfortable. Next, the interviewer might switch to behaviorally oriented questions, which are likely to be the most novel questions for candidates and therefore more difficult to answer.

Third, the interviewer should introduce a series of willingness-to-work questions, followed by a transitional question (e.g., Do you have any other job-related experiences or abilities that we have not discussed so far?). The transitional question ensures that the applicant has had an opportunity to describe completely his or her qualifications for the job. After the transitional question, the interviewer should devote the remainder of the interview to describing the job and organization, answering any questions the applicant may have, and closing the interview by stating how and when the applicant will be notified of the decision.

In sum, careful preparation is necessary for a successful interview. We have described a systematic approach to determining the goals of the interview, the questions to ask, and the questions to avoid. We also suggest that careful attention be paid to question standardization and the sequencing of the applicant-interviewer exchange within the interview event.

Conducting the Interview

Although the contributors to this volume pay considerable attention to what the interview is measuring and how interviewers make decisions, there is relatively little discussion in the preceding chapters of the effective *conduct* of the interview. This lack of attention to conduct may be partially explained by the emphasis on structured interviewing, which attempts to eliminate extraneous variance by standardizing the interviewer-applicant interaction. Selection interview research in the past 10 years has therefore focused on the interview as a test, rather than on the interpersonal interface between the interviewer and the applicant. In addition, structured interviewing has emphasized psychometric and legal considerations and has for the most part ignored applicant reactions. We believe that the increasingly recognized importance of applicant reactions to the interview process (e.g., Borman, Hanson, & Hedge, 1997) suggests that both researchers and interviewers must consider the conduct of the interview far more carefully than heretofore has been the case.

We divide the following discussion into five, sometimes overlapping, issues: using panel interviews, building rapport, communication tactics, providing opportunity for questions, and note taking. Although there has been only limited research in most of these areas, we offer some practical suggestions for interviewers.

Using Panel Interviews

Despite the popularity of panel interviews, there appears to be little systematic research on this topic. As Tullar and Kaiser note in Chapter 16 of this volume, there are many reasons an interview panel is often preferred, including better recall of information, reduction of idiosyncratic biases, and the opportunity for panel members to challenge each others' opinions. The findings of the research comparing the validity of panel versus individual interviewers have nevertheless been mixed (e.g., compare McDaniel, Whetzel, Schmidt, & Maurer, 1994, with Wiesner & Cronshaw, 1988); despite the many assumed advantages of having multiple interviewers, the gains in validity may not necessarily outweigh the additional costs (e.g., time) involved. We conclude that the most compelling reason for an organization to use a panel interview is to pass legal muster (see Roehling et al., Chapter 3, this volume). A second reason to use panel interviews is that the process may lead to greater acceptance of hiring decisions by others in the department and organization. Coworkers who have had input in the hiring process may be more willing to accept the candidate who is hired.

Despite this somewhat pessimistic conclusion, there may be ways to increase the validity of panel interviews. We suspect that diffusion of responsibility or social loafing is a likely culprit for the limited increase in validity of panel interviews, particularly if panel members expect that their ratings will simply be averaged or that they will be required to agree with the dominant opinion that emerges (see Eder, Chapter 11, this volume). To reduce the likelihood of this happening, interviewers should be instilled with a greater sense of accountability. Interviewers should be informed before they interview applicants that they will be expected to share their decision rationales with others and to contribute actively to the group decision.

We do encourage interviewers to consider interviewing in pairs. As Gilliland and Steiner suggest in Chapter 4, the use of more than one interviewer may increase applicant perceptions of fairness, but the use of more than two interviewers at the same time is likely to increase the applicant's stress level. Use of two-person interview teams may increase interviewers' sense of responsibility for doing an effective interview, increase judgment reliability with a second observer, increase recall of job-relevant information, make better use of interviewer and applicant time when multiple interviews are expected, and provide interviewers with the opportunity to discuss the interview experience and learn how to improve interviewing skills from one another. Two-person interview teams may also benefit by dividing up the questioning, which permits one interviewer to take notes and the applicant to focus on just one interviewer's questions at a time. In sum, use of multiple interviewers can be advantageous. The way in which multiple interviewers will operate, however, should be carefully planned to be optimally effective.

Building Rapport

Despite calls for more research to address exactly what interviewer behaviors are likely to help build rapport (Harris & Fink, 1987), little has been achieved in this regard (Rynes, Bretz, & Gerhart, 1991). In a review

Table 21.3 Improving Interviewer-Applicant Rapport: Suggestions for the Interviewer

1. Warmly greet and introduce yourself to the applicant; ask the applicant what name he or she prefers you use (e.g., Dave or David; Jan or Janice).

2. Begin the interview with small talk, but remember that not everyone enjoys discussing sports or the high school he or she attended. Also, be aware that some seemingly innocuous topics for small talk may be inappropriate (e.g., "Where are you from?" "Do you have kids in school?"). The idea is to "break the ice" with easy conversation.

3. Share the interview purpose with the applicant and indicate the mutual benefit to both of you (e.g., "I would like to start out by learning more about your job-related experiences and abilities and, later in our discussion, give you time to ask me questions about the job or the company, so that we can *both* make a good decision").

4. Begin with relatively familiar topics, such as the applicant's most recent job, so that he or she becomes comfortable talking.

5. Maintain occasional eye contact with the applicant and a pleasant facial expression. Be polite; avoid interrupting the applicant unless absolutely necessary.

6. End the interview on a pleasant note, such as by saying, "I enjoyed talking with you."

---

of previous literature, Harris (1989) found only a handful of studies examining the relationship between interviewer and applicant dynamics. The most relevant study, conducted by McComb and Jablin (1984), indicated that only one (i.e., number of interruptive statements) of nine behaviors coded (e.g., number of probing questions, use of encouraging statements) was related (negatively) to applicants' perceptions of interviewer empathic listening. Although there has been little research conducted, then, to examine which behaviors may increase rapport in the interview, we offer some suggestions in Table 21.3 based on our own reading and experience in the area.

Communication Tactics

In Chapter 17 of this volume, Jablin, Miller, and Sias discuss some interesting findings regarding the communication tactics used by *applicants*. For example, they summarize research indicating that successful applicants (defined as candidates who were highly rated by interviewers) spend less time answering questions and more time talking outside of question-answer sequences compared with less successful applicants. Other research reported by Jablin et al. examined dominant statements (i.e., statements that try to limit the options of the other party) and submissive statements (i.e., statements that cede control to the other party) of interviewers and applicants. Successful applicants were found to be more likely to use complementary exchanges (i.e., responding to an interviewer's dominant

Table 21.4 Recommended Communication Tactics for Interviewers

1. Be sure not to give away too much information about the job and desired KSAs, work requirements, and so forth early in the interview; otherwise, the applicant may try to answer questions to reflect those desired factors. However, it may be helpful to give the applicant a list of basic functions performed in the job at the beginning of the interview.

2. Allow the applicant to do most of the talking during the selection part of the interview; actively listen to what the applicant is saying.

3. Do not show surprise or disapproval in response to any of the applicant's answers.

4. Use silence, head nodding, and similar tactics to encourage the applicant to continue his or her answers.

5. Use empathic statements (e.g., "That sounds like a difficult experience you had") when appropriate, such as when the applicant describes a difficult situation that he or she has encountered.

6. Avoid arguing with the applicant over the answers he or she provides; conversely, avoid coaxing the answers you want out of the applicant.

7. Avoid using nonverbal cues (e.g., moving forward when you are starting to listen carefully) that may signal the applicant that he or she is relaying some negative information.

statement with a submissive statement or responding to an interviewer's submissive statement with a dominant statement) than symmetrical exchanges. Unsuccessful applicants were more likely to use symmetrical responses, and were particularly likely to follow a dominant statement by the interviewer with a dominant act. Unfortunately, the implications of these findings are not clear. Whether the communication styles exhibited by successful applicants are actually the cues used by interviewers, and whether these cues are valid predictors of job-related criteria, is unknown. These results do, however, corroborate the importance of communication tactics during the interview.

In terms of communication tactics for interviewers, the popular literature is replete with suggestions. We summarize what we consider to be some of the most important recommendations for interviewers in Table 21.4. We want to emphasize, however, that there is practically no research on these suggestions, although they seem to make good sense.

Providing Opportunity for Applicant Questions

In Chapter 4, Gilliland and Steiner discuss several aspects of the interview process that might affect applicants' reactions. In our opinion, one of the most important aspects of the process is the opportunity for the applicant to ask questions. It is noteworthy in this regard that several of the items tapping recruiter competence in a study by Harris and Fink

(1987) were related to how well questions were answered by the interviewer. Gilliland and Steiner assert that providing the applicant with an opportunity to ask questions and to gain more information about the job and organization will increase the perceived fairness of the interview. Choice attributes may enhance applicant attraction, an important complementary objective in a successful selection process. Although it is unlikely that an organization would fail to provide *any* opportunity for the applicant to ask questions about the job and organization, interviewers differ widely in terms of how much *time* they allocate for this purpose, how *willing* they appear to be to answer inquiries, how *informative* their answers are, and how much they view the interview as an opportunity to recruit as well as to select. Thus, rather than the issue being simply *whether* the opportunity to ask questions is offered, what may be important is how *helpful* the interviewer is in answering the applicant's questions and how *persuasive* the interviewer is in elevating applicant interest. In any case, the opportunity to ask questions and the way in which inquiries are answered may be important determinants of applicant reactions to the interview and the eventual likelihood of acceptance if the applicant is offered the position.

We therefore recommend that interviewers be sure to consider ahead of time what important facts they should relay to candidates about the job and organization, anticipate what questions might be asked, and set aside sufficient time in the interview to answer the applicant's questions. Relatedly, interviewers should be careful to schedule plenty of time between candidates to allow for the possibility that some interviews may go on longer than expected. Organizations should also consider the benefits of providing information about their history, structure, culture, mission, and key values on a company Web page that may aid applicants seeking information prior to the interview.

Note Taking

Despite exhortations to interviewers to take notes during the interview, there has been little research regarding the effects of note taking on validity, applicant reactions, or other criteria of interest. One exception is a study by Houdek and Macan (1997) that used college students viewing a videotaped interview to compare two types of note taking (i.e., key points versus verbatim) to a "no note taking" condition. Houdek and Macan found that although note taking increased recall accuracy, it had no effect on the accuracy of the ratings.

Although we recommend that interviewers take notes during interviews, we also caution that they should be careful not to overdo this behavior. It is both rude and disconcerting to the applicant for the interviewer to be looking down constantly at a piece of paper or a computer screen. Rather, the interviewer should focus his or her note taking on entering "key points" onto an interviewer report form either during or immediately after the interview. The interviewer report form depicts the rating factors that will be used to assess applicant qualifications and provides the interviewer with a cognitive schema within which to attend to and store relevant information. This can reduce the necessity for excessive note taking while providing a meaningful context for the "key notes" that are taken. The report form with notes can also aid in documenting the interviewer's judgment.

In sum, properly conducted interviews are likely to have positive effects on applicants' perceptions of the organization and to reduce the probability of lawsuits being filed. Hiring managers should also be reminded that applicants may be current or future customers (e.g., of a retail store chain or fast-food company).

Using Interview Information

After interviews are conducted, the hiring manager should organize and integrate information as it pertains to the relevant factors and make a selection decision. One study found that mechanical combination of interview ratings was superior to subjective combination of interview ratings (Conway, Jako, & Goodman, 1995). Thus, we recommend that hiring managers make ratings for each question (or each KSA) and combine the ratings in an objective manner (e.g., simple sum) to obtain an overall score.

In this section we focus on several key issues that interviewers should consider in making their ratings: candidate impression management tactics, determining the veracity of interview information, and evaluating unfavorable information.

Candidate Impression Management Tactics

A list of some impression management tactics is provided in Table 21.5. As Gilmore, Stevens, Harrell-Cook, and Ferris observe in Chapter 18 of this volume, impression management tactics do in fact affect interviewer perceptions, but not all of the effects are positive. For example, extremely high levels of impression management seem to backfire against the candidate. The main limitation of this research is that it is not known whether these variables reduce or enhance the *validity* of the interview ratings. On the one hand, impression management tactics presumably increase error variance because they would seem to constitute non-job-related information. On the other hand, perhaps applicants who exhibit inappropriate (i.e., too little or too much) impression management behavior are reflecting a lack of common sense, or perhaps such applicants will behave similarly on the job. On that basis, impression management behaviors may constitute valid information.

Although there has been little research on the validity of impression management ratings in the interview context, our experience suggests that

Table 21.5 Candidate Impression Management Tactics

Enhancement: Statements about particular events or outcomes that indicate greater responsibility on the part of the candidate than most people would expect; for example, "I sold more merchandise than all 250 salespeople in the country."

Other-enhancement: Statements that compliment or praise the interviewer; for example, "I would really enjoy working with someone as impressive as you!"

Opinion conformity: Statements that express beliefs, attitudes, or opinions similar to those the candidate might expect the interviewer to hold; for example, in interviewing with a small company, the candidate says, "I prefer small organizations because of the impact each employee has."

Justification: Statements in which the candidate expresses responsibility for his or her behavior but rejects the negative outcomes of that behavior; for example, "Our division didn't have the best ideas, but we certainly tried our best."

SOURCE: Adapted from Stevens and Kristof (1995).

interviewers are often fooled by applicants who effectively use such tactics. Even intelligent, critical interviewers can be unduly influenced by applicants who display impression management behavior. We believe that there are two ways to avoid this problem. First, interviewers must be taught to recognize what impression management tactics are and how their presence may inflate (or possibly deflate) their ratings of candidates. Second, and most important, although there is no empirical research to support our recommendation, we believe that the development and use of detailed scoring guides as a basis for interview ratings will reduce the effects of impression management tactics.

Determining the Veracity of Interview Information

Given that a significant number of job seekers apparently are falsifying at least some aspects of their credentials and work experience, interviewers are faced with the onerous task of determining which information is truthful. Whereas some information is potentially verifiable (e.g., dates of employment), other information may be impossible to verify (e.g., career goals). Despite the potential importance of this subject and some literature regarding deception on personality tests (e.g., Hough, Eaton, Dunnette, Kamp, & McCloy, 1990), none of the chapters in this volume addresses applicant deception, and we are not aware of any such research in the industrial and organizational psychology literature with regard to interviewing.

There is, however, a relatively large literature in *social psychology* regarding deception (DePaulo, 1992). Overall, observers tend to believe that people are honest, even if they know the people "may be lying some of the time" (DePaulo, 1992, p. 220). This research nevertheless has identified a number of cues that might be used to detect deception, including increased blinking of the eyes, greater hesitation in speaking, and increased fidgeting. Observers, on the other hand, erroneously believe that attempts at deception are accompanied by a shifting of gaze and body (DePaulo, Stone, & Lassiter, 1985).

Can interviewers detect deception with any accuracy? In a fascinating study using a simulated interview, Toris and DePaulo (1985) found that merely being warned that candidates may be lying did *not* lead to improvements in interviewers' abilities to identify deception. Moreover, being made aware that candidates may be lying had a negative effect on some of the interpersonal dynamics. Without specific training on what to look for, even if warned that some candidates are lying, interviewers appear limited in their capacity to detect deception.

Given that most organizations rely heavily on interviews in making hiring decisions, it appears that detection of deception by candidates could increase the validity of this selection tool. However, as we observed earlier, a well-designed interview has reasonably high validity without consideration of deception. It therefore remains questionable whether the costs (e.g., increasing negative applicant reactions) of having interviewers devote more effort to identifying deception in the interview context are worth the *possible* increased validity. Although hiring managers are aware that applicants sometimes lie about their experiences and credentials, they may have a particularly difficult time detecting falsification, because as interviewers they are busy talking, listening, and taking notes (DePaulo, 1992). With the increasing diversity in the workplace, we believe that the meaning of nonverbal cues may have less value for indicating deception than research indicates. In the final analysis, we recommend that interviewers spend less time trying to assess whether deception is occurring and more time attempting to verify information provided by candidates through follow-up questions and contacts with references.

Understanding Unfavorable Information

In the interview, there are two basic types of negative information: directly negative information, such as being fired from a job, and indirectly negative information, such as the inability to respond to a question or not answering the question actually asked (see Kacmar & Young, Chapter 13, this volume). Unfavorable, or negative, information appears to be heavily weighted in interviewing decisions, particularly when such information is presented early in the interview. This in turn suggests that interviewers need to consider negative information, and especially indirectly negative information, carefully to ensure that they do not accord it greater attention than is appropriate. For example, follow-up questions may be needed to determine whether an applicant's response is indeed poor or whether the applicant simply misheard the question.

Table 21.6 Critical Suggestions for Interviewing

1. Prior to conducting the interview, determine

   what your goals are (e.g., relative emphasis on selection versus recruitment);
   what factors, weighted or unweighted, you are trying to measure;
   what set of questions you will ask that are designed to tap your factors; and
   how you will score each question or factor.

2. Make sure that all of your questions are legally acceptable and relevant for the position.

3. Determine ahead of time the sequence of the questions you will ask all applicants and the information that you will provide to applicants during the interview.

4. Take notes during the interview. It may also be particularly helpful to record your assessments and transcribe key notes to aid recall and documentation on an interviewer report form for each applicant.

5. Maintain a positive rapport with the candidate throughout the interview.

6. Allow adequate time toward the end of the interview for applicant questions.

7. Avoid falling prey to candidate impression management tactics and other factors that are not likely to be relevant.

We have presented a large number of suggestions for line managers who will be conducting interviews. By way of summary, Table 21.6 contains seven critical suggestions for interviewers. We turn next to recommendations for HRM staff who are seeking to implement and maintain structured interviewing practices in their organizations.

Introducing, Implementing, and Maintaining Structured Interviewing Practices: Advice for HRM Staff

As Schmitt notes in Chapter 20 of this handbook, minimal research attention has addressed the implementation of a new (e.g., structured) interviewing system as an organizational intervention, susceptible to organizational politics. Although there has been some limited research on how *applicants* react to structured interviews (e.g., Smither, Reilly, Millsap, Pearlman, & Stoffey, 1993), there has been practically no research investigating how *interviewers* feel about structured interviews (Harris, Dworkin, & Park, 1990). The evidence that does exist is rather mixed. Maurer et al. indicate in Chapter 9 that interviewers have positive attitudes toward the situational interview compared with the traditional interview. However, the results of the survey reported by Dipboye and Jackson in Chapter 15 would suggest that interviewers may harbor negative feelings toward a structured interview approach. Specifically, as Dipboye and Jackson note, a majority of respondents believed that interviewers should be allowed to ask any question desired and *disagreed* that the same questions should be asked of all applicants. Even more surprisingly, a majority of respondents disagreed with the statement that an interviewer should base questions on specific job qualifications. Our experiences with several organizations may offer some clarification to these conflicting interviewer reactions. First, as evidenced by the practitioner discourse on the HRNET listserv and widespread adoption of structured interviewing training, there is growing acceptance and positive support by hiring managers for doing more structured employment interviewing. However, we have both noted that when experienced hiring managers are first exposed to structured interviewing questions, they dislike the restraint placed on their asking the "pet questions" they have come to rely on over the years. They do see the structured interview as generating more job-relevant questions and augmenting the documentation process, but resent the loss of independence that results in how they conduct *their* interviews. Given that hiring managers may resist using structured interviewing practices, careful thought should precede any proposed change in staffing procedures that would result from the introduction of structured interviewing.

This section of the chapter is devoted to the introduction, implementation, and maintenance of structured interviewing practices. By *structured interviewing practices,* we refer to the recommended interviewing practices discussed earlier, including job analysis procedures to develop questions, asking the same basic set of questions of all applicants, and using predetermined scoring guides. By way of comparison, we use the term *unstructured* to refer to interviewing practices in which no systematic job analysis is performed, each applicant is asked a largely different set of questions, and no predetermined scoring guides are used.

We begin with a discussion of the introduction phase of structured interviewing in which we describe potential sources of resistance and offer suggestions for ways these sources of resistance might be addressed. We then review implementation issues, focusing primarily on training programs. Finally, we discuss the importance of assigning accountability to interviewers as a means of enhancing effective interviewer decision making.

Managerial Resistance to Structured Interviewing: Causes and Some Solutions

We believe that user resistance poses a major challenge to HRM staff who are responsible for implementing and maintaining structured interviewing practices. Every interview training program should explicitly address user resistance. Although there has been little scholarly or practitioner discussion of this issue, we speculate that there are four major factors that contribute to managers' reluctance to use structured interviewing practices: loss of control, preferred informality, the importance of "gut feelings," and time constraints.

Loss of Control

The HR function has been the target of some pointed criticism during the past few years (e.g., Stewart, 1996). A dominant theme of this criticism is that HR staff place unnecessary restrictions on line managers' decisions while devoting relatively little effort to solving line managers' problems (McCallum, 1996). HR staff prescriptions that line managers use a core set of questions that must be asked of all applicants and formal scoring guides may be perceived by line managers as a further constraint on their independence in the hiring process and another example of unwanted staff control over managers.

A solution to this problem is for HR staff to explain to line managers how structured interviewing practices can help improve their hiring effectiveness. Case examples of organizations that have effectively adopted such interviewing practices may be particularly helpful (Johns, 1993). Various exercises and media (e.g., videotapes) can be used in training programs to convince managers that structured interviewing is a better way to make selection decisions. Of even greater importance is the need to involve line managers in the construction of interview questions and interviewing processes (e.g., scoring guides) to help them develop a sense of ownership. If they participate in the development of interviewing questions, managers should be less likely to resist using structured interviews.

Preferred Informality

As we have noted, the employment interview often serves multiple purposes. In addition to being used to assess applicants, the interview serves as a recruitment and public relations opportunity. In some cases, a job applicant is also a potential customer. As Gilliland and Steiner observe in Chapter 4 of this handbook, standardized interviewing techniques may create negative reactions because applicants prefer a more casual process, which they may regard as a better setting for explaining their qualifications. In today's more informal business atmosphere, a structured interview may seem out of place. Anticipating this potential negative applicant reaction, managers may resist the use of structured interviews.

To address the problem of preferred informality, we offer two recommendations. First, HR staff should remind managers that the interview is intended to achieve a variety of purposes, all of which are important to the organization. An extemporaneous interview may underachieve one or more of these purposes; hence, the interview needs to be well planned and well executed. To the extent that the interview is a critical component in the selection process, which is often the case, managers need to be reminded of the organizational and personal costs associated with making poor selection decisions. Incremental increases in ability typically do yield substantial gains in workforce productivity, even before one applies additional training and motivational practices. Beyond selection, managers need to be reminded that how they conduct the interview can also affect further applicant interest in the position. They should also be reminded of the negative public relations, or even potential lawsuits, that may arise when an unstructured casual conversation wanders into questions that are legally inappropriate. The senior author of this chapter once talked with a sales manager who indicated that he informed the applicant at the beginning of an interview that he asked the same questions of everyone in order to compare them objectively. Perhaps such information would provide applicants with a better understanding of the need for standardized practices and increase confidence in the fairness of whatever decision is made.

Second, a structured interview need not be an interview that is delivered with mechanical stiffness or by a nonresponsive interviewer. Though perhaps finding the questions asked to be more challenging than those in unstructured interviews, applicants often are impressed with and appreciative of the professional manner and obvious preparation that go into structured interviews. Effective rapport-building strategies should always be incorporated into interviewer training programs, particularly for structured interviewing, where we believe communication issues may have a tendency to be somewhat ignored. As we have discussed above, there are various tactics that managers can use to build a positive atmosphere during the interview. We would also note that the use of a more informal, unstructured interviewing style does not guarantee good applicant rapport. Thus, communication issues are not unique to structured interviews, and should be addressed in any interview training program.

The Importance of "Gut Feelings"

Despite the emphasis that structured interviews place on assessing and quantifying whether applicants meet job requirements, managers may place greater value on their "gut feelings" and base their assessments on factors other than job-related KSAs. For example, Rynes and Gerhart (1990) describe the presence of other, perhaps less tangible, applicant characteristics that interviewers may consider important, such as use of leisure time, hobbies, and political orientation. Because structured interviewing practices are based on KSA-oriented questions and scoring guides, managers may feel that this approach negatively affects their ability to make accurate judgments.

Furthermore, use of structured interviews may prevent managers from asking their "pet" questions. In a recent conversation about staffing, a colleague (a former HR manager) described his favorite interview question to the senior author of this chapter: "Why should I hire *you*?" As this colleague explained, the candidate's answer to this question revealed his or her persuasive ability. Because this question is unlikely to be asked in a structured interview, we suspect that this individual might resist adopting structured interviewing practices.

One strategy for reducing manager reliance on "gut feelings" is to explain the legal need for using clearly defined job-related factors. Describing recent lawsuits, such as the restaurant that will be monitored by a judge to ensure that it "drops what it described in court as its 'gut-feeling' approach to hiring in favor of one based on a questionnaire drafted with help from an industrial psychologist" (Simon, 1997, p. B8), may increase manager awareness of the consequences of relying too heavily on "gut feelings." Second, managers should be told that "gut feelings" are useful, but only as a signal for the need to probe further on a specific rating factor of concern. Using analogies, such as the purchase of a home or a car, may also be helpful in explaining the importance of making selection decisions on the basis of well-defined, job-related factors. Even if one becomes enamored of a particular home or car, it is wise still to examine systematically whether that home or car meets or exceeds previously established criteria.

Time Demands of Structured Interviewing Procedures

Structured interviewing techniques are likely to take more time than the unstructured interview. The need for a carefully documented job analysis may seem superfluous to a hiring manager who has supervised employees in the position for many years. Managers may believe that the requirement to ask all applicants a standard set of questions makes little sense if an applicant is clearly giving poor responses early on. To a busy manager, a lengthy structured interview may be perceived as an unjustifiable waste of his or her limited time.

We believe that this may be one of the most pernicious sources of manager resistance. It is noteworthy that the time-consuming nature of effective HR practices has been identified as a problem elsewhere, particularly performance management activities (Harris, 1994). The key, in our opinion, is that the organization must place greater value on the HR activities managers perform. In particular, top management should recognize and reward managers who take the time to manage human resources effectively, which would include using structured employment interviews. Without clear, consistent support from top management, it is quite likely that managers, once trained in structured interviewing practices, will regress back to unstructured interviewing when faced with conflicting demands and inadequate time.

In conclusion, HR departments need an effective partnership with line managers, who often conduct the critical employment interviews in the selection process. It is important for HR staff to be aware of likely sources of manager resistance to adopting structured interviewing practices, to address these sources of resistance proactively, and to gain line manager commitment to implement structured employment interviews on a continuing basis. Once manager commitment has been obtained, the full potential of line manager training in structured interviewing can be realized.

Implementing Effective Interviewing Practices: The Role of Training

Interviewer training is essential for effective implementation of structured interviewing practices. As suggested by the preceding remarks, training is not only to instruct hiring managers in *how* to interview properly, it is also to convince managers to *use* structured interviewing practices. There is virtually no published research on persuading managers to adopt structured interviewing practices. Yet with the widespread offering of 1- or 2-day workshops on structured interviewing, the opportunity exists to test directly the workshop facilitator's ability to address several of the sources of practitioner resistance noted previously. Next, we discuss two issues: first, whether or not interviewer training is effective, and second, some potential differences in training experienced versus inexperienced interviewers.

Does Interviewer Training Work?

Despite the ubiquity of interviewer training, there is little empirical evidence regarding its effects. What little research has been conducted has provided mixed conclusions about the efficacy of such programs. As Palmer, Campion, and Green observe in Chapter 19 of this volume, a study comparing three different types of training programs found that only one had an effect on interviewing practices. Even less is known regarding which components of interview training programs are most effective and which are least effective. What is clear in the literature is the minimal impact interviewer training likely has when that training focuses only on the avoidance of rating errors (e.g., leniency, halo, central tendency, range restriction). Training interviewers to reduce rating errors assumes one can pinpoint the sources of interviewer bias, distinguish what constitutes "true" perception, and make a permanent change in subsequent judgment processes. What appears more promising is to engineer the interview to be more structured and standardized, which appears to have the dual effects of increasing predictive validity and removing any meaningful differences in validity across interviewers (see the study described by Graves & Karren in Chapter 14). In other words, the adoption of structured interviewing techniques that include interviewer training can create a situation in which all, or most, interviewers are equally effective.

Furthermore, there may be potential value in different interviewer training components. For example, Connerley (1997) considered interviewers' self-perceptions and applicants' perceptions of interviewer inter-personal skills and overall effectiveness in a college campus recruitment context. Quite interestingly, although interviewers' self-perceptions were *not* related to having attended a training program, applicants gave slightly higher ratings on both interpersonal skills and overall effectiveness to recruiters who had undergone training. Recruiters who had the opportunity to role-play in the training program, received information on what to tell applicants, and were provided instruction regarding administrative issues perceived themselves to be more interpersonally skilled and effective than those who did not receive such training. Conversely, applicants were somewhat more favorable toward recruiters who were trained in what questions to ask. Thus, line managers who participate in training are likely to feel more comfortable as interviewers. Perhaps most noteworthy is that those aspects of training that made interviewers feel most confident and those that made applicants feel best about interviewers were not the same.

Should Training Be Different for Experienced and Inexperienced Interviewers?

An interesting question that might be raised is whether experienced interviewers require a different training approach than do inexperienced interviewers. Maurer and Fay (1988) contend that one reason the 8-hour training program in their study had no effect was the possibility that the interviewers trained were all highly experienced. Dipboye and Jackson (Chapter 15, this volume), as well as Connerley (1997), found that interviewing experience was correlated with self-ratings of effectiveness in this role. In light of earlier comments about line manager resistance, as well as the effect of ingrained habits, we believe that more experienced interviewers might require somewhat different training strategies than inexperienced interviewers.

Examination of Dipboye and Jackson's contribution to this volume indicates some potentially important information in this regard. Specifically, these authors suggest that experienced interviewers may use automatic, rather than deliberate, information processing, thereby reducing their effectiveness. This is particularly troubling in light of research indicating that experienced interviewers suffer from the same biases (e.g., being influenced by physical attractiveness) as inexperienced interviewers. It seems possible, then, that experienced interviewers will be more resistant to new interviewing tactics and less thorough in making selection decisions. Experienced interviewers may be particularly likely to resist using new effective interviewing strategies because they sense a loss of control or they believe that they should rely on "gut feelings" for selection decisions. Training of experienced interviewers may need to focus more on the advantages of structured interviews and on the need for more deliberate decision processes. A specific comparison of the advantages of newer

394 ■ COMMENTARY ON THEORY, RESEARCH, AND PRACTICE

interviewing approaches versus traditional interviewing may be helpful in this regard, with case examples illustrating how the former approach is superior.

Clearly, more research is needed on the important question of how best to incorporate interviewer training on structured interviewing techniques. HR staff would be well-advised to instruct interviewers in not only what questions to ask, but also what information to provide candidates, how to build and maintain rapport, and how to address various legal issues to reduce liability (e.g., as relates to the ADA). If many of the participants are experienced interviewers, trainers will need to give additional attention to conveying the merits of moving to structured interviewing. HR staff will also need to monitor whether newly trained managers are following structured interviewing procedures, to prevent reversion to more informal and unstructured interviewing styles. There is both published research (e.g., Latham & Saari, 1984) and anecdotal evidence (e.g., we heard of one situation where, in order to save time, the hiring manager was using only a sample of the required questions from a highly structured interview) showing that hiring managers may revert to their "old" or "simpler" ways of conducting interviews. Thus, we believe that effective maintenance of effective interviewing practices is critical to success.

Maintaining Structured Interviewing Practices: Holding Managers Accountable

HR staff should design the selection process to hold interviewers accountable for the quality of their assessments (for a review of the accountability literature, see Eder, Chapter 11, this volume). The simple expectation that one may have to justify a forthcoming decision appears to reduce information primacy effects and judgment overconfidence, increase recall of significant information, and activate a more multidimensional information-processing framework. However, it is critical that the accountability context be created for the decision maker prior to his or her gathering of information. In contrast, felt postjudgment accountability (i.e., being told only after the interview that one will have to justify one's assessment) produces more variance in interviewer decision levels, though not necessarily more accuracy, when compared with a nonaccountability context. In other words, it is not enough to inform interviewers after the fact that they will be expected to justify their judgments. Expressed rationale will be equally as elaborate as under the preaccountability intervention, but it will yield no more accurate judgments. One cannot easily undo the information-gathering and integration process once it has already occurred. HR staff need to convey accountability expectations to interviewers prior to the start of interviewing.

There is also a political, impression management side to accountability that can produce perverse effects that should be minimized, if possible. To the extent that interviewers engage in impression management tactics (see Gilmore et al., Chapter 18, this volume) and they know the persons to whom they will have to justify their assessments, interviewers may simply adopt the other party's position and seek to rationalize their choices. In this case, increased accountability toward a known target audience (e.g., having to justify one's assessment to a particular supervisor whose personal selection criteria and preferences are well-known) may undermine self-critical thinking and exacerbate interviewer judgment biases. To offset the politicizing of interviewer deliberations, HR staff should encourage documentation and judgment justification around the evaluation criteria that were established prior to interviewing in an atmosphere of open, self-critical analysis. Not knowing exactly to whom they will have to justify their assessments, or the particular bias that person holds about how the selection decision should be made, likely has the positive effect of causing interviewers to be thorough and highly rational in their assessments. However, experienced organizational members likely know well in advance how discussions are likely to go and the agendas others are likely to promote. This suggests there may be some value in constructing mixed groups of interviewers (e.g., asking a few managers from other work units to interview and offer their perspectives) rather than using the same group of interviewers each time.

There may also be value in having someone from the HR staff sit in occasionally on an interview or during final deliberation among the interviewers to monitor the interviewing process. As Harris (1994) explains in the context of performance appraisal, a rater's supervisor will induce little sense of accountability in the rater unless the supervisor takes the review process seriously and holds the rater accountable for doing a high-quality assessment. By the same token, if the HR staff member or other credible party is perceived as encouraging a high-quality judgment process, collective accountability will increase and more accurate judgments will likely result. In particular, research evidence suggests that it is more important to hold interviewers accountable for the *process* they employed (e.g., Were the right questions asked? Were scoring guides used?) than it is to hold them accountable for the *outcome* of their decisions (i.e., Was the applicant hired a success?) (Simonson & Staw, 1992). In the interview context, we believe that accountability for the process is far easier to regulate and monitor than is accountability for the outcome. Hence, we recommend that particular emphasis be placed on making hiring managers accountable for following effective interviewing procedures, such as the questions asked, the scoring guides used, and how responses were evaluated. Thus, the individual responsible for monitoring would make inquiries of the managers involved in the hiring to determine whether the proper steps were followed. The responsibility of HR staff does not end with interviewer training. HR staff must also monitor interviewing practices to ensure that they are neither misused nor disused. By way of summary, Table 21.7 provides several

Table 21.7 Suggestions for HR Staff When Implementing Structured Interviewing Practices

1. View the process of implementing a new interviewing program as a means of partnering with line managers.

2. Anticipate sources of resistance from managers to the use of structured interviewing techniques.

3. Train interviewers on both the questions that should be developed (e.g., SI or BDI questions) and the standardized procedures to follow that will enhance interview structure. Include in the training how to establish positive applicant rapport and how to be responsive to applicant questions about the organization and the job.

4. Include in the training a credible rationale for why managers should adopt structured interviewing procedures, especially for experienced managers, who may resist change.

5. Hold managers accountable for the quality of their interviewing procedures, information gathering, and judgment formation. Follow up to ensure that structured interviewing procedures are being implemented appropriately.

suggestions to HR staff charged with the responsibility to implement structured interviewing practices.

In conclusion, we have offered advice, based on the chapters in this book as well as other sources, for hiring managers who must interview applicants and for HR staff who are responsible for introducing new interviewing practices into their organizations. Although both research findings and anecdotal evidence strongly support the use of structured interviewing practices, hiring managers may resist their use. HR staff must be prepared to address managers' concerns as they arise. When properly implemented, structured interviewing should be highly beneficial to organizations, both for selecting top candidates and for defending legal challenges.

References

Barber, A. E., Hollenbeck, J. R., Tower, S. L., & Phillips, J. M. (1994). The effects of interview focus on recruitment effectiveness: A field experiment. *Journal of Applied Psychology, 79*, 886-896.

Borman, W. C., Hanson, M. A., & Hedge, J. W. (1997). Personnel selection. *Annual Review of Psychology, 48*, 299-337.

Breaugh, J. A. (1992). *Recruitment: Science and practice*. Boston: PWS-Kent.

Campion, M. A., Palmer, D. K., & Campion, J. E. (1997). A review of structure in the selection interview. *Personnel Psychology, 50*, 655-702.

Connerley, M. (1997). The influence of training on perceptions of recruiters' interpersonal skills and effectiveness. *Journal of Occupational and Organizational Psychology, 70*, 259-272.

Conway, J. M., Jako, R. A., & Goodman, D. F. (1995). A meta-analysis of interrater and internal consistency reliability of selection interviews. *Journal of Applied Psychology, 80,* 565-579.

DePaulo, B. M. (1992). Nonverbal behavior and self-presentation. *Psychological Bulletin, 111,* 203-242.

DePaulo, B. M., Stone, J. I., & Lassiter, G. D. (1985). Telling ingratiating lies: Effects of target sex and target attractiveness on verbal and nonverbal deceptive success. *Journal of Personality and Social Psychology, 48,* 1191-1203.

Gatewood, R. D., & Feild, H. S. (1998). *Human resource selection.* Fort Worth, TX: Dryden.

Harris, M. M. (1989). Reconsidering the employment interview: A review of recent literature and suggestions for future research. *Personnel Psychology, 42,* 691-726.

Harris, M. M. (1994). Rater motivation in the performance appraisal context: A theoretical framework. *Journal of Management, 20,* 737-756.

Harris, M. M., Dworkin, J., & Park, J. (1990). Pre-employment screening procedures: How human resource managers perceive them. *Journal of Business and Psychology, 4,* 279-292.

Harris, M. M., & Fink, L. S. (1987). A field study of applicant reactions to employment opportunities: Does the recruiter make a difference? *Personnel Psychology, 40,* 765-784.

Houdek, C., & Macan, T. H. (1997, April). *Interview note-taking.* Paper presented at the annual meeting of the Society for Industrial and Organizational Psychology.

Hough, L. M., Eaton, N. K., Dunnette, M. D., Kamp, J. D., & McCloy, R. A. (1990). Criterion-related validities of personality constructs and the effect of response distortion on those validities. *Journal of Applied Psychology, 75,* 581-595.

Huffcutt, A. I., & Arthur, W., Jr. (1994). Hunter and Hunter (1984) revisited: Interview validity for entry-level jobs. *Journal of Applied Psychology, 79,* 184-190.

Johns, G. (1993). Constraints on the adoption of psychology-based personnel practices: Lessons from organizational innovation. *Personnel Psychology, 46,* 569-592.

Latham, G. P., & Saari, L. M. (1984). Do people do what they say? Further studies on the situational interview. *Journal of Applied Psychology, 69,* 569-573.

Maurer, S. D., & Fay, C. (1988). Effects of situational interviews, conventional structured interviews, and training on interview rating agreement: An experimental analysis. *Personnel Psychology, 41,* 329-344.

McCallum, T. (1996). HR under fire. *Human Resources Professional, 13*(3), 12-14.

McComb, K. B., & Jablin, F. M. (1984). Verbal correlates of interviewer empathic listening and employment interview outcomes. *Communication Monographs, 51,* 353-371.

McDaniel, M. A., Whetzel, D. L., Schmidt, F. L., & Maurer, S. D. (1994). The validity of employment interviews: A comprehensive review and meta-analysis. *Journal of Applied Psychology, 79,* 599-616.

Pulakos, E. D., & Schmitt, N. (1995). Experience-based and situational interview questions: Studies of validity. *Personnel Psychology, 48,* 289-308.

Rynes, S. L., Bretz, R. D., & Gerhart, B. (1991). The importance of recruitment in job choice: A different way of looking. *Personnel Psychology, 44,* 487-521.

Rynes, S. L., & Gerhart, B. (1990). Interviewer assessments of applicant "fit": An exploratory investigation. *Personnel Psychology, 43,* 13-35.

Simon, C. (1997, October 7). Restaurant seeks waitresses after suit. *Wall Street Journal*, p. B8.

Simonson, I., & Staw, B. M. (1992). Deescalation strategies: A comparison of techniques for reducing commitment to losing courses of action. *Journal of Applied Psychology, 77,* 419-426.

Smart, B. (1983). *Selection interviewing.* New York: John Wiley.

Smither, J. W., Reilly, R. R., Millsap, R. E., Pearlman, K., & Stoffey, R. W. (1993). Applicant reactions to selection procedures. *Personnel Psychology, 46,* 49-76.

Stevens, C. K., & Kristof, A. L. (1995). Making the right impression: A field study of applicant impression management during job interviews. *Journal of Applied Psychology, 80,* 587-606.

Stewart, T. (1996, May 13). Human resources bites back. *Fortune, 133,* 175-176.

Toris, C., & DePaulo, B. M. (1985). Effects of actual deception and suspiciousness of deception on interpersonal perceptions. *Journal of Personality and Social Psychology, 47,* 1063-1073.

Wiesner, W. H., & Cronshaw, S. F. (1988). A meta-analytic investigation of the impact of interview format and degree of structure on the validity of the employment interview. *Journal of Occupational Psychology, 61,* 275-290.

Index

About the Editors

Robert W. Eder (Ph.D., business administration, University of Colorado–Boulder) is Professor of Human Resources at Portland State University, School of Business Administration. Trained in organizational behavior and human resource management, he has research interests in the areas of the employment interview, strategic staffing, managerial effectiveness, and human resource management practices in a quality business environment. He has authored or coauthored more than 40 articles, which have been published in scholarly outlets such as *Journal of Management, Organizational Behavior and Human Decision Processes, Research in Personnel and Human Resources Management, Advances in International Comparative Management,* and *Educational and Psychological Measurement.* He is also coeditor, with Gerald R. Ferris, of *The Employment Interview: Theory, Research, and Practice* (1989). Dr. Eder has held managerial and professional positions in both the private and public sector, and regularly conducts research and/or consults with numerous service and high-technology firms. He has conducted many workshops in the areas of management development, strategic staffing, employment interviewing, and employee relations in North America, Europe, Asia, Australia, and Africa. He was honored in 1979, 1985, and 1997 with teaching excellence awards, with the Ascendant Scholar Award for his research from the Western Division of the Academy of Management in 1992, and with his election as the 1997 Chair of the Research Methods Division of the Academy of Management.

Michael M. Harris (Ph.D., industrial and organizational psychology, University of Illinois–Chicago) is Professor of Management at the School of Business Administration, University of Missouri–St. Louis. His area of interest is human resource management, and he has conducted research on a variety of related topics, including interviewing, assessment centers, and performance management. His work has appeared in such publications as the *Journal of Applied Psychology, Personnel Psychology,* and the *Journal of Management.* He has served on the editorial boards of several journals, including the *Journal of Applied Psychology,* and is author of the textbook *Human Resource Management: A Practical Approach.* He is the columnist for "Practice Network," which appears in *The Industrial-Organizational Psychologist,* the official newsletter of the Society for Industrial and Organizational Psychology. He regularly conducts workshops on employment interviewing and has served as an expert witness in several legal cases, three of which involved the use of an interview.

About the Contributors

Anthony J. Adorno is a partner of the DeGarmo Group, a human resources/management consulting firm located in Bloomington, Illinois. He received his B.S. degree in psychology and M.S. degree in industrial/organizational psychology from Illinois State University. He conducts research on the fairness and validity of personnel selection processes, focusing primarily on assessment center and employment interview contexts. He has presented research and served as an invited speaker at both regional and national conferences, and he currently manages an Internet-based HR forum for professionals of the call center industry. He has consulted with organizational clients on projects such as turnover reduction, employee career development, managerial assessment, selection system design and validation, EEO compliance, and training design and implementation. In collaboration with John Binning, he is developing structured personality assessment systems to measure job candidates' congruence with discomforting and stressful job demands, to better manage employee turnover in organizations. As part of this effort, he has coordinated an international research study that includes organizational representatives from five countries.

Richard D. Arvey (Ph.D., University of Minnesota) is Professor and Land Grant Chair in the Department of Industrial Relations at the University of Minnesota. He has taught at the University of Tennessee and the University of Houston, and has been a Visiting Professor at the University of California at Berkeley as well as UC-Irvine. His areas of interest and research include the selection and placement of employees, training and development, and organizational behavior. He has served as academic adviser to more than 50 graduate students working toward their master's or Ph.D. degrees and has published more than 75 articles, chapters, or technical reports. One of his best-known works is his book *Fairness in Selecting Employees* (1979; revised edition, 1988). He serves or has served on the editorial boards of several national professional journals, is a Fellow of the Division of Industrial/Organizational Psychology, American Psychological Association, and has held a variety of professional offices and positions. He has served as an expert witness in a number of court cases and has been a consultant to such firms as Mead Paper Company, Shell Oil Company, the Mayo Clinic, and the American Petroleum Institute.

Howard M. Berkson is a doctoral student at the Institute of Labor and Industrial Relations at the University of Illinois at Urbana-Champaign. He has research interests in organizational politics, employment interviews, performance appraisals, and absence. He has published in peer-reviewed journals, including *Human Resource Management Review,* and has consulted on a variety of human resources topics with local and regional nonprofit organizations.

John F. Binning is Associate Professor of Industrial/Organizational Psychology at Illinois State University. He received his M.A. and Ph.D. degrees from the University of Akron, and a B.A. from Butler University. His research focuses on factors affecting selection decisions in assessment center and employment interview contexts and has appeared in the *Journal of Applied Psychology, Academy of Management Journal, Organizational Behavior and Human Performance,* and *Human Resource Management Journal.* For 18 years he has consulted with organizational clients on selection system design and validation, EEO compliance, performance appraisal, training program design, and managerial succession planning. He currently is developing personality assessment systems to measure job candidates' congruence with discomforting and stressful job demands, thus enhancing predictions of emotional exhaustion and assisting clients in managing employee turnover.

M. Ronald Buckley is Professor of Management and Professor of Psychology and the John and Mary Nichols Research Fellow at the University of Oklahoma. His current research interests encompass the employee socialization process, specifically the efficacy of the employment interview and those processes that facilitate the socialization of new organization entrants. He has published more than 70 articles in scholarly research journals and practitioner-oriented journals.

Daniel M. Cable (Ph.D., Cornell University) is Assistant Professor of Human Resource Management at the Kenan-Flagler Business School at the University of North Carolina. His current research interests include person-organization fit, the organizational entry process, organizational selection systems, job choice decisions, and career success. His research has been published in the *Journal of Applied Psychology, Personnel Psychology, Academy of Management Review, Academy of Management Journal, Organizational Behavior and Human Decision Processes,* and *Human Relations.*

James E. Campion (Ph.D., University of Minnesota) is Professor of Psychology at the University of Houston, where he heads the Ph.D. program in I/O psychology and directs the Personnel Psychology Services Center and the Interviewing Institute. The Interviewing Institute was created in 1952, when the first employment interviewing workshop was conducted. These workshops have been offered on a continuous basis since then, making this program the longest running of its kind in the country. His research interests and consulting practice are in the areas of assessment, training, recruitment, and the employment interview.

Michael A. Campion is Professor of Management at Purdue University. His previous industrial experience includes 4 years each at IBM and Weyerhaeuser Company. He holds an M.S. and a Ph.D. in industrial and organizational psychology and has published more than 50 articles in scientific and professional journals. He has also given numerous presentations at professional meetings on such topics as interviewing, teams, work design, testing, training, turnover, promotion, and motivation. He is past editor of *Personnel Psychology* and past president of the Society for Industrial and Organizational Psychology. He is an active consultant with a wide range of private and public sector organizations on a broad variety of topics.

Robert L. Dipboye is Chair of Psychology and Professor of Psychology and Management at Rice University. Previous to his current position, he held faculty positions at the University of Tennessee and Purdue University. He graduated from Purdue University with his M.A. (1970) and Ph.D. (1973) degrees. His research interests include staffing, training, job analysis, group behavior, and organizational behavior. He is associate editor of the *Journal of Applied Psychology* and is on the editorial boards of the *Journal of Organizational Behavior* and SIOP's Frontier Series. He is the author of *Selection Interviews: Process Perspectives and Industrial and Organization Psychology: An Integrative Approach* (with C. Smith and W. C. Howell). He is a fellow of the American Psychological Association, the Society of Industrial and Organizational Psychology, and the American Psychological Society. In addition to teaching courses in organizational psychology, he has served as a consultant to organizations on problems of human resources management.

Thomas W. Dougherty is Professor of Management at the University of Missouri in Columbia, where he has worked since starting as an Assistant Professor in 1979. He received his B.B.A. degree in accounting as well as his M.A. and Ph.D. in industrial/organizational psychology from the University of Houston. While a doctoral student, he served as an intern in the Personnel Research Group at Exxon Company U.S.A. in Houston, where he also conducted his dissertation research on the measurement of role stress. His research interests include mentoring processes and career success, employment interviewing and recruiting, role stress, and job burnout. He has published in journals including the *Journal of Applied Psychology, Academy of Management Journal, Academy of Management Review, Personnel Psychology,* and *Organizational Behavior and Human Decision Processes.*

Gerald R. Ferris (Ph.D., University of Illinois at Urbana-Champaign) is Professor of Labor and Industrial Relations, of Business Administration, and of Psychology, and Caterpillar Foundation University Scholar at the University of Illinois at Urbana-Champaign. He also served as the Director of the Center for Human Resource Management at the University of Illinois from 1991 to 1996. In July 1999 he will move to the University of Mississippi, where he will hold the Robert M. Hearin Endowed Chair in Business Administration. He has research interests in the areas of interpersonal and political influence in organizations, performance evaluation, and strategic human resources management, and he is the author of numerous articles that have appeared in such publications as the *Journal of Applied Psychology, Organizational Behavior and Human Decision Processes, Personnel Psychology, Academy of Management Journal,* and *Academy of Management Review.* He serves as editor of the annual series Research in Personnel and Human Resources Management and has authored or edited a number of books, including *Handbook of Human Resource Management, Strategy and Human Resources Management,* and *Method and Analysis in Organizational Research.*

Stephen W. Gilliland (Ph.D., Michigan State University) is Associate Professor and the FINOVA Fellow of Management and Policy in the College of Business and Public Administration at the University of Arizona. His primary research interests are in the justice and fairness of human resource practices and policies. Through a merging of social, legal, and managerial issues in this area, he has authored or coauthored more than 50 published papers and conference presentations. He serves on the editorial boards of the *Academy of Management Journal, Journal of Applied Psychology,* and *Personnel Psychology.* He is the 1997 recipient of the Ernest J. McCormick Award for distinguished early career contributions from the Society for Industrial and Organizational Psychology. His consulting and executive education work has addressed issues involving managerial communication and goal setting, team development, and designing and implementing effective performance management systems.

David C. Gilmore is an industrial/organizational psychologist and has been on the psychology faculty at the University of North Carolina at Charlotte since 1979. He received his M.A. and Ph.D. in industrial/organizational psychology at the Ohio State University. He has taught at Illinois State University and the University of Southampton, England. In addition to teaching, he has consulted with many organizations on a variety of human resource issues and currently has an adjunct relationship with the Center for Creative Leadership. His research interests are in leadership, organizational politics, job design, and the employment interview. He was one of the founding members of the North Carolina Industrial/Organizational Psychologists and is a member of the Society for Industrial and Organizational Psychology and the Academy of Management.

Laura M. Graves is Associate Professor of Management at the Graduate School of Management at Clark University. Prior to joining the faculty at Clark, she worked in Corporate Human Resources at Aetna. Her research has addressed issues related to leadership, employee selection, and workforce diversity. Her current work examines bias in employment interviewers' decision processes and the effects of demographic diversity on work groups. Her research has appeared in the *Academy of Management Review, Journal of Applied Psychology,* and *Personnel Psychology,* as well as other journals, and she is currently Chair-Elect of the Gender and Diversity in Organizations Division of the Academy of Management.

Paul C. Green began consulting in 1970, when he earned his doctorate in industrial organizational psychology from the University of Memphis. During the first 20 years of his professional life he conducted approximately 5,000 individual assessments. His research and consulting have been focused primarily on the selection interview, with his most recent interests being directed to the development of behavioral competencies to link interviews to appraisal, coaching, and training. He introduced the "Behavioral Interviewing\reg Seminar" in the early 1980s. A unique aspect of this seminar was the introduction of a special-purpose job analysis technique that enables job experts to create a structured interview very quickly. He is also the primary contributor to eight training videos, including *More Than a Gut Feeling,* a widely adopted dramatization of behavior-based interviewing. Paralleling these activities, his book *Get Hired* is designed to instruct job candidates on how to prepare for a behavior-based interview.

Gloria Harrell-Cook is Assistant Professor of Management in the College of Business and Industry at Mississippi State University. She received her Ph.D. from the Institute of Labor and Industrial Relations at the University of Illinois at Urbana-Champaign. Her main research interests are in the areas of strategic human resources management and organizational politics with regard to human resource management and decision making. Her work has appeared in such journals as the *Journal of Management, Journal of Organizational Behavior,* and *Human Resource Management Review* as well as a number of other scholarly publications.

Fredric M. Jablin is the E. Claiborne Robins Chair in Leadership Studies in the Jepson School of Leadership Studies at the University of Richmond. His research has been published in a wide variety of communication, psychology, personnel, and management journals, and he is coeditor of *Handbook of Organizational Communication: An Interdisciplinary Perspective* (1987). He is also coeditor of the *New Handbook of Organizational Communication* (1999, Sage Publications). His research has examined various facets of leader-member communication in organizations, group problem solving, interaction in the employment interview, and communication processes associated with organizational entry, assimilation, and exit. He has been a member of the editorial boards of more than a dozen professional journals and has been the recipient of numerous awards for his research.

Stacy L. Jackson is Assistant Professor of Organizational Behavior in the Olin School of Business at Washington University in St. Louis. Prior to his current position at Olin, he spent several years as a Senior Manager with Ernst and Young's Management Consulting Practice and in Organization Development at NASA/Johnson Space Center. In the former position, he advised a variety of Fortune 100 clients on selection and performance assessment issues. He received his Ph.D. in industrial/organizational psychology from Rice University in 1997. In addition to human resource selection, his research interests include power and politics as well as performance assessment (e.g., 36-degree assessments). He has a specific interest in applying his understanding of these areas to nonprofit organizations.

K. Michele Kacmar (Ph.D., Texas A&M University) is Director of the Center for Human Resource Management and Associate Professor of Management at Florida State University. Her research interests include impression management and organizational politics. She has published more than 35 articles in such journals as *Journal of Applied Psychology, Journal of Management,* and *Human Relations.* She has received numerous teaching awards, a variety of research awards, and was selected as one of five Developing Scholars at Florida State for 1998. She is on the board of directors of the Society for Human Resource Management Foundation, is Editor-designate for the *Journal of Management,* and serves as the Newsletter Coeditor for the Human Resource Division of the Academy of Management.

Paula R. Kaiser holds M.S. and Ed.D. degrees from Indiana University. She currently teaches management communications and organizational behavior at the University of North Carolina at Greensboro. She has held several administrative positions at her current institution and formerly held administrative positions at the University of Cincinnati, Xavier University, and Indiana University. She has also key leadership roles in graduate management education, including serving as a member of the board of directors of the Graduate Management Admission Council, an international corporation that sponsors the Graduate Management Admission Test and other activities to benefit graduate business schools. She has consulted with corporate clients in several major cities in the United States and Canada and is the author of several articles in management communications areas.

Ronald J. Karren is Associate Professor of Management at the University of Massachusetts-Amherst. He received his B.A. degree (1971) from Rutgers University in psychology, his M.A. degree (1973) from the New School for Social Research in psychology, and his Ph.D. degree (1978) from the University of Maryland in psychology. He has served as a Research Personnel Psychologist at the U.S. Office of Personnel Management and as the Ph.D Director for the School of Management at the University of Massachusetts. His research on utility assessment, drug testing, the interview, person-organization fit, and human resource decision making has appeared in several scholarly journals, including the *Journal of Applied Psychology, Personnel Psychology,* and *Organizational Behavior and Human Decision Processes.*

Gary P. Latham is the Secretary of State Professor of Organizational Effectiveness at the University of Toronto. He is a Fellow of the American Psychological Association, the American Psychological Society, the Canadian Psychology Association, the Academy of Management, and the Royal Society of

Canada. In 1997 he was the first recipient of the award for "Distinguished Contributions to Industrial-Organizational Psychology" from the Canadian Psychological Association. In 1998 he was awarded the "Distinguished Contributions to Psychology as a Profession" from the Society of Industrial-Organizational Psychology. He is currently President of the Canadian Psychological Association. Among his creative accomplishments is the development of the situational interview for selecting employees and behavioral observation scales for performance appraisal.

James M. LeBreton received his B.S. in psychology (1995) and his M.S. in industrial/organizational psychology (1997) from Illinois State University. He is currently a doctoral candidate in the Industrial/Organizational Psychology Program at the University of Tennessee. His research interests and publications are in the areas of alternative methods of personality assessment, assessing nonnormal personality types, person-organization fit issues, and assessment center technology. He is particularly interested in the application of structural equation modeling to personality and assessment center data. He also has published research on the effects of cognitive load on interviewers' preinterview impressions of job candidates.

Robert C. Liden (Ph.D., University of Cincinnati) is Professor of Management at the University of Illinois at Chicago, where he is Director of the Ph.D. Program. His research focuses on interpersonal processes as they relate to such topics as leadership, groups, and employment interviews. He has published more than 45 articles, including 21 in the *Academy of Management Journal, Academy of Management Review, Journal of Applied Psychology,* and *Personnel Psychology.* He has served on the editorial boards of the *Academy of Management Journal* and the *Journal of Management* since 1994. He is the 1999 Program Chair for the Academy of Management's Organizational Behavior Division, a position that will be followed by Division Chair-Elect (1999-2000) and Division Chair (2000-2001).

Steven D. Maurer is Associate Professor of Management at Old Dominion University. His research has focused on recruitment, selection, and retention of engineering and scientific employees, with special emphasis on the potential of the situational interview for recruiting graduate engineers. His work has appeared in *The Employment Interview: Theory, Research, and Practice* (edited by Robert W. Eder and Gerald R. Ferris, 1989) as well as in the *Academy of Management Review, Personnel Psychology, Journal of Applied Psychology, Human Resource Management Review,* and the *Journal of High Technology Management Research.* He was employed for 10 years as a project engineer and engineering employment manager for AT&T and has served for 5 years as the coeditor of the Academy of Management's HRM newsletter. He also has published articles on legal issues in employee selection, has served as an expert witness in federal court pleadings, and has presented numerous management seminars on employment methods, sexual harassment, and HR skills.

Vernon D. Miller (Ph.D., University of Texas at Austin) is Associate Professor in the Department of Communication at Michigan State University. His research interests in the communicative aspects of newcomer assimilation into organizations include campus and on-site employment interviews, organizational socialization tactics and content, new hire information-seeking behaviors, and employee role negotiation activities. He has also examined the role of communication in organizational change efforts, including reorganizations and downsizings.

Stephan J. Motowidlo is the Huber Hurst Professor of Management and Director of the Human Resource Research Center in the Warrington College of Business Administration at the University of Florida. He received his Ph.D. from the University of Minnesota in 1976 in Industrial and organizational psychology. His current research interests are in the areas of performance models, performance evaluation, and behavioral assessment procedures such as job simulations and selection interviews. With his students, he has done several studies on effects of nonverbal interview cues on the favorability and validity of interviewers' judgments and effects of interviewer accountability and note-taking on interview validity. His research has been published in the *Journal of Applied Psychology, Personnel Psychology, Human Performance, Academy of Management Journal, Academy of Management Review, Organizational Behavior and Human Decision Processes,* and other journals. He serves or has served on the editorial boards of the *Journal of Applied Psychology, Human Performance,* and the *Journal of Management.*

David K. Palmer is Assistant Professor in the College of Business and Technology at the University of Nebraska at Kearney. He holds a Ph.D. from Purdue University's Krannert Graduate School of Management in organizational behavior and human resource management. His previous work experience includes 3 years in international trade/customhouse brokerage and 10 years in the food service/hospitality industry. His research interests include interviewing and selection, job search behaviors, and the perception and use of time by individuals in organizations. His articles have appeared in *Current Directions in Psychological Science, Journal of Business and Psychology, Journal of Managerial Psychology,* and *Personnel Psychology,* and he has participated in more than 25 conference presentations.

Charles K. Parsons is Professor of Organizational Behavior in the DuPree College of Management at the Georgia Institute of Technology. He received his Ph.D. in 1980 from the University of Illinois in industrial/organizational psychology. He has been on the faculty of the DuPree College of Management since 1979. He has also performed in various administrative capacities in the college, including Acting Associate Dean and Director of the Ph.D. Program (most recent). He has taught undergraduate and graduate courses in organizational behavior and human resource management. His special teaching interests are in the areas of (a) human resource management in the legal and regulatory environment and (b) organizational and behavioral aspects of advanced manufacturing technology. He has also recently begun teaching a course on international human resource management. His research interests include employment interviewing, the impact of performance feedback on employee motivation and performance, and employee responses to technological change.

Mark V. Roehling is currently Assistant Professor of Management in the Haworth College of Business, Western Michigan University. He received his Ph.D. in human resource management from Michigan State University, and juris doctor degree from the University of Michigan. His research focuses on recruitment, selection, and legal issues associated with human resource practices. His work has appeared in leading academic journals such as *Personnel Psychology* and the *Journal of Applied Psychology*. He teaches courses in staffing, and human resource management. He also has professional experience as a HRM practitioner and as an attorney in the field of employment law.

Craig J. Russell received his Ph.D. in business administration from the University of Iowa in 1982, majoring in human resource management and minoring in applied statistics. He is currently the J. C. Penney Chair of Leadership at the University of Oklahoma, where he teaches in the undergraduate, M.B.A., and Ph.D. programs. He also holds a joint appointment in the Department of Psychology, where he teaches in the master's and doctoral industrial/organizational psychology programs. His research focuses on advancing theory and practice in selection and development of organizational leaders. His work has appeared in the *Academy of Management Journal, Applied Psychological Measurement, Human Resource Management Review, Human Relations, Journal of Applied Psychology, Journal of Management, Journal of Occupational and Organizational Psychology, Leadership Quarterly, Personnel Psychology,* and *Research in Personnel/Human Resources Management.* He also serves on a number of editorial boards.

Neal Schmitt received his Ph.D. from Purdue University in 1972 in industrial/organizational psychology and is currently University Distinguished Professor of Psychology and Management at Michigan State University. On sabbatical from the university this year, he is also serving as Director of Applied Research at the Human Resources Consulting Group of Aon. He served as editor of *Journal of Applied Psychology* from 1988 to 1994 and has served on the editorial boards of 10 journals. He has also been a Fulbright Scholar at the University of Manchester Institute of Science and Technology. He is coauthor of the textbooks *Staffing Organizations* (with Ben Schneider), *Research Methods in Human Resource Management* (with Richard Klimoski), and *Personnel Selection* (with David Chan), and is coeditor of *Personnel Selection in Organizations* (with Walter Borman). He has also published approximately 130 articles in a large number of different journals.

Patricia M. Sias is Associate Professor of Communication in the Edward R. Murrow School of Communication at Washington State University. Her research centers on workplace relationships—in particular, on the development of peer relationships and workplace friendships and the ways such relationships influence, and are influenced by, the organizational context. She has published articles in a variety of academic journals, including *Communication Monographs, Human Communication Research, Communication Research, Western Journal of Communication, Communication Quarterly, Communication Reports,* and *Communication Research Reports.* In 1993, she received the W. Charles Redding Award for the Outstanding Dissertation in Organizational Communication.

Dirk D. Steiner is Professor of Psychology at the Université de Nice-Sophia Antipolis in Nice, France. He earned his Ph.D. in industrial/organizational psychology at the Pennsylvania State University and began his academic career at Louisiana State University before moving to France. He has published research on topics such as job satisfaction, selection-related attitudes, and performance appraisal in journals such as the *Journal of Applied Psychology, Journal of Occupational and Organizational Psychology,* and *Human Relations.* Currently, he is working on research related to organizational justice in personnel selection and on individual differences in time orientation. He is an Associate Editor of the journal *Revue Internationale de Psychologie Sociale/International Review of Social Psychology,* which publishes articles in both French and English.

Cynthia Kay Stevens (Ph.D., University of Washington) is Associate Professor of Human Resource Management and Organizational Behavior at the University of Maryland Business School at College Park. Her research interests are in the areas of staffing (interviews, job search and choice, recruitment), training (interpersonal skill acquisition, maintenance and transfer), decision making, and the creation of intellectual capital. Her work has been published in *Personnel Psychology,* the *Academy of Management Journal,* and the

Journal of Applied Psychology. She worked for three years as an instructional development consultant at the University of Washington and has won several awards for teaching effectiveness at the University of Maryland. She has also consulted with several organizations on diversity-related issues and on the development and implementation of behavioral performance-appraisal procedures.

Christina Sue-Chan earned her Ph.D. in management, specializing in organizational behavior and human resource management, from the Joseph L. Rotman School of Management, University of Toronto, in 1998. She is currently a lecturer in the Department of Organisational and Labour Studies, the University of Western Australia, where she teaches human resource management and organizational behavior. Her research interests encompass social cognitive, goal-setting, and institutional theories as applied to selection, performance appraisal, and other human resources management issues in the not-for-profit sector. She has presented her work at numerous conferences, including those of the Academy of Management, the American Psychological Association, the Canadian Psychological Association, and the Society for Industrial and Organizational Psychology. She has published her work, coauthored with her doctoral supervisor, Gary P. Latham, in monographs as well as journals.

William L. Tullar is Associate Professor in the Department of Business Administration of the Bryan School of Business and Economics at the University of North Carolina at Greensboro. He was a Research Fellow at the International Research Institute for Management Science in Moscow, Russia, in 1990 and 1991, and a Visiting Professor at the University of Applied Sciences in Worms, Germany, in 1993-1994. He has consulted for a number of organizations in both North America and Europe. His most recent publications are *Compensation Consequences of Reengineering* and *Group and Electronic Meeting Systems*. His current research interests include panel interviewing via the Internet, cognitive processes in interviewing decisions, organizational life cycles and organizational trust during the last days of the Soviet Union, and Russian entrepreneurial motivation.

Daniel B. Turban is Associate Professor of Management at the University of Missouri, Columbia. He earned his B.A. in psychology from the University of Hawaii at Manoa and his M.A. and Ph.D. in industrial organizational psychology from the University of Houston. His research interests include employment interviewing, recruitment processes and organizational attractiveness as an employer, supervisor-subordinate relationships, and mentoring relationships. He has published research in the *Journal of Applied Psychology*,

Academy of Management Journal, Journal of Vocational Behavior, and *Journal of Organizational Behavior,* and he currently serves on the editorial board of the *Academy of Management Journal.*

Angela M. Young received her Ph.D. in organizational behavior and human resource management from Florida State University and is currently an Assistant Professor at California State University, Los Angeles. She teaches several different human resource management and related management courses. Additionally, she is on the board of directors of the Professionals in Human Resources Association (PIHRA) as the Student Chapter Liaison and Cochair of the PIHRA Foundation, which is active in providing scholarships to deserving students. She has published research in the areas of mentoring, employment interviewing, and other human resource topics, and has presented her research at numerous academic conferences. Her current research interests include mentoring relationships and other dyadic exchanges in the organization (e.g., leader-member exchange), the interview process, and perceptions of equity in the workplace. Prior to her academic experience, she worked in corporate management information systems for several years and started her own business, which dealt with developing and conducting computer training classes.